THE BHAGAVAD GITA
AND THE WEST

RUDOLF STEINER (1913)

THE BHAGAVAD GITA
AND THE WEST

The Esoteric Significance of the Bhagavad Gita
and Its Relation to the Epistles of Paul

Fourteen Lectures Held in Cologne and Helsinki
December 28, 1912-January 1, 1913
and May 28-June 5, 1913

EDITED, WITH INTRODUCTION, DESCRIPTIVE OUTLINES
AND NOTES BY ROBERT MCDERMOTT

FOREWORD BY CHRISTOPHER BAMFORD

INCLUDING THE TEXT OF THE BHAGAVAD GITA
TRANSLATED BY EKNATH EASWARAN

RUDOLF STEINER

SteinerBooks

CW 142/146

Copyright © 2009 by SteinerBooks

SteinerBooks
Anthroposophic Press
610 Main Street, Great Barrington, Massachusetts 01230
www.steinerbooks.org

This book comprises volumes 142 and 146 in the Collected Works (CW) of Rudolf
Steiner, published by SteinerBooks, 2006. Translated from shorthand reports unre-
vised by the lecturer. This is a translation of two volumes in German *Die Bhagavad
Gita und die Paulusbriefe*, GA 142 and *Die okkulten Grundlagen der Bhagavad Gita*, GA
146, published by Rudolf Steiner Verlag, Dornach, Switzerland, 1961. The lecture in
the appendix is translated from *Das Markus-Evangelium*, GA 139, and was published
in *The Gospel of St. Mark*, Anthroposophic Press, 1986. Part I: *The Bhagavad Gita and
the Epistles of Paul* was translated by Lisa D. Monges and Doris M. Bugbey. Part II: *The
Esoteric Significance of the Bhagavad Gita* was translated by George and Mary Adams
and amended by Doris M. Bugbey. Both translations were revised for this edition by
Mado Spiegler. The lecture in the Appendix was translated by Conrad Mainzer and
edited by Stewart C. Easton. Part III: The text of the Bhagavad Gita, translated by
Eknath Easwaran, is reproduced with kind permission from Nilgiri Press, Berkeley,
CA, 2007. Copyright 1985, 2007 by The Blue Mountain Center of Meditation.

Library of Congress Cataloging-in-Publication Data
Steiner, Rudolf, 1861-1925.
    [Okkulten Grundlagen der Bhagavad Gita. English]
    The Bhagavad Gita and the West : the esoteric significance of the Bhagavad Gita
and its relation to the epistles of Paul / Rudolf Steiner ; edited and introduced by
Robert McDermott ; foreword by Christopher Bamford.
        p. cm.
    "Including the text of the Bhagavad Gita translated by Ekrath Easwaran."
    "Fourteen lectures held in Cologne and Helsinki, December 28, 1912-January 1,
1913 and May 28-June 5, 1913."
    Includes bibliographical references and index.
    ISBN 978-0-88010-604-7
    1. Bhagavadgita–Criticism, interpretation, etc. 2. Bible. N.T. Epistles of
Paul–Criticism, interpretation, etc. 3. Anthroposophy. I. McDermott, Robert
A. II. Easwaran, Eknath. III. Steiner, Rudolf, 1861-1925. Bhagavad Gita und die
Paulusbriefe. English. IV. Bhagavadgita. English. V. Title.
    BL1138.67.S7413 2008
                        294.5'924046—dc22
                                2008014774

Printed in the United States

CONTENTS

PART II
THE ESOTERIC SIGNIFICANCE OF THE BHAGAVAD GITA

1.

HELSINKI, MAY 28, 1913

The recognition of the Bhagavad Gita and its relevance for the present time. A statement on this by Wilhelm von Humboldt. The starting-point of the Bhagavad Gita: a battle of brothers. The reluctance of Arjuna to be involved in worldly battle. The opposite picture of Socrates as proclaimer of the immortality of the soul. Arjuna as the representative of the world of the group soul, and Krishna as the leader for the experience of the individual ego.

2.

HELSINKI, MAY 29, 1913

The artistic composition of all ancient esoteric documents. A shattering soul experience as the starting point of esoteric experiences. Widening of interest as a prerequisite of spiritual training. Arjuna's spiritual development in accordance with such prerequisites. Thinking in general concepts as a new acquisition at the time of the Bhagavad Gita. Ideas and concepts as the beginning of clairvoyance. The teaching of Krishna: turning away from the word of the Vedas and turning toward treading the path of Yoga. Undergoing the feeling of solitude and the first steps to supersensible knowledge.

3.

HELSINKI, MAY 30, 1913

The connection of dream pictures with everyday experiences. The intrusion of spiritual experiences into the world of dreams as a result of spiritual-scientific practices. The overcoming of the usual sympathies and antipathies as a precondition for such experiences. Examples of the difficulties of achieving this. Attaining a new attitude to one's own destiny. The necessity of strengthening self-awareness for the ascent into higher worlds. The reflection of such facts in the meeting between Arjuna and Krishna.

4.

Helsinki, May 31, 1913

The last remains of clairvoyance in people at the time of the Bhagavad Gita. The feeling of the senselessness of a merely physical existence as a spur to spiritual research. The attainment of higher knowledge through conscious penetration into the region of the spiritual world otherwise only experienced during sleep. The recognition of the necessity of evil in the world. The indignation of public criticism toward insights brought down from the "sleep region." The truth of the two Jesus children as an example. The words of Krishna as a revelation from this spiritual region.

pages 136–149

5.

Helsinki, June 1, 1913

The deficiency of all definitions. Characterization of the cyclic course of the processes of upbuilding and degradation in the nervous system through the alternation of sleeping and waking. Helen Keller as example for the resilience of hereditary forces against organic damage. The cyclic law of life in the course of history and alternation between periods of preparation and of fulfillment. The formation of a new organ in the human brain between the fourteenth and fifteenth centuries and the beginning of spiritualistic thinking in the present. Examples of the after effects of a materialistically superficial mode of thinking. Woodrow Wilson's views on national life. The preparation of self-consciousness through Krishna during the time of division into castes and ancestor worship. Arjuna's becoming conscious of this process.

pages 150–160

6.

Helsinki, June 2, 1913

An error of today's abstract scientific knowledge: the interpretation of ancient religious documents as philosophical systems. The meeting of Arjuna with Krishna bringing about self-consciousness. The artistic crescendo of the first songs of the Bhagavad Gita to the ninth song: from comprehension of the eternal through outer phenomena to deepening in Yoga, to experiencing the Krishna spirit in imaginative pictures. The meaning of the Krishna impulse for the individual human soul, and of the Christ impulse for all humanity.

pages 161–171

7.

8.

9.

APPENDIX: From *The Gospel of St. Mark*

BASEL, LECTURE 5, SEPTEMBER 19, 1912

Buddha and his predecessor Krishna. Krishna's teachings an esoteric revelation. Teachings of modern idealist philosophers equally "esoteric" but conceptual in the post-Christian era. In the Vedas and the Bhagavad Gita, Krishna's teachings summarized a world perceived by ancient clairvoyance in the third cultural epoch before the loss of clairvoyance. Buddha's teachings some centuries later show nostalgia for the lost world of Krishna. Buddha looked backward to Krishna, John the Baptist looked forward to Christ.

PART III

Complete Text of the Bhagavad Gita

Translated by Eknath Easwaran

FOREWORD

by Christopher Bamford

The two sets of lectures on the Bhagavad Gita (December 28, 1912 through January 1, 1913 and May 28 through June 5, 1913), were given at a critical juncture—an epochal moment—for both Rudolf Steiner and Anthroposophy.

Cosmically, and in terms of human and earthly evolution, 1912 was important on several counts. Above all, perhaps, because, based on the earthly life of Christ Jesus, it marked the close of the first thirty-three-year cycle, after the cosmic-spiritual-earthly event of 1879. This was the moment when, according to the traditional sequence of the archangelic regents of the time periods, the Archangel Michael assumed responsibility for the next three hundred-and-twenty years or so of earthly guidance. Most significantly, Michael, who is the "countenance of Christ," was simultaneously also "elevated" in the angelic hierarchies from the rank of Archangel to Principality (Archai or "Time Spirit"), to more powerfully aid humanity in what would be a new and difficult undertaking in the service of cosmic evolution.

For Michael's deed of overcoming the Dragon and casting down its "spirits of darkness" into the earthly sphere had placed humanity's destiny before us in a new way; and "Evil" was now given an unavoidable, earthly-human reality, at once seductive and accessible to free, independent, conscious moral thinking. At the same time, the cosmic intelligence of the spiritual world, whose ruler was Michael, was opened to humanity to aid it in the overcoming of evil (and striving for the good). In other words, it is the will of heaven that after 1879 human beings who turn toward the spiritual world will receive the healing influx of cosmic intelligence through the mediating power of the Archangel Michael without illusion or fantasy.

These two intimately related spiritual realities—the Christ event revealed through the Mystery of Golgotha and the Michael event revealed to those able to cognize it in 1879 in the spiritual world, and thereafter on Earth—framed Steiner's life and mission as well as the mission of Anthroposophy. (Steiner once said that Anthroposophy was born in 1880, the first year of Michael's rule.)

As Guenther Wachsmuth writes in *The Life and Work of Rudolf Steiner*, in the opening of his chapter on the year 1912:

> There are certain years, the spiritual hallmarks of which attain eminence not merely by reason of external chance. There is such a thing as a time organism of history in which law is inherent and which possesses rhythm and structure like all else that is living. Rudolf Steiner endeavored repeatedly to awaken a consciousness of the inward obedience to law of great human lives. He showed how the rhythm of thirty-three years that characterized the life of Christ, secret yet open to cognition, is incorporated in the rhythm of world events; that again and again in history the rhythm of thirty-three years may bring maturity and fulfillment to a spiritual genesis. He also demonstrated by reference to a diversity of world-historical phenomena that the year 1879 must be regarded in esoteric teaching as a point at which a decisive spiritual revolution came to pass, which at the same time denoted the opening of a new world epoch. Up to the year 1912, thirty-three years had passed since that turning point, a germ had matured, a fruit had ripened, able to bring forth new seeds, new fruit.

Not surprisingly, then, it was in 1912 that Steiner first published the *Calendar of the Soul*, which begins with Easter, and is explicitly dated "1879, after the birth of the I am"; that is, from the thirty-third year of the Common Era, when, through the crucifixion and resurrection, the "I am" united forever with the Spirit of the Earth.

Neither is it surprising that this same year (1912) saw the birth of the Anthroposophical Society.

From 1902, although he wholeheartedly committed to the principles of Theosophy, Steiner had always had an uneasy relationship with its earthly manifestation. For, while subscribing to its principles, he taught from his own experience, and on that basis sought to bring into Theosophy a future-oriented esoteric Christian and Western element. Neither the independence of his teaching, nor esoteric Christianity's increasingly central role in it, met with anything like universal approval. In a word, they were controversial. But, it was not until 1906-7, when the leading Theosophist and clairvoyant, Charles Leadbeater, was forced to resign for sexual misconduct that the tensions which had been simmering beneath the surface began to come to a head. Steiner attributed this moral lapse to Leadbeater's esoteric path, which Steiner held to be "dangerous and apt to mislead," because it was not appropriate for the evolving consciousness of the modern West.

Following this debacle, Steiner was given permission to separate his own path—now more and more explicitly esoteric Christian and Rosicrucian—from the main Indian-based stream of Theosophy. For a short while everything was quiet. Then, in 1909, Leadbeater discovered the young Jiddu Krishnamurti, and announced him to be the new World Teacher in tones that suggested a "Second Coming of the Christ." Steiner dissented; but his dissent went unheeded. Meanwhile, the Krishnamurti movement only gained in strength. By early 1911, to prepare for the imminent advent of the new World Teacher, "The Order of the Rising Star" had been formed and soon became "The Order of the Star in the East," the very name announcing, as it were, Christ reincarnated: a second Bethlehem. For Steiner, this was not only false; it was palpable nonsense and contradicted the very meaning of the Mystery of Golgotha. So he, too, began to prepare. In December 1911, those who stood with him assembled to form an association, which, as its statutes stated, had "nothing to do with the Theosophical Society either in form or content." The association continued to meet through 1912. In August, Steiner proposed that the name of the new society be the "Anthroposophical Society." Finally, in December, all members of the Order of the Star in the East were expelled from the German Section and Annie Besant was declared to have betrayed the fundamental Theosophical principle "No Knowledge Higher than the Truth." On December 11, a telegram was sent demanding her resignation.

And so it happened that, on December 28, without celebration of formality, the Anthroposophical Society was founded in Cologne. Then on January 1 and 2, 1913, the General Meeting for the Foundation of the Anthroposophical Society was held. Members and friends from many countries attended. On January 14, Annie Besant revoked the foundation document of the German Theosophical Society. Less than a month later, on February 2 and 3, the matter was concluded and the first, constitutive General Meeting of the Anthroposophical Society was held.

Such is the context of the lectures collected here.

More precisely, *The Bhagavad Gita and the Epistles of Paul* began concurrently with the foundation of the Anthroposophical Society on December 28 and concluded on January 1, the first day of the General Meeting for the Foundation of the Anthroposophical Society. Those who attended, therefore, would have been the members of the Theosophical Society who, together with Rudolf Steiner, created the Anthroposophical Society. Not surprisingly, perhaps, the focus of Steiner's lectures was the harmony and consonance that exists between the essence of Eastern wisdom and esoteric Christianity.

The second set of lectures, on the "esoteric foundations" of the Bhagavad Gita came after the first General Meeting of the Anthroposophical Society in February. It constitutes the third lecture course that Steiner gave following that decisive moment. The first, given at the meeting itself, was entitled *The Mysteries of the East and of Christianity* (CW 144). In these four lectures, Steiner traced the evolution of the initiatory Mysteries from ancient Persia, Egypt and Greece to the paradigmatic "Grail" initiation of the esoteric Christian West exemplified by Parzival. Following that, in Holland, within the now unfolding context of the Anthroposophical Society, he spoke on "the meaning of esoteric development for the human sheaths and the human self" (CW 145). The emphasis was on inner work within a Western framework. Then, in June, in Helsinki, he again turned eastward and gave the lectures on the Bhagavad Gita printed here.

In other words, contextually, these are transitional lectures. Considered in the light of their context, they help map out how Rudolf Steiner brought Theosophists into the new terrain of Anthroposophy.

The same is also true of the preceding 1912 lectures. Here, however, the predominant emphasis is on inner development and the inner life of the soul. The *Calendar of the Soul* sets the tone. Then, in April, again in Helsinki, Steiner gives his incomparable lectures on *The Spiritual Beings in the Heavenly Bodies and the Kingdoms of Nature* (CW 136), presented not so much as theory but more as experience, available to all. *The Spiritual Foundations of Morality* (CW 155) followed in May in Copenhagen. Again, it was a call to develop spiritually. July, in Münich, saw the unveiling both of the third, and perhaps most inward, Mystery Drama, *The Guardian of the Threshold*, and the revolutionary little book, *A Way of Self Knowledge* (CW 16), which taught the inner path through eight stages in eight meditations. Lectures followed that helped one to grasp, and perhaps achieve, the "threshold" experience so important for inner work and for one's inner life. At the end of August, Steiner gave the lecture series *Initiation, Eternity and the Present Moment* (CW 138), while fall saw lectures on St. Mark's Gospel (CW 139) and *Life Between Death and Rebirth* (CW 140). Thus, Rudolf Steiner led the way into the new world that was calling. It may seem astonishing that with all that was going on behind the scenes politically, Steiner was able to be so outwardly active and creative. But, in fact, the one demanded the other. Without the teaching, the politics would be just that: unredeemed.

Rudolf Steiner, of course, taught Anthroposophy from the beginning. For most German Theosophists, he was the teacher. Nevertheless, stepping out of Theosophy was a radical and revolutionary event. Certainly, most of those who made the move with him—and they were the majority—had a good understanding of what was involved. But some others, probably those more involved with Blavatsky's teachings (and their reframing by Annie Besant), clearly needed a helping hand. From one perspective, these lectures helped provide a bridge. This is not to say that, as with all of Steiner's work, they do not have a profound significance and deep meaning in themselves: they do, as Robert McDermott beautifully articulates.

PREFACE

by Robert McDermott

In his *Essays on the Gita*, Sri Aurobindo recommends approaching the Gita as a great revelation to humanity, while warning the reader that the great interpreters of the past have agreed only to disagree with each other on the core meaning of this great scripture. Because the differences of interpretation tend to reflect each interpreter's biography, rather like the many interpretations of the New Testament, it would seem appropriate for me as editor of this volume to share something of my relation to this text, to the Indian spiritual tradition, to various modern interpreters of the Gita, and particularly to Rudolf Steiner, the primary interpreter of the Gita in this volume.

I first encountered the Bhagavad Gita thanks to a copy given to me by Thomas Berry in 1963 as I began doctoral studies at Boston University, but I did not really fathom its depth or significance until I read Sri Aurobindo's *Essays on the Gita* in 1970. It was Sri Aurobindo who enabled me to see the vast revelation of Krishna as well as the specific significance of each Yoga, and the harmony of all the Yogas in theory and practice.

From 1968 to 1975, I was a devoted student of Sri Aurobindo (1872–1950), the foremost yogic philosopher and spiritual teacher of modern India. By 1975 I had published *The Essential Aurobindo* and had come to recognize Krishna as an avatar and his teaching in the Bhagavad Gita as a profound revelation to humanity. In 1975 I published a review of Western interpretations of the Bhagavad Gita.[3] As I considered my bibliographical essay to have been comprehensive, I was very surprised on first meeting Fred Paddock at the Anthroposophical Library to be handed two volumes of lectures on the Bhagavad Gita by Rudolf Steiner—and shown approximately two hundred other volumes by Steiner—all of which were entirely unknown to me at that time.

---

3. "Indian Spirituality in the West: A Bibliographical Mapping," *Philosophy East and West*, April 1975, pp. 213–39.

Even after I read Rudolf Steiner's two volumes of lectures on the Gita, I continued to read, ponder, and be influenced by Sri Aurobindo's Integral Yoga, including particularly his *Essays on the Gita* and his two-volume study, *Synthesis of Yoga*, the fullest expression of his Yoga teaching. In 1976 I wrote and co-edited with Nuala O'Faolain an Open University/BBC film entitled *Avatar: Concept and Example*, devoted to the teaching and legacy of Sri Aurobindo in the context of the Bhagavad Gita. Since joining the faculty of the California Institute of Integral Studies in 2000 (after serving as its president for nine years), I have each year taught a graduate course called "Krishna, Buddha, and Christ" in which the interpretations of the Gita, particularly by Gandhi, Sri Aurobindo, and Rudolf Steiner, play a significant role.[4]

My contributions to this volume are respectfully dedicated to two mentor-friends, Haridas Chaudhuri, founder and first president of the California Institute of Integral Studies, and Thomas Berry, founder and first president of the American Teilhard Association, in gratitude for their profound appreciation of Asian and Western spiritual traditions.

4. See also my essay, "Participation Comes of Age: Owen Barfield and the *Bhagavad Gita*," in Jorge Ferrer and Jacob Sherman, eds., *The Participatory Turn* (Albany: State University of New York Press, 2008), and available online: pcc.ciis.edu/faculty.

The Lord's Song [is] the most beautiful philosophical song existing in any known tongue.

— J. Robert Oppenheimer [1]

The scriptures cannot be understood but by the same spirit that brought them forth.

— *George Fox* [2]

Only those scriptures, religions, philosophies which can be thus constantly renewed, relived, their stuff of permanent truth constantly reshaped and developed in the inner thought and spiritual experience of a developing humanity, continue to be of living importance to humankind.

The rest remain as monuments of the past, but have no actual force or vital impulse for the future.

— Sri Aurobindo, *Essays on the Gita*

The significance of such a philosophical poem as the Bhagavad Gita, or similar works of world literature, can only be rightly valued by one to whom they are not mere theory but a destiny.

— Rudolf Steiner, *The Bhagavad Gita and the Epistles of Paul*

From what alone can truth and genuine reverence for the divine worlds and divine wisdom spring? Only from real self-knowledge, self-discipline, and self-development. May the forces streaming and pulsating through the anthroposophical movement serve this purpose.

This is the reason for giving this particular cycle of lectures at the start of this anthroposophical movement. They should prove that we are not dealing with something narrow, but that our movement's horizon can extend over distances that encompass Eastern thought as well.

— Rudolf Steiner, *The Bhagavad Gita and the Epistles of Paul*

1. Kai Bird and Martin J. Sherwin, *American Prometheus: The Triumph and Tragedy of J. Robert Oppenheimer* (NY: Vintage Books, 2005), p. 99.
2. Ralph Waldo Emerson's "cardinal principle of criticism." Robert D. Richardson, Jr., *Emerson: The Mind on Fire* (Berkeley, CA: University of California Press, 1995), p. 163.

INTRODUCTION
by Robert McDermott

PART ONE

I. The Bhagavad Gita: Revelation and Transformation

1. Approach to the Gita

This volume presents an interpretation of the Bhagavad Gita ("The Song of the Lord") by Rudolf Steiner, the early-twentieth-century philosopher, educator, esoteric teacher, and founder of Anthroposophy. Steiner interprets the Gita within the context of the Western spiritual and esoteric tradition. The editor's introduction treats the Bhagavad Gita as a (and perhaps *the*) distinctively Indian scripture, and the revelation of the Hindu god Krishna to the warrior Arjuna as having universal significance. As the volume is focused on the Gita and the West, the introduction explains interpretations of the Gita by Indian spiritual teachers important in the modern West as well as Western interpreters. Revealed in India in approximately the sixth century B.C.E., the Gita has since helped to shape its country of origin. For two and a half millennia the Gita has been embedded in the core of Indian mythic, religious, and spiritual consciousness. For the past century and a half it has increasingly had a significant influence in the West.

The Gita has been as foundational for India as the Bible has been for the West. Because it issued from the *Mahabharata*, the ancient defining tale of Indian mythic culture, the Gita is also comparable in its definitive cultural influence to the *Iliad* or the *Odyssey*. As the Gita is chanted daily throughout India by pandits (religious teachers, pronounced "pundits"), it continues to be alive for many millions of Indians, including many who cannot read Sanskrit, and no doubt many who are illiterate. It has been interpreted by the major figures in the Indian religious and philosophical tradition, including Shankara, Ramanuja, Chaitanya, Madhva, Vivekananda, Radhakrishnan (former president of India and perhaps the foremost Indian philosopher of the twentieth century), and especially Sri Aurobindo (the foremost twentieth-century Indian spiritual teacher).

Among the twentieth-century Indian interpreters of the Gita, M. K. (Mahatma) Gandhi offers a particularly distinctive rendering, one that would be difficult to defend at a scholarly level but has proven very influential. Gandhi insists that the battle that provides the occasion for the revelation of the god Krishna to the warrior Arjuna is a mythic (non-historical) battle. Gandhi's interpretation in effect changes Krishna's counsel to Arjuna: Instead of Krishna instructing Arjuna to fight in the great civil war, Gandhi insists that Krishna's directive should be understood to mean "go and fight the battle within the self, the battle between compassion and selfishness." The interpretation of Sri Aurobindo, in a stunning contrast between two of India's great teachers of the first half of the twentieth century, insists that Krishna was indeed instructing Arjuna to fight—just as Aurobindo himself instructed India, in direct opposition to the counsel of Gandhi, to fight with the British against Germany in the Second World War.

The revelation of the divine Krishna would seem to be of great significance for humanity at the present time. Surely the Yogas (spiritual disciplines) of knowledge, action, love, and mediation, as taught in the Gita, must increasingly guide humanity as it faces the unprecedented deterioration, and perhaps irreversible destruction, of the entire ecosphere. Further, a reflective person cannot act confidently without a deep knowledge of the rightness of motive and effect. Action and knowledge are most efficacious when joined by love or devotion to a divine reality.

Increasingly, humanity must also work in relation to the teachings of the Gita concerning divine beings who sacrificially enter human history in times of peril and loss of vision.[5] With this expectation affirmed, it is perhaps possible for twenty-first-century persons to see the incarnational reality not only of Krishna, but also of Buddha and Christ, and ideally of all three. The Bhagavad Gita, particularly as

---

5. In Jewish tradition, according to Proverbs 29:18, "where there is no vision, the people perish." In the Hindu tradition, when there is no vision, the Avatar comes.

interpreted by Rudolf Steiner, could encourage contemporary humanity to see Krishna, Buddha, and Christ, and perhaps other such beings, as teachers and saviors of humanity and the Earth. The claim that one can be a disciple of Krishna, or Buddha, or Christ, but never more than one of these, could become passé.

The Gita, however, is not an easy or obvious text for a person of twenty-first-century Western consciousness. It sets its hearer at least two challenges. The first difficulty is submission to a guru, in this case Krishna. How is such submission compatible with the ideal of individual freedom and responsibility that characterizes contemporary life in the West? Second, how can a spiritual teaching conclude with the command, from a god, for a warrior on the front line to throw spears, knowing that the fabric of society will be torn asunder? For us as for Arjuna, despondency in the face of war makes sense. Arjuna begins in bewilderment and depression and ends in action—in fact, the most dramatic action imaginable: hand-to-hand combat in a war between cousins. According to Krishna, who reveals himself to be the god Vishnu and one with Brahman (Ultimate Reality), to the extent that Arjuna would be conscious of Krishna, he must participate in this civil war.

Presumably, the essential teaching of a great scripture cannot be so simple as to affirm a just war and instruct a warrior to fight. Virtually all of the interpreters of the Gita invite the reader to look behind the words of the text to a revelation expressed, perhaps metaphorically or allegorically, in the Gita's ninety pages. According to some interpreters, Rudolf Steiner and Sri Aurobindo most prominently, the reader is invited to consider the possibility that behind the words there are spiritual beings or realities, particularly the god Krishna; and behind or above Krishna an infinite, eternal, original principle or cause, a divine presence or creativity. In the passage quoted at the front of this introduction, Sri Aurobindo invites the reader to work at this text spiritually, so as to get past the pictures, past the words, to the meanings behind, to the speaker behind, to the being behind the speaking, and then to the Being (Brahman) behind the beings.

With effort it may be possible to see Arjuna not merely as a warrior in a long-ago civil war but as the representative of humanity receiving the spiritual teachings necessary for the next epoch in the evolution of human consciousness. It may also be possible to see Krishna as a god who is one with God, with Brahman, the absolute divinity. As Christ in Jesus could assert, "Before Abraham was, I am" (John 8:58), Krishna could be heard to assert that before the Earth, before humanity, before the other gods, before he was the god Krishna, he was God, Brahman.

Whatever its true revelations, the Gita did not come as an abstract theological treatise but as a story through which are woven many insights, explanations, directives, and opportunities for a higher vision. The way to these revelations begins with the story in the Indian mythic and spiritual tradition prior to its evolution as a separate text.

2. The Bhagavad Gita in the Indian Spiritual Tradition

Although books on Hinduism from the perspective of comparative religions tend to emphasize the concept of absolute oneness as well as absolute infinity and eternity, the Bhagavad Gita features a personal God in conversation with a single human being at a particular time in history. The Upanishads, the mystical-philosophical texts composed several centuries before the Gita, contain the famous texts that announce the absolute unity of the divine: All creation, every particular, is Brahman, the One without a second. The Upanishads are the foundational texts for Vedanta, the main philosophical tradition within Hinduism. The Upanishads also serve as a background for the Gita, but unlike the Upanishads, the Gita emphasizes the personal nature of the divine, the god Krishna. The Upanishads and Vedanta are generally, though not uniformly, monistic—"All is One"— whereas the Gita is essentially theistic—God is a reality distinct from creation. In the Gita the oneness of the divine is affirmed but not emphasized. The Gita presents God in the form of Krishna, who puts things right in the world. It is Krishna who is to be known and adored, and is the only true and right guide of human action.

The Gita begins: "Taught by the blessed Narayana" (i.e., Vishnu) to Arjuna, "compiled by Vyasa the ancient seer, in the middle of the *Mahabharata*, the blessed of eighteen chapters, the bestower of the nectar of non-dualistic wisdom, the destroyer of rebirth, the *Bhagavad Gita*." *Maha* means great and *bharata* refers to the tale of India, the mythic reality of the Indian soul. *Gita* means song, and *Bhagavad* means the Lord, specifically Krishna, the incarnation of Vishnu, who with Brahma (the creator) and Shiva (the destroyer) comprises the triune deity of Hinduism. This trinity invites comparison with the Christian doctrine of the Trinity—Father, Son, and Holy Spirit—an association strengthened by the obvious similarity between Krishna, the avatar-savior of the Gita, and Christ, the Son-savior of the New Testament.

Though it has its own history as a separate text of fewer than a hundred pages, the Bhagavad Gita originated as and remains part of the *Mahabharata*, the great encyclopedic epic poem that evolved from approximately the eighth to the sixth centuries B.C.E., adding episodes and characters to what eventually became a text of 24,000 verses. The main story line of the *Mahabharata* traces the rivalry between two sets of cousins for control of the family kingdom.

The Kaurava family had two sets of cousins, the five sons of Pandu, called the Pandavas, and the 100 sons of Dhritarastra, called the Kuru princes. The Pandavas were known to be virtuous, while the Kuru princes were known for their bad character. The eldest son of Pandu was Yudhisthira; the oldest son of Dhritarasthra was Durudana. When Pandu died, his sons were not old enough to rule and so came under the care of his brother, Dhritarastra. Yudhisthira was tricked in a game of dice and lost the Pandava kingdom. He and his brothers and their family were exiled for thirteen years, at the end of which they were to rule again.

When the terms of the agreement had been met, Durudana, supported by the other sons of Dhritarasthra, even under the threat of war, refused to honor the terms of the agreement. When all efforts to negotiate failed, Yudhisthira reluctantly gave approval to the war. The rival sides each gathered together an enormous army of allies for a final showdown on the field of Kurukshetra, "the field of the Kurus," pitting the Kurus's sons and their teachers Bhisma and Drona against the Pandavas, including the great warrior Arjuna (younger brother of Yudhisthira) and his charioteer, Krishna. At this critical moment Arjuna, greatest of the Pandava warriors, rode to the forefront of the battle line with his charioteer Krishna and began the discourse known as the Bhagavad Gita. Faced with this battle, he asks: "What is my dharma (duty)? Should I fight or not fight?"

In the *Mahabharata*, this story, which appears in the sixth of eighteen books, serves as the vehicle for the revelation of Krishna in the Bhagavad Gita, which is presented on the same level, or in a way completely consistent with, the rest of the *Mahabharata*. Krishna appears to be a very special, somewhat divinely endowed human being, and in book XVI Krishna dies accidentally and ascends gloriously to heaven. However, in the chapters of the *Mahabharata* that become the Bhagavad Gita as a separate text,[6] the story evolves into a decidedly spiritual, or mystical, revelation (a *shruta*, "that which is heard"). That is, those who recited this tale on behalf of Vyasa[7] (the blind seer) began to tell it differently from the way it first appeared in the *Mahabharata*. For some interpreters this is just a distortion or inflation of the original tale, a myth with a life of its own. For the mainstream of Hinduism, however, the Bhagavad Gita is *shruti*, "knowledge by hearing."

In the Gita version of this conflict and Krishna's counsel, there appear passages that seem multidimensional, symbolic, and mystical, with allusions to Indian spiritual teachings and disciplines. It appears that Krishna has access to amazing realities and can lift his pupil to astonishing heights of vision and insight. In the middle of the dialogue Arjuna seems to be in ecstasy, outside of and higher than his ordinary self. He appears transformed from a self to a Self, from an individual human *jiva* to a divine *Atman*. After the first chapter, which sets the scene with the two clans prepared to slaughter one another, the remainder of the dialogue, the next seventeen chapters, is really a

---

6. For a counter to this position, see J. A. B. van Buitenen, *The Bhagavadgita in the Mahabharata* (Chicago, IL: University of Chicago Press, 1981): "The Bhagavadgita was conceived and created in the context of the *Mahabharata*. It was not an independent text that somehow wandered into the epic. On the contrary, it was conceived and developed to bring to a climax and solution to the dharmic dilemma of a war which was both just and pernicious" (p. 5).

7. Vyasa, who was believed to have had a miraculous birth and, like most tellers of ancient tales, to have been physically blind and spiritually sighted, was credited with creating many important Hindu texts.

monologue of teacher to pupil that mysteriously takes the reader (or in India more likely a listener) beyond ordinary consciousness.

The first chapter of the Gita presents Arjuna on the battlefield at the head of his side in a civil war. As a member of the *ksatriya varna* (warrior caste), his life task is to protect his society, by war when necessary. His charioteer, Krishna, is behind him. Arjuna recognizes that once this battle begins in earnest, it will result in the death of both armies, threatening their families and the society to which they all belong. He wonders whether the battle will uphold or destroy dharma, the divine order that holds all of these parts in proper relationship. As he looks across the field he sees teachers, relatives, and friends armed with spears and arrayed as the enemy of his side in this impending fratricidal slaughter.

Horrified, Arjuna says, in effect, "Hell, no, I won't go. I will not fight this war that will not only kill most of the combatants but will destroy the world as we know it." "Arjuna's Despondency," the title of chapter I, refers to his clear-eyed, almost existential realization that once the war begins, not only will the warriors be slain but the temples, schools, livestock, and farms will all fall into chaos. His feelings seem entirely justified. The next seventeen chapters are essentially Krishna's response to Arjuna's despondency and to the human condition at that time. In the process, Krishna provides a glimpse of the spiritual world from the Hindu perspective and with relevance for the whole of humanity. To follow Krishna's instruction to Arjuna requires an understanding of Sanskrit terms used throughout the text. These terms have a long history before and after the Gita.

3. Dharma, Karma, Yoga(s) and Other Important Sanskrit Terms

Zen Buddhist teachers are fond of telling their students not to mistake the finger pointing to the Moon for the Moon itself. All of the traditions make a similar point: Do not confuse ritual—its methods, techniques, concepts, or instruments—with the divine or whatever spiritual reality is the goal of one's effort. Employing a host of metaphors, spiritual teachers urge the student not to mistake the preparation for the achievement, or the practices and aids for the spirit itself. That said, tools such as key terms are essential for an understanding of the path (the finger, the practice) and the goal (the Moon, enlightenment). Textual knowledge, with appropriate distinctions and explanations, is essential to the Gita's meaning and to the practices each reader is encouraged to follow in an effort to replicate Arjuna's experience of Krishna consciousness.

Anyone who seriously aspires to knowledge of spiritual liberation or of the god Krishna, or to selfless action, or to devotion to the divine, or to an efficacious silence, will require the use of certain terms. Effort toward the transformation of consciousness will also be needed. A third necessary component will be an affinity with the experience of Arjuna, his inner turmoil at the bottom rung of the ladder of consciousness or spiritual awareness. It is this ladder that each reader/listener is invited to climb with Krishna's assistance. While one does not need knowledge of Sanskrit in order to understand the Gita's message, one does need to understand, and to work meditatively with, certain key concepts, a partial list of which would include the following: *dharma, karma, moksha, avatar, maya, Sankhya,* three *gunas,* and most especially the four *Yogas—jnana, karma, bhakti,* and *raja.* These terms will be explained in the following several pages and used throughout this introductory essay. (As dharma, karma, yoga, maya, and avatar are now familiar in English, they will not be italicized in the pages that follow.)

Dharma refers to the total correct context of an event, and especially the context of a person's obligations, according to age and caste. Every aspect of traditional Hindu life has its own set of obligations or duties. Arjuna's dharma, for example, is that of a warrior; his presumed duty in the total historical, divinely ordained order would be to fight in an unavoidable civil war. Arjuna's position in society and his particular work as a *ksatriya* were prescribed by his birth family, and that birth is understood as having been determined by his previous life. Like every person of his religious culture, Arjuna had to reconcile four dharmas, as follows:

Sva-dharma, one's own personal obligation consistent with one's inner self or nature, including one's karma (below).

Varna, caste. The Hindu tradition acknowledges four vocational classes, *brahmin* (priest, teacher), *ksatriya* (ruler, leader), *vaishya* (businessman—in traditional India there were no businesswomen), and *shudra* (farmer, laborer). (Untouchables are technically not a caste but a group of people who in effect have been systematically and cruelly relegated to a position below the *shudra* caste.)

Ashrama, successive roles in life, including child/student, house-holder, and retired person, each with its particular duties.

Mokshadharma, or *moksha*, means spiritual liberation, specifically release from the burden of negative karma built up over one or more lifetimes of unenlightened deeds and thoughts. *Moksha* should be understood as extraordinary dharma, a set of duties that one should assume only after one has demonstrated a disciplined practice of ordinary dharma.

Arjuna was expected to express his interior purpose, his karma, in the context of his multiple duties, his dharma. His despondency arose from the limitations of this established world order and an inability to imagine a new cultural framework. From this questioning a new order was about to be born, for this was the beginning of a time when, as W. B. Yeats said of the early twentieth century, "the centre cannot hold."[8] When a culture enters a period of uncertainty or chaos, it doesn't usually return to an old status quo but instead ushers in a new cultural framework, thereby revising the cultural dharma and the dharma of representative individuals such as Arjuna.

In a traditional culture defined by karma and dharma, it would be unthinkable for a warrior on the front line of a civil war to question whether he should fight. To the extent that dharma presides, that it is coherent and effective, the question that Arjuna asks in the first chapter of the Gita should not arise. There should be no conscientious objectors or warriors refusing to fight in the Gita, just as there

---

8. W. B. Yeats, "The Second Coming" (1921): "Things fall apart; the centre cannot hold."

should be none in Homer's *Iliad*, or in the army of Alexander the Great. It takes an entirely new situation for a warrior in this culture to say, "Even though I am born a warrior and even though this is a civil war, maybe I should not fight." Such a statement suggests existential anxiety. More than fear, it expresses fundamental confusion and loss of direction in one's life and the situation in which one is expected to act. A new age, a new paradigm, a new dharma, would seem to be dawning through Arjuna's human despondency and Krishna's divine reply.

In his despondency, Arjuna does not understand that this life and this task are a result of previous lives and a preparation for the next life. When Krishna tells him that he must lift his consciousness, Arjuna in effect replies that he does not know how to do that. Perhaps, he thinks, he should change his life as a warrior to that of a monk. Instead, beginning in the second chapter, Krishna undertakes to lead Arjuna through the kind of transformation that will enable him to understand the whole sweep of karma and rebirth, and the ways in which one's dharma discloses and guides one's life task. He also shows some of the ways in which, through the Yogas, a person can develop spiritual awareness and, ultimately, liberation from the round of births.

Karma, usually thought of as a law, refers to the positive or negative value that accrues to the person who performs any deed or thought, both in a given lifetime and over many lifetimes. It is a chain of rebirth in which a life is a link, such that each life begins as the exact product of the essential spiritual results of the previous life. Arjuna's karma, for example, landed him at the head of his side of a civil war with sufficient capacity to see the horror of war, sufficient conscience to question it, and sufficient spiritual alertness to benefit from Krishna's revelation.

An avatar is a divine being who enters human history during a time of *adharma* (when the context for human action has fallen into chaos). That Arjuna would question whether, or why, he should fight in the civil war shows the need for Krishna to intervene and to restore dharma—which in a time of transition would be the restoration of order, but in a way that absorbs some significant change. Krishna is certainly considered an avatar, and many would consider Sri Ramakrishna, the nineteenth century Hindu mystic, an avatar. Some claim that Mahatma Gandhi must be an avatar, and others would regard Sri Aurobindo and The Mother, the twentieth-century mystic teachers of Integral Yoga, as co-avatars.

The Bhagavad Gita is not only the revelation *by* Krishna, it is more importantly the revelation *of* Krishna, the reincarnation of Vishnu, one with Brahman, an avatar, divine teacher, and rescuer of a confused humanity. This one-hundred-page book in eighteen chapters constitutes both a divinely inspired revelation and a revelation of the divine. A revelation can be considered divinely inspired not because it takes place without human agency, but because it claims both a divine source and the active, co-creating participation of one or more human beings. Such a revelation would seem to be neither universal nor arbitrary but exactly what is needed for a specific time, place, problem, or an entire culture. It is disseminated through a specific language, set of concepts, and worldview. It is intelligible to and significant for a specific community.

In the fourth chapter, Krishna replies to Arjuna:

5 You and I have passed through many births, Arjuna. You have forgotten, but I remember them all.

6 My true being is unborn and changeless. I am the Lord who dwells in every creature. Through the power of my own maya, I manifest myself in a finite form.

7 Whenever dharma declines and the purpose of life is forgotten, I manifest myself on earth.

8 I am born in every age to protect the good, to destroy evil, and to reestablish dharma.

9 Those who know me as their own divine Self break through the belief that they are the body and are not reborn as separate creatures.[9]

---

9. *The Bhagavad Gita*, trans. with introduction by Eknath Easwaran, with chapter introductions by Diana Morrison (Tomales, CA: Nilgiri Press, 1985), pp. 85–86. See the full text of this translation at the back of this volume, pp. 235-313.

Krishna comes into the world because *adharma* has arisen, because humanity as represented by Arjuna has lost its way. Krishna remembers his previous lives, but Arjuna does not. Because Arjuna reveals that he has lost track of his place in the great chain of lives and karmically determined duties, Krishna will need to lead him to an understanding of dharma, karma, rebirth, and the Yogas by which he might begin to think and act not as a despondent isolate but as a willing member of the entire cosmos sustained by the god Krishna.

Maya, a term that is prominent in the Upanishads (mystical and philosophical texts recited for several centuries prior to the Gita) and throughout the Hindu philosophical tradition, refers to the gap between unenlightened consciousness, the way each particular entity grasps reality, and the divine, i.e., Brahman, itself.

Sankhya is a system of philosophy that provides an account of the reality of particulars, called *prakriti*, in a dynamic relationship with the divine, called *purusha*; it provides the philosophical concepts for the *Yoga Sutras*, the systematization of Yoga practice written by Patanjali in the sixth century B.C.E.

Guna refers to three kinds, or levels, of soul: *sattvic*, characterized by light; *rajasic*, characterized by energy; and *tamasic*, characterized by darkness and lethargy.

In the Gita there are four Yogas, or spiritual paths to liberation: action, knowledge, devotion, and meditation.

Karma-Yoga is the spiritual discipline of selfless action, acting without attachment to the fruits of one's action. With respect specifically to Arjuna, he should fight because it is his duty to do so according to the multi-lived history that landed him in the dharma described at the beginning of the Gita. This discipline requires an evenness of mind in the execution of his duty to fight, specifically, a lack of desire for the benefits to himself that would come with victory, and an absence of hatred for the enemy.

The Gita begins its Yoga teaching in response to Arjuna's consternation concerning the action he is expected to perform, namely, throwing spears at the enemy—or receiving a spear thrown at him! This is the initial problem of the Gita: should Arjuna fight in this fratricidal battle knowing that it will lead to the slaughter of friends and relatives and leave countless families in grave circumstances? Krishna teaches Arjuna to act according to his dharma and karma, following one or more of the Yogas. Krishna's complete teaching will include several other Yogas, but the initial focus is entirely on the problem of action and the *karma*-Yoga solution.

In chapter II Krishna explains that Arjuna cannot avoid action; action is a necessity. The question is whether Arjuna will act out of a despondent, self-pitying "little self" or out of a Self that is cosmic and in harmony with Krishna. *Karma*-Yoga requires Arjuna to act without concern for the way that his action will affect him and others—whether he or his friends and relatives will be killed, and his family bereft, or worse. In every deed that he performs he must be indifferent to the results, including his own death or his causing the death of another. If not concern for the fate of his kinsmen and himself, what must his motive be? The Bhagavad Gita teaches that the only true motive of action is the divine will. Arjuna must become conscious of what Krishna prescribes, in this case that he follow his dharma as a warrior. This leads to the disturbing thought that Krishna teaches divinely inspired killing. In the same thought, however, he teaches a divinely inspired act of being killed and of upholding dharma. Arjuna is to act without concern for whether he will experience pleasure or pain, killing or being killed. This ideal of equanimity, equal acceptance of pleasure and pain, is taught by the Buddha as well as by Christian saints, Sufis, and other spiritual teachers worldwide, but the Gita's application of selfless action in hand-to-hand combat in a civil war is surely the most extreme application of this ideal.

Jnana-Yoga is the spiritual discipline of knowing, or at least trying to know, the divine. According to this Yoga, Arjuna needs to learn that the self that he knows himself to be by empirical (ordinary) knowledge is in fact part of a larger, universal Self, *Atman.* This knowledge is necessary in order for the ordinary self to give way to the Self, and thereby to act with the universality of the divine—in this case with the consciousness of Krishna. In the event of a war, a warrior must know what action to perform. While his life as a warrior is predetermined, his specific responsibilities require knowledge. He needs to understand the place of the civil war in the whole divine economy and his place in his society, his caste duty, and his sequence of lives. He will need to join *jnana-* or knowledge-Yoga to the other Yogas. After the first few chapters, it becomes clear that Krishna is focused as much on knowledge as on action. Krishna teaches that Arjuna cannot know himself except by knowing Krishna. Krishna reveals (*shruta*), and Arjuna is invited to knowledge by hearing (*shruti*). Further, Arjuna can only act rightly by knowing his place within the divine reality that is none other than Krishna—recognizing that he is truly identical with Krishna. Arjuna must come to know this by replacing his ignorant perception of Krishna as a charioteer with the true vision of Krishna the god. In the early chapters Krishna responds in terms of Arjuna's predicament because he knows that at the early stage of the dialogue Arjuna cannot see anything divine, neither his divinely appointed task nor the divine being who is trying to instruct him.

In urging Arjuna to know himself Krishna is urging Arjuna to know his own divinity, to know himself as the very essence of Krishna. If Arjuna but knew his actual identity he would know that Krishna is his higher self. Of course, in addition to being the higher self of Arjuna, Krishna is the higher self of all human beings. This is essentially the directive of the Delphic Oracle to Socrates—"Know yourself." If you do, you will have knowledge, not merely opinion, of the divine. It is also the directive of Paul: to know the self is to know Christ, because Christ lives within the human soul and is its essence.

This kind of knowledge comes from selfless thinking or thinking with the mind of the divine. It is thinking and knowing with the consciousness of Krishna—who is, as Arjuna eventually comes to understand, none other than Brahman, the Divine One, the God beyond all gods. To attain *Jnana*-Yoga is to see the divine in the human and earthly. Ordinarily human beings see only surfaces or appearance, such as Krishna in his charioteer guise, and fail to see the reality of Krishna as the God of all universes, and of all gods. If Arjuna were to see Krishna in his own right, or Krishna as the higher self of all selves, he would be able to see that both sides of the battle are held lovingly by Krishna, are part of Krishna. Arjuna would see Krishna in each warrior—and in each spear!

The first half of the Gita essentially teaches a combination of *karma*-Yoga and *jnana*-Yoga: one has to know Krishna, or divinity, in order to know what to do, how to act selflessly. One has to know who one truly is, which is the same as knowing Krishna. Or, if one knows Krishna, one truly knows oneself; Krishna is Arjuna's true self. Whether by knowing oneself truly (as Krishna) or by knowing Krishna (as the one who knows oneself and All), one knows reality. It would not be enough to act Krishna-like, whatever that would mean, without real knowledge of Krishna. One has to know the extent of Krishna, the god who includes lifetimes, civilizations, eons, and universes. Short of this knowledge, it is likely that a warrior such as Arjuna would think that throwing or not throwing a spear would be the most important thing that ever happened. Once Arjuna comes to know the reality of Krishna, he will know that the spear, the warrior, the battle, the right rulership of India, India itself, humanity, the Earth, the cosmos, are all but an instant, a speck, in the all-knowing extent and duration that is Krishna.

According to the Gita, the third Yoga to be practiced is the path or discipline of love, surrender, devotion to the divine. *Bhakti*-Yoga is the spiritual path of devotion to the divine, and specifically in the Gita, it is love of Krishna. The aim of this Yoga is an experience of the splendors of the Divine, including the action of the play of the divine in the world, called *lila*, and the subsequent ability to live within that play with total *ananda*, delight. In practicing *bhakti*, one is extending God's love through the universe. As the enemy is as much a manifestation of God as Arjuna is—though, of course, in the early chapters of the Gita, Arjuna is very far from knowing this—to love Krishna brings with it Krishna's love for the enemy. To throw a spear while loving Krishna in effect would be to throw a spear at oneself, or at everyone Krishna loves. As there is no non-Krishna in the world, to throw a spear at anyone is to throw a spear at Krishna. Understanding this, one can throw one's spear calmly, without attachment to the fruits of action, and, more importantly, with love for Krishna, for all that He is, all that He holds and reconciles. Such a loving, equanimous deed, equal in pleasure and pain, equal in response to killing or being killed, suffused with love of Krishna—this is the epitome of *bhakti*-Yoga, the discipline of love in action.

Hence, in this most extreme action of throwing a spear into the body of another warrior, Arjuna must act calmly and without self-interest, extending God's love through the universe. The enemy, after all, is as much a manifestation of God as Arjuna, even though in social, political, historical terms Arjuna's side in the civil war is right and just. The civil war and the killing on both sides are part of the *lila*—the divine drama.

Raja-Yoga means the royal way, the spiritual discipline of meditation, the practice of withdrawing the senses and calming the mind. In addition to the Yogas of action, knowledge, and love, the Gita also teaches the Yoga of meditation based on the Yoga system of Patanjali. This Yoga system, summarized in the *Yoga Sutras* in the sixth century B.C.E., consists of eight steps:

1. *Yama.* Five moral abstentions
2. *Niyama.* Five moral observations
3. *Asana.* Balanced posture
4. *Pranayama.* Regularity of breath
5. *Pratyahara.* Withdrawal of senses
6. *Dharana.* Concentration
7. *Dhyana.* Meditation
8. *Samadhi.* Contemplation

While there is no chapter or series of verses in the Gita that summarize the eight steps of the *Yoga Sutras*, throughout the Gita there are verses that refer to yogic breathing, withdrawal of sense, or meditation, and finally to contemplation of the divine—which in the *Yoga Sutras* is the abstract principle *purusha*, but in the Gita is the personal god Krishna. The Gita teaches that anyone who would have clear consciousness of his or her inner life, where the divine is to be found as readily as it is to be found transcendently, must exclude all distractions to the senses, to breathing, and to thinking. By stilling the body and the mind the Yoga practitioner can see each action more clearly, in a divine light, unclouded by *tamas* (darkness). This kind of stillness of mind is particularly strong in the Buddhist tradition but it is also in the Indian tradition, and particularly in Patanjali's *Yoga Sutras* and thereby in the Gita.

Krishna's revelation draws upon several spiritual and philosophical traditions, including the Vedas, Upanishads, and particularly Sankhya philosophy, one of the six so-called orthodox philosophical systems in the Indian tradition. Sankhya developed during the century prior to the emergence of the Bhagavad Gita and was formulated systematically many centuries later in the *Sankhyakarika* ("Treatise on Sankhya") by Ishvara Krishna (an Indian philosopher named after Lord Krishna). Sankhya posits an ultimate metaphysical dualism: *purusha* (spirit), which is conscious but inactive and without content, and *prakriti* (matter), which is unconscious and active. *Purusha* neither produces nor is produced; it does, however, "'entice' *prakriti* into activity by 'dancing before it,'" with the result that *prakriti* is induced to go from an unmanifest state of pure potentiality into manifestation, pure activity or evolution; as a result the worlds are brought forth."[10]

Sankhya is a combination of metaphysics and epistemology and lends itself to spiritual disciplines such as the Yogas of the Bhagavad Gita. Metaphysically, Sankhya posits a dualism of *purusha* and *prakriti* similar to the dualism of Brahman and maya developed by Vedanta: *purusha*, like Brahman, is ultimate and changeless; *prakriti* and maya are plural and changing and not quite real. There are also three important differences between Sankhya and Vedanta: whereas Vedanta, though monistic, accounts for various gods, and in a sense includes theism, Sankhya does not posit a divinity at all. Similarly, in contrast to Vedanta, which only qualifiedly affirms the tentative reality of matter, matter in Sankhya is explained at great length and precise details in the context of evolutionary cycles. Finally, whereas Vedanta is ultimately a monism—Brahman is the only reality, all else being various degrees of unreality—Sankyha posits a dualism such that *purusha* and *prakriti* are parallel realities that do not interact. Each human being must come to understand and live the difference between *purusha* and *prakriti*. Clearly, this philosophy well serves as the ideal foundation for the Yogas of the Gita.

---

10. A. L. Herman, *An Introduction to Indian Thought* (Englewood Cliffs, NJ: Prentice Hall, 1976), p. 179.

II. The Gita according to Interpreters and Activists, East and West

1. Classic American Interpreters: Emerson to James

The Bhagavad Gita has been an influential text for the American intellectual and literary tradition for more than a century and a half,[11] beginning with Emerson and his friend Bronson Alcott, both of whom read the Gita regularly, quoted from it, and referred to it in their journals and during their frequent conversations.[12] It must be admitted, however, that with the possible exception of Emerson and Thoreau, American thinkers in the nineteenth century did not think through texts such as the Upanishads and the Bhagavad Gita on their own terms or consider the implications of such texts for the modern Western worldview. Rather, nineteenth-century American thinkers tended to see the Upanishads and the Gita as confirmation of some of their own ideas, particularly as the Gita joins thought and action. Emerson and Thoreau both ignored the *bhakti* (devotional) teaching of the Gita.

Emerson found in the Upanishads and the Gita echoes of his own qualified belief in reincarnation, but except for his poem "Brahma," he discussed his affinity with Asian texts only in his journal. In "The Present Age," a lecture he delivered and reworked throughout the 1840s, he wrote a passage with strong overtones of reincarnation as assumed throughout both the Upanishads and the Bhagavad Gita:

---

11. According to J. J. Clarke, Charles Wilkins (1749–1836) produced the first translation of the Gita into English in 1785. Clarke also mentions "Thomas Colebrooke (1765–1837) whose *Essays on the Religion and Philosophy of the Hindus* introduced the public to many hitherto unknown facets of Indian culture and was widely read in the nineteenth century." *Oriental Enlightenment: The Encounter between Asian and Western Thought* (NY: Routledge, 1997), p. 58.

12. For a thorough and reliable treatment of the influence of Asian texts on American thought, see especially Arthur Versluis, *American Transcendentalism and Asian Religions* (NY: Oxford University Press, 1993), and several books cited in the Guide to Further Reading at the end of this volume.

As the wandering seabird which crossing the ocean lights on some rock or islet to rest for a moment its wings, and to look back on the wilderness of waves behind, and onward to the wilderness of waters before, so stand we perched on this rock or shoal of time, arrived out of the immensity of the past and bound and road-ready to plunge into immensity again.[13]

Henry David Thoreau, like Emerson a Unitarian of an essentially universalist outlook, sympathetic to Jesus but not to orthodox Christianity, and particularly unsympathetic to any exclusivist claims, found in the Vedas, the Upanishads, and the Gita an eloquent expression of his own universalism and perennialism. Just before his rather sudden departure at the end of his two-year stay at Walden Pond, Thoreau wrote: "In the morning I bathe my intellect in the stupendous and cosmogonal philosophy of the Bhagavad Gita ... in comparison with which our modern world and its literature seem puny and trivial.... The pure Walden water is mingled with the sacred water of the Ganges."[14]

Thoreau had the clarity of mind to have been confused by Krishna's directive to Arjuna to fight in the civil war. He differed with Arjuna in that he could not find a reason based on Krishna's advice that would have justified the war. "Arjoon may be convinced but the reader is not."[15]

In his classic Gifford Lectures of 1901–02, *The Varieties of Religious Experience*, the unsurpassed study of the scope of religion, saintliness, conversion, mysticism, and other topics, William James includes the following passage in his chapter on "The Value of Saintliness":

Anyone who is genuinely emancipated from the flesh will look on pleasure and pain, abundance and privation, as alike irrelevant and indifferent. He can engage in actions and experience enjoyments without fear of corruption and enslavement. As the Bhagavad

---

13. Quoted in Robert D. Richardson Jr., *Emerson: The Mind on Fire* (Berkeley: University of California Press, 1999), p. 336.
14. Quoted in Versluis, p. 83.
15. Quoted in Robert D. Richardson, Jr. *Henry Thoreau: A Life of the Mind* (Berkeley, CA: University of California Press, 1986), p. 206.

Gita says, only those need renounce worldly actions who are still inwardly attached thereto. If one be really unattached to the fruits of action, one may mix in the world with equanimity.[16]

Although Rudolf Steiner read both Emerson and James, there is no indication that he was aware of their interest in Asian texts. He was very definitely interested, however, in the interpretations of the Gita by a series of theosophical writers, beginning with references by H. P. Blavatsky in *The Secret Doctrine* (1888).

2. H. P. B. and Theosophical Interpreters

H. P. Blavatsky died in London in 1891, ten years before Steiner entered upon his work as an esoteric teacher. Blavatsky considered it to be part of her life work, and of the mission of Theosophy, to show and to foster the harmony, and even the essential identity, of all religions. While it is true that much of Steiner's esoteric teaching, particularly in early foundational works such as *Theosophy* (1904) and *An Outline of Esoteric Science* (1909), closely resembles the writings of H. P. Blavatsky in overall conception and in details, it is also true that after Steiner's break with Annie Besant and the Theosophical Society in 1912, he increasingly emphasized the distinctively different contributions of great spiritual teachers and religious traditions within the specific time frames of the evolution of consciousness. As is evident in the lectures in this volume, delivered in the intense environment following the separation of Steiner and hundreds of his followers from the Theosophical Society,[17] Steiner opposed the universalizing and perennializing

---

16. William James, *The Varieties of Religious Experience* (Cambridge, MA: Harvard University Press, 1985), p. 288.
17. In 13 lectures delivered in 1915–16 and in 1923 Rudolf Steiner demonstrated his continuing interest in the Theosophical Society and his continuing respect for Madame Blavatsky. See Rudolf Steiner, *Spiritualism, Madame Blavatsky, and Theosophy: An Eyewitness View of Occult History* (Great Barrington, MA: Anthroposophic Press, 2001). See also Christopher Bamford's foreword to this volume.

tendency of Theosophy—the position that all spiritual truths are identical and unchanging throughout the history of humanity.

Whereas the Theosophists, beginning with H. P. Blavatsky, emphasized the eternal and universal significance of Krishna and the Bhagavad Gita, Steiner focuses on Krishna and the Gita as having made a historically specific contribution, namely a contribution to humanity at the dawn of the Axial Age,[18] the age of the beginning of individual self-consciousness. For H.P.B., as Blavatsky referred to herself, Krishna, Buddha, and Christ were very nearly interchangeable figures, all teaching selfless service to the one infinite and eternal spirit. This teaching was an essential part of her attempt to show that ancient esoteric teachings are completely relevant for the present time without modification. For Steiner, as for Sri Aurobindo, the Gita was the most advanced teaching of its age but would not be an adequate spiritual guide for contemporary humanity, Indian or Western.

Robert Ellwood's *Theosophy: A Modern Expression of the Wisdom of the Ages*, which appears to be the most immediately intelligible brief introduction to Theosophy, has only one reference to the Bhagavad Gita, but that reference is very helpful:[19]

> The theosophical concept of duty is based on the Hindu idea of dharma. Dharma is a Sanskrit word related to our word "form," and embraces the general form or order of the world with special emphasis on one's moral obligations toward society that help keep it running.
>
> That obligation implies something else: *svadharma*, one's own personal dharma or place in the vast organism, which is the world. Ancient Indian texts like the Bhagavad Gita, a favorite of Theosophists, give a picture of the world of conditioned reality as like a huge game in which each piece must move in accordance with its rules in order to keep the whole going smoothly.

---

18. The concept of the Axial Age was introduced by Karl Jaspers in his *Origin and Goal of History* (New Haven, CT: Yale University Press, 1953), pp. 1–21.

19. Robert Ellwood, *Theosophy: A Modern Expression of the Wisdom of the Ages* (Wheaton, IL: Theosophical Publishing House, 1986).

3. Contrasting Interpretations of M. K. Gandhi and Sri Aurobindo

M. K. (Mahatma, "Great Soul") Gandhi based his life work on the Bhagavad Gita. He did not read Sanskrit, but he translated the Gita from an English translation into his native Gujarati, and provided an interpretation of the Gita that has been influential ever since. His devotion to the Gita, and particularly to his interpretation of it as a message of steadfast nonviolence, figured prominently throughout his forty-year career as a moral and religious leader—initially of India and thereafter of the world.

Gandhi wrote this text for a monthly publication, *Young India*, in 1925, while he was the leader of the Nationalist Movement to secure India's independence from Britain. The Bhagavad Gita gave Gandhi his deepest and most systematic understanding of the religious dimensions of political and moral action. Here are his often-quoted words:

> I find a solace in the Bhagavad Gita that I missed even in the Sermon on the Mount. When disappointment stares me in the face, and all alone I see not a ray of hope, I go back to the Bhagavad Gita. I find a verse here and a verse there and I immediately begin to smile in the midst of overwhelming tragedies—and my life has been full of external tragedies. And if they have left no visible, no indelible scar on me, I owe it all to the teachings of the Bhagavad Gita.[20]

For Gandhi, the practical, moral, and religious are not only inseparable, they are indistinguishable. The most important concept in Gandhi's teaching is *satyagraha*, or "truth force." The truth-force that Gandhi practiced and taught for ten years in South Africa and for thirty years in India is essentially the *karma*-Yoga of the

---

20. M. K. Gandhi, *Young India* (1925), quoted in S. Radhakrishnan, *The Bhagavad Gita* (London: George Allen and Unwin, 1948), p. 10.

Bhagavad Gita. *Karma*-Yoga teaches non-attachment to the fruits of one's actions. The vows that Gandhi required of his followers focus on four variations on the same idea: Do not possess, do not control, do not use anyone or anything merely for pleasure. Do not be attached to the fruits of your action with respect to possessions, sex, or power.

Furthermore, Gandhi's understanding of the Gita matches his teaching and practice of nonviolence—despite the fact that throughout the Gita Krishna does not alter, and in fact reinforces, Arjuna's obligation to perform his duty as a warrior on the frontline of a civil war. In response to this apparent conflict between the Gita and Gandhi's teaching of *satyagraha*, Gandhi says, in effect: This text, this revelation, this scripture is a battle not on a field of dirt soon to run with blood, but within the human heart, between the forces of good and evil. According to Gandhi, when Krishna says go and fight, he means one must go and fight all of one's lower impulses, go and fight so as not to cling to these rewards (whether psychological or material), not to cling to the benefits of one's actions. One must be equally disposed to one's enemy as to oneself.

And again, in Gandhi's own words:

Let it be granted that according to the letter of the Gita it is possible to say that warfare is consistent with renunciation of fruit [of action]. But after forty years' unremitting endeavor fully to enforce the teaching of the Gita in my own life, I have, in all humility, felt that perfect renunciation is impossible without perfect observance of *ahimsa* (nonviolent action) in every shape and form.[21]

Gandhi, of course, came to be known throughout the world as an Arjuna figure, but one who insisted on a novel interpretation of the Gita: he taught *karma*-Yoga, the discipline of non-attachment to the

---

21. Mahadev Desai, *The Gospel of Selfless Action or the Gita according to Gandhi* (Ahmedabad, India: Navajivan Publishing House, 1946), pp. 133–34.

fruits of action, but he ignored the middle chapters in which Krishna reveals his divinity. Gandhi emphasizes *karma*-Yoga to the exclusion of the otherYogas. He does not at all focus on the Yoga of spiritual knowledge. His approach could be described as rationality or common sense. His ideas and his devotion to them might be unusual—and unusually heroic and influential—but in all of his writings (which run to ninety volumes), speeches, and actions, Gandhi was completely rational, patiently offering explanations and justification for his every position.

Similarly, Gandhi did meditate faithfully, but he did not emphasize this Yoga in reference to the Gita. Perhaps most strikingly, Gandhi scarcely ever referred to Krishna or to Vishnu (of whom the Krishna of the Gita is believed to be a reincarnation), but focused instead on Rama, the avatar-king who precedes Krishna in the line of Vishnu avatars. Gandhi's commentary on the avatar passage, IV.7 ("Whenever dharma declines and the purpose of life is lost, I come forth…") treats Krishna, and the avatar concept, as righteousness rather than as a personal God:

> Here is comfort for the faithful and affirmation of the truth that right ever prevails. Wrong has no independent existence. Knowing this let man cease to arrogate to himself authorship and eschew untruth, violence and evil. Inscrutable Providence—the unique power of the Lord—is ever at work. This fact is *avatara*, incarnation. Strictly speaking there can be no birth for God.[22]

The influence of Gandhi, and of his interpretation of the Bhagavad Gita as a text that teaches nonviolence, can be seen in the commentary of his charismatic follower Vinoba Bhave, author of *Talks on the Gita*.[23] At the present time, Satish Kumar, founder of Schumacher College and editor of *Resurgence Magazine*, is advancing with respect to contemporary problems the legacy and nonviolent life of his teacher, Vinoba Bhave, thereby extending the Gandhian legacy.

22. *Ibid.*, p. 196.
23. New York: Macmillan, 1950.

As Gandhi served as the most visible and inspiring representative of nonviolence in the first half of the twentieth century, in the second half of the twentieth century there are at least four great exemplars of the Gandhian approach to nonviolence, two in the Christian tradition and two in the Buddhist: Martin Luther King, Jr. (until he was assassinated in 1968 at age thirty-nine); Thomas Merton, the Roman Catholic monk who wrote passionately about peace and justice in the 1960s; His Holiness the Dalai Lama, who has advocated nonviolence in reply to the genocide of the Tibetan people by the People's Republic of China; and Aun Sang Suu Kyi, the peaceful leader of the democratic movement in Burma/Myanmar.

Of these four, only Merton wrote on the Bhagavad Gita. By virtue of his own mystical experience, he was able to grasp the truth to be found in mystical texts outside his own Roman Catholic tradition.[24] Fortunately, someone in the International Society for Krishna Consciousness (ISKCON, popularly known as the Hare Krishnas) asked Merton to write an introduction to the edition of the Bhagavad Gita translated with commentary by Maharishi Mahesh Yogi, the founder and spiritual leader of ISKCON. The following passage is revealing of both Merton and the Gita:

> The Gita sees that the basic problem of man is his endemic refusal to live by a will other than his own. For in striving to live entirely by one's own individual will, instead of becoming free, man is enslaved by forces even more exterior and more delusory than his own transient fancies. He projects himself out of the present into the future. He tries to make for himself a future that accords with his own fantasy, and thereby escape from a present reality which he does not fully accept. And yet, when he moves into the future he wanted to create for himself, it becomes a present that is once again repugnant to him. And yet this is what he had "made" for himself—it is his karma. In accepting the present in all its reality as something to be dealt

---

24. With John Wu, Merton translated the Chinese mystical text by Chuang Tse.

with precisely as it is, man comes to grips at once with his karma and with a providential will which, ultimately, is *more his own* than what he currently experiences, on a superficial level, as "his own will." It is in surrendering a false and illusory liberty on the superficial level that man unites himself with the inner ground of reality and freedom in himself which is the will of God, of Krishna, of Providence, of Tao. These concepts do not all exactly coincide, but they have much in common. It is by remaining open to an infinite number of unexpected possibilities which transcend his own imagination and capacity to plan that man really fulfills his own need for freedom.[25]

Merton wrote these words in 1968, at a time in his life when he, like Arjuna, was questioning his own karma. He sounded restless, eager for greater depth and expanse of experience. Following a lover's quarrel with his own Trappist monastery in Lexington, Kentucky, and in spiritual turmoil with his own life, Merton knew firsthand the relationships between knowledge, action, devotion, and meditation, and all of these in relation to the transforming power of the divine presence, whether in terms of Krishna, Buddha, Tao, or Christ. Merton saw in the Gita a message for a soul in transit, in the midst of discovery, and in the polarity between a new consciousness and an old dharma. The Gita, after all, begins with the dilemma of the lost soul, the one for whom the center does not hold. Merton recognized that the Gita, like the New Testament, teaches awareness of an inner truth that exceeds the grasp of human thought and the ordinary capacity of will. (It would be interesting to know what Merton might have thought of Sri Aurobindo's spiritual teaching in general and particularly his interpretation of the Gita.)

Tenzin Gyato, His Holiness the Fourteenth Dalai Lama, whom many believe to be Avalokiteshvara, the bodhisattva of wisdom and compassion, in recent decades has vividly represented the reality of nonviolence and also exemplifies all of the Yogas of the Gita. At the

---

25. Merton's essay appears both as a preface to the ISKCON edition, entitled *The Bhagavad Gita As It Is*, and in his last work, *The Asian Journal of Thomas Merton* (NY: New Directions, 1975).

same time the Dalai Lama is articulating a new dharma for humanity, one in which each individual would vow to work for the reduction of suffering of all sentient beings. In his Nobel Prize Speech, the Dalai Lama acknowledged that the Nobel Prize "is also a tribute to my mentor, Mahatma Gandhi, whose example is an inspiration to so many of us."[26]

Any list of great twentieth-century spiritual teachers would include His Holiness the Dalai Lama, perhaps at the top; Sri Aurobindo (1872–1950) would also be included on such a list, though he is still so little known. Among seekers and scholars of spiritual teaching, Sri Aurobindo and his spiritual colleague, The Mother (Mira Richard), are regarded as among the most amazing of spiritual figures. Sri Aurobindo's relative obscurity is due at least in part to his physical obscurity: he lived in retreat in southeast India for the last forty years of his life. During the year that Aurobindo Ghose (his name until 1914 when he came to be called Sri Aurobindo) spent a year in the Alipore Jail in Calcutta, he meditated on the Bhagavad Gita and came to see the prisoners and jailers in the same way that Arjuna came to see the two sides of the civil war he was expected to fight. Krishna enabled Aurobindo, as he had enabled Arjuna, to see that there is no difference between slayer and slain, and that he, Krishna, holds all such polarities in his one indivisible nature. Aurobindo came to see jailers and murderers dancing together. While seeing themselves as enemies, they are nonetheless doing a wonderful Krishna dance, one in which opposites are reconciled.

Sri Aurobindo and his spiritual collaborator, The Mother, offered themselves as co-avatars, as figures who say, with Krishna, "When *adharma* (chaos) arises we take up this form and we take on the task of helping humanity." They devoted their spiritual powers to the transformation of civilization, culture, and physical realities, including the human body. They worked spiritually to advance a process of evolution along the lines that the divine is indicating—that is nevertheless

---

26. Sidney Piburn, ed., *The Nobel Peace Prize and the Dalai Lama* (Ithaca, NY: Snow Lion Publications, 1990), p. 40.

voluntary. Sri Aurobindo and The Mother developed a new Yoga for lifting the whole of humanity to a new dharma. This dharma will be defined not by birth but by ideals, and by international, multi-ethnic, multi-generational communities based on their vision for a new humanity, a new civilization. This is precisely the meaning of Auroville, a golden city, or city of dawn, which The Mother founded in 1968.

This vision and discipline for the transformation of humanity is the far-reaching result of the process that Aurobindo Ghose initiated in the Alipure Jail. The identification of Aurobindo with the vision and discipline of Krishna continued through his years of spiritual research, spiritual experience, writing, collaboration with The Mother, and meeting with a stream of visitors to the Ashram, giving to each a task, an insight, a blessing. Sri Aurobindo frequently referred to his experience in November 1926 as the descent of the Overmind; he also referred to this event as the descent of Krishna. Both Sri Aurobindo and The Mother described this event as the descent of Krishna into the physical body.[27]

Sri Aurobindo obviously regarded Krishna as an avatar. As he understood Krishna to be both God and the rescuer of struggling humanity in a particular time and place, he understood himself and The Mother to be serving a similar function, specifically the task of bringing into human consciousness the divine force, which he referred to as Supermind or the Supramental.

Unlike Gandhi, Sri Aurobindo seems to have identified himself and The Mother more with Krishna than with Arjuna, and especially with the co-avatar transformative force, similar to what Krishna brought to Arjuna on the battlefield. It is of course a deep question whether Sri Aurobindo and the Mother might be of the same spiritual substance, or somehow an extension or manifestation of Krishna.

---

27. See Robert McDermott, Introduction, *The Essential Aurobindo* (Great Barrington, MA: Lindisfarne Press, 1987), pp. 17, 27, 30; see also K. S. Shrinivas Iyengar, *Sri Aurobindo: A Biography and a History* (Pondicherry, India: Sri Aurobindo Ashram Press, 1972), Vol. I, pp. 987–89.

From 1914 until 1921 Aurobindo wrote commentaries on the Bhagavad Gita that were subsequently published as *Essays on the Gita*.[28] In this book, and in a more comprehensive work, *The Synthesis of Yoga*, Aurobindo explores each of the Yogas of the Gita—the Yogas of divine knowledge, divine action, and divine love. He then tries to show how each of these Yogas can and should be understood and practiced in our time. Then he gathers the three primary Yogas of the Gita into a larger framework that he calls *purna*-Yoga or Integral Yoga. In the second half of *The Synthesis of Yoga* Sri Aurobindo addresses each of these Yogas to the task of the evolution of humanity. To the Bhagavad Gita he adds the evolution of consciousness, including especially the evolution of humanity. Sri Aurobindo regarded the Gita as an absolutely splendid revelation in its time but acknowledges that in the present age it is necessary to understand dharma, karma, and the Yogas in more contemporary terms.

Both M. K. Gandhi and Sri Aurobindo looked to the Gita as the foundational text for their spiritual work, but in relation to the Second World War their respective interpretations of the Gita, to which they had been committed for several decades, led them to opposite positions. Consistent with his commitment to nonviolence and his insistence that violence always leads to violence, Gandhi opposed the invitation from the British to the leaders of the Indian Nationalist Movement for India to fight with the Allies in exchange for Indian independence after the war. (The leaders of the Nationalist Movement disagreed with Gandhi, and India fought with the British against the Axis powers.) In a particularly controversial example of his commitment to nonviolence, Gandhi wrote to Martin Buber during the Nazi holocaust of the Jews that it would be better in the long term if the Jews practiced nonviolence in response to their exterminators.[29] By contrast, Sri Aurobindo saw Nazis as agents of

---

28. These writings immediately followed Rudolf Steiner's two series of lectures on the Gita published in the present volume. Unfortunately, Sri Aurobindo makes no reference to these volumes, nor does he mention Rudolf Steiner or any of his writings.

29. See Louis Fischer, *The Essential Gandhi* (NY: Vintage, 1963), p. 329; for Buber's compelling letter to Gandhi dated February 24, 1939, to which Gandhi did not reply, see Nahum N. Glatzer and Paul Mendes-Flohr, eds., *The Letters of Martin Buber* (NY: Schocken Books, 1991), pp. 476–86.

negative spiritual forces in the world working against the evolution of humanity toward freedom and dignity. Which of these two positions, Gandhi's or Sri Aurobindo's, is truer to the teaching of the Gita?

Gandhi focuses on the early chapters, the ones in which Krishna leads Arjuna from depression to effective action by teaching him to practice non-attachment to the fruits of action. For Gandhi, the Gita is not about war, except as a metaphor, but is entirely about the conflict between the higher and lower self. Aurobindo focuses on the chapters that reveal Krishna as avatar and his instructions for the transformation of humanity. In 1914, at the start of World War I, Aurobindo wrote in *Essays on the Gita* that the war in the Bhagavad Gita was not metaphorical or symbolic but historical and that Krishna did mean for Arjuna to fight while focused on Krisha with maximum equanimity. For Gandhi, violence or nonviolence is a matter of morality to be decided by careful thinking. For Aurobindo, it is a matter of darkness or light, of missing or seeing the divine intent, which one can come to know through the Yoga of knowledge. Gandhi is also concerned with the struggle between dark and light but always in a particular situation, whether British vs. Indian rulers, mill owners vs. workers, or upper-caste Indians vs. untouchables, and not in relation to a larger reality.

Borrowing terms from the two major divisions of Buddhism, Theravada (literally, the way of the elders, the teaching that focuses on the path of the individual without regard to divine assistance) and Mahayana (literally, the greater way, the teaching that focuses on the path of the individual in relation to the saving power of Buddha, or Buddha nature), we might say that Gandhi offers a Theravada reading of the Gita and Aurobindo offers a Mahayana reading. Or, borrowing terms from Western philosophy, we might say that Gandhi is a nominalist concerning the gods of Hinduism—i.e., Rama and Krishna are the symbolic names of ideals or processes but not necessarily of actual beings—while for Sri Aurobindo, Rama and Krishna, along with many other figures in the Hindu tradition, including it would seem, himself and The Mother as co-avatars, are real beings, active in history and in the lives of individuals who, with the help of Yoga practice, are paying attention to them. Gandhi's allegorical interpretation, though less scholarly, has clarity, simplicity, and practicality on its side, and it has had many influential followers. Sri Aurobindo's interpretation is scholarly and deep, but too metaphysical and subtle for many readers. While presumably no one can avoid the question of action and its consequences as raised in the early chapters of the Gita (the ones on which Gandhi focuses), an appreciation of Sri Aurobindo's interpretation requires a confrontation with the mysteries of the avatar and his revelation in chapters IX to XI.

III. Rudolf Steiner on Krishna and the Gita

1. Rudolf Steiner's Approach to Krishna, Buddha, and Christ
According to Steiner, 1899 marked the end of the five-thousand-year period called Kali Yuga, the traditional Hindu conception of a dark and chaotic period. It is also the year that Steiner had a life-transforming experience of Christ as the central event in cosmic and human history:

> During the period when my statements about Christianity seemed to contradict my later comments, a conscious knowledge of real Christianity began to dawn within me. Around the turn of the twentieth century, this seed of knowledge continued to develop. The soul test described here occurred shortly before the beginning of the twentieth century. It was decisive for my soul's development that I stood spiritually before the Mystery of Golgotha[30] in a deep and solemn celebration of knowledge.[31]

Steiner thought that the twentieth century would continue in relative darkness—a characterization that proved all too true—but would at the same time be an opportunity for human beings to develop the

---

30. Steiner used this phrase to refer to the events relating to the crucifixion, death, and resurrection of Jesus Christ.
31. Rudolf Steiner, *Autobiography* (Great Barrington, MA: SteinerBooks, 1999), p. 239.

capacity for a more individualized and freer experience of the spiritual world. Though surely less evident, it may also be true that in 1879 the archangel Michael replaced the archangel Gabriel as the primary guide of the age. This double transition—the beginning of the reign of the archangel Michael and the end of the Kali Yuga—represents the beginning of an age ideal for the development of the capacities taught in the Gita. For the three major Yogas—knowledge, action, and love—Steiner uses the terms thinking, willing, and feeling. Within five years after his experience of the Cosmic Christ, in his view the decisive influence on the evolution of human consciousness, Steiner wrote two of his several foundational books, *How to Know Higher Worlds*[32] and *Theosophy*.[33] In 1909 he wrote his most comprehensive single volume, *An Outline of Esoteric Science*.[34]

From 1902 until 1912 he lectured out of his own experience to members of the Theosophical Society throughout Europe. He served as general secretary and primary teacher of the Berlin Branch of the Theosophical Society from 1902 to 1911. He delivered the two sets of lectures reprinted in this edition during 1912 and 1913, the years immediately following his break from the Theosophical Society, during which a group of followers was founding the Anthroposophical Society. In 1911, while lecturing in Copenhagen, Steiner received word that Annie Besant, in collaboration with her colleague, C. W. Leadbeater, had announced that the sixteen-year-old J. Krishnamurti was none other than the world teacher Jesus of Nazareth returned. Steiner was sufficiently disturbed by this announcement that he delivered three lectures under the title "The Spiritual Guidance of the Individual and Humanity,"[35] revised them for publication (as

---

32. *How to Know Higher Worlds: A Modern Path of Initiation*, trans. Christopher Bamford (Hudson, NY: Anthroposophic Press, 1994).
33. *Theosophy: An Introduction to the Spiritual Processes in Human Life and in the Cosmos*, trans. Catherine E. Creeger (Hudson, NY: Anthroposophic Press, 1994).
34. *An Outline of Esoteric Science*, trans. Catherine E. Creeger (Hudson, NY: Anthroposophic Press, 1997).
35. *The Spiritual Guidance of the Individual and Humanity: Some Results of Spiritual-Scientific Research into Human History and Development*, trans. Samuel Desch (Great Barrington, MA: Anthroposophic Press, 1992).

he seldom did), and thereafter considered his separation from the Theosophical Society to be a significant esoteric fact.

By 1911, after nine years of lecturing to large audiences of Theosophists throughout Europe, Steiner was known as one of only a few spiritual teachers able to speak from his own esoteric research. He was also known for his conviction, not shared by the founders or the leaders of the Theosophical Society, that Christ was and will ever be the central fact in the evolution of human consciousness. H. P. Blavatsky, and her two successors as president of the Theosophical Society during Steiner's life, Col. Olcott (1891–1907) and Annie Besant (1907–1933), regarded Krishna and Buddha, and perhaps Buddha preeminently, as the loftiest spiritual beings with the greatest significance for all humanity. Christ, they believed, though an important teacher for the West, did not share this status. The difference between Steiner and Annie Besant was prominent from the beginning of their relationship and intensified until 1911 when the Krishnamurti announcement made inevitable the separation of Steiner and the Christian-Rosicrucian-anthroposophical esoteric movement from the Hindu-Buddhist theosophical movement.

According to Rudolf Steiner, Christ is not only a teacher of the spiritual life but is an active presence, the decisive transformative force in human life. For Steiner, Christ the Logos (Word, Light, and Life) is announced in the Prologue to the Gospel of John: "In the beginning was the Word and the Word was with God and the Word was God." Almost alone among Western spiritual teachers of the early twentieth century, Steiner speaks of Krishna as an avatar and Buddha as a spiritual being close to Christ in stature and significance for the whole of human history. He describes at length the profound and essential contributions they each made to the spiritual evolution of humanity. He also sees each of these three spiritually lofty beings as representing a progressively deeper incarnation, i.e., deeper into *carne*, into human matter. Whereas Krishna seems hardly to have incarnated, Buddha "the enlightened one" lived as Gotama for eighty years and Christ incarnated into the exquisitely prepared body of Jesus of Nazareth. Jesus was born of another exquisitely prepared human being, a Jewish teenager named Miriam, who was crafted of spiritual and physical substances from very highly evolved beings who had already lived through a purification process in previous lives. The body of Jesus of Nazareth also partook of other spiritually advanced souls such as Adam, Hermes, Moses, Zoroaster, Krishna, and Buddha.

Steiner states that Christ the Logos–Sun being took up residence in Jesus for three years, from his baptism at age thirty until his crucifixion at age thirty-three. The Jesus that Christ joined contained the soul of Krishna, thereby joining in a profound way the spiritual teachers of India and the Christian West. According to the spiritual scientific research of Rudolf Steiner, this Krishna soul, joined to Jesus of Nazareth at birth, would seem to have been the visage of the resurrected Christ that was experienced by Mary Magdalen. It was also Christ speaking through the light form of Krishna[36] that Paul heard in his conversion experience on the road to Damascus. In this way, the vast wisdom of the Yogas taught by Krishna in the Bhagavad Gita came into Christianity through the revelation of Krishna-Christ to Paul, the apostle to the entire non-Jewish Mediterranean world and the primary source of Christian theology.

2. Krishna and the Gita in Evolving Consciousness

Rudolf Steiner interprets the Bhagavad Gita and the Yoga teachings of Krishna within an evolving historical context. According to Steiner, the evolution of consciousness, which is the invisible underlying cause of what is observable historically, consists of two opposite processes: a gradual diminishment from the ancient past to the present of a mystical, intuitive, unitive consciousness, and a simultaneous increase in temporality, materiality, and other particularities that followed directly from the development of intelligence. The most advanced expression of mature intelligence would seem to be the distinctive consciousness of the modern West—an expression that has certainly proven to be

---

36. Emil Bock, *Saint Paul* (Edinburgh: Floris Books, 1993), pp. 80–84 and 264–66.

not entirely positive. Several decades before Karl Jaspers introduced the widely accepted concept of the Axial Age, the period around the sixth century B.C.E. when the foundational ideas of several significant worldviews came to expression, Steiner was describing the different modes of consciousness of particularly significant historical periods.

According to Steiner's accounts of the evolution of consciousness, detailed in hundreds of lectures (fourteen of which are contained in the present volume), the sixth century B.C.E. was characterized by an imaginal consciousness, one that was able to access the gods and spirits very directly. The paradigmatic individuals doing the access- ing and reporting, though identifiable, were only at the beginning of a process that would eventually lead to fully formed historical indi- viduals; i.e., individuals who would be able to combine a thoroughly realized individuality and a conscious relationship to the whole of humanity. Steiner regards Socrates and Paul as two very early exam- ples of this ideal. Until the seventh or sixth century B.C.E., revelations tended to be through a single person—e.g., to the pharaohs, the *rishis* (seers, spiritual teachers) of the Vedas and Upanishads, Moses, or Homer—and were intended for a people. The spiritual guides of and for the people were acknowledged in conscious life. By contrast, Arjuna does not recognize the transcendent divinity of Krishna until more than halfway through the Gita, and Buddha seems not to have emphasized the influence of the gods, or spiritual beings. (Personally, I do not quite believe that Buddha was as disconnected from higher beings as many of the early Buddhist texts seem to suggest.)

Steiner emphasizes in many of his lectures that the Gita is created at a time in human evolution when there was around the globe a dramatic jump in a certain kind of awareness. In the same part of the world there came another profound historical consciousness-shatter- ing experience rooted in a kind of existential awareness. Gotama, not yet the Buddha, observed what have come to be known as "the three sorrows," illness, old age, and death. He suffered loss, and the realiza- tion that for all pleasures and for all positive experiences there is some kind of terminal point or limit; there is a transitoriness to everything. All these are ways of giving a meaning to the Sanskrit word *dukkha*, unsatisfactoriness. Gotama looked to the bottom of the human cup, found it empty, and resolved to find a solution. He committed to an extraordinary dharma; his success changed the course of human history. As a result of his enlightenment experience under the Bo tree, Gotama the Buddha explained that the way off the wheel of rebirth was and is to awaken to the reality of suffering, to see that suffering arises in desire, to see that it is curable, and to see that the cure is the eightfold path. These are the four noble truths at the foundation of all Buddhist teaching.

At the same time as Krishna of the Gita and Gotama the Buddha, in Israel the prophets Jeremiah and Second Isaiah were preaching a more interior and individuated Hebraic morality. Simultaneously, in the Greek world Pythagoras, Heraclitus, and Parmenides developed their systems of philosophy. Zoroaster was the great teacher in Persia while in China there were Confucius and Lao Tse. There was a kind of explosion of awareness made possible by each of these figures who came in response to a crisis, usually to an experience of loss or devolution. This dialectic is characteristic of the evolution of consciousness: first a loss, then a breakthrough solution. A loss of spiritual capacity made possible the insight and practices at the root of the world's major religious traditions. It would seem that each of the major religions teaches a foundational loss, lack, or break to be overcome by a teaching concerning the loss as well as practice concerning the way to make restoration, whether understood as liberation, enlightenment, or salvation.

As the human consciousness in which the Gita takes place is significantly different from modern Western consciousness, it is also different from stages of consciousness that preceded it, e.g., the time of the Vedas in India or of Moses and the Pharaohs in Egypt. Each period is a transition. In the sixth century B.C.E., approximately the time of the Bhagavad Gita, Indian consciousness was characterized by the reality of the gods and the spiritual world, and the fixed nature of dharma. Arjuna's dharma as a warrior remains a given throughout the Gita. Although Arjuna questioned his dharma as a warrior, Krishna did not take this questioning seriously. Rather, Krishna affirmed Arjuna's dharma—stay a warrior and fight, but change your focus from yourself to Me. What is distinctive about the Gita, and characteristic of sixth-century consciousness, is that Arjuna questioned his dharma at all. That is the great fact about the Gita, and about Gotama, who also questioned his dharma as a prince.

The experience and teaching of Buddha constitute a new dharma, more radical than the dharma of the Gita: Gotama left his princely dharma in order to strive for the realization of an extraordinary dharma, not as a son, husband, father, and prince, but as a meditator and enlightened spiritual teacher. But the Gita was radical in its Yoga teaching—four ways to realize the divine without changing one's dharma, each leading to *moksha* or liberation right in the thick of battle! Prior to the Gita and to the experience of Buddha, the relationship between individuals, even great historical figures, tended to be intimate and direct. Beginning with the Gita and the Buddha, the experience of the great individuals—and a major part of their being considered great—was precisely this questioning of dharma at the very beginning of a new consciousness, one in which the individual is more a partner in dialogue with the divine than an unconscious recipient of a comprehensive and fixed revelation.

3. Steiner's Approach to the Gita

In Steiner's view, Krishna is an avatar who carries the Indian spiritual and esoteric tradition, and indirectly prepared the way for Buddha and for Christ. In particular, Krishna made possible the line of great spiritual teachings, including the Yogas of Hinduism and its great spiritual teachers such as Shankara, Ramanuja, Chaitanya, Ramakrishna, Vivekananda, Ramana Maharshi, and Sri Aurobindo— as Buddha made possible great Buddhist teachings such as Theravada, Mahayana, Zen, and Vajrayana, and great teachers such as Dogen, D. T. Suzuki, and the fourteen Dalai Lamas. Whereas these teachings and these great spiritual teachers were once limited to particular languages and cultures, as Francis and Clare were once limited to the Christian West, with the dawn of global consciousness, all spiritual traditions are now increasingly contributing to other traditions, east and west, north and south. Based on his own esoteric research,

Steiner offers detailed explanations of the esoteric relationships among Krishna, Buddha, and Christ.

In the process of explaining the global significance of Krishna, Buddha, and Christ, he also explains, again based on his own experience, the mission since 1879 of the Archangel Michael, a servant of Christ working on behalf of human freedom. As a result of the esoteric research of Rudolf Steiner and some other twentieth-century interpreters of more than one spiritual tradition, it is now possible to imagine and to engage with the ways in which these great beings have been working collaboratively on behalf of humanity and the Earth. Steiner's lectures "The Bhagavad Gita and the Epistles of Paul" invite meditation on the picture of the resurrected Christ transmitting the soul of Krishna and the Yogas of the Gita into Saul on his way to a new life as Paul, the apostle to the non-Jewish Mediterranean world.[37] Steiner also gives us an opportunity to contemplate the amazing image of St. Francis, in a previous life, as a disciple of the Buddha living near the Black Sea in the sixth century.[38]

In addition to offering an important solution to the apparent conflict of religions that has been a source of so much misunderstanding and violence, Steiner's esoteric research concerning Krishna, Buddha, and Christ also gives the reader important assistance in approaching each of these figures and their works. He states:

> Above all, we must firmly realize how the human soul, under certain conditions, can meet the being whom we tried to describe from a certain aspect, calling him Krishna. Far more important than any dispute as to wheather Sankhya or Vedic philosophy is contained in the Bhagavad Gita is the realization that, under certain conditions, Arjuna meets that Spirit who prepared the age of self consciousness. (163)[39]

37. See below, p. 91.
38. Rudolf Steiner, *The Spiritual Foundations of Morality: Francis of Assisi and the Christ Impulse* (Great Barrington, MA: Anthroposophic Press, 1995), p. 33.
39. References to *The Bhagavad Gita and the Epistles of Paul* and *The Esoteric Meaning of the Bhagavad Gita* in this volume will be given in parenthesis following each passage.

It is important to try to imagine the god Krishna within or behind the appearance of Krishna the charioteer. The spiritual Krishna really does include universes—and gods. The Gita climaxes with Krishna exclaiming, "Behold, before any of the gods were, I am"—in a way that resembles Jesus's statement "Before Abraham was, I am" (John 8:58).

Although Steiner says that Krishna incarnated for the first time as the avatar of the Gita, his treatment of Krishna in these lectures does not focus on his humanity—as do his treatment of Christ and Buddha—but on his soul and what appear to be references to his etheric body. Because he appeared to function primarily as an etheric body or soul rather than as a fully incarnated human, Krishna did not bring his divine nature to bear on physical reality. This is one of the ways that Sri Aurobindo understood his own spiritual mission, in collaboration with The Mother, to be an extension of Krishna: He sought to bring the divine more fully and effectively into the whole of physical reality, including especially the human body. By his human life, Gotama the Buddha, following almost immediately the Gita event, did bring his exquisite four-part reality—physical (his human body), etheric (his life body, subtle body, ghost body), astral (his soul), and "I" (his eternal reality)[40]—to the service of suffering humanity. It was then possible for Christ, building on the contributions of Krishna and Buddha, to penetrate and heal the human body and the Earth. In joining his resurrected, or etheric, body to the Earth, Christ also brought the Yogas of Krishna and the enlightenment experience of Buddha, both part of the body of Jesus of Nazareth that communicated itself fully to Christ at His death, into a saving relationship to humanity and the Earth. Christ absorbed and then gave back to humanity and the Earth the great soul of Krishna. Steiner writes:

---

40. Admittedly, it appears from Buddhist texts that Buddha did not acknowledge a part of the human being that Steiner refers to as "I." Concerning the reality of the "I" as such, Buddha was silent. This may not indicate a denial of the "I," an eternal essence, as much as a teaching about the need to overcome the lower self, and particularly the spiritual disadvantage of a concern for one's immortality.

So much in the revelations of the Testaments, even if in scattered fragments, comes from the ancient teaching of Krishna. But that teaching became something for all humanity because the Christ as such is not merely a human ego belonging to humankind, but belonging to the upper hierarchies. (91)

PART TWO

The Bhagavad Gita and the Epistles of Paul

DESCRIPTIVE OUTLINE

1. The Merging of Three Spiritual Streams in the Bhagavad Gita

December 28, 1912

Rudolf Seiner opens the first of five lectures on the Bhagavad Gita and the Epistles of Paul, delivered during the days of the founding of the Anthroposophical Society, by placing the Gita and the new Anthroposophical movement within the context of an evolution of consciousness divided into historical periods. For Steiner, the present is a time of increasing opportunity for conscious spiritual knowledge within a larger context, and over against a rapidly increasing darkness of consciousness. While his lectures describe in broad outline—and with some amazing details—the first and second historical periods after the disappearance of Atlantis, periods dating from the eighth through the fourth millennium, they focus more intensely on the three periods that began in the third millennium to the present.

The period that Steiner refers to as the third of the present seven epochs (which he usually refers to as post-Atlantean, a term that is understandably problematic for most readers) was characterized by the consciousness of the Egyptian-Chaldean-Babylonian cultures. It began in the third millennium and lasted until the eighth century B.C.E.

Steiner characterizes the fourth epoch of the present evolutionary cycle (the fourth post-Atlantean) by reference to the consciousness of the Greek, Roman, and Christian cultures. It began in the West in approximately the eighth century B.C.E. and ended at the beginning of the fifteenth century C.E.

The fifth epoch of the present cycle (the fifth post-Atlantean) is characterized by the materialistic, scientific, and the very individualistic consciousness of the modern West. The fifth epoch began in the fifteenth century, in the Renaissance of the West, characterized by such figures as Leonardo, Michelangelo, and Raphael, and will, or should, last until the thirty-sixth century C.E. What Rudolf Steiner refers to as the present is perhaps best understood as the late nineteenth and early twentieth centuries, but with the understanding that the consciousness he is describing can be expected to prevail, while continuing to evolve for better and worse, for many centuries (3-4).

In this lecture, Steiner states that it was only in the fourth epoch, essentially with the Greeks, that outstanding personalities such as Socrates, Plato, and Aristotle begin to arise. Steiner refers to this impress of personality as being characteristic of the last three thousand years, though it should be noted that the personalities he mentions do not extend back past twenty-five centuries, prior to the Greece of Pericles.

The Bhagavad Gita is revealed approximately at the transition from the consciousness of the third to the consciousness of the fourth epoch. Steiner's account of the evolution of consciousness typically uses Western markers—Egyptians, Hebrews, Greeks, Romans, and various periods in the history of the Christian and post-Christian West, or individuals such as Moses, Homer, Plato, Christ and the New Testament, Aquinas, Raphael, Kepler—but in this lecture series, and the subsequent one entitled "The Esoteric Significance of the Bhagavad Gita," he emphasizes the contribution of Krishna to the evolution of Western consciousness. When Steiner refers to "the East" in these two volumes of lectures he means the spiritual tradition and consciousness of India in approximately the seventh and sixth centuries B.C.E., exactly at the transition from the consciousness of the third to the fourth cultural epoch. In other lectures, his references to "the East" can mean either the Hindu and Buddhist teaching of south Asia, or, in lectures on East and West, he might mean eastern Europe, but he seems never to mean the East Asia of China, Korea, or Japan.

Turning to the significance of the Bhagavad Gita, Rudolf Steiner identifies three streams that are woven throughout this text: the Vedas, the Indian texts dating from 1000 B.C.E.; the Sankhya system of Kapila, a classical philosophical system formulated just prior to the experience described in the Gita; and the Yoga system of Patanjali, the handbook for the practice of Yoga summarized around the time of the Gita. "It is the greatness of the Gita that it describes in such an all-inclusive way how the spiritual life of the East receives the contributions of these three streams." Questionably, Steiner identifies the Vedas with the Word, Sankhya with law, and Yoga with devotion. "Word, Law, Devotion—these are the three streams by which the soul can carry on its development." (13) Steiner states that Krishna shows his pupil that all three spiritual streams must be developed harmoniously.

"The Vedic stream is most pronouncedly a philosophy of unity, the most spiritual monism imaginable, and it comes to completion in the Vedanta." (5) Monism here refers to the view that reality is an absolute spiritual oneness.[41] The Vedas are texts that were first spoken by spiritual teachers, *rishis*, concerning teachings and practices of pre-Hindu Brahmanism. The Upanishads, texts that are more mystical and philosophical than the Vedas, followed the Vedas. Vedanta is the system of thought that is identified with monism, due to one particularly influential version of Vedanta, the Advaita (non-dual) Vedanta found in many of the Upanishads and brilliantly formulated by Shankara, the eighth-century spiritual philosopher who interpreted the Upanishads in the light of strict monism.

It seems not quite clear whether Steiner's reference to the Vedic philosophy refers to the Vedas, i.e., the ancient texts, or to the Upanishads, or to the philosophical system of Shankara—or indeed all of these—but it is clear that he identifies the Vedic tradition with spiritual knowledge: "What the Veda tells us is the Word of God, which is creative and which is born again in human knowledge." (7) The Sankhya philosophy also contributes to the Gita a teaching about

---

41. See Robert McDermott, "Monism," Mircea Eliade, ed., *Encyclopedia of Religion* (New York: Macmillan, 1987), 10:57–65.

knowledge, but instead of a monism it teaches a radical dualism—
purusha and *prakriti*, with *prakriti* itself a radical pluralism. Sankhya
is the philosophy that Patanjali used to undergird the Yoga practices
summarized in his handbook, *The Yoga Sutras*. Both of these Yoga
practices and their supportive philosophical ideas are prominent in the
verses of the Gita that focus on *raja-* (meditation) Yoga.

Steiner compares Sankhya philosophy to the atomistic philosophy
of the eighteenth-century philosopher Leibniz. Both philosophies
are extremely complex: the primary elements in Leibniz's system
are "windowless monads," but this same system includes individual
personalities and God; similarly, the components in the Sankhya
system are not just atomistic units with absolutely no unity and no
feeling, but include seven levels of reality all in complex relation to
an ultimate non-physical reality called *purusha*. The Sankhya system
includes three *gunas*, each of which figure prominently in the later
chapters of the Gita: *sattva* is usually understood as light, *rajas* as
energy, and *tamas* as darkness. "Sankhya observes the soul's sheaths,
and Yoga leads it to ever higher stages of inner experience." (10)

In these five lectures, Steiner offers many references to the importance of Krishna's contributions to the evolution of consciousness. In
this first lecture he describes Krishna as the great teacher "for the new
age set free of the old blood-ties." Toward the end of this first of five
lectures, Steiner examines the relationship between the Gita and the
New Testament under three headings: Word, Law, and Devotion.
He sees the Veda, Sankhya, and Yoga, three important strands in
the Gita, as preparation for the Christ, the living embodiment of the
Word, law, and devotion:

> The Vedas approached humanity in abstract form. The divine
> Logos of which the Gospel of John speaks is the living, creative
> Word itself. What we encounter in the Sankhya philosophy as the
> lawful ordering of cosmic forms—transposed historically into the
> old Hebraic revelation—becomes what Paul refers to as the Law.
> Faith in the risen Christ proclaimed by Paul appears as the third
> member of the Trinity. The Yoga taught by Krishna is carried over
> by Paul into faith, which should take the place of the Law. (13)

Thus, Veda, Sankhya, Yoga are the dawn of what later rose as the sun. Veda arises again in the being of Christ himself, appearing actually in historical development, not poured abstractly into the expanses of space and time, but as a separate individuality, the living Word. (13-14)

We shall see that through precisely grasping the connection between the great Bhagavad Gita and the Epistles of Paul the deepest mysteries are revealed concerning what may be called the activity of the spirit in the collective education of the human race. (14)

2. The Fundamental Concepts of the Gita: The Veda, Sankhya, and Yoga

December 29, 1912

At the start of this lecture Steiner refers to the Gita as "the spiritual horizon surrounding the great Buddha, out of which he developed." (16) He considers it significant that Buddha was born in Kapila, the birthplace of Kapila, creator of the Sankhya philosophy. (29) He describes this time as one in which clairvoyance, the seeing of spiritual realities, was not unusual.

According to Sankhya, a multiplicity of individual souls plunged into *prakriti*, reality in its plural forms, and developed downward from the highest differentiated form of the primal flood to coarse bodies. Having arrived at this physical stage, the souls evolve back upward again to the primal flood. With the help of Sankhya philosophy, which like all orthodox Indian philosophies is also a path of spiritual liberation, souls can then free themselves and enter into pure *purusha*. In this process of descent and return, the soul experiences a combination of three levels of consciousness, three *gunas*: the soul can be in a state of sleep, or *tamas*; it can be in a dynamic state, called *rajas*; or it can be in spiritual state, called *sattva*.

In this lecture Steiner discloses that, according to his spiritual scientific research, Aristotle, who had no remembrance of the ancient knowledge found in Sankhya, nevertheless developed a color theory (the text of which was lost) that shows the influence of the Sankhya theory of color. Further, in the late eighteenth century Goethe developed an extremely original, significant theory of color that reiterates the Sankhya theory of the *gunas.* "Goethe's division of color phenomena represents the three states of *sattva, rajas,* and *tamas.*" (28)

Toward the end of this lecture Steiner turns to the central theme of the Gita, Krishna's directive to Arjuna to fight. Steiner interprets this directive in the context of Krishna's attempt to lift the soul of Arjuna from the situation in which he is caught by a conflict of obligation to "a higher stage in which it will feel itself elevated beyond everything transitory." (34)

3. The Joining of the Three Streams in the Christ Impulse

December 30, 1912

Continuing the idea introduced at the end of the second lecture that in the Gita Krishna set out to lift Arjuna out of the transitory, Steiner again states that Krishna "lifts us above everyday human experiences, above all passions and everything that disturbs the soul." He continues:

> We are transported into a sphere of serenity, clarity, calm dispassion, and freedom from emotion, into an atmosphere of wisdom, when even one part of the Gita is allowed to work upon us. Reading it, our humanity is raised to a higher stage. Through it all, we feel that if we wish to allow the divine character of the Gita to affect us in the right way, we must first free ourselves from a good deal that is only too human. (38)

Steiner then contrasts the calm created by Krishna, a "universal man," with the agitation and passion created by Paul, the author of the very personal New Testament letters. "What Paul says comes from a person who is passionately indignant at what has happened." (38) Steiner asserts that Krishna as teacher and avatar is preparatory for the incarnation of Christ in that when the human soul looks to Krishna it finds its "own highest Self," whereas, according to Steiner, Christ advances the evolution one step further by bringing not just a teaching, nor even the highest reality of the individual soul, but a presence and force for the transformation of humanity and the Earth.

It is worth noting that Steiner's statement, "Krishna teaches the highest human wisdom, the highest that humanity can attain" (42) is an excellent example of how an isolated statement taken from one of Steiner's lectures without the rest of the lecture, or the rest of the lectures in a series, and ultimately, without the rest of his entire work, can be very misleading. In this case, the statement means what it seems to say, but without the added information on how Christ not only taught but represented, and continues to represent, a force in the soul, one could mistakenly think that Krishna's contribution was the highest ever, irrespective of the subsequent and greater contribution of Buddha and Christ. Similarly, if one were to take any number of Steiner's statements on the unique contributions of Buddha, or of Christ, one could easily assume, mistakenly, that Buddha's contributions were possible without those of Krishna or Christ, or that Christ's contributions were possible without those of Krishna or Buddha.

One way of understanding the result of Krishna's great contribution to humanity in the Bhagavad Gita is to say that Krishna leads Arjuna to fight without entanglement in the passions of the battle and without regard to the results of the battle. He enables Arjuna to battle as an onlooker, as one who lets it happen—i.e., as a practitioner of *karma*-Yoga. Another way, perhaps a higher way, is to say that after the transformation of Arjuna's consciousness into a unity with Krishna, the Gita reveals that Krishna remains as the expression of the highest in the human being. In chapters IX to XI of the Gita, Krishna reveals himself as the unity of all forms, human and divine, and the leader of humanity. (47) This revelation of Krishna's being is available only to one who comes to him directly, not through the Vedas, sacrifices, and rituals; but as one in solitude looks upon Krishna reverently—"only he can recognize me in the form you have seen, and can become one with me." (XI.47-49)

4. The Essence of the Bhagavad Gita
and the Significance of the Pauline Letters

December 31, 1912

In this, the fourth of five lectures, Steiner turns to an explicit comparison between the Gita and the Epistles of the Apostle Paul. He regards the Gita as "a fully ripened fruit" whereas the Pauline Epistles are "the seed of something entirely new." (56) The revelation of Krishna recounted in the Bhagavad Gita, as well as the enlightenment experience and teaching of Buddha, both took place at the beginning of what Steiner refers to as the fourth epoch of the current set of seven, the one that began in approximately the eighth century B.C.E., whereas the incarnation of Christ took place after seven centuries of astonishing development of human consciousness, the most remarkable of which was the contribution of the Greeks. Whereas many Christian theologians and historians tend to think of the Christian tradition being continuous almost exclusively with the Hebraic tradition, Steiner, and esotericists generally, interpret the Christian tradition equally in terms of the Jewish and Greek traditions.

Steiner also takes account of the change of consciousness summarized by the term Axial Age, the foundational change of human consciousness due to the explosion of genius around the Earth in approximately the sixth century, including the Hebrew prophets Isaiah and Jeremiah, the Persian prophet Zoroaster, the Gita and the Buddha in India, Confucius and Lao Tse in China. All of these changes, according to Steiner, were important in their own right but were also preparatory for the transformation of human consciousness brought about six centuries later by Christ. None of the Axial Age developments, however wide and profound, even when viewed together, were as transformative as the descent of Christ into Jesus of Nazareth and the events that Steiner refers to as the Mystery of Golgotha, i.e., the incarnation, crucifixion, and resurrection of Jesus Christ: "After the Mystery of Golgotha, the Christ impulse worked within the soul, as if the soul were a self-illuminating body radiating light from within." (57)

Clearly, Steiner's account of the evolution of consciousness is very complex: Christ brought a profound and decisive transformation to the Earth and to the whole of humanity, and yet human consciousness continues to devolve, to lose awareness of the spiritual world. Despite the Mystery of Golgotha and many positive spiritual deeds of great souls, the present certainly seems to be characterized by *tamas*, increasing darkness.

Krishna is also part of this paradoxical development: he led Arjuna to the practice of the Yogas, and specifically to the transformation of his knowing, his action, and his devotion, but only after, and because, Arjuna had experienced profound *adharma*. The Bhagavad Gita represents a great gift for an age simultaneously advancing and devolving; it is losing contact with the spiritual world and beginning to develop individual consciousness, the great achievement of the Axial Age. Arjuna's confusion and despondency, presumably not previously possible, and not symptomatic of his time and culture, was a darkness of consciousness that made possible his transformation by Yoga, and by his experience of Krishna.

Similarly, but later and more decisively, the Roman world exhibited a consciousness that was growing increasingly estranged from the spiritual world, and into that culture, at what Steiner calls "the turning point of time," came the ultimate avatar, the rescuer of human consciousness from overwhelming materialism. It is the core of Steiner's teaching that a similar, though more powerful, materialism dominates modern Western consciousness, and again there is need for a new relationship to Krishna and Buddha, and more urgently to Christ. Steiner also emphasized that throughout the twentieth century Christ would reappear in the etheric, as a kind of envelope of the Earth.[42]

Steiner regards the Gita as a philosophical poem in contrast to Paul's intensely personal account of the crucified and resurrected Christ. Paul had to "show the contrast between this darkening

---

42. See Rudolf Steiner, *The Reappearance of Christ in the Etheric* (Great Barrington, MA: Anthroposophic Press, 1983).

influence common to all and the seedling to be brought to life in the human soul as the Christ impulse. He also is to point out every aspect of materialism, every possible vice that his message must battle against." (68)

Steiner then adds a significant contrast between the experience of Krishna at the time of the Gita and the experience of Christ since the Mystery of Golgotha, namely, the role of the tempters, Lucifer (the one who tempts human beings to spiritual presumption) and Ahriman (the one who tempts human beings to believe that there is nothing but matter). Steiner says that these beings attained great power over humanity between the time of Krishna (and Buddha) and the time of Christ, a time of increasing *tamasic* consciousness. Because of the increased persuasiveness of Lucifer and Ahriman, the Christ impulse has been all the more necessary.

Steiner concludes this lecture with a startling disclosure: he seems to state that Krishna lived a full life as the son of Vasudeva and the revealer of the Gita. This statement is significant because in the text of the Gita it is not altogether clear whether, in contrast to accounts of Buddha and Christ, the revealer of the Gita is fully incarnated. In the *Mahabharata*, Krishna is obviously presented as an incarnated being, even if more fictional than historical, but in the more mystical Gita one could easily imagine that Krishna's revelation took place in a particular time and space but that Krishna himself might have appeared to Arjuna as a soul, or etheric figure. Given Steiner's amazing—though not infallible—capacity for reading spiritual events of the past, it is certainly worth noting that he refers to Krishna as having lived a full life in the same culture as Arjuna.

Steiner then notes that a human being was able to serve as the vessel for the God Krishna but that the Christ being would have been too powerful for a human being to hold, beginning at conception, and that Jesus of Nazareth, with the "I" of Zarathustra, had to develop to age thirty in order to receive the Christ ego at the baptism.

*5. The Spirituality of Maya. Krishna, the Luminosity of Christ.
Paul's Experience and Teaching of the Risen Christ*

January 1, 1913

Along with "The Mission of Gotama Buddha on Mars," which
Steiner delivered three weeks earlier, this lecture is one of the most
astonishing of all of Steiner's six thousand lectures. In the lectures
on Buddha, Steiner discloses that according to his spiritual-scientific
research, Buddha performed a sacrifice in the Mars sphere (perhaps
best understood astrologically or archetypally) similar to Christ's
sacrifice on Earth.[43] In this fifth lecture in "The Bhagavad Gita and
the Epistles of Paul," Steiner offers two astonishing statements: that
Krishna was the sister soul of Adam, and that the Yogas taught by
Krishna streamed from the resurrected Christ into Paul, the first and
foremost teacher of Christianity. Both of these statements deserve
thoughtful and reverent consideration.

In a particularly complex disclosure, Steiner explains that the
sister soul of the first human, called Adam (*adamah*, "out of earthly
substance"), incarnated for the first time in, or as, Krishna, and for the
second time as the soul of Jesus of Nazareth: "The only time this sister
soul of Adam became physically visible before its embodiment in the
Luke Jesus boy was in Krishna." (90) "In the Luke Jesus boy lived a part
of the human being that had never before entered human evolution

---

43. The full text reads as follows: "Christian Rosenkreutz realized that to bring about a
certain purification needed on Mars [in the Mars sphere], the teachings of Buddha were
eminently suitable. The Christ being, the essence of divine love, had once descended
to the Earth to a people who were in many respects alien; in the seventeenth century,
Buddha, the prince of peace, went to the planet of war and conflict, Mars, to execute his
mission where souls were warlike and torn with strife.

Thus, Buddha performed a sacrificial deed similar to the deed performed in the
Mystery of Golgotha by the bearer of the essence of divine love, Christ. To dwell on Mars
as Buddha was a deed of sacrifice offered to the cosmos. He was, as it were, the lamb
offered up in sacrifice on Mars, and to accept this environment of strife was for him a kind
of crucifixion. He undertook this deed on Mars in the service of Christian Rosenkreutz.
So do the exalted beings who guide the world together, not only on Earth, but from one
planet to another." ("The Mission of Gotama Buddha on Mars," Neuchatel, December
18, 1912, in *From Buddha to Christ*, NY: Anthroposophic Press, 1978, p. 99).

on Earth." (86) The Luke Jesus boy refers to the soul of the boy Jesus described in the Gospel of Luke, a pure boy with the etheric body of Buddha and the soul of Krishna, as distinct from the boy described in the Gospel of Matthew, a worldly boy with the ego of Zarathustra.[44] The Krishna who revealed his divine nature to Arjuna was the sister soul of Adam and, subsequently, the soul that gave itself to the make-up of Jesus of Nazareth prior to the entrance into that body of the Christ being when Jesus, at age thirty, was baptized by his cousin John.

It is now possible to grasp the amazing picture that Steiner reveals at the conclusion of this lecture, in which the resurrected Christ, which is essentially the soul of Krishna, appears to Saul, persecutor of Jewish converts to Christianity, and transmits to him, and thereby to the whole of Christianity forever after, the soul of Krishna, the teacher of Arjuna, the arch-yogi of the Bhagavad Gita. It is by design, then, that the Christian dharma (teachings and spiritual practices) includes the Yoga teachings of Krishna as transmitted from the resurrected soul of Christ to Paul the Apostle.

> As Paul journeyed to Damascus, it was the Christ who appeared to him. The flood of light that enveloped him was Krishna. Because Christ took Krishna as his own soul sheath, through which he then continued to work, everything that once was the content of the sublime Gita streamed from him. So much in the revelations of the Testaments, even if in scattered fragments, comes from the ancient teaching of Krishna. (91)[45]

This is not to say, however, that Paul's teachings simply repeat the Yogas of Krishna. Whereas the Yogas of the Gita require each individual soul to aspire to its higher self (i.e., to Krishna), Paul

---

44. For Steiner's account of the two Jesus children, see Rudolf Steiner, *According to Luke: The Gospel of Compassion and Love Revealed*, Introduction by Robert McDermott (Great Barrington, MA: Anthroposophic Press, 2001), Lecture Four and pp. 232–37.

45. Robert Powell, esotericist and Sophiologist, reported to me in conversations that the late Willi Sucher, noted astrosophist, shared with Robert his conviction, based on his reading of Rudolf Steiner, that Arjuna was reborn as St. Paul, so that the Resurrected Christ, who had absorbed the astral body of Krishna, was again instructing Arjuna, this time as Paul.

emphasizes that the resurrected Christ is present to all of humanity corporally considered: "For as the body is one, with many members, all the single members forming together one body, so is it also with Christ" (1 Cor. 12:3-31). (79)

Finally, in this extraordinary lecture Steiner offers three additional perspectives: the view of the created world that he finds in the Gita in contrast to the view that he finds in the Epistles of Paul; his claim that the Pauline understanding of Christ is universal, or is compatible with and transcends all religious traditions; and, in conclusion, his claim that these lectures on the Bhagavad Gita should help to establish that the newly formed Anthroposophical Society would not be narrow or sectarian.

First, Steiner claims that whereas the purpose of "this Eastern [i.e., Indian] method of development ... is toward becoming free from material existence, from the outer world of nature, which, according to the Vedic philosophy, is *maya*, illusion," Paul's purpose is to affirm that the revelations of God and His Spirit live everywhere in the created world. (84) The following is a summary of Steiner's own view, one that he also finds in Paul's epistles:

> [Christ] came in order to bring us into true harmony with the world, that we might learn to overcome the power in Lucifer's temptations, to penetrate the veil of maya, to see divine revelation in its true form; that we recognize Christ as the One Who reconciles human beings and their world, and leads them into the reality of divine manifestation, so that through Him those primal words may be understood: "Behold, all is very good." (93)

Second, Steiner makes the following claim concerning the Christ impulse:

> Once a person grasps the world-historical significance of the Christ impulse, nothing more is needed from this or that Christian doctrine in order to proceed. Particularly in our time, one can even take a start from an anti-Christian point of view, or a feeling of indifference. When one looks deeply into what our

time is able to bring to spiritual life, when one sees the contradictions and foolishness of materialism, one is perhaps led most genuinely to the Christ these days, more so than if one came to Him through some special creed. Therefore, when it is said outside our circle that we set out from a special kind of Christian belief, it can be regarded as an especially vicious slander. For it is not a matter of starting out from some kind of denominational doctrine, but from the demands of spiritual life itself. Everyone—Muslim, Buddhist, Jew, Hindu, or Christian—can understand the Christ impulse in its full meaning for humanity's evolution. (83)

Third, in the conclusion of these five lectures to former members of the Theosophical Society, then in the process of committing to a new society with Rudolf Steiner as its teacher, Steiner urges that this new society should avoid sectarianism:

From what alone can truth and genuine reverence for the divine worlds and divine wisdom spring? Only from real self-knowledge, self-discipline, and self-development. May the forces streaming and pulsating through the Anthroposophical Society serve this purpose.

This is the reason for giving this particular cycle of lectures at the start of the Anthroposophical Movement. They should prove that we are not dealing with something narrow, but that our movement's horizon can extend over distances that encompass Indian thought as well. (94-95)

Due to the mixed success of the society that his followers formed at this time, twelve years later, at Christmas 1923 Steiner refounded the Anthroposophical Society and joined his own destiny to its mission.

PART THREE

The Esoteric Significance of the Bhagavad Gita

DESCRIPTIVE OUTLINE

Less than five months after his momentous five lectures on the Bhagavad Gita and the Epistles of Paul, delivered at the time of the founding of the Anthroposophical Society, Steiner gave nine lectures on the specific content of the Gita itself, not in comparison with Paul's epistles, but as an in-depth and detailed study of the text very much on its own terms.

In this series Rudolf Steiner says several times, in as many different ways, that this dialogue between Arjuna and Krishna in approximately the seventh century B.C.E. signals the beginning of a new soul consciousness. The discussion between Krishna and Arjuna is one of the early indications, maybe even the first, of this new soul mood, one in which there is a strong sense of self-consciousness. It is not as strong as a modern Western sense of self, but it represents the beginning of a process that led to a modern Western experience of self as the center of the world and as the locus of value.

Rudolf Steiner offers two pictures, one of Krishna as revealed in the Bhagavad Gita and one of Socrates bidding farewell to his students as he is about to be executed. Steiner often uses such pictures or images to show a quality of consciousness characteristic of a past time or event. In the first picture, in which Krishna brings spiritual wisdom to a combatant in a civil war, consciousness is characterized as spiritual vision— Arjuna the warrior is allowed to see Krishna in a vast and powerful context, and is thereby enabled to continue in battle confident that he does so in accordance with Krishna's divine plan. Socrates, by contrast, has only a dim sense of the spiritual world, and so attempts to raise the vision of his students to a spiritual height by rational argument.

As Steiner interprets the Gita, Krishna is a god who incarnated in order to enable Arjuna, and thereafter humanity, to deal with earthly affairs. Arjuna, the warrior on the front line of battle, needs Krishna to give meaning to action in the world—specifically in the battle about to be fought, with its inevitable suffering, deaths, and chaotic aftermath. Steiner says that Arjuna was at home in the spiritual, or supersensible, and wanted no part of the world of action. Arjuna needs Krishna, the god who by precept and example teaches fidelity to action, to strengthen his acceptance of the inevitability of life and death.

Lecture 1 : May 28, 1913

In this first lecture Steiner refers to the Bhagavad Gita as "one of the greatest and most penetrating manifestations of the human spirit." Ancient though it is, as an example of the clairvoyance characteristic of the third epoch, it nevertheless "comes before us with renewed significance at the present time." Indeed, Steiner makes a very bold claim on behalf of this scripture: "We shall see that there is little in the world to approach the glory of this description of how the teacher's sublime spirit form is revealed to the clairvoyant eye of his pupil." (103)

Steiner develops a contrast between Arjuna, struggling at the end of the age of clairvoyance and in need of having this world explained, and the dying Socrates, who stands at the start of a tradition of questioning knowledge of the spiritual world, and knowledge *per se.* The most significant difference between Arjuna and Socrates, however, is simply that Arjuna felt himself to be part of a group defined by family, and not at all an isolated individual, whereas Socrates, though surrounded by friends and students, felt himself to be a unique individual defined by his ideas. (Steiner does not say so, but Socrates also considered himself defined by his city, Athens, his conception of the civilized world.) Yet Steiner's idea of Arjuna's group identity is unusual in that he sees Arjuna defining himself as "nothing else than myself, and I admit the world's existence only in so far as it is I!" The "I" with which Arjuna identifies himself is not the ego that will come to dominate Western consciousness increasingly throughout the fourth epoch, but rather a group "I" in the beginning of the Gita, and at the end of the Gita an "I" that has been absorbed back into Krishna.

By contrast, neither Socrates nor his students need an introduction to, or justification of, the ordinary world—though it has often been argued that the philosophy of his student Plato does sacrifice the reality of the physical world to a world of ideal forms. Of course, Socrates is not as deeply imbedded in the world as we are, or even as Aristotle was only two generations later, but he was obviously more at one with the ordinary world than Arjuna was. Steiner sees Socrates as one of the last great figures who had a direct glimpse, an intuitive awareness, of the spiritual world—the world to which Socrates confidently argued he would return just as soon as he drank the poison hemlock prescribed by his enemies, political Athenians who opposed him because they opposed free inquiry.

Steiner makes it clear that these two events—the revelation of Krishna to Arjuna and Socrates leaving the earthly realm in favor of the afterlife—represent important stages of consciousness, different ways of thinking and feeling about the divine, the world, and the self. He invites us to reflect on figures such as Krishna and Socrates—as well as Buddha, Jesus, and other paradigmatic religious figures—as a way of tracing the evolution of human consciousness, the path by which we have come to think and feel as we do in the modern West. Steiner depicted the inner life of Krishna and Socrates as a way of enabling us to experience the change in awareness that each brought about in the past. Unlike some thinkers who urge that we imitate or return to a spiritual thinking of a previous age, and others who argue that the spiritual experience of every age is essentially the same, Steiner tries to show that the experiences of Socrates and Krishna are quite different from each other, and radically different from our own. He urges that we understand and appreciate the quality of their awareness (of the divine, the world, and the self), but he does not recommend that we try to cultivate their awareness. They belong to a mode, or quality, of consciousness that is past and therefore inappropriate for our time.

In addition to depicting the various kinds of awareness evident in the history or evolution of human consciousness—of which Buddha and Krishna, Socrates and Jesus are dramatic examples to be studied—Steiner above all stresses the need for a way of thinking that is exactly right for the present age. While it is important, and certainly intriguing, to follow Steiner's accounts of these great figures (and innumerable others in every historical period and many cultures), he is primarily committed to showing the contrast between these old ways of awareness (whether seeing, feeling, or speaking) and a way of thinking that includes feeling and willing, and was not possible in previous ages. This new way of thinking, of which we can find the first traces in Socrates (and less in Buddha and none at all in Krishna), offers the individual human being, for the first time in the history of the world, the possibility of thinking that is fully conscious, will-filled, individual, and free. In order to prove his case for a way of thinking that is far advanced of both the most advanced ways of thinking in the past and the ordinary ways of thinking in the present, Steiner poured out his ideas, some but not all clairvoyantly attained, through a dozen carefully argued books and, incredibly, more than six thousand lectures. He offers thousands of examples of a new, free, and will-filled way of seeing-thinking, concerning entities and events past and present, material and spiritual.

Steiner's way of seeing-thinking the past—e.g., progressively from the revelation of Krishna to Arjuna, to the awakening experience of the Buddha, to Socrates's attempt to bridge the spiritual and material worlds—emphasizes both the power and the limitations of these great experiences. More importantly, however, he shows the way in which each of these experiences, and countless others, have contributed to making possible the seeing-thinking, or conscious intuition, that he recommends for the present age.

Lecture 2 : May 29, 1913

In this lecture, Steiner sees the Gita proceeding through three stages: from Arjuna's despondency, to instruction in thinking, to identification with the cosmos.

First, Steiner emphasizes the depth of Arjuna's despondency: "Destiny is hammering at Arjuna's soul, shaking it to its very depths." (115) This is the kind of upheaval that is necessary at the initial stages of esoteric development. To enter the spiritual world, "we must learn to suffer the convulsions of our soul with outward equanimity and calm." (113)

Second, as a way of calming Arjuna, Krishna teaches him that spirit is eternal, immortal; and so in killing his enemies (who are his cousins) he is not "killing their essential being." (116) Krishna leads Arjuna to consider this idea, and others concerning the nature and significance of reincarnation. In the process of giving to Arjuna "the power of abstract judgment, he is thereby giving him for the first time in the whole of evolution the starting point for the knowledge of higher worlds." (120) In this second stage of the uplifting of Arjuna's soul, Krishna in effect teaches him to "hold fast in Yoga," i.e., stay bound (Yoga, to yoke) to Krishna, who is none other than Arjuna's true Self, his essential eternal identity.

In the third stage of Arjuna's development, Krishna leads him to an experience of his identity with the cosmos, which, of course, is part of Krishna. Steiner explains: "If we gradually reach a point where we no longer consciously live and feel and know *in oneselves*, but live and feel and know *together with the whole Earth*, then one grows into a higher level of consciousness where the things of the sense world vanish for us as they do in sleep." (123)

At the conclusion of this third stage of Arjuna's overcoming his despondency and his evolution toward the realization of his higher self, Steiner summarizes Krishna's message as follows:

"All that lives in your soul has lived often before, only you know nothing of it. But I have this consciousness in myself when I look back on all the transformations through which I have lived, and I will lead you up so that you may learn to feel yourself as I feel myself." This is a new moment of dramatic force, as beautiful as it is deeply and esoterically true! (125)

Lecture 3 : May 30, 1913

This lecture includes a discussion of the importance of dreams both at the time of the Gita and at present, particularly the ways in which dreams can bring a solution to a struggling soul in a way not possible in ordinary consciousness. Dreams will be more effective to the extent that they are not limited by the sense experience of daily life. Steiner explains that in the Gita, Arjuna:

stands at the boundary between the everyday world and that of dreams. He lives his way into that region because through his destiny he has a more powerful self in that realm than he needs in his ordinary life…. Krishna lifts him out of the self he has acquired in ordinary life, and thus he becomes a different person from what he would have been if his expanded self had not met Krishna. (134-135)

Lecture 4 : May 31, 1913

In the fourth lecture, Steiner explains that Arjuna had not performed esoteric exercises in preparation for his meeting Krishna, but instead was able to rely on the primeval clairvoyance still available at that time. Because this clairvoyance was beginning to fade, it was necessary for Krishna to teach Arjuna the four Yogas. Speaking of the present time (during which the ancient clairvoyance is generally unavailable, because Lucifer has the power to deprive an ill-prepared aspiring soul of the light-air it needs, and will thereby suffocate that soul) Steiner cautions the spiritual seeker against entering the spiritual realm without sufficient moral and spiritual preparation. (142-143)

Toward the end of this lecture Steiner refers to the third realm, the one in which a spiritual seeker can find Krishna as well as the experience of the two Jesus children. The first and second realms seem to be dream consciousness and dreamless sleep, though they are not identified as such. What is clear is that it is the third realm where one may come to "understand the origin of the strange and wondrous truths that Krishna speaks to Arjuna—truths that sound so altogether different from anything that is spoken in ordinary life." (148)

Lecture 5 : June 1, 1913

In this lecture, midway through the series of nine lectures, Steiner continues his characterization of the consciousness of Arjuna and Krishna and the dramatic interaction of these two archetypal figures. In the process, he makes a startling claim about the brain of humanity at the present time.

Steiner describes the sudden change of consciousness that led Arjuna from despondency in the face of the ensuing civil war to the healing counsel of Krishna. He says, in effect, that if a person such as Arjuna were to withdraw his "understanding and feeling from the fires of sacrifice and reverence for the ancestors," i.e., from his traditional *dharma*, he would be provided an opportunity "to gaze into the supersensible worlds" to see Krishna in the process of preparing the way for self-consciousness. (159) Steiner also explains that for centuries prior to his revelation to Arjuna on the battlefield, Krishna had worked to prepare humanity to be capable of developing self-consciousness. (160)

In a particularly stunning claim, Steiner says that in the present centuries, Western people have developed an organ in the forehead, and that the forces that built this invisible organ are now available to help humanity gain spiritual knowledge. This is the kind of statement that makes some readers close the book; others react positively because they believe what Steiner says; and some just hold it in suspension, aware that there seem to be no criteria for judging a claim so far outside the boundaries of mainstream knowledge.

Lecture 6 : June 2, 1913

This extremely full lecture returns to some of the themes developed in the lectures "The Bhagavad Gita and the Epistles of Paul." As he did in the third lecture in that series, Steiner here offers two complementary statements that initially appear to be contradictory. First, that the Bhagavad Gita is "one of the greatest creations of the human spirit, a creation that has never been surpassed in later times." And then: "What entered the world with the revelation inherent in the Christ impulse is something altogether different, something to which the Bhagavad Gita could not attain even if its beauty and greatness were increased a hundred times." (162)

Steiner then asserts that "these statements do not contradict each other" because the Gita offers a teaching that enlists the highest aspirations of individual consciousness, whereas Christ brought a presence and a force for transformation of the whole of human consciousness. Again, concerning Krishna, he says:

In the whole range of the world's life, there is nothing to be found that kindled the human self more mightily than the living force of Krishna's words to Arjuna. (162)

The highest impulse that can speak to the individual speaks through Krishna to Arjuna. The highest to which one can lift oneself by raising to their full pitch all the powers that reside within one's being—that is Krishna. The highest to which one can soar by training oneself and working on oneself with wisdom—that is Krishna. (170)

And concerning Christ:

But something came toward humanity *from outside*, which humans could never have reached through the forces that lived within themselves, something bending down to each individual. Thus, the souls that were separating and isolating themselves encountered the same being who came down out of the cosmic universe into the age of self-consciousness from outside. It came in such a way that it belonged to the whole of humanity, to all the Earth. This other impulse came from the opposite side. It was the Christ. (171)

This is one of the most important parts of Steiner's view of humanity: he emphasizes the development of the individual out of the group (e.g., Arjuna's sudden increase in self-consciousness, or the jump in self-knowledge that came about three centuries later through Socrates) but the goal of this development is a very particular combination, namely, the individual in self-conscious, free, and loving unity with humanity. For Steiner, Christ is the guide of the individual and the lord of karma, but also the savior of the whole of humanity. By the revelation of Krishna, "a continually increasing individualization was prepared and brought about in humankind, and then those souls who had the impulse to individualize themselves more and more were met by the Christ impulse, leading them once more together into a common humanity." (90)

Clearly impressed by the majesty of Arjuna's vision of Krishna in Chapters IX–XI, Steiner says one fears to reproduce Arjuna's words.

The Krishna that Arjuna sees imaginatively—which for Steiner means in actual truthful images—is the Krishna who had poured his grace into individual human souls just as Christ poured his grace into the Earth and into humankind. Steiner further states that prior to the appearance of Krishna in the Gita, each soul was on a trajectory toward individual self-consciousness; the Christ impulse was needed to bring individual souls into a unity.

Lecture 7 : June 3, 1913

As in the discussion of the two Jesus children in the fifth lecture of "The Bhagavad Gita and the Epistles of Paul," Steiner explains that Krishna had been a human soul, and specifically "the sister soul of Adam," during the Lemurian age, but had not incarnated until it did so as Krishna—and again as the soul of the Jesus boy in the Gospel of Luke. He writes:

> This wonderful mystery [the presence of Krishna in the Luke child, later joined by the Zarathustra child] is enacted that the innermost essence and self of the human being, which we have seen hailed as Krishna, permeates the Jesus child of the Luke Gospel. In this child are the innermost forces of humanity, the Krishna forces, for indeed we know their origin. (180)

Lecture 8 : June 4, 1913

In a claim not especially related to the Gita but interesting in its own right, Steiner states that the nineteenth-century thinkers Fichte and Hegel, both German, and Soloviev, Russian, advance the Advaita Vedanta philosophy, the "great spiritual and philosophical achievement of Shankara in the eighth century," not by an old clairvoyance but "*quite naturally*, almost as a matter of course!" (189)[46]

---

46. In several places in the lectures following, Steiner omits this surprising reference to Soloviev in this context and more appropriately adds Schelling to Fichte and Hegel.

Lecture 9 : June 5, 1913

1. Western humanity is indebted to Krishna for the transformation of consciousness as summarized in the Gita, and for the "continued working" of the Krishna impulse for the spiritual striving of the individual human being.

2. The Christ impulse was and is more universal than the Krishna impulse.

3. The claim, as had been recently announced by Annie Besant, the president of the Theosophical Society, that a young man, Jiddu Krishnamurti, was the reincarnated world teacher, Jesus, the savior of humanity, is false and runs counter to the striving of thinking, feeling, and willing that together constitute the essence of spiritual science or Anthroposophy.

4. Anthroposophy should be "a means of shedding light on all religions." This should be accomplished not by fusing all religions into one vague spiritual perspective or "by saying they all have the same essence," but rather by a clear understanding of each religion and its founders, teachers, and practices in the context of the evolution of the whole of humanity to which Krishna, Buddha, Christ, and lesser beings have made important, distinctive, and culture-specific contributions.

Within the context of these four very significant interpretive points, Steiner discusses the *gunas* and introduces a new perspective on the relationship between Lucifer, Krishna, and Christ. Steiner recommends the ideal of the *sattva* person, one he characterizes as a modern Western person able to attain objective knowledge of the mineral kingdom. The *rajas* person, however, characteristically does not give in to the object of knowledge and so in effect meets his or her own subjective self. The *tamas* person typically does not attempt to know the world but apathetically gives in to his or her own physical existence. Steiner regards contemporary consciousness as increasingly *tamasic,* which he identifies with materialistic—and spiritualist—passivity. He sees religion as characterized by *rajasic* consciousness, and Anthroposophy by *sattvic* consciousness.

Of course, it is possible to study Anthroposophy and be a supportive member of the Anthroposophical Society at a *rajasic* level, by turning Anthroposophy into a set of religious beliefs, or at a *tamasic* level by consuming some of Steiner's teachings as a substitute for one's own thinking, feeling and willing. At the present time, when Anthroposophy or spiritual science is intended to replace religious faith, Steiner insists that "the soul must be more active than it was in the age before the origin of the Bhagavad Gita."

In the end, Steiner finds the Gita to be limited to its time, unable to provide the necessary encouragement for the soul's full and necessary engagement with the world: "Tearing the self away from the environment, no longer asking what goes on in external processes of perfection, but asking how shall one perfect *oneself.* This is the teaching of Krishna." (206-207)

Whereas Krishna "closes the individual to the external world," the tempter Lucifer does the opposite. "Christ is the synthesis of these extremes."

Through Lucifer, humanity would have been condemned to live one-sidedly in the external conditions of *sattva, rajas,* and *tamas.* Through Krishna, they were to be educated for the other extreme; to close their eyes and seek only their own perfection. Christ took sin upon himself. He gave to humanity what reconciles the two one-sided tendencies. He took upon himself the sin of self-consciousness, which would close its eyes to the world outside. He took upon himself the sin of Krishna, and of all who would commit his sin. He took upon himself the sin of Lucifer and of all who would commit the sin of fixing their attention on externalities. By taking both extremes upon himself, he makes it possible for humanity by degrees to find a harmony between the inner and the outer world, because in that harmony alone the salvation of humanity is to be found. (208)

And, in conclusion: "No one should ever imagine that the Krishna impulse could have been dispensed with. No one should ever think either that one human spiritual movement is fully justified in its one-sidedness. The two extremes—the Luciferic and the Krishna impulses—had to find their higher unity in the mission of Christ." (209)

ROBERT MCDERMOTT, Ph.D., philosophy, Boston University, is president emeritus and chair of the department of Philosophy, Cosmology, and Consciousness at the California Institute of Integral Studies (San Francisco). He taught at Manhattanville College and is professor emeritus and former chair of the department of philosophy at Baruch College, CUNY.

He was secretary of the American Academy of Religion and secretary-treasurer of the Society for Asian and Comparative Philosophy. He was a Senior Fulbright Lecturer at the Open University where he co-produced an OU-BBC film, *Avatar: Concept and Example*. He directed the National Endowment for the Humanities project for the review of audio-visual materials for the study of Hinduism and Buddhism.

He was a member of the council of the Anthroposophical Society in America, president of the Rudolf Steiner Institute, and chair of the board of Rudolf Steiner College and Sunbridge College. He is the founding chair of the board of the Sophia Project (two homes in Oakland, CA, for mothers and children at risk of homelessness), and has been chair of the board and president of several other institutions.

His publications include *Radhakrishnan, The Essential Aurobindo, The Essential Steiner, The New Essential Steiner: An Introduction to Rudolf Steiner for the 21st Century* (2009), and the Introduction to *Essays in Psychical Research* by William James (Harvard University Press). Robert McDermott's essays have appeared in *International Philosophical Quarterly, Cross Currents, Journal of the American Academy of Religion*, and *Philosophy East and West*.

THE BHAGAVAD GITA
AND THE WEST

Rudolf Steiner

PART I

The Bhagavad Gita and the Epistles of Paul

1

THE UNIFIED PLAN OF WORLD HISTORY

THE MERGING OF THREE SPIRITUAL STREAMS
IN THE BHAGAVAD GITA

DECEMBER 28, 1912

TODAY we stand at the point of founding the Anthroposophical Society, in its narrower sense.[1] This seems an opportune moment to remind ourselves of the importance and significance of our cause. Indeed, what the Anthroposophical Society desires to be for modern culture should not be different in principle from what we have always cultivated within our circles as *Theosophy*. But giving it a new name may perhaps call to mind again the earnestness and dignity with which we intend to work within our spiritual movement. The theme of this cycle of lectures was chosen from this viewpoint. At the beginning of our anthroposophical initiative, we will discuss a subject that in a variety of ways may point to the importance and meaning of our spiritual movement for the cultural life of the present time.

---

1. This is a reference to Steiner's break with the Theosophical Society in 1912 and the formation of the Anthroposophical Society. See Günther Wachsmuth, *The Life and Work of Rudolf Steiner: From the Turn of the Century to His Death* (NY: Whittier Books, 1955); Rudolf Steiner, *Spiritualism, Madame Blavatsky, and Theosophy—An Eyewitness View of Occult History* (Great Barrington, MA: Anthroposophic Press, 2001); as well as the foreword by Christopher Bamford and the editor's introduction in the present volume.

Some people may be surprised to find brought together two such different spiritual streams as the great Eastern poem of the *Bhagavad Gita* and the letters written by one so closely connected with the founding of Christianity, namely the Apostle Paul. We can best recognize the nearness of these two spiritual streams if we first indicate the place held in our time by the great Gita and everything connected with it, and then the incoming thrust that laid the foundation of Christianity, the thought and work of Paul. Much in spiritual life today differs from what existed only a relatively short time ago, but just this difference makes necessary a spiritual movement such as Anthroposophy.

Just think: as I had pointed out in my Basel and Munich lecture cycles,[2] not so long ago, someone entering the spiritual life of his or her time had to consider three periods of a thousand years each: one pre-Christian millennium, and the two that have followed, the last not quite completed, but both saturated with the spiritual outstreaming of Christianity.[3] What might a person have thought, when standing within the human spiritual life of that very recent time, at a point when one could not yet see the point of a theosophical or anthroposophical movement as we understand it today? That person might have said: Something is entering spiritual life now, whose source must be sought in the millennium before the Christian era. For only at that time do individuals as personalities begin to have any importance for spiritual life. However great and overpowering much in the spiritual

---

2. Steiner delivered a lecture series on the Gospel of Mark in Basel, September 15–25, the fifth lecture of which is published as an appendix in this volume. See *The Gospel of St. Mark*, trans. C. Mainzer and Stewart Easton (Hudson, NY: Anthroposophic Press, 1986). In August 1912 Steiner gave a series of lectures published as *Initiation, Eternity, and the Passing Moment* (Hudson, NY: Anthroposophic Press, 1980).
3. Steiner usually divides the first three periods of the evolution of consciousness in the West, following the presumed sinking of Atlantis, by 2100-year periods, beginning with the eighth millennium, eighth century C.E., and ending with early fifteenth century C.E.; here, however, he refers to three 1000-year periods beginning 500 B.C.E., 500 C.E., and 1500 C.E. Although this volume follows current usage in referring to dates before and after the birth of Christ as the pre- and post-Common Era, if we were to reflect Steiner's conviction, it would be more appropriate to use the previous practice, namely, B.C. for dates before the birth of Christ and A.D. (*anno domini*, in the year of Our Lord) for dates after the birth of Christ.

streams of earlier times may appear to us, the personalities, the individualities as such, did not stand out from the foundation of those streams. We need only look back to the spirituality of the old Egyptian or Chaldean-Babylonian epochs; here we are looking at a spiritual life that is all of one piece. Personalities as such, spiritually vigorous, only came into prominence in the following Greek period. In the Egyptian age, we can find great teachings, and a sweeping outlook into the far reaches of the cosmos, but only with the Greeks are distinct individual figures beginning to arise, particularly persons such as Socrates, Pericles, Phidias, Plato, or Aristotle. *Personality* as such comes upon the scene. I mean by this not only the *important* personalities, but the impress of spiritual life upon every person as an individual. That is the outstanding characteristic of spiritual life in the last three thousand years, and thereby the spiritual streams become significant to the extent that personalities feel a need to take part in them, finding in them inner comfort, hope, peace, bliss, and security.

Until a comparatively short time ago, we were only interested in history insofar as it proceeded from one person to another, and thus we lacked a deep understanding of what had occurred before the last three thousand years. With Greek civilization began that history that was the only history we understood until a very short time ago. All that was connected with the great being of Christ Jesus occurred at the turn of the first to the second millennium. In the first millennium, the distinctive contribution of Greece, whose source lay in the Mysteries, predominated. We have often described what flowed out from the Mysteries to the great poets, philosophers and artists in every domain—for we must look to the Mysteries to truly understand Aeschylus, Sophocles, Euripides, Socrates, Plato, and Aristotle, not to mention so towering a figure as Heraclitus. You can read about him, and how he relied entirely on the Mysteries, in my book *Christianity as Mystical Fact.*

Then we see how, with the second thousand years, the Christ impulse poured into spiritual development, gradually spreading through Greek culture and uniting itself with it. The course of this second millennium united the powerful impulse of Christ with what has come down to us from the Greeks as living tradition. Quite slowly, we see Greek wisdom, feeling, and art merging organically with this Christ impulse. So passed the second thousand years.

Then the third millennium of personality culture began. How differently the Greek influence affects this epoch! We see it when we consider artists like Raphael, Michelangelo, and Leonardo da Vinci. No longer does one observe Greek culture externally as something historically great, as was done in the second millennium. In the third period, people had to turn directly to what came from Greece. We see that these three great artists let themselves be influenced by the great works of art coming to light again; Greek culture was absorbed ever more consciously, in contrast to its unconscious influence in the second millennium. We see that this Greek influence was consciously embodied in world conceptions—for instance, in the philosophy of Thomas Aquinas, how it was necessary for him to unite what flowed from Christian philosophy with Aristotle's philosophy. Greek influence was assimilated so that, together with the Christian influence, it poured out in philosophical form—and with Raphael, Michelangelo, and Leonardo, in artistic form. This whole line of development was prolonged in spiritual life, even if certain religious conflicts appeared with Giordano Bruno and Galileo. In all the people, not merely in the educated or the more highly cultured but also among the simplest souls, such a spiritual life arose, consciously, out of the flowing together of Greek and Christian impulses. From university to peasant's hut, concepts taken from Greek and Christian ideas made their way into culture.

Then in the nineteenth century something quite unique entered: something actually formed and was first brought to light by what is called *Theosophy* or *Anthroposophy*. There we see a single example of mighty forces in action. When, for the first time, the wonderful poem of the Bhagavad Gita became known in Europe, leading thinkers were enraptured by the greatness of this poem, by its profound content. We shouldn't forget that as wise a spirit as Wilhelm Humboldt[4] said after reading it that it was the most profound philosophical poem ever

---

4. Wilhelm Humboldt (1767–1835), linguist, educator, diplomat, and friend of Schiller and Goethe.

to come before his eyes. He made the beautiful comment that being able to become acquainted with the Bhagavad Gita, the great spiritual song resonating from the primeval holiness of Eastern antiquity, was his reward for living to be as old as he was. How beautiful it is that slowly, without yet reaching a wide circle, much of Eastern antiquity poured out from the Bhagavad Gita into the nineteenth century. For this poem is unlike other writings that came over from the ancient East—writings that always convey Eastern thought and feeling from one or another point of view. In the Bhagavad Gita, however, we meet with the confluence of all the various streams and points of view to be found in Eastern thinking, perception, and feeling. That is the significance of the Bhagavad Gita.

Now let us look at ancient India. Overlooking unimportant features, we find, rising up out of dim prehistoric times, three subtly shaded spiritual streams. One definite stream we encounter is in the earliest Vedas; we then see its further development in the later Vedic poems. It is a very definite stream, although perhaps a one-sided one. We then find a second stream in the Sankhya philosophy, and a third, different one in Yoga. Thus we have put before our souls the Sankhya system of Kapila, the Yoga philosophy of Patanjali, and the Vedas, with quite distinct nuances, each bringing out a certain one-sidedness in which their actual greatness resides. It is the harmonious interpenetration of the three streams that comes to expression in the Bhagavad Gita. What Vedic philosophy had to say reappears for us in the Bhagavad Gita; what Patanjali Yoga had to give humanity can be found in the Bhagavad Gita; and what the Kapila Sankhya had to give is in the Bhagavad Gita. And we don't find it as a conglomerate, but as a harmonious blending into one organism, as if they had belonged together originally. It is the greatness of the Gita that it shows in such an all-inclusive way that the spiritual life of the East receives the contributions of these three streams. Let me briefly characterize what each of them can give us.

The Vedic stream is most pronouncedly a philosophy of unity, the most spiritual monism imaginable, and it comes to completion in the Vedanta. If we are to understand the Veda philosophy, we must keep in mind that it is based on the idea that human beings find the deepest reality within themselves, that it is their own Self. The self that acts in ordinary life is an expression, or imprint, of this Self, and as that Self develops, they gradually bring forth its depths from the foundations of the soul. This higher Self is as if slumbering in them. Present day human beings do not know it directly, but it works in them as the aim toward which they are developing. According to the Veda philosophy, when humans achieve what lives in them as their Self, they will become aware that this Self is one with the all encompassing Cosmic Self—that they not only rest with their Self entirely in this Cosmic Self, but are one with it, relating to it in a twofold way.

We could say the Vedantist conceives the relationship between the human Self and the Cosmic Self as an in and out-breathing. As outside is air in general, and within us is the portion of it we have breathed in, so outside is the great Self actively alive in and permeating everything. When we give ourselves over to observing it, we breathe it in. We breathe it in spiritually with every feeling we have of it, with everything we receive into our souls. All knowledge, wisdom, thinking, feeling, is spiritual breathing. What we take into our souls as part of the Cosmic Self—but which remains bound up organically with it—is Atman, breath, indistinguishable from the Cosmic Self in general, as the air we inhale is indistinguishable from the air surrounding us.

As we breathe out physically, so too the soul goes out in devotion to this Cosmic Self, giving the best that it has, in prayer and sacrifice. That is spiritual out-breathing—Brahman. Atman and Brahman, like the in and out-breath, make us participants in the all encompassing Cosmic Self. In the Vedas, we encounter a monistic spiritual philosophy that is at the same time a religion. Their blossom and fruit brings blessing and assurance to the innermost and the highest reaches of the soul: the feeling of union with the universal, world-encompassing and world-permeating Self, the undivided nature of the cosmos. Vedic philosophy deals with the unity of the world, with human existence within the whole spiritual cosmos. According to the Vedic conception, the word *Veda* was itself breathed out by the all-encompassing, unitary being, and can be breathed in by the human soul as the highest form of cognition. Accepting the Vedic philosophy means taking in the best part of the all-powerful Self. It means becoming conscious of the connection between each human Self and the all-encompassing Cosmic Self. What the Veda tells us is the Word of God, which is creative and which is born again in human knowledge. Thus human knowledge is joined with the creative, permeating principle underlying all existence. Therefore, what is written in the Vedas was considered Divine Word, and those who were filled with it were the possessors of the Divine Word. In a spiritual way, this Word came into the world, and was set forth in the Vedic books. Those who mastered these books took part in the world's creative principle.

Things are different in Sankhya philosophy. When it first meets us, as handed down by tradition, we see exactly the opposite of a teaching of unity. We can compare it to the philosophy of Leibniz. Sankhya philosophy is a pluralistic philosophy, but it does not attempt to trace to a unified source the separate souls that confront us; human souls and divine souls. Yet they are considered as existing singly from eternity, so to speak, or at least as souls that did not originate in unity. The plurality of souls is what meets us in Sankhya philosophy. The independence of each single soul is sharply brought out; the soul pursues its development in the world enclosed within its own being. Against this pluralism Sankhya philosophy affirms the *prakriti* element. We cannot translate *prakriti* adequately with the modern word *matter* because this word for us has a materialistic meaning, which is not what is meant in Sankhya philosophy. Here what is substantial counterpoints the multiplicity of souls and does not come back again into a unity with them. As used in Sankhya philosophy, this is not the meaning intended in using the word *substance*, matter, which contrasts with the multiplicity of souls, yet without leading back to unity. We can say that the multiplicity of souls has a material basis, a primal flood streaming through the world, spatially and in time, out of which souls take the elements of their outer existence. They must clothe themselves in this material element, which is not led back to unity with the souls themselves. In Sankhya philosophy this material element—which, like the single soul, has been thought of from eternity—is primarily and carefully studied, but not much attention is given to the separate souls. Each is considered a reality, entangled and bound up with the material basis, and in this materiality it assumes the most varied forms, showing itself outwardly in the most varied ways. It is the study of these material forms that meets us especially in the Sankhya philosophy.

Above all, then, we have the most primeval form of this material element as a kind of primal, spiritual flood in which the soul is submerged. If we were to look at the beginning of evolution we would find an undifferentiated material element, and a multiplicity of souls dipping into it to carry on their evolution. The first to meet us as form— not yet differentiated from the unity of the primal flood—is spiritual substance itself at the beginning of evolution. Next comes *buddhi*, with which souls individually can clothe themselves. If we think of the soul clothed by the primal flood substance, its appearance is not yet distinguishable from the general surging flood. Enclosed as it is in this first form of the general flood, it can then be enveloped by *buddhi*.

The third element that then emerges, through which the soul can become more and more individualized, is *ahankara*. This is the continually descending form of primal matter. So there is primal matter, whose next form is *buddhi*, and the next, *ahankara*. A fourth form is *manas*; following this are the sense organs; next, the finer elements; finally, the material elements that we have in our physical environment. This, we may say, is the line of evolution according to Sankhya philosophy. Above is the most supersensible element of a spiritual primal flood, gradually condensing into the coarse elements from which the coarse human body is built. In between are the substances out of which our sense organs are woven, and the finer elements that give rise to our etheric or life body. Note that according to Sankhya philosophy, all of these constitute sheaths for the soul. Even that which arose from the first primal flood is a sheath of the soul, which is contained in it. Thus, when Sankhya philosophers study *buddhi*, *ahankara*, *manas*, and the senses, the finer and coarser elements, they study the ever-denser sheaths in which the soul comes to expression.

We must see clearly that the way the Veda and Sankhya philosophies come to us is only possible because they were formulated in those ancient times when some degree at least of primal clairvoyance still existed. These philosophies came into being in different ways. The Vedas depended on a primal, yet (for that earliest humanity) naturally existing inspiration that humans had no part in creating, except that they prepared themselves in their whole being to receive, quietly and passively, this spontaneous divine inspiration. It was otherwise in the development of the Sankhya philosophy, however; there one could say that there was something similar to our present method of learning, only that we are not permeated by clairvoyance, while they were. It was clairvoyant science, inspiration bestowed by grace from above, that produced the Vedic philosophy. Science as we cultivate it today, but carried on by people endowed with clairvoyance—this was Sankhya philosophy. Therefore this latter science left the pure soul element as such undisturbed. It said: Souls express themselves in what one can study in the outer, supersensible form, and we study those outer forms in which souls clothe themselves.

A soul nature that has submerged in outer form but has proclaimed and revealed itself as soul nature lives in the *sattva* element. A soul immersed in form that is, so to speak, overwhelmed by the form and cannot rise above it, lives in the *tamas* element. When the soul can, to some extent, keep in balance between its own element and its formal expression, it lives in the *rajas* element. *Sattva, rajas, tamas,* the three *gunas,* are the essential characteristics of what we call Sankhya philosophy. So we find a developed system of forms as they meet us in the world—as we in our science find the totality of nature's facts, except that in Sankhya philosophy, one advances to a supersensible observation of phenomena. Though attained through clairvoyance, this philosophy remains a science of outer forms, not pressing on into the realm of the soul, which remains untouched by the study. Those who devote themselves to the Vedas feel their religious life entirely united with the life of wisdom. Sankhya philosophy is science; it is knowledge of the forms in which the soul expresses itself. At the same time its adherents can feel, alongside their science, a religious devotion. How the soul element then inserts itself into the forms—not the soul itself, but the way it is inserted—can be discerned in the Sankhya philosophy. We can see in Sankhya philosophy how the soul increasingly guards its independence, or descends further into matter. We are dealing with soul nature, which indeed descends, but in its material forms protects its own being.

Again, it is otherwise with the spiritual stream that comes down to us as Yoga. This deals immediately with the soul's nature, and seeks ways of taking hold of the soul directly so that it might rise to ever higher stages from its present situation. Thus Sankhya observes the soul's sheaths, and Yoga leads it to ever higher stages of inner experience. Therefore devotion to Yoga signifies a gradual awakening of the higher forces of the soul, so that it may experience what is beyond everyday life and discover ever higher stages of existence. Yoga then is the way to the spiritual worlds; the way to freeing the soul from its outer forms; the way to independent inner life.

Yoga is the other side of the Sankhya philosophy. It acquired great importance when that inspiration from on high given by grace in the Vedas could no longer descend. Yoga was the resort of those souls who, belonging to a later human epoch, no longer received any direct revelations but had to work their way up from lower stages to the heights of spiritual existence.

Thus in ancient Indian times there arose three sharply differentiated spiritual streams: the Veda, the Sankhya, the Yoga. Today we are called upon to bring them together again by lifting them out of the foundations of the soul and the depths of the cosmos in the way best suited to our present age. You can find all three streams in our spiritual science. Only read what I presented in my *Outline of Esoteric Science*, in the first chapters on the human constitution, sleeping and waking, life and death. You will find there what can be called Sankhya philosophy in modern terms. Then read what I said there about the world's evolution from Saturn to our time, and you have a contemporary version of Veda philosophy. In the last chapters dealing with humankind's development, you have Yoga for the present time. Our age must unite in an organic way what radiates over to us out of ancient India in these three philosophical streams. For that reason, we must also concern ourselves with the wonderful Bhagavad Gita, which in a deeply poetic way summarizes the three streams reaching so deeply into our age. We must seek something like congeniality between our spiritual striving and the deeper content of the Bhagavad Gita. There are points of contact with the older spiritual streams, not just in the totality of our present-day spiritual streams, but in the details as well.

You will have recognized that in my *Outline of Esoteric Science*, I made an effort to present things entirely out of their own inherent nature, never borrowing anything from history. No one who really understands what I said there concerning Saturn, Sun and Moon will find any assertion taken from historical sources. Statements are made out of the subject itself. But how remarkable it is that what bears the imprint of our age harmonizes in critical places with what resonates to us from ancient times! Here is one small example. At a certain place in the Vedas we read something like the following about cosmic evolution: "In the beginning, darkness was enveloped in darkness; everything was an undifferentiated flood. There arose a great void, which was everywhere permeated by warmth." Now I ask you to recall what was taken from the event itself concerning the constitution of Saturn, where its substance was spoken of as comprised of warmth. Feel how what is newest in spiritual science coincides with what is said in the Vedas. The next passage runs: "Then the Will first arose, which was the first seed of thinking, connecting existence with non existence.... And this connection is found in the Will." Remember how in new terms the Spirits of Will were mentioned. In all that we have had to say in the present time we have not sought to be in accordance with the old; the harmony came of itself, because truth was sought there, and was sought again here on our own ground.

In the Bhagavad Gita we encounter at once a poetic glorification of the three spiritual streams we have described. What is presented to us is the great teaching given to Arjuna by Krishna himself at a crucial moment of world history—crucial for that ancient time. The moment is important because it was the time when the old blood ties were loosening. In everything that I shall say in these lectures on the Bhagavad Gita, remember what I have often referred to, namely, that the ancient blood ties, racial connections, tribal kinships, had special significance and only gradually ceased. Recall everything I said in my *Occult Significance of the Blood.*[5] Loosening those blood ties caused mighty warfare to break out, described for us in the *Mahabharata*, of

---

5. October 1, 1911, Basel. Also translated as "The Etherization of the Blood." See in Rudolf Steiner, *The Reappearance of Christ in the Etheric* (Great Barrington, MA: Steiner-Books, 2003), 116–39.

which the Gita is an episode. There we see that the descendants of two brothers, still tied by blood, part ways in their spiritual direction. What had previously given them a unified point of view, through the blood, now takes different paths, and so there is conflict, because conflict must arise from this separation, wherein the blood ties also lose their importance for clairvoyant knowledge. With this separation, then, the later course of spiritual development is set.

To those for whom the old blood ties have no significance, Krishna appears as the great teacher. He is to be the teacher for a new age set free of old blood ties. We shall describe tomorrow how he does that. Let's say for now what the Gita poem as a whole shows: that Krishna deals with the three spiritual streams we mentioned as an organic unity, and imparts this to his pupil.

How then must this pupil appear before us? In one direction he looks up to his father, in the other to his father's brother. The cousins are no longer to stay close; they must separate, but now each line is picked up by a different stream. Arjuna is dominated by the question, "How will it be when the blood ties no longer hold?" How is one's soul to find its place in spiritual life if this life can no longer flow along as before, under the influence of the old blood ties? Everything must come to ruin!" Or so it seems to Arjuna. Krishna's great teaching is that things must be different but without such an outcome.

Krishna now shows his pupil, who is to live through the transition from the one epoch to the other, how the soul, to maintain its harmony, must absorb something from all three spiritual streams. The Vedic teaching of unity is rightly presented in the teaching of Krishna, likewise the essence of the Sankhya teaching, and of Yoga. For what is it that lies behind all that we are to learn from the Gita? Krishna puts it somewhat like this: "There is a universal creative Word that contains the creative principle itself. As the air undulates and comes alive with the sound of the human voice, the Cosmic Word surges and lives in all things, creating and ordering existence. So does the Vedic principle breathe through all things. It can be taken up by one's understanding into one's soul life. There is a ruling, surging Creator Word and an echo of this in the Vedas. This Word is the creative force in the world, and it is revealed in the Vedas." That is one part of the Krishna teaching.

The human soul is able to understand how the Word comes to expression in the world's forms, for we learn to know the laws of existence in seeing how the separate forms show an orderly expression of the soul. The teaching about these world-forms, about the laws underlying them and their ways of working—this is Sankhya philosophy, the other part of Krishna's teaching.

Even as he makes clear to his pupil that behind all existence there is the World-Creating Word, he emphasizes that human understanding can recognize the separate forms, that human beings can incorporate Cosmic Laws into their own being. Cosmic Word—Cosmic Law—echoing in the Vedas, in Sankhya—this is what Krishna reveals to his pupil. He also speaks to him of the way that leads individual pupils to the heights where they can share in knowledge of the Cosmic Word. Krishna also speaks of Yoga. Threefold is his teaching: of the Word, of the Law, and of reverent devotion to the Spirit.

Word, Law, and Devotion—these are the three streams by which the soul can carry on its development. In one way or another, they will always be working on the soul. We certainly have seen how the new spiritual science, in its new manner of expression, must seek these three streams. But epochs differ, and the threefold form of the world-picture is brought to the soul in the most varied ways. Krishna speaks of the World Word, the Creator Word; of the structure of existence; of the devotional deepening of the soul, of Yoga. The same trinity meets us again, only in a more concrete, living way, in a being thought of as walking the Earth, embodying the divine creative Word! The Vedas approached humanity in abstract form. The divine Logos of which the Gospel of John speaks is the living, creative Word itself. What we encounter in the Sankhya philosophy as the lawful ordering of cosmic forms—transposed historically into the old Hebraic revelation—becomes what Paul refers to as the Law. Faith in the risen Christ proclaimed by Paul appears as the third member of the Trinity. The Yoga taught by Krishna is carried over by Paul into faith, which should take the place of the Law.

Thus, Veda, Sankhya, and Yoga are the dawn of what later arose as the Sun. Veda arises again in the being of Christ himself, appearing actually in historical development, not poured abstractly into the expanses of space and time, but as a separate individuality, the living Word. In Sankhya philosophy, we met the Law in what was shown there as the material basis, *prakriti*, evolved down to coarse substance. The Law reveals how the world came into being, and how individual human beings are formed in this world. This is expressed in the old Hebraic doctrine of the Law, in all that Moses represents. Insofar as Paul points to this Law of the ancient Hebrews, he points to Sankhya philosophy. Insofar as he points to faith in the risen Christ, he indicates the Sun preceded by the dawn in Yoga. Thus arises, in a remarkable way, that which met us in its first elements as Veda, Sankhya, Yoga.

What came before us as the Veda appears now in a new but actual form as the living Word, out of which all things were made and without which nothing is made, and which in the course of time became flesh. Sankhya appears as the historic, Law-founded representation of the way in which the world of phenomena, the world of coarse substances, came into being out of the world of the elohim.[6] Yoga is transformed into what Paul expressed in the words "Not I but the Christ in me," which means that when the power of Christ permeates and absorbs the soul, the human being rises to the heights of the divine.

Thus we see the existence of a unified plan throughout world history: how Eastern philosophy prepared it, and how what first emerged in abstract form appeared in such a remarkable way in more concrete forms in Paul's Christianity. We shall see that through precisely grasping the connection between the great Bhagavad Gita and the Epistles of Paul the deepest mysteries are revealed concerning what may be called the activity of the spirit in the collective education of the human race. Because one must feel such a new element in this new era, this modern age must look back beyond the time of Greece and develop an understanding of what lay behind the first pre-Christian millennium for what appeared as Veda, Sankhya, and Yoga. So, just as Raphael in art and Thomas Aquinas in philosophy had to turn back

---

6. Elohim, plural of Eloah, derivative of El, or God.

to Greek culture, we will see how in our time a conscious adjustment must be made between what the present time seeks to achieve, and what existed before the Greek age, reaching into the depths of Eastern antiquity. We can allow the depths of ancient culture to come closer to our soul when we observe these different spiritual streams in their wonderfully harmonious unity as they meet us in what Humboldt called that greatest philosophical poem, the Bhagavad Gita.

2

THE FUNDAMENTAL CONCEPTS OF THE GITA: THE VEDA, SANKHYA, AND YOGA

DECEMBER 29, 1912

As I mentioned yesterday, the Bhagavad Gita has been called the most significant philosophical poem ever produced, and anyone who studies it seriously will find this statement fully justified. These lectures will draw attention to the artistic merits of the Gita, but above all to the significance of its mighty underlying thoughts and the sublime knowledge of the world from which it grew and for whose glorification it was created. Looking thus into the foundations of the Gita becomes especially important because in all its essentials, particularly those related to thought and knowledge, it is unquestionably transmitted to us from a pre-Buddhist age. So we can say that, in the contents of the Gita, the spiritual horizon surrounding the great Buddha, out of which he developed, is characterized for us. It lets us see the spiritual constitution of the ancient, pre-Buddhist Indian civilization.

We have already emphasized that the thoughts of the Gita are an organic blending of three spiritual streams, moving and interpenetrating one another in such a way that we perceive them as a unity. What we find in the Gita as a unified whole, as a spiritual expression of primeval Indian thinking and perception, is a beautifully grand and immeasurable view of spiritual knowledge, so vast that modern humans unacquainted with spiritual science cannot but doubt the grandeur of its dimensions, for they have no way of penetrating these depths of knowledge. Ordinary modern methods of research do not help in this endeavor. At most, these methods make it possible to look upon the Gita as a beautiful dream that humankind once dreamed, which may inspire wonder but can have no value for science.

Those who have studied spiritual science, however, will be amazed at the depths of the Gita, and will admit that in primeval ages the human spirit penetrated into knowledge that can only be attained again through the gradual development of spiritual organs. This arouses admiration for the insights shown in those past ages, because we are now able to rediscover and confirm its truth, out of world-content itself. How wonderful it was that those primeval humans were able to raise themselves to such spiritual heights!

To be sure, humankind in those days was especially favored in possessing the remains of an old clairvoyance that was still alive in human souls. Not only were people led into the spiritual worlds through the use of special meditative exercises, but the science of that time was impregnated in a certain sense with the knowledge and ideas provided by the remains of the old clairvoyance. Today we recognize for quite different reasons the accuracy of what was handed down to us from that source. But we must understand that in that ancient time, delicate distinctions concerning the human being were arrived at by other means than they are today. Subtle, astute concepts were drawn from what humans could know—concepts that were clearly outlined and could be applied to spiritual as well as to external physical reality. We thus find it possible to understand their ancient point of view, in some instances merely by transposing the terms we use today for our changed point of view.

In our spiritual research, we have tried to present things as they appear to contemporary clairvoyant perception, so that our kind of spiritual science represents what spiritually minded people can attain today out of their own effort. In the early days of theosophical teaching, less was done by means derived directly from esoteric science than by methods relying on the designations and nuances of concepts used in the East, namely those carried over by old traditions from the time of the Gita right into our present time. For this reason, the older form of theosophical development, to which have now been added our present methods of esoteric investigation, worked more through concepts preserved in tradition, especially those of Sankhya philosophy. Sankhya philosophy itself, however, underwent a gradual change through the alteration of thinking in the East, and at the beginning of the Theosophical Movement the secrets of the human being and nature were described in the later terminology of Shankaracharya,[7] the great reformer of Vedic and other Indian knowledge in the eighth century C.E. We will pay less attention today to the expressions chosen at the beginning of the Theosophical Movement, but in order to get to the foundations of the knowledge and wisdom of the Gita, let us look rather into the ancient Indian wisdom found especially in the Sankhya philosophy.

We will best understand how Sankhya philosophy considered the human being and nature if we keep in mind the fact that a spiritual seed is inherent in every human being. This fact has often been expressed by saying that in the human soul are slumbering forces that will gradually emerge in the course of human evolution. The highest we can see now, and that humanity will attain in the future, we call the *spirit human*. Even when we have risen to the *spirit human* stage, we will still need to distinguish between the soul that dwells within us and the *spirit human* itself, just as today a distinction must be made between our innermost soul and the sheaths that enclose it—the astral, etheric, and physical bodies.

For the present human cycle, the soul is divided into three parts: the sentient, intellectual, and consciousness souls. In the future, the soul will be divided in a way corresponding to these three parts, and the sheath nature will have reached the stage of development we call the *spirit human*. Though the sheath in which the spirit-soul core of our being will be enclosed—the *spirit human*—will only be meaningful for humanity in the future, that into which a being is to develop is always in existence. The substance of the *spirit human*, in which our

---

7. Shankara, Advaita (non-dual) mystical philosopher; *acharya* means spiritual teacher.

souls will one day be sheathed, has always been in the great universe; it is there already. Today other beings already possess sheaths that will some day form our *spirit human.*

The existence of the substance of the future *spirit human,* a fact derived from our teaching, was already known to the old Sankhya doctrine. What exists in the universe in an undifferentiated, non-individualized state, flowing like spiritual water, filling space and time and providing the basis from which all forms past, present and future come forth, was known by Sankhya philosophy as the highest form of substance. It is that substance which this philosophy considered as continuing from age to age. Just as we speak of the beginning of our Earth evolution and of how all to which the Earth has since evolved was present in spirit as substantial spiritual being, so did Sankhya philosophy speak of its original substance, its primordial flood, from which all forms, physical and super-physical, have developed. This highest form is not yet relevant for human beings today, but, as I showed earlier, the day will come when it will be.

The next form to evolve out of this primal flowing substance, coming from above downward, we recognize as the second principle of humanity, the *life spirit*—or, to use an Indian expression, *buddhi.* Again, our teaching tells us that in the normal course of things, humanity will develop *buddhi* only at a future stage. But as a spiritual form-principle, it has always been present in other hierarchic beings, and was thus the first form differentiated from the primal flowing substance. According to Sankhya philosophy, *buddhi* arose out of the first form of non-soul, substantial existence.

If we now consider the further evolution of the substantial principle, there appears a third form, which Sankhya philosophy calls *ahankara.* Whereas *buddhi* stands, as it were, on the border of the principle of differentiation and merely suggests individualization, the form of *ahankara* appears as completely differentiated. When *ahankara* is spoken of, therefore, we must imagine *buddhi* as organized downward into independent, real, substantial forms that have individual existence in the world. To create a picture of this evolution, let us imagine the primal substantial principle as an equally distributed mass of water. It wells up so that forms appear—not as separate drops but as forms that emerge like little mounds of water from the common substance, with their bases still in the primal common flow. This condition would represent *buddhi*. If we further imagine these mounds of water detaching themselves into drops, into independent spheres, we would have the form of *ahankara*. Then, through a certain thickening of the individualized form of each separate soul form of *ahankara*, there would originate what is designated as *manas*.

Here we must admit that the naming of these sheaths differs slightly from our designations. In considering human evolution from above downward according to our teaching, *spirit self*, *manas*, follows after life spirit, or *buddhi*. This designation is absolutely correct for the present cycle of humanity, and in the course of these lectures it will be shown why. We do not insert *ahankara* between *buddhi* and *manas*; rather, according to our concepts we combine it with manas, and the two together are called *spirit self*. In those past ages, it was quite justifiable to consider them as separate for a reason that I shall only mention today, and develop later. At that time one could not use the important characteristic that we must employ today if we want to be understood. I am speaking of the influences of Lucifer on the one side and of Ahriman on the other. This characteristic is absolutely lacking in the Sankhya philosophy. For in a human constitution that had no occasion to look toward these two principles, because it could not yet feel any trace of their force, it was quite justifiable to slip in the differentiated form of *ahankara* between *buddhi* and *manas*. So, when *manas* is spoken of in the sense of the Sankhya philosophy, it is not the same as when it is spoken of in the sense of Shankaracharya, who considered *manas* identical to *spirit self*.

Let us then consider human beings living in the world of the senses. They live in such a way that they perceive the reality of their surroundings by means of their senses. Through their sense of touch, by means of their hands and feet, by handling things, walking and speaking, they have an effect upon the surrounding physical world. So expressed, this agrees entirely with Sankhya philosophy. But how does a person perceive the surrounding world by means of the senses? Well—with our eyes we see light and color, brightness and darkness, and the shape of things. With our ears we perceive sounds, with our olfactory organs we sense odors, and with the organs of taste we receive taste impressions. Each separate sense is a means of becoming aware of a particular part of the external world. We open ourselves to it through these doors of being called the senses. But with each sense, we approach one limited area of the world.

Something like a unifying principle in us combines these different areas of the outer world for us, as even our ordinary language shows. We speak, for instance, of warm and cold colors, although we know that this is only a manner of speaking and that in reality we become aware of cold and warmth through the organs of touch, and light and dark colors through the organ of sight. When we speak of warm and cold colors out of this feeling of inner relationship, we are using terms appropriate to one sense in describing the others. We express ourselves in this way because in our inner being there is a kind of intermingling between what we perceive through sight and what impresses us through the sense of warmth. More delicately sensitive people can inwardly form ideas of color upon hearing certain sounds. They may, for example, associate certain tones with red, others with blue. Some activity within us, therefore, holds together the separate senses and makes out of their separate activities a unity for the soul.

A sensitive person can go even further. There are people who may experience yellow upon entering a town. In another town, they may experience red, in others, white or blue. A great part of all our impressions expresses itself inwardly to us as color. The separate sense impressions are united inwardly in an overarching collective sense that does not belong to any one sense alone. It lives in our inner being and floods us with its quality of wholeness by incorporating the individual sense impressions into it. It may be called the inner sense, all the more so because all the usual inner experiences of sorrow and joy, passions and emotions, are united again with what this inner sense offers us, so that we can also describe some emotions as dark and cold, others as warm and full of light. Thus we can also say that our inner life in turn has an effect upon what forms the inner sense.

Therefore, in contradistinction to the several senses directed to different areas of the external world, we can speak of one sense that fills the soul. It is not connected with any single sense organ, but uses the whole being as its instrument. To describe this inner sense as *manas* is quite in the spirit of Sankhya philosophy. According to it, what organizes this inner sense into substance develops out of *ahankara* as a later product in the world of forms. It can be said that there was first the primal flood, then *buddhi*, then *ahankara* and then *manas*, found within us as our inner sense. If we want to understand this inner sense today, we proceed by taking the individual senses and observing how they help us gain particular representations insofar as the sensations from the separate senses join in a common inner sense.

This is the way we proceed at present, because our process of cognition travels in reverse. If we look at the evolution of our cognition, we are forced to say that it starts out from the differentiated givens of the individual sense and seeks to rise up to the common meaning. Evolution in the larger sense proceeds in the opposite direction. In the evolving world, *manas* first evolved out of *ahankara*. Then the primal substances—the forces that formed the separate senses as we carry them within us—differentiated themselves. This does not refer to the material sense organs that belong to the physical body, but to the forces underlying these organs, the formative forces that are wholly supersensible. So, when we descend through the stages of the evolution of forms, Sankhya philosophy would say that we come down from *ahankara* to *manas*. Then *manas* differentiates into separate forms and yields those supersensible forces that build up our separate senses. Because the soul is involved in viewing these separate senses, it is possible to bring the content of Sankhya philosophy into harmony with our teaching.

This philosophy tells us that, inasmuch as *manas* has differentiated into the separate world-forces of the senses, the soul has immersed itself in these different forms but has remained distinct from them. It works through these sense-forces, is interwoven with and entwined in them. As a result, the soul, as spirit-soul being, places itself in connection with the external world in order to feel pleasure and sympathy in it. For instance, the forces that constitute the eye have become differentiated out of *manas*. At an earlier stage, when the human physical body did not exist in its present form—so says Sankhya philosophy—the soul was immersed only in the forces that constitute the eye. We know that today's human eye was laid down as a seed in the old Saturn time. Yet only after the withdrawal of the warmth organ, which can be found today in a stunted form in the pineal gland, did the eye develop, which is to say comparatively late. The forces out of which it evolved were already there in supersensible form, and the soul lived within them.

Sankhya philosophy conceived it in the same way; insofar as the soul lives in these principles of differentiation, it is attached to and develops a thirst for existence in the external world; in a sense it sends out feelers through the sense organs. We call this connection of forces, seen as a sum of forces, the human astral body. Sankhya philosophy speaks of the combined working of separate sense forces, which at this stage are differentiated from *manas*. Out of these sense forces arise the finer elements that we understand as the human etheric body. This etheric body is a comparatively late development.

We must picture to ourselves evolution taking place in the following order: primal flood, *buddhi, ahankara, manas,* the substances of the senses, and the finer elements. In the outer world of nature, these finer elements also exist in plants as an etheric body. In the sense of Sankhya philosophy, we should imagine that the development of every plant has its origin in the primal flood, which has carried out a whole evolution from above downward. In the case of the plant, however, this all takes place in the supersensible realm, and only becomes real in the physical realm when it condenses into the finer elements that live in its etheric body. Things are different with the human being. In its present development, the higher forms and principles of *manas* have already revealed themselves physically. The separate sense organs have appeared externally. With the plant, we first find that later product that arises when the sense substance condenses into the finer etheric elements, whose further condensation produces the coarse elements that make up all the physical things we encounter in the outer world.

When we go upward we can see, in the sense of the Sankhya philosophy, how the human being is membered into a coarse physical body; the finer etheric body; an astral body (an expression not used in Sankhya philosophy, which refers instead to a "force body" that constitutes the sense organs); an inner sense, *manas*; then *ahankara,* the principle underlying human individuality, which enables the human being to have an inner sense not only for perceiving the separate areas of the senses in the outer world but also for feeling itself as a separate, individual being. Following *ahankara* comes the higher principle that first appears as *buddhi*, and what other Indian philosophies customarily call *atma*, its cosmic meaning being recognized by Sankhya philosophy as the spiritual primal flood previously described. Thus in Sankhya philosophy the human constitution is presented completely: how in the past, present, and future, the human soul is sheathed in the substantial, external nature principle—the word "nature" meaning not only the outwardly visible but all stages of *nature*, up to the invisible.

In *prakriti*—that is, in all the *forms* from the coarse physical body up to the primal flood—dwells *purusha*, the spirit-soul element, which is imagined as being monadic in every individual soul. The separate monadic souls, therefore, must be thought of as without beginning and without end, just as the material *prakriti* principle—which is not material in our materialistic sense—is also thought of as without beginning or end. We should imagine a multiplicity of individual souls plunged into the *prakriti* principle and developed downward from the highest differentiated form of the primal flood with which they surrounded themselves, to incarnate in coarse physical bodies. After reaching this lowest stage, when they overcome the physical body they turn back and evolve upward again, thus returning to the primal flood. Finally, they free themselves even from it and enter as free souls into pure *purusha*. When we allow this knowledge to act upon us, we see that this primal ancient wisdom is based upon what we can attain again today by means of our meditation.

Sankhya philosophy also demonstrates insights into the way the soul may be united with each of these form principles. The soul may, for example, be connected with *buddhi* in such a way that within *buddhi* it realizes its full independence, as much as is possible in it. In such a case the soul nature, not *buddhi*, predominates. The opposite may also occur. The soul may fold its independence in a sort of sleep, and envelop it in lassitude and laziness so that the sheath nature is most prominent. This may also take place with external physical nature, consisting of coarse substance. We need only observe humans. A person may bring his or her soul and spirit to expression in such a way that every movement, gesture, and look communicated by the coarse physical body recedes before the fact that the spirit-soul nature is expressing itself within it. As the coarse physical body stands there, in its movements, gestures, and look, something appears that makes us say, "This person is entirely spirit and soul, and only needs the physical principle as a means of expression. The physical principle does not overpower; it has been mastered in all things."

This condition, in which the soul is master of the external sheath principle, is the *sattva* condition. It may manifest in the soul's relation to *buddhi* and *manas* as well as in its relation to the body with its fine and coarse elements. To say that the soul lives in *sattva* means nothing else than a certain relation of the soul to its envelope, of the spiritual principle in the soul to the nature principle, of the *purusha* principle to the *prakriti* principle.

But we can also see how a person's coarse physical body may be dominant. (No reference to moral characterizations is intended here, but purely objective characterizations, in the light of Sankhya philosophy. When seen with spiritual vision, no moral consideration whatever is involved.) Such a person may appear to walk about weighed down by the physical body and may have put on so much flesh that the whole appearance seems influenced by weight, making it difficult to express the soul in the external physical body. When a person's facial muscles move in harmony with the speaking of the soul, the *sattva* principle is master. When quantities of fat imprint a special physiognomy on a person's face, the soul principle is overpowered by the external sheath condition, and the soul's relation to the nature principle is that of *tamas*. When a balance exists between the *sattva* and the *tamas* states, when neither the soul has mastery as in the *sattva* state, nor the external sheath nature as in the *tamas* condition, but both are in equilibrium, the condition may be called *rajas*. *Sattva, rajas,* and *tamas* are the three *gunas*, and are of special importance.

We must distinguish, then, between the characteristics of the separate forms of *prakriti* and the highest principle of undifferentiated primal substance, down to the coarse physical body. This sheath principle is one characteristic. The other is what Sankhya philosophy characterizes as the relation of the soul nature to the sheaths, regardless of what the particular form of the sheath may be. This characteristic is revealed through the three conditions—*sattva, rajas,* and *tamas*.

When we realize the profound depths of such knowledge and attempt to visualize how deep an insight into the secrets of existence this science had, in order that it might give such a comprehensive description of living beings, our souls become filled with admiration. We say to ourselves that it is one of the most amazing occurrences in the evolutionary history of humankind that a knowledge appearing today in our spiritual science out of dark spiritual depths should have already existed in those ancient times, obtained as it was by different methods. All this knowledge existed previously, and it is perceived again when our spiritual attention is directed to those primeval times.

Let us now turn to the succeeding ages. We see what is usually referred to as the spiritual life of the successive periods—the old Greek age, the Roman age that followed, and the Christian Middle Ages. We turn from these older cultures to modern times, to our age in which spiritual science brings us something that has grown out of the primal wisdom of humankind. As we survey all this, we can say that throughout these ages even the smallest glimmering of that primeval knowledge is often lacking. Gradually, the knowledge of that lofty sphere of existence, with its supersensible, all embracing, ancient perception, was lost. Indeed, the purpose of evolution for three thousand years has been to replace that primal wisdom with external knowledge of the material, physical plane.

Nevertheless, it is interesting to see that in the age of Greek philosophy there still remained on the physical plane something like an echo of the old Sankhya knowledge. We can still find in Aristotle echoes of the real nature of the soul, but they are no longer such as can be clearly connected with the ancient Sankhya knowledge. Aristotle still divides the human being into the coarse physical body—though he scarcely mentions it—and what he believes to be the soul nature, whereas the Sankhya philosophy knows these are only the sheaths. Then there is the vegetative soul, which would coincide with the finer elemental body in the sense of the Sankhya philosophy. Where Aristotle believes he is expressing something soul-like, he characterizes only the relations between soul and body, the *gunas*. In this he describes merely sheath forms.

Then Aristotle designates as a soul principle that which reaches out into the sphere of the senses—into what we call the astral body. He no longer distinguishes clearly the soul from the body, because for him the soul has already been submerged in the bodily shape. He differentiates rather the *aisthetikon,* and distinguishes further in the soul the *orektikon, kinetikon,* and *dianoetikon.*[8] To him, these are gradations of the soul, but there is no longer a clear distinction between the soul and its various sheaths. Aristotle believes he is presenting a classification of the soul, while Sankhya philosophy grasped the soul in its own being as a monad, and all its differentiations were, so to speak, covered by the sheath, or the *prakriti* principle.

Therefore, with Aristotle there is no longer any remembrance of that ancient knowledge found in the Sankhya philosophy. However, in the material domain, when he speaks of light and darkness in colors, what he has to say is like a lingering echo of the principle of the three conditions. Some colors, he says, have more darkness in them and others more light, and still others are between the two. In the colors ranging between blue and violet, darkness predominates over light, so a color is blue or violet because darkness prevails in it. It is green or greenish yellow when light and darkness are more nearly in equilibrium. A color is reddish or orange when the light principle overrules the dark.

Sankhya philosophy contains this principle of three conditions for the whole compass of world phenomena. It is *sattva,* for example, when the spiritual predominates over the natural. Aristotle uses the same characteristic when speaking of colors. He did not use the word *sattva,* but it would be correct to say that red and reddish yellow represent the *sattva* condition of light. Without using its terminology, Aristotle retained the principle of the old Sankhya philosophy where green represents the *rajas* condition as regards light and darkness, and blue

---

8. Frederick Hiebel explains these terms in the following way: "The human physical body as a mere mineral substance is *sarx*; this Greek word, *sarx*, for flesh, means that which is contained in the sarcophagus, the coffin. The principle that makes the body alive and lets it rise from the 'sarcophagus' is the *threptikon*: the vegetative or nutritive soul. Furthermore, the living being has the soul of sensitiveness, *aisthetikon*; the soul of desiring, *orekticon*; and the soul of moving and understanding, *kinetikon*. The human being alone among living beings has reason, *noesis*: this appears in its highest aspect as *dianoetikon*. The *dianoetikon* comes from the spiritual world, from *nous*...." *The Gospel of Hellas* (Hudson, NY: Anthroposophic Press, 1949), p. 247.

and violet, in which darkness predominates, represent the *tamas* condition. The whole way of thinking that we find in the Sankhya philosophy regarding its spiritual grasp of world conditions shone into him, hence his teachings on color were an echo of this old philosophy.

Even this echo, however, was lost. We find the first glimmering of the reappearance of the three conditions—*sattva, rajas,* and *tamas*—in the external world of color in the hard battle fought by Goethe. For after the old Aristotelian division of the world of color into conditions of *sattva, rajas,* and *tamas* had been completely obliterated, it reappeared in Goethe. Today the Goethean system of color, brought to birth out of the principles of spiritual wisdom, has been excoriated by modern physicists. From their own standpoint, of course, they are right in disagreeing with Goethe. But it only shows that in these matters they have been abandoned by all the good gods.

If genuine modern science wanted to establish any connection with esoteric principles, it ought to take a stand in favor of Goethe's theory of color. For in it we can find again, in the midst of our scientific culture, what once reigned as the spiritual principle within Sankhya philosophy. You can understand why many years ago I set myself the task of bringing forward Goethe's color theory to be evaluated as a physical science, while resting upon esoteric principles. For it is entirely relevant to say that Goethe's division of color phenomena represents the three states of *sattva, rajas,* and *tamas.* So, gradually, as out of spiritual darkness into a new chapter of spiritual history, new methods bring forth what humanity once attained by entirely different means.

This Sankhya philosophy was pre-Buddhist, as is obvious from the legend of the Buddha.[9] Indian teachings rightly relate that Kapila was

---

9. Sankhya ideas are included in various Upanishads, beginning in 900 B.C.E. The oldest Sankhya text, *Sankyakarika,* a summary of Sankhya ideas by Ishvarakrishna, is thought to have been composed between 350 and 550 C.E. (see Edeltraud Harzer, "Sankhya," in Mircea Eliade, ed., *Encyclopedia of Religion,* 13:47–51). The Buddha's title, Sakyamuni, "Sage of the Sakya Clan," clearly suggests that he was born in the region of the Sakhya (in what is now Nepal), the capital of which was Kapila Vastu. Some Indian archeologists claim that Buddha was born in Piprahwa, Uttar Pradesh, India. For the Buddha's birthplace and lineage, see Hajime Nakamura, *Gotama Buddha: A Biography Based on the Most Reliable Texts,* Vol. 1, trans. Geynor Sekimori (Tokyo: Kosei Publishing Co., 2000), pp. 29–53.

the founder of Sankhya philosophy. The birth of Buddha in the dwelling place of Kapila, in Kapila Vastu, indicates that he had his roots in Sankhya teachings. His very birth placed him at the spot where that personality once worked who was the first to formulate the great Sankhya philosophy.

Now imagine the relation of this Sankhya doctrine to the other spiritual currents we have mentioned, although not in the way many Asians, present it today. In various parts of ancient India lived people who had become differentiated in accordance with these three spiritual streams, since by that time the primal state of human evolution no longer existed. In northeast India, for example, human nature was such that it inclined to the concepts given in the Sankhya philosophy. In an area more to the west, the tendency was to conceive of the world according to the Vedic doctrine. The different spiritual nuances arise, therefore, out of the differently gifted human natures in the different parts of India. Only later, through the Vedantists carrying their work further, was much of Sankhya philosophy integrated into the Vedas as we now have them. Yoga, the third spiritual current, arose because the old clairvoyance had gradually diminished and new approaches to the spiritual world had to be sought. Yoga differs from the Sankhya point of view in that the latter is the view of a genuine science, a science of outer forms, that actually grasps only these forms and the way the human soul is interrelated with them. Yoga indicates how the soul is to develop in order to reach the spiritual worlds.

What was an Indian to do at a comparatively later time to develop in a way that would not be one-sided? What was one to do if one wished not merely to advance by concerning oneself with external forms, but to raise one's soul nature so as to achieve again the illumination that the Vedas had originally given as if by grace? An answer to this is provided by Krishna to his pupil Arjuna in the sublime Gita. Such a soul would have to undergo a development expressed like this:

Yes, it is true that you see the world in its outer forms, and when you are permeated with the knowledge of the Sankhya philosophy you will see how these forms have developed out of the primal flow. You will also see how form after form changes. Your vision can follow the origin and dissolution of forms, your eyes see the birth and death of forms. But, when you consider thoroughly how these forms change, how form after form arises and vanishes, then you are led to contemplate what comes to expression in all these forms. Accurate observation will lead you to the spiritual principle living in all these forms, transforming itself within them, sometimes more according to the *sattva* condition, at other times more after the forms of the other *gunas*, yet always freeing itself again from these forms. Such a thorough observation will direct you to something permanent, which, compared to form, is imperishable. The material principle, to be sure, is constant, but not the forms you see, which come into being, arise and fade, and go through birth and death. Yet the soul-spiritual element is ongoing. Direct your attention to that!

In order, however, to be able to experience this soul-spiritual element within and around you and to identify it with yourself, you must develop the slumbering forces in your soul. You must yield yourself to Yoga, which begins with looking up devotionally toward the soul-spirit element of existence, and with the practice of certain exercises leading to the development of these slumbering forces.

In this way the pupil rises from stage to stage by means of Yoga. Devotional reverence for the spiritual element of the soul is the other way leading the soul forward to that spirit living in unity behind the changing forms—that element once proclaimed by the Vedas through grace and illumination. The soul will recapture through Yoga what we look for behind all changing forms. Thus, a great teacher might have told a pupil:

Study the knowledge given in the Sankhya philosophy, in its forms, in the *gunas*, considering the conditions of *sattva, rajas,* and *tamas*, through all the forms, from the finest down to the coarsest substance. Study these with your understanding, then admit that there must be something permanent, something unifying in it all. Then, by thinking, you will have penetrated to the eternal.

But you can also begin with devotion. By means of Yoga you can push on from stage to stage and ultimately reach the spiritual that is at the base of all forms. From two sides you can approach the eternal—through a thoughtful contemplation of the world, and through Yoga [II.39–41]. Both will lead you to what the great teacher of the Vedas describes as the unitary Atman-Brahman that lives in the outer world as well as in the inmost being of the soul, which in oneness exists at the world's foundation. On the one side you will attain it by thinking through the Sankhya philosophy; on the other through devotion by means of Yoga.

As I have shown in my booklet *The Occult Significance of the Blood*, it is possible to look back to those ancient times when clairvoyant power was still united with human nature through the blood. But humankind has gradually advanced from that blood-bound clairvoyance to a kind more truly soul-spiritual. In order not to lose this connection with the soul-spiritual, naturally attained in those ancient times of close tribal and folk blood relationships, new methods and ways of teaching had to be found during the transition from the period of blood relationships to the time when these relationships no longer prevailed.

It is the sublime song of the Bhagavad Gita that leads to this transition to new methods and tells of the battle fought between the descendants of the two royal brothers of the lines of Kuru and Pandu. On one side is represented the age that was already past when the story of the Gita begins, the time in which the old Indian perception still existed and humans still based their way of life upon it. In the blind King Dritarashtra of the house of Kuru, we see the line that reaches from ancient times into the new era. We see the king in conversation with his charioteer. He stands on one of the warring sides. On the other side are the sons of Pandu, who are related to the others by blood but who are fighting them because they are in a state of transition from the old times to the new.

King Dritarashtra, who is characteristically described as blind because it is not the spiritual in this line but the physical that is to be transmitted, is told by his charioteer what is happening on the other side among the sons of Pandu. To them is to pass, for future generations, what is of a more soul-spiritual nature. The charioteer tells the king how Arjuna, the representative of the Pandu warriors, is instructed by the great Krishna, the teacher of humankind. He tells him how Krishna gives to his pupil Arjuna all the knowledge of which we have been speaking: of the possibility of achieving again—if thinking and devotion are developed through Sankhya and Yoga—what the great teachers of humankind had incorporated in the Vedas. In grandiose language, as much philosophical as poetical, we are told of the instruction given by Krishna, the great teacher of the new age that had abandoned the old blood relationships.

Here something else shines through to us out of those ancient times. In the basic considerations of the booklet *The Occult Significance of the Blood*, and elsewhere, I have indicated how the evolution of humankind proceeded from the time of the old blood relationships to later differentiations, whereby the striving of the soul was transformed. The noble song of the Bhagavad Gita leads directly to this transition. Through Krishna's instructions to Arjuna it becomes clear how humans, who no longer possessed the old clairvoyance dependent upon the blood, must press on to what is imperishable. The Gita thus stands as an illustration of what I have often mentioned, from direct observation out of the events themselves, as an important transition in the evolution of humankind.

What particularly attracts us in the Bhagavad Gita is the penetrating perception with which it speaks of the human path, of the way we must take in order to gain the enduring as opposed to the transitory. At the beginning of the poem the charioteer, relating the happenings on the battlefield to King Dritarashtra, pictures Arjuna standing there, his soul torn over the prospect of having to fight the Kurus, his blood relatives. Arjuna asks himself, "Must I fight against those who are linked to me by blood? Those who are my father's brothers' sons? There are many heroes among us who must turn their weapons against their own relatives. On the opposite side there are heroes just as honorable who must direct their weapons against us." In great torment he continues, "Can I win this battle? Ought I to win it? Do brothers dare to raise the sword against each other?"

Then Krishna, the great teacher, comes to him and says,

> First of all, give thoughtful consideration to human life and examine the circumstances in which you find yourself. In the temporal bodies of the Kurus against whom you are to fight, there live soul beings that are eternal, that only express themselves in these temporal forms. In your fellow warriors also live eternal souls who only express themselves in the forms of the outer world. You will have to fight, for your law ordains it. This is for you to accomplish, decreed by the outer, earthly evolution of humanity. You must do battle; this is the will of the moment that signifies the transition from one period to the other. Should you mourn the fact that forms fight against other forms? Forms in transition battling against other changing forms? Whichever of these forms will lead the others to death—what is death? what is life?—the changing of forms is death, and it is life. Similar are the souls of those who are to be victorious to those who will now go to their death. What is this victory and what is this death compared with that to which a thoughtful study of the Sankhya philosophy leads you, compared to these eternal souls now opposing each other yet remaining beyond the reach of battle? [II.18–28]

In this magnificent manner, out of the situation itself, we are led to see how Arjuna is shown that he should not suffer torments in his innermost being, but only do his duty calling him to battle; that he should look beyond what is passing and involves fighting to the eternal that lives on, whether as conqueror or as the conquered. So a powerful tone is sounded in the sublime Gita, a tone heralding a significant event in human evolution, the perishable confronting the imperishable.

In the Bhagavad Gita, we can see verified a statement once made about the philosophy set forth in it: "The Indian philosophy was so much a religion in those ancient times that a person devoted to it, however great and wise he may have been, was not without the deepest religious fervor. And the simplest person, who only lived the religion of feeling, was not without a certain amount of wisdom." We are on the right path if, instead of having abstract thoughts about the matter, we let its feeling contents work upon us. We proceed in the right way when we perceive that Krishna's instructions are designed to raise Arjuna's soul from the stage at which it stands, entangled in the net of transitoriness, to a higher stage in which it will feel itself elevated beyond everything transitory, even when the transitory presents itself to the soul directly involved in such a distressing form as victory or defeat, as inflicting death or suffering it.

We feel this when we see how the great teacher, Krishna, not only influenced the thoughts of his pupil Arjuna, but also worked directly into his feeling, bringing him to contemplate the transitory and the torments of the transitory existence. In such a significant situation, he raises Arjuna's soul to a height far above everything transitory, above all its miseries, pain, and sorrow.

3

Joining the Three Streams in the Christ Impulse

December 30, 1912

T HE significance of a philosophical poem such as the Bhagavad Gita, or similar works of world literature, can only be rightly valued by one to whom they are not just theory, but destiny, for world conceptions may be destiny for humankind. In the last few days we have met with two different concepts of world philosophy—Sankhya and Yoga—as well as a third, the Veda. When rightly viewed these two show how world conceptions can become destiny for the human soul.

In the Sankhya philosophy one can bring together all that a person is able to achieve in cognition, in conceiving ideas, in surveying world phenomena—everything in which the life of the soul finds its expression. In the normal contemporary human being, something of this world conception can be scientifically expressed, although it stands at a much lower level spiritually than Sankhya philosophy. Hence we can say that even in our own age we can still feel as destiny that which in Sankhya philosophy was felt as destiny. Of course, this will only be experienced as destiny by those who devote themselves single-mindedly to such a philosophical study—persons one might call scientists in the strict sense, or Sankhya philosophers. What would be the soul experience of such persons, their attitude toward the world? These questions can only really be answered out of experience. One must know what takes place in a soul that devotes itself solely to one aspect of a world conception. Such a soul can study in detail the various forms of world phenomena. It can come to the most complete understanding of that which comes to expression as active forces in the world, as ever-changing forms. If, in one of its incarnations, this soul through its capacities and karma only finds the opportunity to live into world phenomena so as to acquire knowledge chiefly through reasoning, this must lead to a certain coldness in the entire soul life, whether or not it was illuminated by clairvoyance. According to the temperament of that soul it might, to a greater or lesser degree, take on a character of ironic dissatisfaction with world phenomena. Or it might lose interest altogether and feel a general discontent with such knowledge as it skips from subject to subject, from one phenomenon to another.

Everything that so many souls in our time feel when confronted by a science conditioned by scholarship, the coldness and barrenness that depress them, the nagging dissatisfaction—all this can be perceived when we examine such a soul's attitude. It would feel desolate and uncertain of itself. It might well ask itself: what if I gain the whole world and know nothing of my own soul; if I feel nothing, sense nothing, experience nothing but inner emptiness? To be crammed full of all the science in the world and yet be inwardly empty—that can be a bitter fate. It would be like being left stranded amid the phenomena of the world, losing everything that would be of value to one's inner being.

We find this condition in many people who possess some sort of learning or abstract philosophy. We find it in those who, dissatisfied and realizing their emptiness, have lost interest in all their knowledge and seem to feel miserable. We also find it when someone comes at us with some abstract philosophy and proceeds to hand out information in abstract terms on the nature of the Godhead, cosmology, and the human soul. We feel that it is all in the person's head, that the heart has no part in it, and the soul is empty. We feel chilled when we meet such a soul. Sankhya philosophy can lead to such a destiny where one realizes that one is lost to oneself, bereft of anything one might call one's own, someone from whose individuality the world can gain nothing.

Let us take the case of a soul seeking development in a one-sided way through Yoga, a soul lost, as it were, to the external world and disdaining to know anything about it. "What good is it to me," such a person says, "to learn how the world came into existence? I want to find out everything out of my own self. I will advance myself by developing my own powers."

This person may perhaps feel an inward glow, and may often give the impression of being self-contained and self-satisfied. Nevertheless, in the long run such a person will not always be so self-complacent, but in time will become prone to a sense of loneliness. A person who led a hermit's life while seeking the heights of soul development may go forth into the world and encounter everywhere world phenomena, perhaps saying inwardly: What do all these things matter to me? If one confronts these glorious revelations as an alien, without understanding, this one-sidedness will lead to a fatal destiny.

How often we meet such people! How can we really get to know those who use all their powers toward the development of their own being, and thus, cold and indifferent, pass by their fellow human beings as though wishing to have nothing in common with them? Such souls can feel lost to the world, while appearing excessively egotistical to others. Only when we see these life connections do we experience how world conceptions become destiny. Behind the great disclosures and world-views we find in the Bhagavad Gita and the Epistles of Paul, we see the influence of destiny. We might say that if we only look a little behind the Gita, and also the Epistles, we find a direct ruling of destiny.

It often says in the Epistles that the real salvation of the soul consists in the so called "justification by faith" in contrast to the worthlessness of external works, because of what the soul can gain when it establishes the connection with the Christ impulse, when it takes into itself the great force that flows from a true understanding of the resurrection of Christ. When we meet this in the Epistles, we feel that the human soul is thrown back upon itself and can become estranged from all external works, thus coming to rely entirely upon grace and justification by faith. But then, the external works are there in the world, and we do not wipe them out simply by turning away from them. We collide with them in the world. Again, destiny rings out in all its greatness! Only when things are looked at in this way can we realize the force of such utterances.

Now, these two mighty works, the Gita and the Epistles, are outwardly quite different from each other, and this external difference acts, in every part of these works, upon the soul. We not only stand in wonder before the Gita for the reasons we have been considering, but also because it strikes us as being so poetically great and powerful. In every verse it radiates the great nobility of the human soul. Everything spoken by Krishna and his pupil Arjuna lifts us above everyday human experiences, above all passions and everything that disturbs the soul. We are transported into a sphere of serenity, clarity, calm dispassion, and freedom from emotion, into an atmosphere of wisdom, when even one part of the Gita is allowed to work upon us. Reading it, our humanity is raised to a higher stage. Through it all, we feel that if we wish to allow the divine character of the Gita to affect us in the right way, we must first free ourselves from a good deal that is only too human.

With the Pauline Epistles all this is different. They have neither sublime poetic language nor serenity. When we let the Epistles work upon us, we feel over and over again that what Paul says comes from a person who is passionately indignant at what has happened. Sometimes the tone is harsh and scolding, one might even say condemnatory. His statements about the great concepts of Christianity—about grace, the law, the difference between the law of Moses and Christianity, the Resurrection—all this is put forth in a tone that is supposed to be philosophical, or in the nature of a philosophical definition. But it is not so, because one hears a Pauline note at every turn. Every sentence reminds us that the speaker is either excited or expressing justified anger. He gives the impression of being a propagandist of the highest concepts of Christianity, and speaks about them in such a way that we feel he is personally involved .

Where could we find in the Gita sentiments of such a personal nature as those we find in the Epistles when Paul writes to one of the communities, "How have we ourselves interceded for Christ Jesus! Remember that we have not become a burden to any, remember that we labored day and night that we might not be a burden to anyone."

How personal all this is! In the sublime Gita, by contrast, a wonderfully pure sphere can be found—an etheric sphere that borders on the super-human, and at times extends into it. Outwardly, therefore, there are enormous differences between these two works. It would be the blindest prejudice to refuse to admit that through the great Song there flowed the union of mighty world conceptions, and that something of sublime purity, impersonal, calm and passionless, was given to the Hindus. By contrast, in the Epistles of Paul, the very first documents of Christianity, we find an entirely personal and often passionate expression, utterly devoid of serenity. Turning away from the truth and refusing to admit these things will not help us know things that we must instead understand in the right way. Let us therefore keep this contrast in mind like an unshakable signpost during the considerations that follow.

I pointed out in yesterday's lecture that the Gita contains the momentous instruction given by Krishna to Arjuna. Now, who exactly was Krishna? This question must be of utmost interest to us. However, we cannot understand who Krishna was unless we are familiar with something I have already mentioned elsewhere, namely that in earlier ages the system of name giving and forms of address was quite different from what it is now. Actually, nowadays it does not matter in the least what a person is called. We know very little about a man once we have learned that he is called Miller or Smith. By the same token, everyone will admit that we really don't know much about a man simply from hearing that he is a privy councilor, or something of the kind. Nor do we learn much about people simply by knowing whether they are to be addressed as "Your Honor," "Your Eminence," or only "Dear Sir or Madam." In short, all these titles do not say much about a person, and it is easy to convince ourselves that other designations in use today do not reveal much either. Things were different in past ages. Whether we use the terms of Sankhya philosophy or those of our own Anthroposophy, we can start from either and make the following observations.

According to Sankhya philosophy, the human being consists of the coarse physical body, the finer elemental or etheric body, the body that contains the natural law-filled forces of the senses, the body called *manas, ahankara,* and so on. But when we observe persons as they stand before us in this or that incarnation, we find they are different. In one, the ether body is more strongly expressed; in another, the laws of the senses predominate; in the third, the inner sense of *manas;* in the fourth, *ahankara*. We do not need to consider the other higher members, as they are not yet, in general, developed. Or, in our own language, there are people in whom the forces of the sentient soul are more active; then others who more strongly express the intellectual soul; still others in whom forces of the consciousness soul predominate; others again in whom something inspired by *manas* plays a part, etc. These differences are to be seen in one's whole manner of life, and point to a person's real nature.

For reasons that are easily understood, it is currently impossible to name people according to their natures in the sense of what I have just said. With the widespread disposition of humanity as it is today, if one were to say that the highest we could attain in our present cycle of development was a trace of *ahankara*, everyone would be convinced of expressing *ahankara* in his or her own being more clearly than anyone else. People would feel hurt to be told that this was not yet the case because a lower principle still ruled in them. It was not so in olden times. Names were given indicating what was most essential in a person. This was especially true when there was a question of ranking one above others, perhaps by giving him or her a leadership role. One would then be given a name expressing one's most outstanding characteristic.

Imagine a man in the past who had brought *manas* to expression within him in the most comprehensive way—someone who had certainly experienced *ahankara* but had allowed this to slip more into the background as a distinct element, so that for the sake of his effectiveness in the outer world he had brought his inner sense, *manas*, to the fore. According to the laws of the older, smaller evolutionary cycles—and only quite exceptional people could have embodied this—such a man would have been called upon to be a great lawgiver, a leader of great masses of people. It would not have been enough to name him as one named other men, but he would have to have been named according to his most outstanding capacity, "a *manas* bearer," while another would be designated merely as "sense bearer." One would have said: There is a *manas* bearer, a "Manu."

A person's name in past ages must be understood as descriptive of the member of the human organization that was foremost in that particular incarnation. Suppose that what specially came to expression in a man was that he felt a divine inspiration; that he had to put aside all question of ruling his studies and actions by what the external world decrees through the senses and through reasoning bound to the brain. Instead, in all things he listened to the Divine Word that spoke to him, and thereby made himself a messenger for the Divine Substance that would speak through him. Such a man would have been called a "Son of God." Even at the time of the Gospel of John, right at the beginning of the first chapter, such men were still called "Sons of God."

The essential point was that everything else was left out of consideration when the significant element was expressed. Everything else was unimportant. Consider two people, one just an ordinary person who allowed the world to act upon him through his senses and who then reflected upon it with cerebral intellect, and the other an individual into whom the Word of Divine Wisdom had streamed. According to those ideas out of the past, one would say that the first person was born of a father and mother, begotten according to the flesh. With the other, the messenger of the Divine Substance, no consideration would have been given to the usual content of a biography. To write such a biography of the second person would have been folly, for the fact of his fleshly body was only incidental, not the essential thing. His fleshly body was, so to speak, only the means through which he expressed himself to other people. For this reason it is said that the Son of God was not born of flesh but of a virgin, directly from the spirit, and that the essential element in him, which rendered him of value to humanity, was descended from the spirit. In past ages, that element alone was stressed.

In certain schools of initiation, it would have been considered a great sin to write an ordinary biography recounting everyday occurrences in the life of a person who was recognized as especially significant for possessing the higher members of human nature.[10] For anyone with

10. Cf. Sri Aurobindo: "My life has not been on the surface for me to see." Epigraph, *Sri Aurobindo on Himself,* Sri Aurobindo Birth Centenary Library, Vol. 26 (Pondicherry, India: Sri Aurobindo Ashram, 1972).

even a faint feeling for the sentiments of those ancient times, biographies such as those written today—of Goethe, for example—must appear as the height of absurdity. If we remember that in those days people lived with ideas and feelings such as these, then we can understand how this ancient humanity could be permeated with the conviction that a Manu, in whom *manas* was the prevailing principle, appeared but seldom and must wait long epochs of time before appearing again.

If we think of the secret forces capable of raising a human being to heights of soul; if we think how this exists in most people only in rudimentary form and rarely becomes the essential principle of a life; if we think of a personality who only occasionally appears in the world in order to be a leader of humanity, who is higher than all the Manus, who dwells as an essence in every human being, and who as an actual person appears only once in a world epoch; if we let such a concept take shape, it brings us near to Krishna's being. Krishna is the universal human being. He is, one might almost say, all humanity thought of as a single being. Yet he is no abstraction.

When people today speak of humankind in general, they speak of it in the abstract. Because we have become so ensnared in the sense world, abstraction has become our common fate. To speak of humankind in general is a vague concept that does not come to life. Those who speak about Krishna in general do not mean that kind of an abstract idea. They say that this being lives potentially in every person, but only once in every world-epoch does he appear and speak human language. With this being, however, it is not the external fleshly body, not the more refined elemental body, not the forces of the sense organs, not *ahankara*, not *manas*, that is significant. The important characteristic is what in *buddhi* and *manas* is directly connected with the great universal substance, with the divine that lives and weaves through the world.

From time to time, beings such as Krishna, Arjuna's great teacher, appear for the guidance of humankind. Krishna teaches the highest human wisdom, the highest that humanity can attain, and he gives it as his own nature, yet in such a way that it harmonizes with every human soul. Everything contained in Krishna's words can be found as a predisposition in every human soul, so when human beings look up to Krishna they are looking up to their own highest Self. But they are also looking up to another being in whom they honor what they themselves are predisposed to become. This other being is separate from the person and bears the same relationship to him or her as a god to humanity.

This is the way we must conceive the relation of Krishna to his pupil. Then the key tone of the Gita will sound out to us as though it concerned every soul, a tone ringing through everyone in such an intimately human way as to make the soul feel guilty if it did not have a longing to listen to these great teachings. On the other hand, it all seems so calm and without emotion, so dispassionate, so sublime and wise, because the highest in every human being speaks here: that which is divine and yet appears incarnated once as a divine human entity in the evolution of humanity.

How exalted are these teachings! So much so that the Bhagavad Gita rightfully bears the name "Sublime Song." Here we meet a teaching given in exalted words: that everything that appears as change in the world, arising and passing away, birth and death, victory and defeat, still contains the expression of something imperishable, eternal, permanent. One who wishes to view the world rightly must struggle through the transitory and reach this eternal element. We have already met this in the reasoned reflections of the Sankhya philosophy on the permanence to be found in everything transitory, on the quality before God of the conquered and the victorious souls when the door of death closes behind them.

But Krishna also tells Arjuna that the soul can be led, by another path, away from thinking of everyday matters, and that is through Yoga. There are two paths by which the soul may develop. One is to pass from one phenomenon to another, making use of the wealth of related ideas, whether or not illuminated by clairvoyance. On the other path, one turns entirely away from the outer world, closes the door of the senses, shuts out all that reason and understanding can say about the outer world, closes off to all memories of ordinary life, then endeavors to enter into one's inmost being. By means of suitable exercises, one tries to draw forth what rests within one's soul, directing one's efforts toward the highest that can be imagined, which, out of the force of contemplation, seeks to arise. When this happens, one can rise ever higher by means of Yoga, eventually reaching those higher levels attainable by first making use of the bodily instrument. One attains those stages in which one is set free of all bodily organs and lives, as it were, outside the body, in the higher principles of the human constitution. In this way one raises oneself to a completely different form of life. The phenomena of life and their activities become spiritualized. One comes ever closer to one's own divine nature, and enlarges one's individual being to that of cosmic being—to God—losing the limits of one's own individuality and merging in the All through Yoga.

The pupil of the great Krishna is then given methods by which he can rise in one way or another to these spiritual heights. First, Arjuna is shown the difference between the two attitudes to be faced in the outer world. It is indeed a tremendous situation that the Gita presents here. Arjuna must fight his blood relatives. That is his outer destiny, his task, his karma, the sum of the deeds he must first accomplish directly in this situation. In these deeds, he lives as an external self, but the great Krishna teaches him that a person only becomes wise, only unites with the eternally divine, when he or she acts because such deeds prove to be necessary in the outer course of nature and of human evolution. Even so, as a wise person one frees oneself from them. One performs these deeds, but at the same time a part of one acts as onlooker, taking no part in the deeds but saying: I do the work, but I could just as well say that I let it happen. One becomes wise by looking at what one does as though it were being done by another, by not allowing oneself to be disturbed by the pleasure the deed gives, nor by the sorrow it causes.

"It is all the same," says Krishna to Arjuna, "whether you are here in the ranks of Pandu's sons, or are over there among Kuru's sons. Whatever you do, as a wise man you must free yourself from the Pandus and Kurus. If it does not affect you whether you are to act with the Pandus as though one of them, or with the Kurus as though you were a son of Kuru; if you can rise above all this and not be disturbed by your own deeds; if you can live in your deeds like a flame quietly burning, protected from the wind, undisturbed by anything outside you, and your soul, undisturbed by its deeds, lives quietly beside them—then do you become wise. Then does your soul free itself from its deeds and no longer inquires as to their results" [II.55–72].[11]

For the results of our deeds concern only our narrowly limited soul. But if we act because the development of humanity or world events require certain actions, then they are performed without regard to consequences, whether they lead us to what is dreadful or glorious, to suffering or delight. This lifting oneself above one's deeds, this standing upright no matter what one's hands may carry out, even to what one's sword may do, or what one speaks—this uprightness of one's innermost self in face of everything one may say or do is where the great Krishna leads his pupil Arjuna.

Arjuna is directed to a human ideal presented in such a way that a person could reflect: "I perform my deeds, but whether I or another performs them, I observe them. What happens by my hand or is spoken by my mouth, I see as objectively as I might watch a loose rock on a mountainside roll down into a ravine. Though I may be in a position to know this or that and to form concepts of the world, I remain quite separate from them. Though there lives in me something that knows, I look on as if it were another one who knows. In this way I free myself even from my knowledge. I can become free of my deeds, free of my knowledge, free of my understanding."

An exalted ideal of human wisdom is presented here! Upon finally reaching the spiritual, whether one encounters demons or holy spirits, one can look upon them externally. One stands there, free from everything going on around one, even in the spiritual worlds. One goes one's own way and takes no part in what is going on, because one has become an onlooker. That is the teaching of Krishna.

As we have heard that these teachings are based on the Sankhya philosophy, it is understandable that in many places this philosophy can be seen shining through, as when Krishna informs his pupil that the soul living in him has various ties: to the coarse physical body, to the senses, to *manas, ahankara,* and *buddhi.* But Arjuna himself is apart from them all. If he regards these entities as external, as sheaths

---

11. These are the verses that Gandhi took to be the essential teaching of the Gita.

surrounding him, if he is conscious that as a soul being he is independent of them all, then he will have understood something of what Krishna has tried to teach him. If he is aware that his connections with the outer world, with the world in general, were given him through the *gunas*, through *tamas, rajas,* and *sattva*, then he has learned that in ordinary life, humans are connected with wisdom and kindness through *sattva*, with the passions, emotions, and thirst for existence through *rajas*, and that through *tamas* they tend to be lazy, idle, sleepy.

Why do people feel enthusiasm for wisdom and kindness in ordinary life? Because they have a connection with the foundation of nature that is designated as *sattva*. Why do some go through ordinary life joyful and eager for outer existence, for life's outer manifestations? Because they have a relation to life indicated by *rajas*. Why do others go through ordinary life sleepy, lazy, inactive, feeling oppressed by their corporeality and finding it impossible to rouse themselves at any moment to prevail over their bodily natures? Because they are connected with the world of external forms, which in Sankhya philosophy is expressed through the condition of *tamas*.

The soul of the wise person, however, must become free from *tamas*. It must sever its connection with the external world expressed in sleepiness, laziness, and torpor. When this is done, then the soul is only connected with the external world through *rajas* and *sattva*. If one further extinguishes one's passions and emotions, one's thirst for existence, retaining only the enthusiasm for kindness, compassion, and knowledge, one remains connected with the external world through *sattva*. But when a person has also become liberated from the urge to goodness and knowledge; when, as a good and wise person, one is independent of how one expresses oneself in the outside world; when kindness has become a natural duty, and wisdom is as something poured out over one, then one has also broken the tie with *sattva*. With the three *gunas* stripped off one has freed oneself from all connection with every external form. Then one triumphs in one's soul, and has come to understand something of what the great Krishna has wanted to make of him or her.

What then does one grasp in striving to become the ideal that Krishna holds up? What does one come to understand? Does one understand the forms of the outer world more clearly? No; rather, having understood these before, one has raised oneself above them. Is one able to comprehend more exactly the relation of the soul to external forms? No; rather, having already understood that, one has raised oneself above it. It is not what one meets in the multitude of forms of the outside world, nor is it one's connection with these forms that one now understands in stripping off the three *gunas*. All of that belongs to earlier stages. As long as one remains in *tamas, rajas,* or *sattva* one has a relationship with the natural foundation of existence. One adapts oneself to social relationships and to knowledge, and acquires the capacities for kindness and sympathy. But when one rises even above all that, one has stripped off all connections with the preceding stages. What comes before one then—what then does one comprehend? There comes before one's eyes *just what these are not.*

What is it that is distinct from everything one acquires along the path within the *gunas*? It is none other than what one finally recognizes as one's own being, for everything belonging to the external has been stripped away. In the sense of what has previously been said, this is Krishna himself. For he himself is the expression of what is highest in humanity. That is to say, when one has worked up to the highest, one stands face to face with Krishna, the pupil to the great teacher, Arjuna to Krishna himself, who lives in all things that exist and who can truly say of himself, "I am not a solitary mountain. When I am among the mountains I am the most gigantic of all. When I appear upon Earth I am not a single man but the revelation of the consummately human, who appears only once in a world epoch as a leader of humankind. That am I, Krishna, the unity in all forms" [see IX.13–17].

In this way the teacher himself sets forth his own being to his pupil. At the same time it is made clear in the Bhagavad Gita that this is an exalted revelation, the highest to which human beings can attain. So, to stand face to face before Krishna as Arjuna did is something that could come about through gradual stages of initiation. It would happen in the depths of a Yoga schooling. It can also be represented as flowing from the evolution of humanity itself, as given to humanity by an act of grace. Thus it is expressed in the Gita—as if in a sudden great leap Arjuna is lifted high and finds Krishna bodily before him.

He does not appear as a man of flesh and blood, however, because such a man would represent the nonessential in Krishna. For what is essential is that which is essential in all human beings. But as the other kingdoms of the world represent fragments of humanity, so all that comprises the world apart from humanity is Krishna. The rest of the world disappears and Krishna stands there as the One. As the macrocosm is related to the microcosm, as humankind as a whole can be compared to a single human being, so does Krishna stand in relation to the individual.

Should a person gain this conception through an act of grace, his or her human comprehension would not be sufficient to grasp it. If one looks at the essential in Krishna—which is only possible to one possessing the highest clairvoyant power—he appears quite different from anything we are accustomed to see. There comes before us at that moment in the Gita the sublime human being beside whom everything else in the world appears trivial in comparison. It is this awesome being before whom Arjuna stands, and his power of comprehension forsakes him. He can only stare, and haltingly try to express what he beholds. That is understandable, for by all the means he has known up to now he has not learned how to take in such a revelation and describe it in words. Arjuna's speech from the depths of his soul as he actually sees the great Krishna is one of the most magnificent outpourings ever given to humanity in connection with art and philosophy. In words he has never uttered before, words such as he is unaccustomed to speaking, and could never have spoken before that moment because he has never seen such a sight, he stands there before Krishna and begins to utter the words that come to him to say:

> O Lord, I see within your body all the gods and every kind of living creature. I see Brahma, the Creator, seated on a lotus; I see the ancient sages and the celestial serpents.
>
> I see infinite mouths and arms, stomachs and eyes, and you are embodied in every form. I see you everywhere, without beginning, middle, or end. You are the Lord of all creation, and the cosmos is your body.

Your wear a crown and carry a mace and discus; your radiance is blinding and immeasurable. I see you, who are so difficult to behold, shining like a fiery sun blazing in every direction.

You are the supreme, changeless Reality, the one thing to be known. You are the refuge of all creation, the immortal spirit, the eternal guardian of eternal dharma.

You are without beginning, middle, or end; you touch everything with your infinite power. The sun and moon are your eyes, and your mouth is fire; your radiance warms the cosmos.

O Lord, your presence fills the heavens and the earth and reaches in every direction. I see the three worlds trembling before this vision of your wonderful and terrible form.

The gods enter your being, some calling out and greeting you in fear. Great saints sing your glory, praying, "May all be well!"

The multitudes of gods, demigods, and demons are all over-whelmed by the sight of you. O mighty Lord, at the sight of your myriad eyes and mouths, arms and legs, stomachs and fearful teeth, I and the entire universe shake in terror.

O Vishnu, I can see your eyes shining; with open mouth, your glitter in an array of colors, and your body touches the sky. I look at you and my heart trembles; I have lost all courage and all peace of mind.

When I see your mouths with their fearful teeth, mouths burning like the fires at the end of time, I forget where I am and I have no place to go. O Lord, you are the support of the universe; have mercy on me!

I see all the sons of Dhritarashtra; I see Bhishma, Drona, and Karna; I see your warriors and all the kinds who are here to fight.

All are rushing into your awful jaws; I see some of them crushed by your teeth. As rivers flow into the ocean, all the warriors of this world are passing into your fiery jaws; all creatures rush to their destruction like moths into a flame.

You lap the worlds into your burning mouths and swallow them. Filled with your terrible radiance, O Vishnu, the whole of creation bursts into flames.

Tell me who you are, O Lord of terrible form. I bow before you; have mercy! I want to know who you are, you who existed before all creation. Your nature and workings confound me. [XI.15–31]

Thus Arjuna speaks when he is alone with that which is his own being, when it appears objectively before him. We are confronted here with a great cosmic mystery—a mystery not because of its theoretical content but because of the overpowering feeling it arouses in us when we are able to grasp it correctly. It is so full of mystery that it must speak differently to all human feeling from anything that was ever spoken before.

When Krishna himself speaks, his words resound to the ear of Arjuna:

I am time, the destroyer of all; I have come to consume the world. Even without your participation, all the warriors gathered here will die.

Therefore arise, Arjuna; conquer your enemies and enjoy the glory of sovereignty. I have already slain all these warriors; you will only be my instrument.

Bhishma, Drona, Jayadratha, Karna, and many others are already slain. Kill those whom I have killed. Do not hesitate. Fight in this battle and you will conquer your enemies. [XI.32–34]

We know that the instruction given by Krishna to Arjuna among the sons of Pandu was related to the blind hero, Dritarashtra, king of the Kurus, by Sanjaya, his charioteer. Continuing this report of what is happening on the battlefield, Sanjaya says that when Arjuna had heard the words of Krishna he trembled, folded his hands, and, though seized with fear, bowed low to Krishna, and with faltering but reverent speech said:

> O Krishna, it is right that the world delights and rejoices in your praise, that all the saints and sages bow down to you and all evil flees before you to the far corners of the universe.

> How could they not worship you, O Lord? You are the eternal spirit, who existed before Brahma the Creator and who will never cease to be. [XI.36–37]

Truly we stand before a cosmic mystery. For what does Arjuna say upon seeing his own self before him in bodily form? He addresses his own being as though it were higher than Brahma himself. We are face to face with a mystery. For when one reaches one's highest Self in this way, Arjuna's words must be understood without anything of the feelings, perceptions, ideas, or thoughts of ordinary life entering into one's understanding. Nothing could put a person in greater danger than to bring into these words of Arjuna a feeling such as one might otherwise have in life. If one were to do this, not realizing that this was something unique, not sensing it as the greatest cosmic mystery—if he were to meet Krishna, his own higher being, with but ordinary feeling—then insanity, megalomania, would be as nothing compared to the illness that would befall him.

> You are the first among the gods, the timeless spirit, the resting place of all beings. You are the knower and the thing which is known. You are the final home; with your infinite form you pervade the cosmos.

> You are Vayu, god of wind; Yama, god of death; Agni, god of fire; Varuna, god of water. You are the moon and the creator

Prajapati, the great-grandfather of all creatures. I bow before you and salute you again and again.

You are behind me and in front of me; I bow to you on every side. Your power is immeasurable. You pervade everything; you are everything.

Sometimes, because we were friends, I rashly said, "Oh, Krishna!" "Say, friend!"—casual, careless remarks. Whatever I may have said lightly, whether we were playing or resting, alone or in company, sitting together or eating, if it was disrespectful, forgive me for it, O Krishna. I did not know the greatness of your nature, unchanging and imperishable.

You are the father of the universe, of the animate and inanimate; you are the object of all worship, the greatest guru. There is none to equal you in the three worlds. Who can match your power? O gracious Lord, I prostrate myself before you and ask for your blessing. As a father forgives his son, or friend a friend, or lover his beloved, so should you forgive me.

I rejoice in seeing you as you have never been seen before, yet I am filled with fear by this vision of you as the abode of the universe. Please let me see you again as the shining God of gods. Though you are the embodiment of all creation, let me see you again not with a thousand arms but with four, carrying the mace and discus and wearing a crown. [XI.38–46]

Truly we are confronted with a mystery when one human being speaks to another in this manner. Again, Krishna speaks to his pupil:

Arjuna, through my grace you have been united with me and received this vision of my radiant, universal form, without beginning or end, which no one else has ever seen.

Not by knowledge of the Vedas, nor sacrifice, nor charity, nor
rituals, nor even by severe asceticism has any other mortal seen
what you have seen, O heroic Arjuna.

Do not be troubled; do not fear my terrible form. Let your heart
be satisfied and your fears dispelled in looking at me as I was
before. [XI.47–49]

Then Sanjaya tells the blind Dritarashtra that when Krishna had
spoken these words to Arjuna, the Immeasurable One, without
beginning and without end, supreme above all powers, vanished; and
Krishna showed himself again in his friendly human form as though
he wished thus to reassure the shocked Arjuna.

Arjuna spoke: "O Krishna, now that I have seen your gentle human
form my mind is again composed and returned to normal" [XI.51].

And Krishna said: "It is extremely difficult to obtain the vision you
have had; even the gods long always to see me in this aspect. Neither
knowledge of the Vedas, nor austerity, nor charity, nor sacrifice can
bring the vision you have seen. But through unfailing devotion,
Arjuna, you can know me, see me, and attain union with me.

"Whoever makes me the supreme goal of all his work and acts without selfish attachment, who devotes himself to me completely and is
free from ill will for any creature, enters into me" [XI.52–55].

Here is a cosmic mystery communicated to humankind at a most
significant cosmic hour, at a time when the old clairvoyance dependent upon the blood ceases, and human souls must seek new paths
to what is unending, to the eternal. So is this mystery brought to our
attention, that at the same time we may observe all that can become
dangerous to us when we are able to see our own being, which we
ourselves have brought to birth.

Further lectures will show how, by using what the Gita reveals
about a certain stage of human evolution, we can throw fresh light
upon another stage, as shown in the Epistles of Paul. If we grasp this
deepest of human and cosmic mysteries, which reveals our own being
through true self-knowledge, there stands before us then the greatest
world riddle. But it may only be put before us when it is revered in

all humility. No intellectual comprehension suffices to approach this cosmic mystery, only the right feeling. No one may approach this mystery, which speaks out of the Gita, who cannot do so reverently. This feeling alone makes possible a complete comprehension of it.

4

THE ESSENCE OF THE BHAGAVAD GITA
AND THE SIGNIFICANCE OF THE PAULINE LETTERS

DECEMBER 31, 1912

I pointed out at the beginning of yesterday's lecture how different our impressions are when we let the calm, dispassionate, wisdom-filled character of the Bhagavad Gita work upon us, then think of the pervasive effect of Paul's Epistles: the personal opinions and aims, passionately expressed, often in a spirit of agitating propaganda, temperamental scolding, or even boiling rage. In the Gita, the way the spiritual content comes to expression reveals a wonderful, artistically rounded form. We can hardly see how it could be more perfect, both as poetry and philosophy. By contrast, one often finds in the Pauline Epistles such an awkwardness of expression as to create a real hindrance in apprehending their deep meaning. In spite of all this, it is true to say that these Epistles give the tone and establish the directives for the development of Christianity, as the harmonized tones of the Indian world concepts come to expression in the Gita.

Indeed, in the Epistles we can find all the significant truths of Christianity: those regarding the Resurrection, the meaning of faith as compared to the Law, the nature of grace, the life of Christ in the soul or in human consciousness, and much else, so that again and again, in presenting Christianity, one must proceed from these Pauline Epistles. Everything in them relates to Christianity, as the Bhagavad Gita relates to the great truths about freeing oneself from the immediate activities of living, so that the soul may sink itself into observing everything, into contemplation, into raising itself to spiritual heights, and purifying itself—in short, in preparing itself for union with Krishna. We see how difficult it is to make comparisons between the two spiritual revelations. Superficially, one would doubtless grant the Gita a higher place because of its purity, serenity, and wisdom. It is as if one were faced with a full-grown plant with a beautiful blossom, and beside it a seed. One might be moved to declare that the plant, with its gorgeous, fully developed blossom, is much more beautiful than the insignificant seed. But it might be that out of the seed would one day come a still more beautiful plant and blossom. One cannot make a true comparison between a fully matured plant and an entirely undeveloped seed. So it is if one compares the Bhagavad Gita and the Epistles of Paul. In the Gita, we have the fully ripened fruit, a wonderfully beautiful outgrowth of human evolution throughout thousands of years, which finally comes to a ripe, wise, and artistic expression in the sublime Gita. The Epistles contain the seed of something entirely new that grows and must continue to grow. Only when one sees it as germinal, as prophetic of what could come of it after thousands and thousands of years of development into the future, can one sense the full significance of this steadily ripening seed laid into human soil by the Pauline Epistles. Any true comparison requires us to take this into consideration. In these Epistles, what should be great someday first had to pour out of the human soul in a homely, chaotic form from the depths of Christianity. Thus the significance of the Gita and the Epistles for the collective evolution of humankind on Earth must be judged differently, not merely according to the beauty, wisdom, and inner perfection of form to be found in a finished product.

For a comparison of the two world conceptions given in the Gita and the Epistles, we must first ask what is their main concern. Being able to view in historical perspective everything connected with these concepts, we see that their chief concern is the entrance of the human ego into the stream of evolution. If we trace this process, we find that in pre-Christian times this ego lacked independence; it was still rooted in hidden depths of the soul. It was still unable to develop itself. This could only come about through the thrusting in of what we call the Christ impulse.

Before the Mystery of Golgotha,[12] the human ego couldn't have felt what Paul expressed in his words: "Not I, but Christ in me." But in the millennium preceding the Mystery of Golgotha, when the Christ impulse was drawing nearer, gradual preparations were made for the entry of this impulse into the human soul. The way of this preparation came to expression in Krishna's deed. After the Mystery of Golgotha, human beings then had to seek the Christ impulse within themselves, in the sense of the Pauline formula, "Not I, but Christ in me." Before that event, this impulse had to be sought as a revelation coming to the human being out of the cosmos. The further back one goes in time, the more brilliant, the more impulsive, one finds this outer revelation to be.

So we can say that prior to the Mystery of Golgotha, a certain kind of revelation came to humankind from outside, like a stream of sunlight. The light of the spiritual Sun illuminated the human soul from outside, enveloping it in light. After the Mystery of Golgotha, the Christ impulse worked within the soul, as if the soul were a self-illumining body radiating light from within. Considered in this way, the fact of the Mystery of Golgotha becomes a significant transition point in human evolution. Before the Christ impulse entered the soul, it was like a drop of water glittering with the light radiating into it from all directions. After this mystery, if the soul had taken in the Christ impulse, light streamed out from it as from an inner flame.

With this in mind, we can express this whole relationship with the terms we learned to know in Sankhya philosophy. If our spiritual eye is turned to a soul that before the Mystery of Golgotha was illuminated from every side by spiritual light, it appears to be in the *sattva* condition. By contrast, after the Mystery of Golgotha occurred, the soul appears as if the spiritual light were hidden in its depths; the soul's own nature concealing it. It is as if the soul substance sheathed the light that contains the Christ impulse! Now, is this not the situation up to our time, especially in our own time, in regard to everything the human being experiences externally? Observe a person

---

12. Steiner's phrase for the death and resurrection of Christ.

today busying with outer knowledge and activities; then how, like a small flame giving a feeble light, the Christ impulse lies deep within, enclosed by the other soul contents. In contrast to the pre-Christian condition of *sattva*, this relationship of spirit to soul is the *tamas* condition.

Viewed in this way, what did the Mystery of Golgotha bring into human evolution? It transformed the manner of spirit revelation from the *sattva* condition to that of *tamas*. As a result, humanity advanced, but it also experienced a deep fall—not occasioned by the mystery but by humanity itself. The Mystery of Golgotha caused the tiny flame to grow ever brighter, but it appears faint compared to the powerful light that shone upon the soul from all sides before the event, because progressing human nature was sinking ever deeper into darkness. Thus, the Mystery of Golgotha is not to be blamed for the *tamas* condition of the soul as it relates to the spirit. Rather, this Mystery made it possible for the *tamas* condition to come again in the distant future into the *sattva* condition, which is now being kindled from within.

In the sense of the Sankhya philosophy, the *rajas* condition lies between that of *sattva* and *tamas*, and is characteristic of the evolutionary period in which the Mystery of Golgotha occurred. As to the manifesting spirit, humanity itself fell from light to darkness, from the *sattva* to the *tamas* condition, during the thousands of years surrounding the Mystery of Golgotha.

To make it more exact:

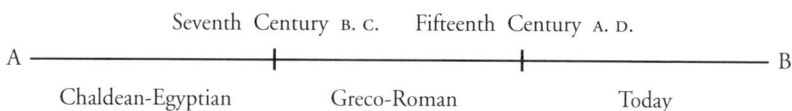

```
                  Seventh Century B. C.    Fifteenth Century A. D.
A ─────────────────────────┼──────────────────────┼─────────────── B
      Chaldean-Egyptian          Greco-Roman                Today
```

If we indicate the evolution of humankind by the line A–B, up to about the eighth or seventh century B.C.E., all human culture was in the *sattva* condition. Then began the age in which the Mystery of Golgotha occurred; and around the fifteenth or sixteenth century C.E., a transition to the *tamas* age definitely set in. Using our customary terms, the first epoch, which for certain spiritual revelations fell into the *sattva* stage, coincided with what we call the Egypto-Chaldean period.[13] What was of the *rajas* condition came in the Greco-Roman epoch[14]; that of the *tamas* condition is in our own age. We know that in the post Atlantean times, this Egypto-Chaldean era is the third, the Greco-Roman the fourth, and ours the fifth. There had to take place, as we might say, according to the plan of human evolution, a deadening of outer revelation in the passage from the third to the fourth period. How was humankind actually prepared for the flashing up of the Christ impulse?

If we wish to be clear about the difference between humanity's spiritual relationships in the Egypto-Chaldean epoch and in later epochs, we must recognize that in this third period the people in all those lands,[15] including India, still possessed a remnant of the old clairvoyance. That means that, at least under certain conditions between sleeping and waking, they not only saw the world through their senses and their cerebral intelligence, but also through the organs of the etheric body. To picture a human being of that era means recognizing that viewing the outer world of nature as we now do, through our physical senses and reason, was but one way of experiencing the world. Humans then did not arrive at knowledge; they only looked at things as they were in action, juxtaposed in space and succeeding each other in time. To achieve knowledge they had to attain a certain condition—not cultivated, as is the case with us, but quite natural— that happened as if by itself as a result of the arousal of the deeper forces of their etheric bodies. All the wonderful wisdom that appeared in the Sankhya philosophy emerged out of such knowledge, as did what has come down to us in Vedantic wisdom, though this belonged to a more ancient time.

Thus human beings attained knowledge in that time, either by bringing themselves into another state of consciousness, or by feeling themselves transported into it. They had an everyday consciousness,

13. Egypto-Chaldean epoch: 2907 B.C.E. to 747 B.C.E. (2160 years).
14. 747 B.C.E. to 1413 C.E. This epoch could as accurately be designated Greco-Roman-Christian.
15. Presumably what is now referred to as the Middle East and South Asia.

in which they used their eyes and ears and carried on activities with their ordinary intelligence. But they used these faculties only for outer, practical affairs. It would not have occurred to them to attain scientific knowledge by such means. For this, they had to employ what came to them in another state of mind, wherein they activated their deeper forces.

We can thus conceive of human beings in that ancient time as having their *everyday body*, and within this, a more subtle, spiritual body—their *Sunday body*, if I may put it so. With their everyday body they did their daily work; with their Sunday body, woven only out of the etheric body, they perceived and developed science. It would be correct to say that a person of that time would be astonished at our ability to attain knowledge using our everyday body, never "putting on our Sunday bodies" when we want to know something about the world.

How then did a person of that time experience all of these conditions? When people gained knowledge through the use of deeper powers—for instance, in developing Sankhya philosophy—they did not feel as people do nowadays who, when wanting to attain knowledge, have to strain their intellect and use head-thinking. To gain knowledge, they felt themselves to be in their ether body, which was only slightly extended into what today is the physical head, but was more defined in the other parts of the body. Humans then thought much more with the other members of the etheric body. The ether body was least developed in the head, so that in thinking one felt lifted out of one's physical body. But in such moments of forming knowledge, of scientific thinking, one felt also as if united with the Earth. When taking off the everyday body and putting on the Sunday body, one felt as though forces flowed through one's whole being, as if forces coursing through the limbs and feet connected one with the Earth, the way hands and arms feel themselves connected with our trunk. Human beings began to feel part of the Earth. On one side, they were aware of thinking and knowing in their ether body, and on the other, of no longer being a separate human being but a part of the Earth. They felt themselves growing into the Earth. Thus the whole inner nature of experience changed when one put on one's Sunday body and set out to attain knowledge.

What then had to happen, to bring this epoch to a close and allow the fourth to emerge? If we wish to understand this, we would do well to feel our way into the old way of designating things.

If we were experiencing what I have been describing in that ancient time, we would say: "The serpent has become active within me." Our being would have been extended into the Earth. We would have felt our physical body not as the active part of the self, but as a serpent-like appendage stretched into the Earth, its head alone sticking out. We would have felt that this serpent was the thinker. This might be indicated as follows:

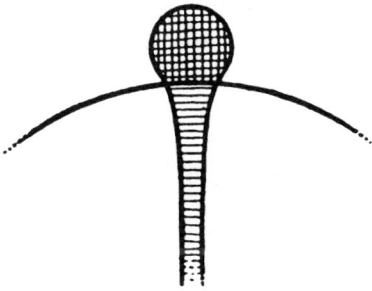

The ether body stretches into the Earth like a serpent, and while the physical being stands outside the Earth, in the activity of thinking and understanding, the ether body penetrates the Earth in thought. So, to apprehend something in ancient times meant: "I stir into action the serpent within me; I feel my serpent nature."

What needed to happen to bring about the new way of knowing? It had to become impossible for human beings to feel themselves extended into the Earth through their limbs and feet. Also, feeling had to die away in the ether body, and had to pass instead into the physical head. If you correctly picture this change, you will find it well expressed by saying, "The human is wounded in the feet, but crushes the serpent's head." This means that the serpent's head ceases to be the organ for thinking. The physical brain kills the serpent, which takes revenge by withdrawing humanity's feeling of belonging to the Earth: it "bites the human being on the heel."

At such times of transition from one form of human experience to another, there is conflict, since the two forms still coexist. Parents live for many years after the children are born, yet the children bear inside them what is descended from the parents. The characteristics of the fourth (Greco-Roman) epoch were present while those of the third epoch were still active in people and nations. Such intermingling naturally accompanies evolution. But the influx of the new, and the receding of the old alongside it, means that they do not understand each other well. The old does not understand the new; the new must protect itself from the old, and must assert its life in the face of it. Yet once the new is there, the ancestors, who have not assimilated the new, project their qualities into their descendants. In this way, we can characterize the transition from the third to the fourth period of human culture.

There now had to be a "hero," one might say, a leader who was an outstanding representative of this process of killing the serpent and being wounded by it, and who at the same time had to rebel against the past. Humanity must go forward in such a way that what entire generations are to experience, one person must first experience in its full greatness. Who was the hero who killed the head of the serpent and rebelled against the significance of the third epoch, leading humankind out of the old *sattva* period into that of *tamas*? This hero was Krishna. How could this be more definitely indicated than by the legend showing Krishna as a son of the gods Mahadeva and Devaki,[16] who entered the world amid wonderful happenings as the harbinger of something new? Continuing with my analogy, Krishna leads humankind to seek knowledge by way of the everyday body; he slays the Sunday body, the serpent. He has to resist what his kindred bring over into the new age. Such a person is something new—and wonderful. So the legend relates that Krishna was surrounded from

---

16. In the Vedas, the mythological parents of Krishna. Vasudeva is also considered to be the father of Krishna. See Heinrich Zimmer, *Philosophies of India* (NY: World Publishing Company, 1951), p. 18, and R. N. Dandekar, "Vaishnavism," in Mircea Eliade, ed., *The Encyclopedia of Religion* (NY: Macmillan, 1987), 15: 168–71.

birth by miraculous occurrences, and that his uncle, Kansa, sought to kill him. In his uncle, we see the thrust of the old forces that Krishna had to oppose in order to kill off the influences of the third epoch, which were hindering humankind's evolution. He had to rebel against Kansa as being of the old *sattva* era. Among the most significant miracles surrounding Krishna, the legend tells of how the powerful serpent Kali wrapped around him, but he succeeded in crushing its head, whereby he was wounded on the heel. Thus the legend directly reflects an esoteric fact, as all legends do. One should not give superficial explanations of legends, but really understand them, see them in the right relation to true knowledge.

Krishna is the hero of the declining third post-Atlantean epoch. The legend tells us that he appeared at the end of this age, so everything hangs together when rightly understood. Krishna is the one who killed the old faculty of clairvoyant perception and cast it into darkness. He did this in his outer manifestations, eclipsing the *sattva* knowledge that had surrounded humankind. He is shown in the Bhagavad Gita as the one who—in order to compensate for what he has taken away—gives instruction to one single person for attaining through Yoga what was being lost to humanity as a whole. For the world, Krishna is the destroyer of the old *sattva* knowledge, and at the same time he appears, at the end of the Gita, as the Lord of Yoga who leads the way back to the knowledge that has been left behind—that knowledge which can only be recovered if humankind ceases to be dominated by what it has drawn about it like everyday clothes, and returns to the old spiritual condition.

Such was Krishna's twofold deed. As a world-historical hero, he crushed the head of the old serpent knowledge and forced humanity to enter into the physical body. Whereas earlier, everything contributing to the human being's ego streamed in from outside, from now on, it would only be possible to develop the ego as a free, self sufficient entity by means of the physical body. Krishna was a world-historical hero. He restored what was once lost to individual humans for meditation, contemplation, and inner discovery. It is this, entering in such a grand way on the Gita scene, that we let work upon our souls at the end of yesterday's lecture: Arjuna confronting his own nature, but seen outwardly, spread out through space, without beginning or end.

If we examine the Gita closely, we come to a place in the text that makes us wonder again at its infinite greatness. People today must find it impossible to explain this passage. There, Krishna reveals to Arjuna the nature of the *avayata* tree,[17] the fig tree, saying that the roots of this tree grow upward and its branches downward; that its single leaves are the pages of the Vedas that together contain the Vedic knowledge. What does this peculiar passage mean?

To understand it, we must go back to the old knowledge and clearly see its effects. Human beings today only gain knowledge through their physical organs. The old knowledge was gained, as we have said, through the etheric body. Not that the total person was etheric, but knowledge came through that part of the ether body that was in the physical. Imagine yourselves for a moment perceiving in your etheric body with its serpent. That was once an objective fact, which no longer exists for human beings today. At present, we observe our environment quite naturally, yet we cannot see our own brain while we are busy observing. We cannot see the marrow of our own spine. But this impossibility ceases if one observes by means of the ether body. A new object appears then, which is otherwise invisible: we see our own nervous system. But we certainly don't see it as an anatomist sees it nowadays. Rather, we feel: "There you are in your etheric nature; you look upward and see how the nerves spread into all the organs, gathering up in the brain. You experience it as a tree with its roots stretching upward, and its branches extended down into all the limbs!"

The wonderful picture of the Gita now lies before us: the tree with its roots going upward, its branches downward, its leaves containing knowledge, and the human being the serpent on the tree. Perhaps you have already seen this picture of the Tree of Life with the serpent. Everything is meaningful when one looks at all these ancient symbols. Here we encounter the tree, its roots extending upward, its branches downward. One has a feeling of being in the reverse position to the Tree of Paradise, and that is deeply meaningful. For the Tree of

---

17. Also *ashvatta* tree.

Paradise stands at the initial point of another chapter of evolution, that which works on into Christianity through the ancient Hebraic era.

The Tree of Life is not experienced as small enough to be contained within our own skin, but as a great world-tree, its roots reaching out into space and its branches downward. One feels oneself as a serpent, seeing the nerve system objectively in front of oneself. Remember my mentioning in earlier lectures that in a certain sense the human being is a plant upside-down. We must combine all our observations in order to understand this remarkable scene in the Gita. Above everything, one marvels at that ancient wisdom which today, using new methods, must be brought to light again out of the depths of esotericism. One then experiences the Vedic knowledge that grows out of this tree as leaves, streaming into the self from outside.

Here, then, is indicated the whole nature of ancient knowledge. When Krishna explicitly says to his pupil Arjuna, "renunciation is the power that makes this tree visible to human eyes,"[18] he indicates that humankind returns to that ancient knowledge by giving up in the subsequent course of evolution everything that was attained, which we described yesterday. This is the glorious gift that Krishna makes to this single individual, his pupil Arjuna, as repayment for what he had to take away from humanity in general for their everyday use. That is Krishna's essence.

What must Krishna's gift to his individual pupil become? It must become *sattva* wisdom. The more clearly Krishna imparts this wisdom to Arjuna, the more profound, serene, and dispassionate it will be. But it will be an old, revealed wisdom, given to humankind from outside in the wonderful words spoken by the noble Krishna himself, and expressed again in his single pupil's response.

Thus Krishna becomes the Lord of Yoga, who leads back to the primal wisdom of humankind. He always seeks to overcome that soul force that even in the *sattva* age concealed the spirit. He wants to bring to his pupil what the spirit was in its primal purity before descending

18. This seems not be an exact quotation; see XV.1–5 for the source of Steiner's approximate rendering.

into material substance. So, in the dialogue with Arjuna presented yesterday, Krishna stands before us in spirit only.[19]

With this, we come to the end of the epoch that saw the last of the old spirituality. We could follow it so as to see the total spiritual light at its beginning, and then its decline into materiality, in order that humankind might find independence, the ego. When the spiritual light had come as far as the fourth epoch, a kind of transition set in, a *rajas* connection between spirit and the outer soul faculty. In this period, the Mystery of Golgotha occurred. Can one describe this era in terms of *sattva*? No. One would miss precisely what belonged to that age. In order to express something correctly in the *rajas* age—using this term in the sense of Sankhya philosophy—one must not speak out of a state of detachment but out of the personal, out of indignation over this and that. In this way, Paul speaks out of the *rajas* condition. Just feel, repeatedly breaking through in his letters to the Thessalonians, the Corinthians, the Romans, the struggle to get free of something, the rage, the all-too-personal characteristics.

Such are the style and character of these Epistles. They must be so, while the Bhagavad Gita must be detached and personality-free, since it is the finest blossoming of the declining age. But to all, it gives a substitute for what is being lost, and leads back to the heights of spiritual life. Krishna had to give his own pupil the highest blossoming of the spirit because he was required to kill the old knowledge for humanity, to crush the head of the serpent. The *sattva* condition had faded out by itself. It was no longer there. Anyone speaking of the *sattva* condition while standing in the *rajas* era that followed could only refer to it as something ancient. A person living at the beginning of the new age had to express what was now the determining influence. Personality had entered human nature, in the search for knowledge by means of the organs and processes of the physical body that it had begun to use. That personal element speaks from the Pauline Epistles. Paul's personality thunders his

19. This is one of several passages suggesting that Steiner envisioned Krishna not as a fully incarnated being but rather as a soul that entered into dialogue with Arjuna at the outset of this civil war. See also fns. 22 and 33, and pp. 112, 116, and 179.

indignation about everything bearing the darkness of materiality. His letters often reverberate with words of anger.

But this also means that these letters cannot speak in the sternly conclusive phrases, with the wisdom-filled, sharply delineated detachment we find in the Bhagavad Gita. Such wisdom can only be spoken when a person is free from outer concerns and is lifted triumphantly to the spirit, becoming one with Krishna. One can describe the wisdom-filled path of Yoga to the greatest heights of soul. The new element in the world, the victory of the spirit over the merely soul-like, could only be described out of the *rajas* condition. The individual who first described it in a way vitally important to human history, did so with utmost enthusiasm, in such a way that people knew he was deeply involved—shaken to his roots—as he encountered the manifestation of the Christ. In that moment, he encountered it personally. For the first time, he faced what henceforth would be working for thousands of years into the future. It took hold of him by personally seizing upon all the powers of his soul. Therefore, he did not describe it in the philosophical, wisdom-filled, definitive concepts of the Bhagavad Gita, but was forced to tell of the resurrection of Christ as an event of direct, personal involvement.

And should it not be a personal experience? Should Christianity not permeate the intimately personal, filling it with warmth and life? Truly, he who described the Christ event for the first time could only do so personally.

In the Gita, the main thought resides in rising to spiritual heights through Yoga; everything else is only touched upon. Why is this so? Because when Krishna is giving instruction, he deals with this one pupil, not with what other humans feel as their relation to the spiritual. Krishna describes what his pupil should become, achieving ever-higher spiritual realms. What he describes leads to ever more mature conditions of soul, therefore to ever more impressive and beautiful pictures. Only in conclusion do we see the contrast between what is spiritual and what is demonic, which somewhat confirms the beauty inherent in the soul's ascent. All those out of whom only the material speaks, who live in materiality, who believe that with death all is finished, are demonic in nature. But that is said merely to enlighten;

the great teacher [i.e., Krishna] really is little concerned with it. His task is above all the spiritualizing of the human soul. Only in passing may Yoga speak of its opponent.

First and foremost, Paul has to do with humanity as a whole, living at the time when darkness is breaking in upon it. He has to orient his view to everything this epoch of darkness brings about in human life. He must show the contrast between this darkening influence common to all and the seedling to be brought to life in the human soul as the Christ impulse. He also is to point out every aspect of materialism, every possible vice that his message must battle against. This message at first is like a tiny, flickering flame in the soul, and can only gain strength if there is enthusiasm behind his words—words pressing to victory, revealing a personalized power of feeling.

This is how remote from each other the presentations of the Gita and the Epistles are: in the Gita, we have detached impersonal description, but Paul must work personal expression into his words. This accounts for the tone and style of both, showing in almost every line. Artistic perfection can be achieved only after maturity. At the beginning of a development, there is bound to be more or less chaos.

Why did all this happen as it did? We find the answer if we return to the striking beginning of the Gita poem, where we saw blood-related warriors opposing each other, the victors and the vanquished alike connected by blood ties. The time had come for passing from the old blood relationships on which clairvoyance depended, to the differentiation and mixing of bloodstreams characteristic of the new age. This involved a transformation of the outer physical nature of humanity and the changes in cognition necessarily connected with it. A different kind of blood-mixing, another meaning for blood, now enters human evolution. If we study this passage from that ancient era to the new one (you may recall my booklet *The Occult Significance of the Blood*) we find that the clairvoyance of ancient times was dependent on people having the same tribal blood, whereas with a mixing of tribes the old clairvoyance was destroyed, and the new cognition bound to the physical body superseded it.

The beginning of the Gita points to something external that is bound to the human form. Sankhya philosophy in particular mentions such formal transformations. What pertains to the soul is left in the background, as we pointed out. The souls in their multiplicity simply exist behind the forms. We found a kind of pluralism in Sankhya philosophy, which we could compare with the philosophy of Leibniz in the modern age. If we thought ourselves into the soul of a Sankhya philosopher, we could imagine saying, "Here is my soul, expressing itself either in the *sattva, rajas,* or *tamas* condition as related to the forms of the external body." But this philosopher would observe that these forms change. One of the most significant changes shows in the different way of using the etheric body, or in the transition in blood kinship that we described. This is an external change in form. The soul is untouched by the concerns of Sankhya philosophy. The outer changes of form suffice for considering the transition from the old *sattva* era to the new *rajas* era, on the boundary of which Krishna stands. Here, the formal transformations more external to the soul come into consideration.

Outer changes in form always had to be considered when one epoch passed into another. The change in the transition from the Persian[20] to the Egyptian era was different from that between the Egyptian and the Greco-Roman eras. Further back, from the primeval Indian to the Persian, another change occurred, although it was yet another change in form. In fact, the passage from old Atlantis to the post-Atlantean world was marked merely by a change in forms. One can follow this through the indications given in Sankhya philosophy, which show that the soul lives in these forms but is not influenced by them. *Purusha* remains untouched.

We thus find a remarkable kind of change that Sankhya philosophy expresses in its own concepts. But behind it stands *purusha*, every person's individual soul quality. So this philosophy merely

---

20. What Steiner refers to as the second post-Atlantean epoch, the first being ancient India, the third being the Egypto-Chaldean (and Hebraic), and the fourth being the Greco-Roman (and Christian) or pre-modern West. Steiner considers the transitions between these epochs after the disappearance of Atlantis to have been changes in form, in contrast to the substantive change that came due to the Mystery of Golgotha.

says that the individual soul element exists in the external relation of the three *gunas*—*sattva, rajas, tamas*—but is undisturbed by them. Unquestionably, the teachings of Krishna, Lord of Yoga, point continually to this soul element. But knowledge as to the real nature of the soul is not forthcoming. Guidance as to how the soul should develop is the highest thing he imparts, and this is concerned with change in the outer forms. There is only a hint at any change in the soul itself. We discover this hint in the following way.

Those wishing to rise through Yoga from the ordinary to the higher soul levels must free themselves from outer activities, from worldly knowledge; they must each become their own witness. By rising above all externalities, the soul gains its inner freedom. This is the case with ordinary human beings. But with a person who enters upon initiation and becomes clairvoyant, this no longer pertains. Outer materiality does not confront this person, for it is *maya*. It is only reality for those who can use their own inner instruments.

What is it that takes the place of matter? This comes before us when we look at the initiation of olden times. While the ordinary person in everyday life confronts matter—*prakriti*—the soul of one becoming initiated through Yoga faces the world of the *asuras*, the world of demonic powers, which must be fought. Matter is that which provides resistance. The *asuras*, the powers of darkness, are the enemy. But all of this is only hinted at; there we glimpse something of the soul, and we begin to feel what the soul is. For the first time, then, in doing battle with the demons, the *asuras*, this soul activity perceives its own being spiritually.

In our language, we would say that this battle becomes visible as spirits in action, when matter shows its spiritual nature, even in miniature, contained entirely within the soul. Then that which was formerly the legion of the spirits of matter grows to a gigantic size, and the soul confronts a mighty foe. Soul stands against soul; the individual soul is pitted against Ahriman's kingdom in the wide expanse of the universe.

The lowest level of Ahriman's kingdom is what one fights in Yoga. But now Ahriman himself confronts us; his full powers, his whole kingdom opposes the human soul. Sankhya philosophy calls the *tamas* condition the relationship of the soul to outer materiality when the latter has the upper hand. One initiated through Yoga is not only in this *tamas* condition, he or she is battling certain demonic powers into which, in the yogic view, matter has been changed. In our conception, we see the soul not only when it relates to the spiritual element in matter, but also when it confronts the purely spiritual, the ahrimanic element.

According to Sankhya philosophy, matter and spirit are in balance in the *rajas* state. They swing back and forth, each rising in turn. When this condition leads to initiation, in the spirit of the old Yoga, one overcomes *rajas* and becomes *sattvic*. For us, initiation does not yet lead to *sattva*, but instead another battle begins here: the battle with Lucifer. Now, as we view it, we confront *purusha*. Sankhya philosophy only hints at *purusha*, and we merely hint at it now. It actually stands right in the center of the battleground against Ahriman and Lucifer, soul opposing soul. In the Sankhya philosophy, *purusha* appears at a primeval distance.

If we go deeper into what plays into the being of the soul, when it is not yet undivided between the luciferic and the ahrimanic elements, we find the relationships between the psychic and the material-substantial only in *sattva, rajas* and *tamas*. In our terms, we now find the soul between Ahriman and Lucifer, vigorously struggling and battling with them. This is something that could first be seen in its true magnitude through Christianity.

In the old Sankhya teaching, *purusha* was, so to speak, left undisturbed. There, a condition was described that arose when *purusha* clothed itself in *prakriti*. When we enter the Christian age and its esoteric foundations, we can penetrate *purusha* itself, characterizing its threefold form as the soul, the ahrimanic and the luciferic elements. We are now concerned with the inner condition of the soul itself in its struggle, as it underwent the transition occurring within the fourth epoch through the Mystery of Golgotha.

What happened then? With the passing from the third to the fourth epoch came what we might describe as merely a change of form, yet it now involved the transition from *prakriti* to *purusha* itself, by which one inwardly felt that *purusha* was completely emancipated from *prakriti.* The human being was torn away, not just from blood ties but also from *prakriti,* from all exteriority, and must now inwardly be finished with it. At this time, the Christ impulse entered the human being, the greatest transition possible in the whole of Earth evolution. No longer does the question arise as to how the soul relates to matter—in *sattva, rajas,* and *tamas*—for then the soul not only had to conquer *tamas* and *rajas* in order to lift itself above them in Yoga, but it was left to itself to fight against Ahriman and Lucifer. Then began the necessity of coming to terms with what the past epoch had required, and with the demands of the new age as it is represented in the song of the Bhagavad Gita. This poem shows us the conflict. There the human soul is revealed, living in bodily sheaths whose forms are continually changing. As long as the soul lives in them, it is ensnared by the ordinary life of *prakriti.* In Yoga the soul escapes this entanglement, breaks out of its restraining sheaths, and enters the spiritual sphere entirely free.

However, it is not enough for the soul merely to free itself. Here we must consider what Christianity, the Mystery of Golgotha, brought into evolution for the first time. Through Yoga, the soul would make itself free; then it could attain a vision of Krishna in his full power. But this would be Krishna as he was before Ahriman and Lucifer had attained their full power. A kind of divinity still concealed the fact that on either side of Krishna—visible in the exalted way we described yesterday—stood Ahriman and Lucifer. Such concealment was possible in old clairvoyance because the human being had not yet descended into matter. But that condition can no longer continue. If now the soul merely passes through Yoga, it confronts Ahriman and Lucifer and has to fight them. But the soul could not take its place beside Krishna without the help of the ally who does battle with Ahriman and Lucifer. *Tamas* and *rajas* do not suffice. This firm ally is the Christ. We thus see how bodily nature frees itself from the body. We could also say that the bodily nature was darkened in the body when the great hero, Krishna, appeared. On the other hand, we see something more powerful: the soul, left to its own devices, becomes exposed to the battle, something only visible in its own domain in the age when the Mystery of Golgotha took place.

I can well understand, my dear friends, someone saying: "Truly, what greater vision can there be than to see in the vision of Krishna humankind's highest ideal, the perfection of humanity?" There can be something higher. It is that which must stand by us, and permeate us, when we first confront the powers in the spirit—not merely *tamas* and *rajas* but the powers we must conquer if we are to gain this exalted human state. The force to help us is the Christ.

So, if we will to see the highest only in what Krishna stands for, it is only our own inability that prevents us from seeing something still higher. Then, too, the preponderance of the Christ impulse over the Krishna impulse is shown in the fact that the being who was incarnated in Krishna was incarnated in his total humanness.[21] Krishna was born and grew to manhood as the son of Visudeva.[22] But in his whole human endowment lived that highest human impulse which we recognize as Krishna. However, the impulse that must come to our aid when we confront Lucifer and Ahriman (this confrontation, which, like all the other things I have described in my Mystery Dramas,[23] still exists only in its beginning and will become comprehensible only in the future)—that is an impulse too great for humankind to contain as yet. That impulse could not even live in such a body as the Zarathustra ego could live in, but only when this body had attained the height of development, that is, when it had reached its thirtieth year. For this reason, the Christ impulse could not have lasted throughout a whole life but only through its ripest years.[24] Thus it is that this impulse was present in the body of Jesus for only three years. It is shown again directly in this fact that

---

21. In this passage, as in some others, Steiner seems to affirm Krishna's actual incarnation as a human being, but see fn. 20.

22. Steiner must mean Vasudeva, Krishna's father in the *Mahabharata*. See fn. 17.

23. See: Rudolf Steiner, *Four Mystery Dramas* (*The Portal of Initiation, The Soul's Probation, The Guardian of the Threshold, The Soul's Awakening*), trans. Ruth and Hans Pusch (Great Barrington, MA: SteinerBooks, 2007).

24. See: Rudolf Steiner, *According to Luke: The Gospel of Compassion and Love Revealed*, trans. Catherine E. Creeger, Intro., Notes, Robert McDermott (NY: Anthroposophic Press, 2001).

the Christ impulse stands higher than that of Krishna from birth onward.

As to how the superiority of the Christ impulse shows itself further, we have still more to say. But from what has already been described, you will have seen and felt that the relation between the great Gita and the Epistles of Paul must truly be as we indicated. Because the Gita is the ripe fruit of many previous epochs, it can be a finished creation. The Epistles, being the first seeds of a ripening, more perfect and comprehensive period in history yet to come, are necessarily much more imperfect. So, in viewing the course of world history, one must recognize the imperfection of the Pauline Epistles when comparing them to the Gita. Those most significant imperfections should not be passed over, but one should understand why these imperfections are inevitably there.

5

THE SPIRITUALITY OF MAYA

KRISHNA—THE LUMINOSITY OF THE CHRIST

PAUL'S EXPERIENCE AND
TEACHING OF THE RISEN CHRIST

JANUARY 1, 1913

In these lectures we considered two significant human documents—characterizing them only briefly due to our limited time—and we saw what impulses had to flow into evolution to allow these two documents, the Bhagavad Gita and the Epistles of Paul, to come into being. It is still important for our understanding of them to show the fundamental differences between the whole spirit underlying them.

We have already mentioned the teachings that Krishna was able to impart to his pupil Arjuna, teachings that, because of their intimate nature, could only be given to one person. Now, however, they are available to anyone, because they came to light in the Gita. Of course, this wasn't the case at the time the poem was composed. These teachings did not then reach all ears, as they were only communicated by word of mouth. In those ancient times, teachers were careful to ascertain a pupil's ripeness to receive such teachings. In our time this is no longer possible for any instruction that has come before the public in one way or another. We live in an age when spiritual life, to a certain degree, is open to all, which is not to say that there is no longer any esoteric science, only that it does not cease to be esoteric science when it is printed or spread abroad. Indeed, there is plenty of esoteric science now. For example, Fichte's scientific teachings, available to anyone in print, are genuine esoteric teachings. Hegel's philosophy also is assuredly an esoteric teaching, as it is very little known and contains many expedients for keeping it secret. That is the case with many things nowadays. These writings of Fichte and Hegel have very simple means for keeping them secret, as they are written so that most people don't understand them and fall asleep after reading the first few pages. This is true of much else now, which many people think they know but really do not, so the things remain secret. In fact, such things as are contained in the Gita remain secret, even though they have become known in the widest circles through print. In its mighty revelations, one person perceives the evolution of his or her own nature, another sees in it only an interesting poem, reducing all its concepts and feelings to so much triviality. Let no one believe he or she has absorbed what lies in the words of the Gita after merely taking in their literal meaning, which may be far from their real meaning. In this way, the profundity of the poem protects it in many respects from being vulgarized. In any case, it is certain that such teachings, expressed poetically, are for each of us to work through for ourselves. We must experience them if we are to lift our souls to a meeting with Krishna, the Lord of Yoga.

What the Great Teacher addresses to each person is a matter of individual concern. It is otherwise with the Epistles of Paul when we view them from this standpoint: everything in them is directed to the community, to the many. But when we look into the innermost core of the Krishna teaching, we find that it is to be expressed in the deep privacy of the individual soul. If I am to find my way back to the primal revelations and experiences of humankind, I can only achieve the meeting with Krishna as a solitary pilgrim. That which Krishna can give must be given for each one singly.

This was not the case with the revelation given to the world through the Christ impulse, which from the outset was to be thought of as directed to all humanity. The Mystery of Golgotha was not accomplished as a deed for single souls. If we consider all of humanity from the beginning to the end of Earth evolution, what took place on Golgotha occurred for everyone. It is, to the greatest possible extent, a deed for the community of humankind. Therefore the style of these Epistles—apart from what I have already pointed out—must be different from that of the sublime Gita.

Bring vividly to mind again Krishna's relationship to Arjuna. As Lord of Yoga, Krishna gave Arjuna specific directions for lifting up his soul, step by step, so as to attain a vision of Krishna. Compare this now with a particularly pregnant section in the Epistles, where a group of followers goes to Paul and asks if this or that thing is true, and whether they are in accord with what he had been teaching. And there is a passage in Paul's instructions that in its greatness is equal in every respect, even artistically, with what is in the sublime Gita, although it is quite different in tone, quite different in its way of expressing a soul experience. It is the passage in which Paul writes to the Corinthians about the variety in human talents present in a group, and how they must be brought to work together. Krishna said to Arjuna, "You must be so and so, do this or that, then step by step your soul will progress."[25] Paul said, "One of you has this gift, another that, a third another. If these work together harmoniously like the members of a human body a spiritual wholeness results, which then can be permeated by the Christ."[26] Thus, through their common situation, he could direct them to the idea of human beings working together as a plurality. He made use of a special opportunity to do this, namely, when the gift of "speaking in tongues" came up for consideration.

Now what is this "speaking in tongues" we find in the Pauline Epistles? It is none other than a survival of ancient spiritual faculties, which, in a renewed but fully conscious way, confront us again at the present time. In our methods of initiation, inspiration is a condition one may attain with the same clear consciousness one has in the everyday use of reasoning and sense perception, but it was otherwise in olden times. Then, the person concerned spoke as if he were an instrument of higher spiritual beings who made use of his organs of

---

25. This seems to be a paraphrased summary of XVII.47–66.
26. Paul's First Letter to the Corinthians, 14:1–25.

speech to express higher truths. Thus, individuals could say things they themselves could not understand at all. Communications were made from the spiritual world that the transmitter did not need to understand directly. This was occurring right in Corinth. A condition had arisen there, in which a number of people had this gift of "speaking in tongues."

Now, if someone has this gift, what he or she brings forth is under all circumstances a revelation from the spiritual world. Nevertheless, it can be that one person says this, another that, because there are many regions in the spiritual world. These differences in inspiration bring it about that the revelations do not always agree. Only when one enters the different regions in full consciousness does one discover how they harmonize. Therefore Paul admonishes his followers: "There are some who have this gift of speaking in tongues and there are others who can interpret the message. They should work together like the left hand with the right. We should not merely listen to the one spoken through, but also to those who may not have this gift but know how to interpret what one or the other spiritual region imparts." In this way Paul again urges them on to achievements as a community, founded on their united efforts.

Connected with this speaking in tongues, Paul gave the discourse that, as I said, is so wonderful that in certain respects it can be compared in still another way with the communications in the Gita. He said (I Cor. 12, 3–31)[27]:

Concerning the spiritually gifted brethren, I will not leave you without directions. You know that in the time of your paganism blind desire led you astray, to dumb idols. Wherefore I give you to understand that as little as one speaking in the spirit of God

---

27. The quotations from Paul's Epistle to the Corinthians have been translated from the German edition, since what Rudolf Steiner offers is somewhat different from the usual English translations. As he has pointed out—for example, in his *How to Know Higher Worlds*—the source of his spiritual research lies beyond the scope of the documents of external history.

says "Accursed be Jesus," so little can he call Him "Lord" except it be through the Holy Spirit.

Now through grace there is a diversity of gifts, but only one Spirit. There is diversity in human beings' achievements, but only one Lord. Individual men have a diversity of strength, but only one God is active in all these forces. To every person are granted manifestations of the Spirit, to each one's profit. Thus, to one is given words of prophecy; to another, knowledge. Again, there are those who live by faith; others have the gift of healing; others have the gift of prophecy; others have insight into human character; to others the gift of tongues; and others can interpret the speaking in tongues. But in every human being works the one Spirit, apportioning to each their due. For as the body is one, with many members, all the single members forming together one body, so is it also with the Christ. For through the Spirit, we are all baptized as one body, whether Jew or Greek, slave or free man. We are all filled with one Spirit, as the body consists not of one but of many members. If the foot were to say, "Because I am not the hand I do not belong to the body," nevertheless it does belong to the body. If the ear were to say, "Because I am not the eye I do not belong to the body," it would even so belong to it. If the whole body were only eye, where then is the hearing? If the whole body were only hearing, where then is smelling? But God has given each member a particular place in the body, as He found it good. If there were only one member, where would be the body?

So, there are many members, and only one body. The eye dare not say to the hand, "I do not need you!" Neither the head to the feet, "I have no need of you." Rather, the apparently weak members of the body are necessary, and those members we hold in low esteem prove to be especially important. God has put the body together and given to the undistinguished members their significance in order that there be no schism in the body but that all members work together in harmony and have care for each other. When one member suffers, all suffer with it; and when one prospers, all rejoice. But you now are the body of Christ. All of you together form His members. Some among you he has appointed to be apostles; others to be prophets; a third portion to be teachers; a fourth to be miracle-healers; a fifth to have other helping tasks; a sixth to be administrators of the community; and a seventh he has appointed to speak with tongues. Should all be apostles, or prophets, or teachers, or healers, or all speak with tongues? Should all be interpreters? Therefore it is right that the various gifts of grace work together—the more they do so the better.

Then Paul speaks of the force that can be active in each one but also in the community, that brings together all the single members of the community as the strength of the body unites the separate members of the body. Krishna said nothing more beautiful to any one person than Paul said to all humanity with its variety of members. Paul then goes on to speak about the power of Christ that unites diverse individuals, as the body unites its various members, the force that thereby can live in each one like the life-force in each member, yet that lives also in the whole entity of a community. He characterized this with powerful words:

Indeed, I will show you the way higher than all the other ways. Though I could speak out of the spirit with the tongues of men or of angels and have not love, my speech would sound as brass and a clanging cymbal. And though I could prophesy, and reveal all mysteries, and communicate all the world's knowledge, though I have faith to move mountains, and have not love, it all would come to nothing. Though I gave to others all my spiritual gifts, yes, though I gave my very body to be burned, and have not love, everything would be in vain.

Love endures. Love is kind. Love does not know envy, nor boasting, nor vanity. It does not violate propriety, nor seek its own advantage. It does not let itself be provoked to anger. It bears no malice toward anyone, nor rejoices over injustice but only over truth. Love encompasses everything, permeates all beliefs, is hopeful in all things, and in all matters practices tolerance.

Love, if it be love, is never lost. A prophecy ceases after it is fulfilled. What is spoken in tongues dies away when it no longer speaks to human hearts. Knowledge vanishes as soon as its subject is exhausted, because all knowledge is fragmentary; likewise all prophesying. But when that which is complete has come, then the fragments have lost their meaning.

When I was a child I spoke as a child, I felt as a child, I thought as a child. Since I have become a man my world of childhood is past. Now we see only dark outlines in the mirror, but one day we shall see the spirit face to face. Now is my knowledge in fragments, but one day I shall know fully what I myself am. Lasting is faith, lasting the certainty of hope, and lasting is love. But love is the greatest of these, therefore it is supreme.

All spiritual gifts may be yours. One who is able to prophesy must also strive to attain love. One who speaks with tongues speaks not among humans but among gods. No one hears, because such a one utters spiritual mysteries. (I Cor. 13.1–14.2)

We see that Paul understands the nature of speaking in tongues. He means: "The speaker is carried away into spiritual worlds and talks among gods. One who prophesies speaks with others to edify them, exhort them, or give them consolation. One speaking in tongues in a certain sense gives oneself satisfaction in doing so, while the prophet edifies the community. Even if all of you were able to speak with tongues, it is much more important that you prophesy. The prophet is greater than the speaker in tongues, unless the tongue-speaker is able to understand what he or she speaks in order that the community understand it. Suppose I come to you as a speaker in tongues, what use am I to you if I cannot tell you the significance of what I say as prophecy, as teaching, as revelation? My speaking would be like the tones of a flute, a zither, which you could not clearly distinguish one from the other. How would one distinguish the playing of a flute from a zither if they did not produce different sounds? If the trumpet did not give out a distinctive sound, who would arm themselves for battle? So it is with you. If you cannot put your tongue-speaking into a distinct language your speaking goes into thin air." [I Cor. 14.1–5].

All this shows that the various spiritual gifts must be distributed among the members of the community, and that the members, as individuals, must work together. With this we come to the point in human evolution when Paul's revelation occurred, and we see how it must differ fundamentally from Krishna's. Krishna's revelation is directed to one particular individual, but actually to every person who is ripe to progress on the soul's path upward, as outlined by the Lord of Yoga. We are directed ever again back to the primeval time of humanity, to which, according to Krishna's teaching, we want to return in spirit. At that time, humans were less individualized, so one could assume that the same teaching and guidance was suitable for everyone. Paul confronted humanity when individuals were becoming differentiated, when they *had* to become differentiated, each with their own special capacities and gifts. One could no longer count on pouring the same thing into every single soul. One had to point to what ruled invisibly over all. That which is in no one person separately, but can be in every single one, is the Christ impulse. This force is again similar to a new group soul for humanity, but one that is consciously sought by humanity.

To clarify the matter, let us imagine a number of Krishna's pupils in the spiritual world and a like number of those who have been deeply impressed by the Christ impulse. Each of Krishna's pupils has been set alight by the same impulse, given them by the Lord of Yoga. In spiritual life, each is like every other. To one as to another, the same instructions were given. But those stirred by the Christ impulse are disembodied in the spiritual world, yet each with their own particular individuality, their own differentiated spiritual forces; so that, in the spiritual world also, one person can function in one way, another in another way. The leader of both, the one who pours himself into each one, however individualized that one may be—this is the Christ. He lives in every soul, and at the same time hovers over them all. Therein, the community is differentiated even when souls are disembodied, while the Krishna-pupils are a unity if they have received direction from the Lord.

Therefore, Krishna speaks as he did in the Gita to his pupil. But Paul has to speak otherwise—actually, he speaks to every person. It is then a matter of individual development whether each one, according to the degree of maturity, stops with exoteric life only at this or that stage of his or her incarnation, and embarks on esoteric development to rise to an esoteric Christianity. One can proceed further and further in

Christianity to the most esoteric heights, but one begins on a different basis from that given in the Krishna teaching. There, one starts from the standpoint of what one is as a human being, and raises the soul, however one can achieve it, as a single person. In Christianity, before one can even begin to advance, one enters upon a relationship to the Christ impulse, so that this transcends all else. The spiritual path to Krishna can only be followed by one who receives Krishna's instructions. Anyone can follow the path to Christ, because he brought the Mystery for all people; all can find a relationship to it. That, however, was consummated on the physical plane. The first step, therefore, is taken on the physical plane—and that is the main point.

Once a person grasps the world-historic significance of the Christ impulse, nothing more is needed from this or that Christian doctrine in order to proceed. Particularly in our time, one can even take a start from an anti-Christian point of view, or a feeling of indifference. When one looks deeply into what our time is able to bring to spiritual life, when one sees the contradictions and foolishness of materialism, one is perhaps led most genuinely to the Christ these days, more so than if one came to Him through some special creed. Therefore, when it is said outside our circle that we set out from a special kind of Christian belief, it can be regarded as an especially vicious slander. For it is not a matter of starting out from some kind of denominational doctrine, but from the demands of spiritual life itself. Everyone— Muslim, Buddhist, Jew, Hindu or Christian—can understand the Christ impulse in its full meaning for humanity's evolution. This is exactly what we see penetrating Paul's entire concept and presentation. He is the personality who sets the tone for the first proclamation of the Christ impulse in the world.

Having described how Sankhya philosophy was concerned with the changing of forms, with what pertains to *prakriti*, we may now say that Paul, in all that underlies his most meaningful Epistles, deals wholly with *purusha*, with what is of the soul. What the soul is destined to become, the manifold ways in which it is to develop throughout human evolution, all this Paul sets forth in quite definite, conclusive ways. There is a fundamental difference between what Indian thinking was still able to produce, and what comes from Paul in such wonderful clarity.

We pointed out yesterday that with Krishna everything depended on the human being finding the way out of the changing forms. But *prakriti* remains external, as something foreign to the soul. All striving within this Indian method of development, even within Indian initiation, is toward becoming free from material existence, from the outer world of nature, which, according to the Vedic philosophy, is maya, illusion. Everything outside us is maya, and Yoga is the way to become free of it. We have noted how, right in the Gita, it is required that human beings free themselves from everything they do, achieve, will, and think, from what they desire and enjoy; and that in their souls they triumph over everything external. The work they do falls away; and so, resting in itself, it finds satisfaction in itself.

Anyone who desires to develop according to Krishna's teaching has in mind becoming something like a *paramahamsa*, a high initiate, who leaves behind all material existence and rises above all his or her deeds in the sense world. Individuals who no longer have any connection with what lives in this sense world as their work are in such a pure, spiritual state as to lose all thirst for incarnating again, and so we are confronted everywhere in the Gita with escape from the illusion of maya, with the triumph over it.

But it is not like this with Paul. If he had encountered this Indian teaching the following words would have risen from the depths of his soul: "So, you want to develop yourself away from everything that surrounds you, away from whatever you have accomplished in the outer world. Do you want to leave all that behind? Is it not the work of God? Is not all that above which you wish to lift yourself the creation of the Divine Spirit? When you disdain that, do you not cast scorn upon God's work? Do not the revelations of God and His Spirit live everywhere in it? Did you not seek above all to reveal God in your own work, with love, and faith, and devotion? And now you desire to triumph over God's work?"

It would be good to inscribe deep in our souls these words of Paul, which, if not actually spoken, ruled in the depths of his soul, for in them comes to light a vital nerve of what we know as Western revelation. Even in a Pauline sense, we speak of the illusion that surrounds us. Indeed, we say, "All about us is maya!" But we also ask, "Is this maya then not divine revelation, the work of Divine Spirit? Is it not blasphemy not to understand that in everything the divine spiritual is at work?"

Now the other question arises: Why is there maya? Why do we see illusion all around us? The West does not stop with asking if everything is illusion; it wants to know why. Here, an answer leads directly into the realm of the soul, into *purusha*. Because the soul once came under the power of Lucifer, it sees everything through the veil of maya, and of itself spreads the veil of illusion over everything.

Is objectivity at fault, then, that we see maya? No. True objectivity would appear as a quality of soul if we were not under the power of Lucifer. It seems to be maya because we are not capable of seeing to the roots of what is spread about us. Lucifer's power prevents it. The fault does not lie with the gods, but with our own souls. By succumbing to Lucifer, we have ourselves changed the world into maya. From the highest spiritual expression of this truth, a direct line leads down to Goethe's words, "It is not the senses that deceive, it is judgment." Philistines and zealots may oppose Goethe and his Christianity all they like, yet he still was entitled to call himself one of the most Christian of men, because to the roots of his nature he thought like a Christian, right into that saying, "It is not the senses that deceive, it is judgment." The soul is at fault in that what it sees does not appear as truth but as maya. What for the Indian world is simply an act of the gods is diverted into the depths of the human soul where the great battle with Lucifer begins.

So, when we truly observe Indian philosophy, we see that in a way it is materialism, just because it does not recognize the spirituality in maya and wishes to rise above matter. Pulsing through the Epistles of Paul, however, is a teaching for the soul, albeit in germinal form and therefore easily misunderstood in our *tamas* time. It is this that in future will leave its imprint throughout the whole world. This unique nature of maya must be understood, for only then will it be thoroughly clear just what the main human concern must be in the further progress of evolution. Then one will understand what Paul meant in speaking of the first Adam, whose soul was victimized by Lucifer and thereby fell ever deeper into matter. This means nothing other than that the soul was ensnared in a false experiencing of matter.

Matter in the external world, as God's creation, is good. What takes place in that realm is good. But that which the soul experienced in the course of human evolution became more and more evil, because in the beginning it was overpowered by Lucifer. Paul named Christ as the second Adam because He entered the world untouched by Lucifer, and could therefore be that friend to humanity who could gradually lead it away from Lucifer, that is, into a right relation to Lucifer. Paul could not communicate to people in his time everything he knew as an initiate. But whoever absorbs the contents of the Epistles will discover that more lies in their depths than comes to expression on the surface. That is because Paul had to speak to a certain community and must therefore reckon with their ability to understand. So there is much in his Epistles that seems to be contradictory. But if one penetrates their depths, one will indeed find everywhere in them the impulse coming from the being of Christ.

Remember how we ourselves described the entrance of the Mystery of Golgotha into human life, how to make it possible, two differing children's histories were mentioned in the Matthew and Luke gospels—because actually there were two Jesus children. We pointed out that according to their physical descent, "after the flesh" as Paul put it, the two Jesus boys stemmed from the House of David, the one from the Nathan, the other from the Solomon line, and that two Jesus boys were born at about the same time. In the child cited in the Matthew Gospel, Zarathustra was incarnated. The other child, described by Luke, was not endowed with an ego such as especially characterizes a human being, rather, in the Luke Jesus boy lived a part of the human being that had never before entered human evolution on earth.[28]

Here we come to a point that is somewhat difficult to explain. But try to imagine how the soul incarnated in Adam—in Adam, as meant in my *Outline of Esoteric Science*—succumbed to Lucifer's temptation, symbolized in the Bible by the fall into sin in Paradise. One can form a

---

28. See Rudolf Steiner, *The Spiritual Guidance of the Individual and Humanity*; *According to Luke*; and *According to Matthew*, for a full exposition of the two Jesus children.

picture of this. Then, further, besides that human element that incarnated in Adam's body, another part remained behind, a human entity that did not enter a physical body but remained purely soul. You need only imagine that before physical human beings arose in human evolution, they were soul, which then divided into two parts. The one part, a descendant of the common soul, incarnated in Adam, and thereby entered the ongoing stream of incarnation, succumbing to Lucifer, and so on. For the other part of the soul, the wise world rulership foresaw that it would not be good if it also were incarnated; it was held back in the soul world, apart from the stream of incarnation. Only those initiated into the mysteries would have any connection with this sister soul. Also, this soul, during the evolution that preceded the Mystery of Golgotha, would not take ego-experience into itself, since that comes only with incorporation into a physical body. Therefore, this soul possessed all the wisdom that could be experienced through the Saturn, Sun, and Moon periods of evolution. It possessed all the love a human soul can attain. It remained innocent of all the guilt that humanity can incur for the purpose of development in the course of its incarnations. This soul was one as could not be encountered outwardly as human, but could only be perceived by means of the old clairvoyance. In this way, it could also be seen communing, one could say, in the Mysteries. Thus there was a soul both within and yet above human evolution, visible only to spiritual perception—a veritable super-human being!

It was this soul[29] that, instead of an ego, incarnated in the Jesus boy of the Luke Gospel. It was similar to an ego, acted quite naturally like an ego as it penetrated the body of Jesus, yet it was different from the usual human ego. I have already mentioned that this boy at birth could speak a language understandable by his mother, and other similar faculties were evident in him.

The Jesus boy described by Matthew, in whom the Zarathustra ego lived, continued to grow up to his twelfth year; likewise, the boy of the Luke Gospel. But the latter showed no special knowledge or erudition,

---

29. That is, the soul—or as Steiner says elsewhere, the "sister soul of Adam"—that had not previously incarnated. See *According to Luke*, Lecture Four.

no particular gift for learning the external things people usually learn; rather, he bore within him divine wisdom and a supreme capacity for sacrifice. We know further that the body of the Matthew boy was forsaken by the Zarathustra ego, which in his twelfth year took possession of the body of the Luke boy. That is the moment indicated as his appearance before the learned rabbis in the temple, teaching them, while being lost from his parents.[30] We also know that the Luke boy bore the Zarathustra ego within him up to his thirtieth year; that then this ego forsook the body of the Luke Jesus, and the sheaths that had surrounded it came into the possession of the Christ—a super-human being from the hierarchies, who only under such circumstances could live in a human body. For Him, a body was provided that had been permeated up to its twelfth year by primeval wisdom, by powers of divine love, and that then was permeated by all that the Zarathustra ego had attained during many incarnations through initiation. One acquires the right esteem, the right reverence, above all the right feeling for the being of Christ through nothing so much as when one tries to understand what kind of a bodily nature was necessary for this Christ ego to enter into humanity at all.

In this presentation of the being of Christ, given by the Holy Mysteries of the modern age, many have found him less intimate, less human, than the Christ Jesus some people have worshipped as he is usually presented—familiar, near to humanity, embodied in the ordinary kind of human organism, which contained nothing like a Zarathustra-"I."

Our teaching has been reproached for presenting Christ Jesus as combining forces from every region of the cosmos. Such reproach only arises from people's lazy thinking and feeling, which will not lift them up to their true heights. Besides, the greatest can only be grasped after exerting the soul to the utmost, so as to attain that inner intensity of feeling needed to raise the soul even to approach the level of the greatest, of the highest there is. One's first feeling is only heightened when the matter is seen in this light.

---

30. See Luke 2:41-52; this event is not found in Matthew, Mark, or John.

In addition, we know how these words of the Gospel are to be understood: "Divine powers are being revealed in the heights, and peace is spreading among people of good will."[31] The tidings of peace and love resound as the Luke Jesus child is born, for the Buddha, that being who had already lived through his last incarnation as Gotama Buddha and had risen to total spirituality, is intermingled with his astral body. So that in the astral body of the Luke Jesus boy, the Buddha was revealed, showing how he had progressed up to the time of the event of Golgotha on Earth.[32]

We have pictured the being of Christ Jesus as it could be given to humanity for the first time, today we may say, out of the foundations of spiritual science. Paul, even though he was an initiate, had to speak in the more easily understood concepts of his time. He could not have assumed that humanity would be able at that time to comprehend such concepts as we have been able to bring to your hearts today. That which came about through his inspiration was due to the initiation bestowed upon him by an act of grace. Because he had not attained it in the regular, prescribed schooling of the ancient mysteries, but through the risen Christ having appeared to him on his way to Damascus, I say this initiation took place through grace. But Paul's experience of this vision was such as to convince him that what had arisen from the grave in the Mystery of Golgotha lives on, bound up with the Earth sphere ever since that event. He recognized the resurrected Christ, and proclaimed Him from that time onward.

How was it that Paul was able to see the Christ just as he did? Here we must enter into the nature of the manifestation of Christ at Damascus, for it was quite a special kind. Only those people who do not want to learn about esoteric facts assume that everything visionary is the same. They do not distinguish between a vision such as Paul's, and the many others that have appeared to the saints in later times.

31. The usual translation of this passage is "Glory to God in the highest and peace to those of good will" [or: "those who enjoy his favor"] (Luke 2:14).
32. For Steiner's account of Buddha's contribution to the body of Jesus of Nazareth, see *According to Luke*, Lecture Five.

What was the reason Paul was able to perceive the Christ in the appearance of Damascus? What was there in it that convinced Paul it was the risen Christ?

This question leads back to another one, namely, what was necessary in order that the total being of Christ could descend completely into Jesus of Nazareth as indicated by the Baptism by John in the Jordan? We have just said what was necessary to prepare the physical body in which the Christ was to dwell. But what was needed for the Risen One to appear to Paul in such a dense soul form? What was that ray of light, so to speak, in which He appeared? What was it? Whence was it taken?

If we are to answer this question, we must add several explanations to what I have already said. I told you of the sister soul present along with the Adam soul, which had entered the sequence of human generations. This sister soul remained in the soul world. It was also the one incarnated in the Luke Jesus boy. But this was not the first time, strictly speaking, that this soul was embodied as physical human being. Previously it had once been prophetically incarnated, and earlier still had been used as a messenger of the Holy Mysteries. It came and went among them; it was cherished and cultivated, and was sent out wherever something important was taking place among humankind. But it could only appear in the etheric body, and therefore could only be perceived as long as the old clairvoyance continued. While that clairvoyance was present, this ancient sister soul of Adam did not need to come down as far as the physical body in order to be seen. Thus, it actually appeared repeatedly within human evolution on earth, and was always sent forth by the Mysteries when important deeds were to be performed. But it did not need to incarnate in ancient times while clairvoyance lasted. This incarnating became necessary for the first time when clairvoyance faded away during the transition from the third to the fourth post-Atlantean epoch. Then it took on a kind of substitute embodiment in order to continue its functions after clairvoyance had ceased.

The only time this sister soul of Adam became physically visible before its embodiment in the Luke Jesus boy was in Krishna. So now we understand why Krishna spoke in such a superhuman way, why he is the best teacher for the human ego, why he appears as an overcoming of the human ego, why his soul qualities are so sublime. Because in that exalted moment we described several days ago, he appeared as the human not yet immersed in the stream of human incarnations.[33] Then he appeared again in order to be embodied in the Luke Jesus boy. Thereby, the height of perfection was reached when the most profound world concepts of India, in the ego of Zarathustra and the spirit of Krishna, united in the twelve-year-old Jesus boy. The one speaking to the learned men in the temple was not only Zarathustra speaking as an ego, but also one having all the resources Krishna had once drawn upon in proclaiming Yoga. He spoke about a Yoga now raised a level higher. He united himself with the power of Krishna, with Krishna himself, in order to continue developing up to his thirtieth year. Only then was that physical organism so completely matured as to be ready for the Christ to take possession of it. Thus do the spiritual streams of humanity flow together. So when the Mystery of Golgotha occurred, there was indeed a working together of the most important leaders of humankind—a summation, a synthesis, of spiritual life.

As Paul journeyed to Damascus, it was the Christ who appeared to him. The flood of light that enveloped him was Krishna. Because Christ took Krishna as his own soul sheath, through which he then continued to work, everything that once was the content of the sublime Gita streamed from him. So much in the revelations of the Testaments, even if in scattered fragments, comes from the ancient teaching of Krishna. But that teaching became something for all humanity because the Christ as such is not merely a human ego belonging to humankind, but belonging to the upper hierarchies. For this reason also, Christ belongs to those times when humanity was not yet separated from what now surrounds us as material existence, and when we were not yet enveloped in maya through our own luciferic temptation. A look back

---

33. This appears to be the most exact statement of Steiner's understanding as to whether, or in what way, Krishna of the Gita is an incarnate being, i.e., he was visible to Arjuna as a charioteer even though, apparently, he was not a fully-incarnated being. It would seem that we are to understand Krishna as the Adam soul who did not fully incarnate until contributing itself to the body of the Luke Jesus child. See p. 179, below.

through the whole of evolution shows that in ancient times there was not yet that sharp division between the spiritual and the material. The material was still spiritual, and the spiritual—if we may put it so—was still manifesting itself outwardly. In the Christ impulse, something entered humanity that completely excluded such a sharp separation as existed in the Sankhya philosophy between *purusha* and *prakriti*, and for this reason, Christ became the leader in taking human beings out of themselves but also toward divine creation. Dare we say then that one must absolutely abandon maya when we recognize that it appears to have been given us through a fault of our own? No. For that would be a blasphemy against the spirit in the world. It would mean assigning to matter qualities that we imposed upon it ourselves under the veil of maya. Instead, we should much rather hope that when we conquer in ourselves that which caused matter to become maya, we may again be reconciled with the world.

Do we not hear sounding out from the world around us that it is a creation of the elohim?[34] That on the last day of creation the elohim looked, and found that all was good?[35] It would be karma fulfilling itself if there were nothing but the teaching of Krishna, for nothing remains in the world that does not fulfill its karma. If in all eternity there had only been a Krishna teaching, then the material world surrounding us, the manifestation of God—of which the elohim said at the beginning of evolution, "Behold, all is very good"[36]—would be met by humanity's judgment, "It is not good, I must abandon it." Human judgment would be placed above divine judgment. This is what we must learn to understand in the words that stand there as a mystery at the beginning of evolution, that we must not set human judgment above divine judgment. If ever all the things that could cling to us as guilt could fall away and only the one offence remained—that we blasphemed the creative work of the elohim—the Earth's karma

---

34. For Steiner on the elohim, see his *Genesis: Secrets of the Bible Story of Creation* (London: Rudolf Steiner Press, 1982), Lectures 4 and 6.
35. Genesis, ch. 1 repeats the statement, "And God saw that it was good."
36. Genesis 1:31.

would have to be fulfilled. Everything in the future would have to crash down upon us, and, thus, karma would have to take its course.

Christ came into the world so that this should not happen. He came in order to bring us into true harmony with the world, that we might learn to overcome the power in Lucifer's temptations, to penetrate the veil of maya, to see divine revelation in its true form; that we recognize Christ as the One who reconciles human beings and their world, and leads them to the reality of divine manifestation, so that through human beings those primeval words may be understood: "Behold, all is very good." For us to learn to attribute to ourselves what we must never attribute to the world, we need the Christ. Even if all other sins were lifted from us, this particular sin must be taken from us by Christ. Transformed into a moral feeling, this reveals a new aspect of the Christ impulse. At the same time, it shows why it became necessary for this impulse, as a higher soul, to envelop itself in the impulse of Krishna.

* * *

My dear friends, the matters I brought before you in this series of lectures should not be taken as mere theory, as a compilation of ideas and concepts to be absorbed passively. They should be received as a kind of New Year's gift, a gift to work influentially through the coming year. From these indications should flow a continuing experience of what one can understand of the Christ impulse and the way it throws light on the words of the elohim, which sounded forth at the beginning of the creation of our world. This must be understood.

Look, too, at what we have endeavored to show as the point of origin of our anthroposophical spiritual stream. Through it, the way human beings can come by themselves to self-knowledge will be made ever more widely known. Self-knowledge cannot be achieved completely yet. *Anthropos* cannot yet attain knowledge of anthropos, human beings cannot yet know the human being, so long as they consider that what they must bring about in their own souls is an affair to be played out between themselves and external nature. It is a requirement set by the gods that we see our world immersed in maya. It is a matter for our own souls' higher self-knowledge that the person be conscious of one's own self within the human situation. It is a concern of Anthroposophy that through it, we first experience what Theosophy can be for humankind.

It should be with the greatest modesty that we feel impelled to belong to the Anthroposophical Movement, a modesty reminding us that if we want to jump over the concerns of the soul and take at once the highest step into the divine, our humility can easily vanish and pride and conceit take its place. May the Anthroposophical Society also be a starting point to this higher moral sphere. Above all, may it avoid the pride, vanity, ambition and lack of earnestness that have so easily slipped into and been a burden to the Theosophical Movement in receiving the highest wisdom. May the Anthroposophical Society at the outset avoid such hindrances by observing what solving the problem of maya entails as a concern of the human soul itself.

One should feel that the Anthroposophical Society is the result of the deepest human modesty. Then out of this modesty will come the greatest earnestness in confronting the holy truths we shall reach when we enter the realm of the supersensible, the spiritual. Let us therefore regard the adoption of the name *Anthroposophical Society* with genuine humility, and say to ourselves: May whatever pride, conceit, ambition, dishonesty, which may have been working under the name of Theosophy, be eradicated as we begin humbly to look up to the gods and divine wisdom. May we dutifully seek likewise to know the human being and human wisdom when we reverently approach Theosophy and dutifully devote ourselves to Anthroposophy. This Anthroposophy will lead us to the gods. If through it we learn to see ourselves truly and devotedly, if we see how we must struggle against all maya and error by means of strict self-discipline and training, then the word *Anthroposophy* will stand above us as if written on a bronze tablet! May it be an admonition to us that above all else we should, through Anthroposophy, seek self-knowledge, humility of self, and in this way endeavor to erect a structure founded upon truth, because truth only blossoms when self-knowledge, in full earnestness, puts down its roots deep in the human soul.

What is the source of all conceit, all untruthfulness? It is failure in self-knowledge. From what alone can truth and genuine reverence for the divine worlds and divine wisdom spring? Only from real self-knowledge, self-discipline, and self-development. May the forces streaming and pulsating through the Anthroposophical Movement serve this purpose.

This is the reason for giving this particular cycle of lectures at the start of the Anthroposophical Movement. They should prove that we are not dealing with something narrow, but that our movement's horizon can extend over distances that encompass Indian thought as well. But let us grasp this humbly, in the anthroposophical way of self-education, arousing our will to self-discipline and training. If you, my dear friends, take up Anthroposophy in this way, it will lead to beneficial results. It will bring a measure of regeneration to every person and to every branch of human society.

These words bring to a close this series of lectures. Perhaps you can take much away from them for the future, much that will be fruitful for our Anthroposophical Movement, for which in these days you have gathered for the first time. May we always meet under the sign of Anthroposophy in a way that will justify our reaffirming the words with which we now conclude, words expressing a spirit of humility, of the desire for self-knowledge, which at this moment we place before our souls as our ideal.

PART II

The Esoteric Significance
of the Bhagavad Gita

1

Helsinki, May 28, 1913

It is more than a year since I was able to speak here[37] about those things that rest so deeply in our hearts, things that we believe must enter more and more into human knowledge. From our time onward, the human soul will feel increasingly that these thoughts belong to its requirements, to its deepest longings. And it is with great pleasure that I greet you in this place for the second time, along with all those who have traveled here in order to show in your midst that their hearts and souls are connected to our sacred work the whole world over.

The last time I was able to speak to you here, we let our spiritual gaze journey far into the wide regions of the universe. This time our task will keep us more in the regions of earthly evolution. Our thoughts will nonetheless penetrate to regions that lead us to the gateway of the eternal manifestation of the spiritual in the world. We shall speak about a subject that apparently leads us far away in time and in space from the here and now. It will not on that account lead us any less to what lives in the here and now, but rather to what lives

---

37. Between April 3 and 19, Rudolf Steiner gave a lecture series in Helsinki called "The Spiritual Beings in the Heavenly Bodies and in the Kingdoms of Nature," published under the same title, Anthroposophic Press, 1992.

equally in all times and all places on Earth, because it will bring us near to the secrets of the eternal in all existence. It will lead us to the ceaseless human search for the wellsprings of eternity, for the springs where they can find the elixir of what humans have called all-powerful love. For wherever we are gathered, we are gathered in the name of the search for wisdom and the search for love; we are gathered in nostalgia for the wellsprings of this love. What we seek is extended out into space and can be observed in the far horizon of the Cosmic All, but it can also be observed everywhere in the struggling human soul. It meets us especially when we turn our gaze to one of those mighty manifestations of the struggling human spirit that is given us in great works, like the one that is to form the basis of our present studies. We are going to speak of one of the greatest and most profound manifestations of the human spirit—the Bhagavad Gita, which, ancient as it is, yet in its foundations comes before us with renewed significance at the present time.

A short time ago the peoples of Europe, and those of the West generally, knew little of the Bhagavad Gita. Only during the last century has the fame of this wonderful poem extended to the West. Only lately have Western peoples become familiar with this marvelous song. But these lectures of ours will show that a real and deep knowledge of this poem, beyond mere familiarity with it, can only come when its esoteric foundations are more and more revealed. For what meets us in the Bhagavad Gita sprang from an age of which we have often spoken in connection with our anthroposophical studies. The mighty sentiments, feelings, and ideas it contains had their origin in an age that was still illumined by what was communicated through the old human clairvoyance. One who tries to feel what this poem breathes forth page by page as it speaks to us will experience, page by page, something like a breath of the ancient clairvoyance humanity once possessed.

The Western world's first acquaintance with this poem came in an age that had little understanding of the original clairvoyant sources from which it sprang. Nevertheless, this lofty song of the divine struck into the Western world like a wonderful flash of lightning, so that a certain Central European man, upon first encountering this Indian song, said that he must frankly consider himself happy to have lived until the time when he could become acquainted with the wondrous things expressed in it. This man was acquainted with the spiritual life of humanity through the centuries, indeed through thousands of years. He was a man who looked deeply into spiritual life—Wilhelm von Humboldt, the celebrated astronomer's brother. Other Westerners, people of widely different origins, have felt the same. What a wonderful feeling it produces in us when we let this Bhagavad Gita work upon us, even in its opening verses!

It seems that, particularly in our circle, my dear friends, we often have to begin by working our way through to a fully unprejudiced position. Despite the fact that the Bhagavad Gita has been known for so short a time in the West, its holiness has so taken hearts by storm that we are inclined to approach it from the start with this sense of encountering a sacred text, and are thus unable to see clearly the poem's actual starting point. Let us look at it quite dispassionately, perhaps even a little excessively so.

We have before us a poem that from the very beginning sets us in the midst of a wild and stormy battle. We are introduced to a scene of action hardly less wild than that into which Homer straightway places us in the *Iliad*. We go on and are confronted in this scene with something that Arjuna—one of the foremost, perhaps *the* foremost of the personalities in the Song—feels from the start to be a fratricidal conflict. He comes before us as one horror-stricken by the battle, for there among the enemy, he sees his own blood relations [I.26]. His bow falls from his grasp when it becomes clear to him that he is to enter a murderous strife with men descended from the same ancestors as himself, men in whose veins flows the same blood as his own. We begin by empathizing with his dropping the bow and recoiling from the awful battle between brothers [I.27].

Then, before our gaze, arises Krishna, Arjuna's great spiritual teacher, and a wonderful, sublime teaching is brought before us in vivid colors. It appears as a teaching given to his pupil, but where is it all leading? That is the question we must first of all set before ourselves, because it is not enough just to give ourselves up to the great, seemingly sacred teaching in Krishna's words to Arjuna. The circumstances of its being given must also be studied. We must visualize the situation in which Krishna exhorts Arjuna not to quail before this battle with his brothers, but to pick up his bow and hurl himself with all his might into the devastating conflict [II.3]. Krishna's teachings emerge amid the battle like a cloud of spiritual light, incomprehensible at first. They require Arjuna not to recoil but to stand firm and do his duty in this battle. When we bring this picture before our eyes, it is almost as though the teaching becomes transformed by its setting. Then again, this setting leads us further into the whole weaving of the song of the *Mahabharata*, the mighty song of which the Bhagavad Gita is only a part.

Krishna's teaching leads us out into the storms of everyday life, into the wild confusion of human battles, errors, and earthly strife. His teaching appears almost like a justification of these human conflicts. If we regard the picture before us quite dispassionately, the Bhagavad Gita will perhaps suggest to us altogether different questions from those that arise when we approach things expecting to understand them, as if they were ordinary human deeds. So it is perhaps necessary to point first to the *setting* of the Gita in order to realize its world-historic significance, and then to be able to see how it can be of increasing and special significance in our own time.

I have already said that this majestic song came into the Western world as something completely new, and almost equally new were the feelings, perceptions, and thoughts that lie behind it. For what did Western civilization really know of Indian culture before it became acquainted with the Bhagavad Gita? Apart from various things that have only become known in the last century, very little indeed! With the exception of certain secret societies, Western civilization has had no direct knowledge of what is actually the central nerve-impulse of this great poem. When we approach such a thing, we feel how inadequate everyday human language, philosophy, and ideas are for it, and how little they suffice for describing such heights of human spiritual life upon Earth. We need something quite different from ordinary descriptions to express what shines out to us from such a revelation of the human spirit.

I would like first of all to place two pictures before you as a foundation for further descriptions. The first is taken from the book itself, the other from the spiritual life of the West. The latter is comparatively easy to understand, whereas for the time being the one from the book appears quite remote. To start with the former, we are told how, in the midst of the battle, Krishna appears and unveils before Arjuna cosmic secrets, immense teachings. His pupil is overcome by the strong desire to see the spiritual form of this soul, to know the one speaking such sublime teachings. He begs Krishna to show himself to him in his true spirit form in whichever way he can do so. Krishna appears to him (we shall return to this description later) in a form that embraces all things—a sublime, glorious beauty, a nobility that reveals cosmic mysteries. We shall see that there is little in the world to approach the glory of this description of how the teacher's sublime spirit form is revealed to the clairvoyant eye of his pupil [IX.17–25].

Before Arjuna's gaze lies the wild battlefield where much blood will have to flow and where the fratricidal struggle is to develop. The soul of Krishna's disciple is to be wafted away from this battlefield of devastation. It is to perceive and plunge into a world where Krishna lives in his true form. That is a world of holy bliss, removed from all strife and conflict, a world where the secrets of existence are unveiled, far away from everyday affairs. Yet the human soul, in its most inward, most essential being, belongs to that world. The soul must learn to know this world, and then it will have to descend from that world again to return to the chaotic, evil battles of this world. In truth, as we follow the description of this picture we may well ask ourselves what is really taking place in Arjuna's soul. What is the matter with this soul? It stands in the midst of a raging battle, as though the battle in which it stands were forced upon it. This soul feels related to a heavenly world in which there is no human suffering, no battle, no death. It longs to rise into a world of the eternal, but with the inevitability that can come only from the impulse of so sublime a being as Krishna, this soul must be forced downward into the chaotic confusion of the battle. Arjuna would gladly turn away from all this chaos, for the life of Earth around him appears as something alien and remote, altogether unrelated to his soul. We can distinctly feel that his soul is still one of those that long for the higher worlds, that would live with the gods, and that perceives human life as something foreign and incomprehensible to them. In truth it is an astounding picture, containing matters of sublime import: a hero, Arjuna, surrounded by other heroes and by the warrior hosts—a hero who feels all that is spread before him as unfamiliar and remote— and a god, Krishna, who is needed to direct him to this world. He does not understand this world until Krishna makes it comprehensible to him.

It may sound paradoxical, but I know that those who can enter into the matter more deeply will understand me when I say that Arjuna stands there like a human soul to whom the earthly aspect of the world must first be made comprehensible.

Now, this Bhagavad Gita comes to Westerners who undoubtedly do have an understanding for earthly things! It comes to humans who have attained such a high degree of materialistic civilization that they have a very good understanding for everything earthly. It has to be understood by souls that are separated by a deep gulf from our observation of Arjuna's soul. Things for which Arjuna shows no inclination, requiring Krishna to force him to "come down to Earth," seem quite intelligible and obvious to the Westerner. The difficulty for Westerners seems rather to be an inability to lift themselves up to Arjuna, to whom must be imparted an understanding of what in the West is easily understood: physicality, earthly materiality. A god, Krishna, must make our civilization and culture intelligible to Arjuna. How easy it is in our time for people to understand what surrounds them! We need no Krishna. It is well for once to see clearly the mighty gulfs that can lie between different human natures, and not overestimate how easy it is for a Western soul to understand a nature like Krishna's or Arjuna's. Arjuna is human, but utterly different from those who have slowly and gradually evolved in Western civilization.

That is one picture I wanted to bring to you, for words cannot lead us more than a very little way into these things. Pictures that we can grasp with our souls can do better, because they speak not only to the understanding, but also to that in us which on Earth will always be deeper than our understanding—to our power of perception and to our feeling.

I now would like to place another picture before you, one no less sublime than that from the Bhagavad Gita but one that stands infinitely nearer to Western culture. We have in the West a beautiful, literary picture that Westerners know well and which is meaningful for them. But first let us ask, to what extent does Western humanity really believe that this being of Krishna once appeared before Arjuna and spoke those words? We are now at the starting point of a concept of the world that will lead us on until it is no mere matter of belief, but of knowledge. We are, however, only at the beginning of this conception, the point of departure of the anthroposophical conception of the world. The second picture is much nearer to us. It contains something to which Western civilization can respond.

We look back some five centuries before the founding of Christianity, to a soul whom one of the greatest spirits of Western lands made the central figure of all his reflections. We look back to Socrates. We watch in our mind's eye the dying Socrates, as Plato describes him in the circle of his disciples, in the famous discourse on the immortality of the soul.[38] In this picture there are but slight indications of the beyond, represented in the "daemon" who speaks to Socrates. Let him stand before us in the hours that preceded his entrance into the spiritual worlds. There he is, surrounded by his disciples, and in the face of death he speaks to them of the immortality of the soul. Many people have read the wonderful discourse wherein Plato described for us the scene of his teacher's death. But people nowadays read only words, only concepts and ideas. There are even those—I do not mean to censure them—in whom this wonderful scene of Plato arouses questions as to the logical justification of what the dying Socrates sets forth for his disciples. These are people who cannot feel that, for the human soul, there is something more important, more significant than logical proofs and scientific arguments. Let us imagine a contemporary of ours, a person of great culture, depth, and refinement, making the same statement Socrates makes about immortality but in a different situation from that of Socrates, under different circumstances. Even if the words of this person were a hundred times more logically sound than those of Socrates, in spite of it all they would perhaps have a hundred

38. See Plato, *Crito* and *Phaedo*.

times less value. This will only be fully grasped when people begin to understand that there is for the human soul something of more value, even if less plausible, than the most strictly correct logical demonstrations. If any highly educated and cultured teacher speaks to students on the immortality of the soul, it can indeed have significance. But its significance is not revealed in what is said—I know it will sound paradoxical, but it is true—its significance depends also on the fact that the teacher, having spoken these words to the students, goes on to look after the ordinary business of life, and the students do the same. Socrates speaks in the hour immediately preceding his passage through the gates of death. He gives out his teaching in the brief moment when his soul is about to be severed from his bodily form.

Let us now imagine one of Socrates's pupils, who could certainly have no doubt of the reality of all that surrounded him, being a Greek, and compare him with Krishna's disciple Arjuna. Think how the Greek must be introduced to the supersensible world, and then think of Arjuna, who can't have any doubt whatsoever about the supersensible world, but is confused instead by his relationship to the sensible/physical world, almost doubting the possibility of its existence. It is one thing to speak about immortality to the pupils he is leaving behind in the hour of his own death—which does not meet him unexpectedly, but as an event predetermined by destiny—and another thing to return to the ordinary business of living after such a discourse. It is not Socrates's words that should work on us, as much as the situation in which he speaks them. Let us take all the power of this scene, all that we receive from Socrates' conversation on immortality, the full immediate force of this picture. What do we have before us? It is the world of everyday life in Greek times, the world whose conflicts and struggles led to the best of the country's sons being condemned to drink hemlock. This noble Greek spoke these last words with the sole intention of bringing the souls of the men around him to believe in something of which they could no longer have knowledge, to believe in what was for them "a beyond," a spiritual world. That it needs a Socrates to lead earthly souls to gain an outlook into the spiritual worlds, that it needs him to do this by means of the strongest proofs—namely by his *deed*—is entirely comprehensible to Western souls. Socrates's culture is quite understandable for Western souls. The image of Socrates standing in front of his students, placing them in the immediate presence of the reality of death, is easily understood by Western souls. We only grasp Western civilization correctly if we recognize that, in this respect, it has been a Socratic civilization for centuries, for millennia.

I know that history, philosophy, and other branches of knowledge may say, with apparently good reason, "Yes, but if you only look at what is written in the Bhagavad Gita and at Plato's works, it is just as easy to prove the opposite of what you have just said." I know too that those who speak like this do not want to feel the deeper impulses, the mighty impulses that arise on the one hand from that picture out of the Bhagavad Gita, and on the other from that of the dying Socrates as described by Plato. A deep gulf yawns between these two worlds, despite all their similarities. This is because the Bhagavad Gita marks the end of the age of the ancient clairvoyance. We can catch there its last echo, while in the dying Socrates we meet one of the first of those who through thousands of years wrestled with this kind of knowledge, these kinds of ideas, thoughts, and feelings, with people who were as if cast off by the old clairvoyance and who continued to evolve in the intervening time because they must prepare the way for a new clairvoyance. Today we are striving toward this new clairvoyance by announcing and receiving what we call the anthroposophical conception of the world. From a certain angle, we may say that no gulf is deeper than the one opening up between Arjuna and a disciple of Socrates.

We now live in a time when human souls, having gone through manifold transformations and incarnations in the search for life in external knowledge, are once more seeking to make connections with the spiritual worlds. The fact that you are sitting here is living proof that your own souls are seeking this reunion. You are seeking the connection that will lead you in a new way up to the worlds so wondrously revealed to us in Krishna's words to his disciple Arjuna. So there is much in the esoteric wisdom on which the Bhagavad Gita is founded that resonates for us, that responds to our deepest longings. In ancient times, the soul was well aware of its bond with the spiritual.

It was at home in the supersensible realm. We are now at the beginning of an age wherein the human soul will once again seek access to spiritual worlds in a new way. We must feel stimulated in this search when we think that such access was once available to human beings. Indeed, we shall find it to an unusual degree in the revelations of the sacred song of India.

As is generally the case with the great human works, we find that the opening words of the Bhagavad Gita are full of meaning. (Are not the opening words of the *Iliad* and the *Odyssey* most significant?) The story is told by his charioteer to the blind king, the chief of the Kurus who are engaged in fratricidal battle with the Pandavas. A blind chieftain! This already seems symbolic. Ancient people had vision into the spiritual worlds. With their whole heart and soul they lived in connection with gods and divine beings. Everything that surrounded them in the earthly sphere was in unceasing connection with divine existence. Then came another age, and just as Greek legend depicts Homer as a blind man, so the Gita tells us of the blind chief of the Kurus. It is to him that Krishna's discourses, in which he instructs Arjuna concerning goings on in the world of the senses, are directed. He must even be told of those things of the sense world that are projections into it from the spiritual world. There is something deeply symbolic in the fact that old men who looked back with perfect memory and a perfect spiritual connection into a primeval past, were *blind* to the world immediately around them. They were seers in the spirit, seers in the soul. They could experience as though in lofty images all that lived as spiritual mysteries. Those who were to understand the events of the world in their spiritual connections were pictured as blind in the old songs and legends. Thus we find the same symbol in the Greek singer Homer as in the figure that meets us at the beginning of the Bhagavad Gita. This introduces us to the age of transition from ancient humanity to that of the present day.

Now, why is Arjuna so deeply moved by the impending battle of the brothers? We know that the old clairvoyance was in a sense bound up with external blood relationships. In ancient times, the flowing of the same blood in the veins of a number of people was rightly looked upon as something sacred, because it was connected to the ancient perception of a particular group soul. Those who not only felt but knew their blood relationship to one another did not yet have the kind of ego that lives in present-day humans. Wherever we look in those ancient times, we find groups of people who did not at all feel that they were each an individual "I," as we do today. Each person's identity was felt *only within the group*, within a community based upon blood ties.

What does the folk soul, the nation soul, signify to a person today? Certainly it is often an object of the greatest enthusiasm. Yet compared with the individual "I" of a person, we may say that this nation soul does not really count. This may be a hard saying but it is true. Once upon a time, a person did not say "I" to him- or herself, but to the tribal or racial *group*. This group-soul feeling was still living in Arjuna when he saw the fratricidal battle raging around him. That is the reason why this battle filled him with such horror [I.28–35].

Let us enter Arjuna's soul and feel his horror when he realized how those who belonged together were about to murder each other. He felt that what lived in all the souls at that time *was about to kill itself.* He felt the way a soul would feel if its body, which is its very own, were being torn to pieces. He felt as though the members of one body were in conflict, the heart with the head, the left hand with the right. In this mood, Arjuna is met by the great teacher Krishna. Here we must call attention to the incomparable manner with which Krishna is pictured in this scene: the holy god, who stands there teaching Arjuna what humanity must discard if we wish to take the right direction in its evolution. And what does Krishna mention? "I," and "I," and "I," and always only "I." "I am in the earth, I am in the water, I am in the air, I am in the fire, in all souls, in all manifestations of life, even in the holy Aum. I am the wind that blows through the forests. I am the greatest of the mountains, of the rivers. I am the greatest among men. I am all that is best in the old seer Kapila" [see IX.17–18; X.25–42]. Truly Krishna says nothing less than this, "I recognize nothing else than myself and I admit the world's existence only in so far as it is I!" Nothing else than "I" speaks out from the teaching of Krishna.

We should see, once and for all, quite plainly how Arjuna stands there as one who does not yet understand himself as an ego, but now must do so. The God confronts him like a cosmic egotist, admitting of nothing but himself, even requiring others to admit of nothing but themselves, each one an "I." Yes, in all that is in earth, water, fire or air, in all that lives upon the Earth, in the three worlds, we are to see nothing but Krishna.

It is of momentous significance for us that one who cannot yet grasp the ego is brought for instruction before a being who demands to be recognized only as his own Self. Let him who wants to see this in the light of truth read the Bhagavad Gita through and try to answer the question, "How can we designate what Krishna says of himself and that for which he demands recognition?" It is *universal egotism* that speaks in Krishna. It does indeed seem as though through the whole of the sublime Gita this refrain resounds to our spiritual ear: "Only if you recognize, you humans, my all-embracing egotism, only then can salvation be for you!"

The greatest achievements of human spiritual life always set us riddles. We only see them in the right light when we recognize that they set us the very greatest riddles. Truly, a hard one seems to be given us when we are now confronted with the task of understanding how a most sublime teaching can be bound up with the announcement of universal egotism. It is not through logic but in the perception of the great contradictions in life that the esoteric mysteries unveil themselves to us. It will be our task to get beyond what seems so strange and come to the truth within maya.

Our task will be to reach truth by overcoming some remarkable aspects of maya, so that we shall know just what it is we call egotism when we speak from inside maya. This riddle will lead us out of maya, to reality, to the light of truth. Our next lectures will examine how to take that step into reality.

2

HELSINKI, MAY 29, 1913

T HE deeper we go into the esoteric records of various ages and peoples, that is to say, into the truly esoteric records, the more we are struck by one feature that meets us again and again. I already indicated this when discussing the Gospel of John, and on a later occasion when speaking of the Gospel of Mark. I refer to the fact that on looking deeply into any such esoteric record it becomes ever clearer that it is really most wonderfully composed, that it forms an artistic whole. I could show, for instance, how John's Gospel, when we penetrate into its depths, reveals a wonderful, artistic composition. With remarkable dramatic power, the story is carried stage by stage toward a great climax, and then continues from this point onward with a kind of renewal of dramatic power to the end. You can study this in the lectures I gave in Kassel on John's Gospel in relation to the three other gospels, especially to that according to Luke.[39]

Most impressive is the gradual enhancement of this inner, dramatic composition which becomes visible in John's Gospel, so that from

---

39. *The Gospel of St. John and Its Relation to the Other Gospels* (Kassel, June 24–July 7, 1909), NY: Anthroposophic Press, 1982.

so-called miracles and signs the supersensible is presented from sign to sign, and from sign to sign there is continual enlargement until we get to the sign of the initiation of Lazarus. It makes us realize how we can always find artistic beauty at the foundation of these esoteric records. I could say the same about the composition of the Gospel of Mark. When we regard such records in their formal beauty and dramatic power, we can indeed conclude that just because they are *true*, such records cannot be other than artistically, beautifully composed, in the deepest sense of the word. For the moment we will only indicate this fact, as we may come back to it in the course of these lectures.

Now, it is remarkable that the same thing meets us again in the Bhagavad Gita. There is a wonderful intensification of the narrative. Let us begin by indicating a few of the outstanding points—and we will confine ourselves today to the first four discourses—because these points are important both for the artistic structure and for the deep esoteric truths that it contains.

First Arjuna meets us. Facing the bloodshed in which he is to take part, he grows weak. He sees all that is to take place as a battle of brothers against brothers, his blood relations. He shrinks back. He will not fight against them. While fear and terror overcome him and he is horror-stricken, his charioteer suddenly appears as the instrument through which Krishna, God, is to speak to him. In this very first episode we have a moment of great intensity and also an indication of deep esoteric truth. Anyone who finds the way, by whatever path, into the spiritual worlds, even though he or she may have gone only a few steps—or even had only a dim presentiment of the way to be experienced—such a person will be aware of the deep significance of this moment.

As a rule we cannot enter the spiritual worlds without passing through a deep upheaval in our souls. We have to experience something that disturbs and shakes all our forces, flooding our soul with intense feelings and sensations. Emotions that are generally spread out over many moments, over long periods of living, whose permanent effect on the soul is therefore weaker—such feelings are concentrated in a single moment and storm through us with tremendous force when we enter the esoteric worlds. Then we experience a kind of inner shattering, which can indeed be compared to fear, terror, and anxiety, as though we were shrinking back from something in horror. Such experiences belong to the initial stages of esoteric development, to entering the spiritual worlds. Just for this reason, great care must be taken to give the right advice to those who would enter the spiritual worlds through esoteric training. We must be prepared so that we may experience this upheaval as a necessary event in our soul life without its encroaching on our bodily life and health, and insofar as the body is included, it must suffer a like upheaval. That is the essential thing. We must learn to suffer the convulsions of our soul with outward equanimity and calm.

This is true not only for our bodily processes. The soul forces we need for everyday living, our ordinary intellectual powers, even those of imagination, of feeling and will—these too must not be allowed to become unbalanced. The upheaval that may be the starting point for esoteric life must take place in far deeper layers of the soul, so that we go through our external life as before, without anything being noticed in us outwardly, while within we may be living through whole worlds of shattering soul experience. That is what it means to be ripe for esoteric development: to be able to experience such inward convulsions without losing one's outer balance and calm. To this end, those striving to become ripe for esoteric development must widen the circle of their interests beyond everyday life. They must get away from the things which otherwise keep us going from morning to night and reach out to interests that move on the great horizon of the world.

We must be able to undergo the experience of doubting all truth and all knowledge. We must have the power to do this with the same intensity of feeling people generally have only where their everyday interests are concerned. We must be able to feel with the destiny of all humankind with as much interest as we usually feel in our own destiny, or perhaps in that of our nearest connections of clan, family or nation. If we cannot do this, we are not yet completely ready for esoteric development.

For this reason modern Anthroposophy, if pursued earnestly and worthily, is the right preparation for true esoteric development in our age. Let those who are absorbed in the petty material interests of the immediate present, who cannot find the interest to follow the anthroposophist in looking out over world and planetary destinies, over the historical epochs and races of humankind—let them scoff if they will! Those who would prepare themselves for esoteric development must lift up their eyes to the heights where the interests of humankind, of the Earth, of the whole planetary system, become their own. The person whose interests are gradually sharpened and widened through the study of Anthroposophy, including esoteric training, to an understanding of esoteric truths, is being rightly prepared for an esoteric path.

There are many people nowadays who have such an interest in the whole of humankind. More often than not, we shall not find them among intellectuals but among people who seem to lead quite simple lives and feel this interest as if by natural instinct. That is why Anthroposophy is in such harmony with the spirit of our age.

First, then, we must experience the mighty upheaval of the soul that has to come at the beginning of esoteric experience. With wonderful truth the Bhagavad Gita sets such a moment of upheaval at the starting point of Arjuna's experience, only he does not undergo an esoteric training but is placed into this moment by his destiny. He is placed into the battle without being able to recognize its necessity, its purpose, or its aim. All he sees is that his relatives are about to fight against each other. A soul such as Arjuna's can be shaken to its innermost core by that experience, for he has to say to himself, "Brother fights against brother. Surely then all tribal customs will be shaken and then the tribe itself will wither away and be destroyed, and all its morality fall into decay! Those laws that place men into castes in accordance with an eternal destiny will be shaken, and then will everything be imperiled—humanity itself, the law, the whole world. The whole significance of humankind will be in the balance" [see I.36–45]. Such is his feeling. It is as though the ground were about to sink from under his feet, as though an abyss were opening up before him.

Arjuna was a man who had received into his feeling something that people nowadays no longer know, but that in those ancient times was a primeval teaching of tradition. He knew that what is handed on from generation to generation in humankind is bound up with *female nature*, while the individual, personal qualities whereby a person stands out from blood connections and family line are bound up with *male nature*. What a person inherits as common, generic qualities is handed on to the descendants by the woman, whereas what forms that person into an unique, individual being, tearing one out of the generic succession, is the part received from the father. "If blood fights against blood must it not then have an evil effect on the laws that rule woman's nature?" Arjuna says to himself [see I.41–42].

Arjuna has now absorbed another feeling, another impression, upon which depends for him what he sees as the healthy course of future human evolution. He feels that the forefathers of the tribe, the ancestors, are worthy of honor. He feels that their souls watch over the succeeding generations. For him, it is a sublime service to offer up sacrificial fires to the Manes,[40] to the holy souls of the ancestors. But now what is he forced to see? Instead of altars with sacrificial fires burning on them for the ancestors, he sees those who should join in kindling the fires assailing one another in battle. If we would understand a human soul, we must penetrate into its thoughts. Above all we must enter deeply into its feelings, because it is in feeling that the soul is intimately bound up with its very life. Think now of the great contrast between all that Arjuna would naturally feel, and the bloody battle of brother against brother that is about to take place. Destiny is hammering at Arjuna's soul, shaking it to its very depths. It is as though he had to gaze down into a terrible abyss. Such an upheaval awakens the forces of the soul and brings it to a vision of esoteric realities that are, at other times, hidden as behind a veil. That is what gives such dramatic intensity to the Bhagavad Gita. The ensuing discourse is thus placed before us with wonderful power, developing of necessity out of Arjuna's destiny, instead of being given us merely as an academic, pedantic course of instruction in esotericism.

Now that Arjuna has been rightly prepared for the birth of the deeper forces of his soul, now that he has an inward vision of these

40. See "Manas, Roman Spirits of the Dean," in Simon Hornblower and Antony Spawforth, eds., *The Oxford Classical Dictionary* (NY: Oxford University Press, 1996), p. 916.

forces, something happens which everyone with the power to behold will understand: His charioteer becomes the instrument through which the god Krishna speaks to him. In the first four discourses, we observe three successive stages, each higher than the last, each one introducing something new. Here in these first discourses we find an accent that is a wonder of dramatic artistry, apart from the fact that it corresponds to a deep esoteric truth. The first stage is a teaching that may appear downright trivial to many Westerners in its given form. Let us admit this at once. (Here I should like to remark, especially for the benefit of my dear friends here in Finland, that I mean by "Western" all that lies to the west of the Ural Mountains, the Volga, the Caspian Sea, and Asia Minor—in fact the whole of Europe. What is to be called Eastern land belongs essentially in Asia. Of course, America too forms part of the West.)

To begin with, then, we find a teaching that may easily appear trivial, especially to a philosophical mind. For what is the first thing that Krishna says to Arjuna as an exhortation to battle? "Look there," he says, "at those who are to be killed by you, those in your own ranks who are to be killed and those who are to remain behind, and consider well this one fact. What dies and what remains alive, in your ranks and in those of the enemy, is but the outer physical body. This deepest being of humanity is not affected in this battle. Rise, Arjuna, rise to the spiritual standpoint, and then you can go and give yourself up to your duty. You need not shudder nor be sad at heart, for in killing your enemies you are not killing their essential being" [see II.18–21].

Thus speaks Krishna, and upon first hearing them, his words are in some sense trivial,[41] yet trivial in a very remarkable way. In many respects, Westerners are shortsighted in their thinking and consciousness. They never stop to consider that everything is evolving. If they say that Krishna's exhortation, as I have expressed it, is trivial, it is as though one were to say, "Why do they honor Pythagoras as such

---

41. Steiner refers to Krishna's words about reincarnation and not to his directive to fight, which is hardly trivial.

a great man when every schoolboy and girl knows his theorem?" It would be foolish to conclude that Pythagoras was not a great man in having discovered his theorem just because every school child now understands it! We see how foolish this is, but we do not notice when we fail to realize that the wisdom of Krishna, which any Western philosopher may recite by rote—that the spirit is eternal, immortal, etc.—was a sublime wisdom at the time Krishna revealed it. Souls like Arjuna did indeed feel that blood relations ought not to fight. They still felt the common blood that flowed in a group of people. To hear it said that "the spirit is eternal" (spirit in the sense of what is generally conceived, abstractly, as the center of the human being)—this stated in abstract and intellectual terms was something absolutely new and epoch-making in its newness when it resounded in Arjuna's soul through Krishna's words. All the people in Arjuna's environment definitely believed in reincarnation, but as Krishna taught it, as a general and abstract *idea*, it was new, especially in regard to Arjuna's situation. This is one reason why we had to say that such a truth can only be called "trivial" in a special sense. That holds true in another respect as well. Our abstract thinking, which we use even in the pursuit of popular science, which we regard today as quite natural—this thinking activity was by no means always so natural and simple.

In order to illustrate what I say, let me give you a radical example. You will think it strange that while for all of you it is quite natural to speak of a "fish," it was by no means natural for primeval peoples to do so. Ancient peoples were acquainted with trout and salmon, cod and herring, but "fish" they did not know. They had no such word as "fish," because their thought did not extend to such abstract generalization. They knew birch trees, cherry trees, orange trees, individual trees, but "tree" they did not know. Even now, thinking in such general concepts is by no means natural to indigenous people. This mode of thinking has indeed only entered humanity in the course of its evolution. In fact, one who considers why it was that logic first began in the time of ancient Greece could scarcely be surprised when the statement is made on esoteric grounds that logical thinking has only existed since the period that *followed* the original composition of the Bhagavad Gita. Krishna impels Arjuna to think logically, to think in abstractions, to a new way of thinking that is only now entering humanity.[42]

But people have the most distorted and unnatural notions about this activity of thinking that human beings have developed and take for granted today. Western philosophers in particular have the most distorted ideas about thinking, for they generally take it to be merely a photographic reproduction of external sense reality. They imagine that concepts and ideas and all of human thinking simply arise out of the external physical world. While libraries of philosophical glossaries have been written in the West to prove that thought is merely something that originates in response to the stimuli of the external physical world, only in our time will thought be valued for what it really is.

Here I reach a point that is most important for those who would undergo esoteric development in their own souls. I want to make every effort to get this point clear. Medieval alchemists used to say—I cannot now discuss what they really meant by it—that gold could be made from all metals, gold in any desired amount, but that one must first have a minute quantity of it. Without that, one could not make gold. Whether or not this is true of gold, it is certainly true of *clairvoyance*. No one could actually attain clairvoyance if one did not have a tiny amount of it already in one's soul. It is generally supposed that people are not—as such—clairvoyant. If that were true they could never become clairvoyant at all, because just as the alchemist thought that one must have a *little* gold to conjure forth large quantities, so must one already be a little clairvoyant in order to be able to develop and extend it more and more. Now you may see two alternatives here and ask, "Do you think then that we all are clairvoyant, if only slightly, *or* do you think that those of us who are not clairvoyant can never become so?" This is just the point. It is most important to understand that there is really no one among you who does not have this starting point of clairvoyance, though you may not be conscious of it. You all

---

42. Steiner seems to mean that Arjuna was to be one of the first to be capable of this kind of thinking which, after two and a half millennia, has only today become a widely shared capacity.

have it. None of you is lacking in it. What is this that all possess? It is something not generally regarded or valued as clairvoyance. Let me make a rather crude comparison.

If a pearl is lying in the roadway and a chicken finds it, the chicken does not value the pearl. Most men and women today are chickens in this respect. They do not value the pearl that lies there in full view before them. What they value is something quite different. They value their concepts and ideas, but no one could think abstractly, could *have* thoughts and ideas, without being clairvoyant. The pearl of clairvoyance is contained in our ordinary thinking from the start. Ideas arise in the soul through exactly the same process as what gives rise to its highest powers. It is immensely important to learn to understand that clairvoyance begins in something common and everyday. We only have to recognize the supersensible nature of our concepts and ideas. We must realize that these come to us from the supersensible worlds; only then can we look at the matter correctly.

When I tell you of the upper hierarchies, of seraphim and cherubim and thrones, right down to archangels and angels, these are beings that must speak to the human soul from higher spiritual worlds. It is from those worlds that concepts and ideas come into the human soul, not from the world of the senses. In the eighteenth century, what was considered at the time a great call was uttered by one of the Enlightenment philosophers, "O, humanity, make bold to use thy power of reason!"[43] Today a great word must resonate in human souls: "O, humanity, make bold to claim thy concepts and ideas as the beginning of thy clairvoyance." What I have just expressed I said publicly many years ago in my books *Truth and Science*[44] and *The Philosophy of Freedom*,[45] where I showed that human ideas come from supersensible, spiritual knowledge. It was not understood at the time,

---

43. Immanuel Kant (1724–1804) exclaimed, "Dare to reason!"
44. Rudolf Steiner's doctoral dissertation: *Truth and Knowledge: Introduction to "Philosophy of Spiritual Activity"* (Great Barrington, MA: SteinerBooks, 2007).
45. London: Rudolf Steiner Press, 1970. Also translated as *Intuitive Thinking as a Spiritual Path* (Hudson, NY: Anthroposophic Press, 1995).

and no wonder, for those who should have understood it were—well, like the chickens! We must realize that at the moment when Krishna stands before Arjuna and gives him the power of abstract judgment, he is thereby giving him, for the first time in the whole of evolution, the starting point for the knowledge of higher worlds. The spirit can be seen on the very surface of the changes that take place within the external world of sense. Bodies die; the spirit, the abstract, the essential being, is eternal. The spiritual can be seen playing on the surface of phenomena. This is what Krishna would reveal to Arjuna as the beginning of a new clairvoyance for human beings.

When you have this experience in your world of ideas, when the full cup of doubt in all existence has been poured out with pain and bitterness over your soul, only then are you ripe to understand how, after all, it is not the infinite spaces and periods of time of the physical world from which your ideas have come. Only then, after the bitterness of doubt, can you open yourself to the regions of the spirit and know that your doubt was justified, and in what sense it was justified. For it had to be, since you imagined that the ideas had come into your soul from the times and spaces of the physical world. How do you now feel your world of ideas, having experienced its origin in the spiritual worlds? Now for the first time you feel yourself inspired. Before, you were feeling the infinite void spread around you like a dark abyss. Now you begin to feel that you are standing on a rock that rises up out of the abyss. You know with certainty, "Now I am connected with the spiritual worlds. They, not the world of sense, have bestowed on me my world of ideas." One thing is necessary for people today if they would attain an inward experience of truth. They must have once passed through the feeling of the fleeting nature of all outer transformations. They must have experienced the mood of infinite sadness, of infinite tragedy, and at the same time the exultation of joy. They must have felt the breath of the ephemeral that streams out from all things. They must have been able to fix their interest on this coming forth and passing away again, the transitoriness of the world of sense. Then, when they have been able to feel the deepest pain and the fullest delight in the external world, they must once have been absolutely alone—alone with their concepts and ideas. They must have had the feeling, "In these concepts, I grasp the

mystery of the worlds; I take hold of the outer edge of cosmic being"—
the very expression I once used in my *Philosophy of Freedom*! This must
be experienced, not merely understood intellectually, and if you would
experience it, it must be in deepest loneliness. Then you have another
feeling. On the one hand you experience the majesty of the world of
ideas that is spread out over the *All*. On the other hand you experience
with the deepest bitterness that you have to separate yourself from space
and time in order to be at one with your concepts and ideas. Loneliness!
It is the icy cold of loneliness. Furthermore, it comes to you that the
world of ideas has now drawn together as into a single point of loneliness. Now you say, I am alone with my world of ideas. You become
utterly bewildered in your world of ideas, an experience that stirs you to
the depths of your soul. At length you say to yourself, "Perhaps all this
is only I, myself; perhaps the only truth about these laws is that they
exist in the point of my own loneliness." Thus you experience, infinitely
enhanced, utter doubt in all existence.

This is the next stage for the evolving soul. It is the stage where we
begin to be deeply in earnest with what has today come to be a trivial,
commonplace truth. To bear this feeling in your heart will prepare
you to receive in a true way the first truth that Krishna gives to Arjuna
after the mighty upheaval and convulsion in his soul: the truth of the
eternal spirit living through outer transformations. To abstract understanding we speak in concepts and ideas. Krishna speaks to Arjuna's
heart. What may be trivial and commonplace to the understanding is
infinitely deep and sublime to the human heart.

We see how the first stage shows itself at once as a necessary conse-
quence of the deeply moving experience that is presented to us at the
start of the Bhagavad Gita. And now to the next stage.

It is easy to speak of what is often called *dogma* in esotericism—
something that is accepted in blind faith and given out as gospel truth.
Let me suggest to you that it would be quite simple for someone to
come forward and say, "This man has published a book on esoteric
science,[46] speaking in it about Saturn, Sun, and Moon evolutions,

---

46. Rudolf Steiner, *An Outline of Esoteric Science*, first published in 1909.

and there is no way of controlling these statements. They can only be accepted as dogma." I could understand such a statement, because it corresponds to the superficial nature of our age—and there is no getting away from it, our age *is* superficial. Indeed, under certain conditions this objection would not be without foundation. It would be justified, for example, if you were to tear out of the book all the pages that precede the chapter on the Saturn evolution. If anyone were to begin reading the book at this chapter it *would* be nothing but dogma. If, however, the author prefaces it with the other chapters, he is by no means a dogmatist, because he shows what paths the soul has to travel in order to reach such conceptions. That is the point, that it has been shown in the book how every individual reaching into the depths of his or her soul is bound to come to such conceptions. Herein all dogmatism ceases.

Thus it may feel natural that Krishna, having brought Arjuna into the world of ideas and wishing to lead him into the esoteric world, now proceeds to show him the next stage, how every soul can reach that higher world if it finds the right starting point. Krishna then must begin by rejecting every form of dogmatism, and he does so radically. Here we come up against a hard saying by Krishna. He absolutely rejects what for centuries had been most holy to the highest minds of that age—the contents of the Vedas. He says, "Hold not to the Vedas, nor to the word of the Vedas. Hold fast to Yoga!" [see IX.20–24]. That is to say, "Hold fast to what is within thine own soul!"

Let us grasp what Krishna means by this exhortation. He does not mean that the contents of the Vedas are untrue. He does not want Arjuna to accept what is given in the Vedas *dogmatically* as do the disciples of the Vedic teaching. He wants to inspire him to take his start from the very first original point whence the human soul evolves. For this purpose all dogmatic wisdom must be laid aside. We can imagine Krishna saying to himself that even though Arjuna will in the end reach the very same wisdom that is contained in the Vedas, still he must be drawn away from them, for he must go his own way, beginning with the sources in his own soul. Krishna rejects the Vedas, whether their content is true or untrue. Arjuna's path must start from himself. Through his own inwardness he must come to recognize

Krishna. Arjuna must be assumed to have in himself what one can and must have if one is really to enter into the concrete truths of the supersensible worlds. Krishna has called Arjuna's attention to something that from then onward is a common attribute of humanity. Having led him to this point, he must lead him further and bring him to recognize what he is to achieve through Yoga. Thus, Arjuna must first undergo Yoga. Here the poem rises to another level.

In this second stage we see how the Bhagavad Gita goes through the first four discourses with ever-increasing dramatic force, coming at length to what is most individual. Krishna describes to Arjuna the path of Yoga. We shall speak of this in more detail tomorrow. He describes the path that Arjuna must take in order to pass from the everyday clairvoyance of concepts and ideas to what can only be attained through Yoga. Concepts only require to be placed in the right light, but Arjuna has to be *guided* to Yoga. This is the second stage.

The third stage shows once more an enhancement of dramatic power and the expression of a deep esoteric truth. Let us assume that someone takes the Yoga path. Such a person will rise at length from his ordinary consciousness to a higher state of consciousness, which includes not only the ego that lies between the limits of birth and death, but also what passes from one incarnation to the next. The soul awakens to know itself in an expanded ego. It grows into a wider consciousness. The soul goes through a process that is essentially an everyday process, but is not experienced fully in our everyday life because we go to sleep every night. As the sense world fades, we become unconscious of it. For every human soul, the possibility exists of letting this world of sense vanish from consciousness as it does when we go to sleep, and then to live in higher worlds as in an absolute reality. Thereby humans rise to a higher level of consciousness. We shall still have to speak of Yoga, and also of the modern exercises that make this possible. But if we gradually reach a point where we no longer consciously live and feel and know *in ourselves*, but live and feel and know *together with the whole Earth*, then we grow into a higher level of consciousness where the things of the sense world vanish for us as they do in sleep.

However, before we can attain this level we must be able to identify ourselves with the soul of the Earth. We shall see that this is possible.

We know that human beings not only experience the rhythm of sleeping and waking but other rhythms of the Earth as well—of summer and winter. When one follows the path of Yoga or goes through a modern esoteric training, it is possible to lift oneself above the ordinary consciousness that experiences the cycles of sleeping and waking, summer and winter. One can learn to look at oneself from outside. One becomes aware of being able to look back at oneself just as one ordinarily looks at things outside the self. Now we observe the cycles in external life. We see alternating conditions. We realize how the body, so long as one is outside of oneself, takes on a form similar to that of the Earth in summer with all its vegetation. What material science discovers and calls *nerves*, we begin to perceive as a sprouting forth of something plant-like when going to sleep. When we return to everyday consciousness we feel how this plant-like life shrinks together again and becomes the instrument for thinking, feeling, and willing in waking consciousness. One feels one's going out from the body and returning into it as analogous to the alternation of summer and winter on the Earth. In effect, we feel something summer-like in going to sleep and something winter-like in waking up—not, as one might imagine, the opposite way around. From this moment onward, we learn to understand what the spirit of the Earth is, and how it is asleep in summer and awake in winter, not vice versa. We realize the wonderful experience of identifying ourselves with the spirit of the Earth. From this moment on, one says, "I live not only inside my skin, but as a cell lives in my bodily organism, so do I live in the organism of the Earth. The Earth is asleep in summer and awake in winter as I am asleep and awake in the alternation of night and day. And as the cell is to my consciousness, so am I to the consciousness of the Earth."

The path of Yoga, especially in its modern sense, leads to this expansion of consciousness, to the identification of our own being with a more comprehensive being. We feel ourselves interwoven with the whole Earth. Then we no longer feel ourselves bound as humans to a particular time and place, but we feel our humanity such as it has developed from the very beginning of the Earth. We feel the age-long succession of our evolutions through the course of Earth evolution.

Thus Yoga leads us on to feel our at-one ment with what goes from one incarnation to another in the Earth's evolution. That is the third stage.

This is the reason for the great beauty in the artistic composition of the Bhagavad Gita. In its climaxes, its inner artistic form, it reflects deep esoteric truths. Beginning with an instruction in the ordinary concepts of our thinking, it goes on to an indication of the path of Yoga. Then at the third stage it describes the marvelous expansion of humanity's horizon over the whole Earth, where Krishna awakens in Arjuna the idea, "All that lives in your soul has lived often before, only you know nothing of it. But I have this consciousness in myself when I look back on all the transformations through which I have lived, and I will draw you to me so that you may learn to feel yourself as I feel myself" [IV.5]. This is a new moment of dramatic force, as beautiful as it is deeply and mysteriously true!

Thus we come to see the evolution of humankind from out of its everyday consciousness, from the pearl in the roadway that only needs to be recognized, from the particular world of thoughts and concepts that are a matter of everyday life in any one age, up to the point from where we can look out over all that we really have in us, which lives on from incarnation to incarnation on the Earth.

3

HELSINKI, MAY 30, 1913

I n the last lecture I was trying to show you how the thinking of the present day, which tends to the formation of abstract concepts, is not really a gift of the outer physical world, but a gift of the spiritual world. I tried to show you how fundamentally this abstract thinking enters the human soul in exactly the same way as the revelations of the beings of the upper hierarchies. The point then is this, that in our ordinary life we have something in us already that is related to clairvoyant perception. And we have something else in us as well, which is even more akin to clairvoyant perception, although in a less obvious way. I am referring to the consciousness that appears between our ordinary waking state and sleep—our dream consciousness. We cannot become familiar in a practical way with the ascent of the soul into higher worlds without trying to get a clear idea of the peculiar life that the soul leads in the twilight consciousness of dreaming. What, then, is a dream, in reality?

Let us begin by considering the dream pictures we have around or before us, which in general are more fleeting, and less sharply outlined than the perceptions of ordinary life. These pictures seem to flit past our souls. When we analyze them objectively in retrospect, we may be struck by the fact that in most cases they have some kind of connection with our life on the physical plane. Of course, there are people who are only too ready to see lofty and wonderful things in their dreams, or to interpret them at once as revelations of higher worlds. There are those who really believe that a dream has given them something altogether new, something that has never been there before. In most cases we shall be mistaken in interpreting our dreams in such a way. In our careless haste we fail to recognize how, after all, some experience or other we have had on the physical plane more or less recently, or perhaps even many years ago, has reappeared in the changing, weaving pictures of our dreams. For this very reason, it is quite easy for the materialistic science of our age to reject the idea that there is anything remarkable in the revelations of our dreams, and to point out instead that dreams are simply copies or reflections of what has been experienced in external life. If you are acquainted with the contemporary science of dreams, you will realize that it is always at pains to prove that the dream contains nothing more than the reflections of the physical world stored in the brain. Admittedly, such an attitude can easily deny any higher significance to our dream life by showing that the exalted revelations many people claim to have are pictures characteristic of the age in which they live, pictures that could not have been seen at all in any other age. So, for example, people today often dream in images derived from inventions and discoveries only made in the nineteenth century. Of course it is easy to prove that images derived from external life steal their way into the ever-changing play of dreams.

Those who would gain a clear idea of their dream experiences, to learn something from them to help them access esoteric worlds, must therefore be exceedingly careful in this realm. They must make a habit to carefully follow out all the hidden connections. By doing so, they will realize that most of our dreams give us no more than was experienced in the outer world. But it is just when we become more careful in analyzing our dream life—and every aspiring esotericist should do so—that we gradually begin to notice how one thing or another wells up before us that we could not possibly have experienced in our external life during this incarnation. Readers following the indications given in my *How to Know Higher Worlds* will notice that their dream life gradually begins to change.[47] Their dreams do actually begin to

---

47. See *How to Know Higher Worlds*, ch. 7.

assume a different character. One of the first experiences may be the following.

Perhaps I have been thinking for a long time about some perplexing problem and have at last concluded that my understanding is not yet equal to solving it, nor is all that I have been able to learn from external sources adequate for solving it. Now it will not generally happen that I am immediately conscious of having a dream in which this problem is solved for me. Even so, I will be able to have a certain higher consciousness at a comparatively early stage. For instance, awaking from a dream I will seem to *remember* something. I can tell myself, "I have not been dreaming about this problem, nor was I conscious of a dream I have had earlier. Yet a kind of memory is arising in me. It is as though some being had come near to me who solved this problem for me by giving or suggesting a solution."

This experience comes fairly easily if one expands one's consciousness by following the indications I have given. One will recall something that was experienced as though in a dream, and will know that at the time one was not aware of experiencing it. Such an experience will seem to shine upward from the depths of the soul and one may say to oneself, "When I wasn't there with my intelligence, my cleverness; when instead, I was protecting my soul from the suggestions of my intellect, then my soul had greater power. My soul could come freely in-touch with the solution to the problem, before which my intellect and understanding were powerless."

Here too, scientists will no doubt often find it easy to give a materialistic explanation for such an experience. But the one who has had it knows full well that what appeared, emerging like the recollection of a dream experience, reveals something quite different from a mere reminiscence of ordinary life. The whole mood of soul following it tells the dreamer he or she has never had such an experience before. It triggers a wonderful feeling of bliss and elation to realize that in the depths of the soul something more is active than is present in ordinary consciousness. This recognition can become still more distinct, and it happens in the following way.

If one carries out energetically the exercises given in my book *How to Know Higher Worlds*, and if one continues to do so for a long time—

even perhaps for several decades—then an experience may arise in the soul quite similar to what I have just been describing. For example, we may recollect an experience in everyday life years ago, perhaps a most disagreeable experience that was felt as a hard blow of fate and could never be recollected without pain and bitterness. Now something like the memory of a dream arises in our consciousness, but it is a strange dream. It tells us that feelings live within us that drew this bitter experience to us with irresistible force, and welcomed it gladly. Something lives in us that felt a kind of *delight* in bringing about all the circumstances that led up to this stroke of fate. When we have had such a dream remembrance, we know full well that while in our usual consciousness, which regulates our external affairs, there has not been a single moment—not one in the whole course of our present life—when we did not feel this stroke of fate with bitter pain. Yet, deep down within us, *something* stands in quite a different relation to this blow of fate. It used all of its power and magnetic force to draw together the circumstances needed to bring about this misfortune. We did not know it at the time. Now we notice that behind our everyday consciousness another, deeper layer of our soul life was wisely at work.

If we have such an experience—and we *shall* have them, if we earnestly carry through the exercises I have indicated—from then onward we will have an extended area of knowledge and conviction. In ordinary life we feel ourselves in a certain relation to the outer world and to the events that come to us in the course of our destiny. We meet these events with sympathy and antipathy. In the case mentioned, this particular blow of fate was felt as a bitter and hateful experience. We did not know that all this time our soul had another, wider life, longing to live through what we felt to be so unwelcome. This feeling is quite different in quality from any recollection of ordinary life, for in our innermost being we are very different from what we imagine. It is just this difference that now becomes evident in our soul. It enters in such a way that we know it has brought us revelations from realms into which our everyday consciousness cannot penetrate. It widens our whole concept of our life of soul. We know then, from experience, that our soul life contains far more than its mere content within the limits of birth and death. Unless we penetrate into these deeper regions, we have no idea that beneath the threshold of consciousness we are quite different beings from what we imagine ourselves to be in everyday life. When a new, significant feeling thus arises, the horizon of what we call our world expands into a new region. We realize why it is that in ordinary life we can enter it only under certain conditions.

In attempting to describe to you what may be called the esoteric development of dream life, I have set before you two quite different conditions. Our ordinary dream life, which most people experience continually at the border of sleeping and waking and which is nourished by images of everyday life, and an altogether new world of inner life that can arise steadily through a certain training. We have the power to plunge into the regions of the dream life in such a way as to find a new world dawning upon us, one in which we have actual experiences of the spiritual worlds. However, if we would have these new experiences between sleeping and waking during the night, one condition must be fulfilled. We must be able to exclude the recollections and images of our ordinary life. So long as these interfere in the realm of dreams, they will become inflated and block the way to real experiences of the higher worlds.

Why is it that the images from our everyday life thrust themselves so insistently into this higher realm? Because, whether we admit it or not, we have the liveliest interest in all that concerns our particular selves in the external world. If some people imagine that they no longer take any special interest in their life, that makes no difference at all. No one who realizes how in this connection people can give themselves up to the grossest illusions, will be misled by such imaginings. After all, people *are* closely attached to the sympathies and antipathies of their everyday lives. If you really try to carry out the exercises I have given for soul development, you will soon realize that it all comes to this, that you must detach your interest from your everyday life. People carry out the directions given in *How to Know Higher Worlds* in all sorts of ways. Many different people read the book, and for many different reasons, and one's reason for looking into it will determine one's attitude to it. Some may begin reading with the most beautiful feelings of how they may gain insight into the higher worlds. Then their curiosity is aroused—and why indeed should we not be curious about this realm? Curiosity often begins to stir even if one begins with the holiest of feelings. That will only carry through for a little while, however, for all sorts of inner feelings start coming in and make us stop, so we give it up.

But the feelings that we do not wish to recognize clearly, and generally interpret wrongly, are just those connected with sympathies and antipathies. We must free ourselves from them in quite another way, if we really mean to carry out these exercises. In fact, we do not free ourselves from them. That is why we stop doing the exercises. Though we say we want to break free of them, we do not do so. But when a person is really in earnest about doing the exercises, the effect they can have is seen very soon. One's sympathies and antipathies toward life change a little. I must say this does not happen very often. When it does happen, the change is of *utmost* significance, because it means we are struggling against the very forces that allow the images from our everyday life to arise in our dreams. If we have come so far as to alter our sympathies and antipathies in any sphere of life, no matter which one, these forces can no longer find their way in.

This alteration in the forces of sympathy need not occur in a high realm of life, but in *some* domain it *must* be carried out, perhaps in the most mundane matters. There are people who say they do their exercises every day, morning and evening, and for hours at a time, and cannot go even one step into the spiritual worlds. Sometimes it is difficult to explain to them how easily one can understand this situation. In many cases they need only realize the fact that they are still grumbling about the same things they were grumbling about twenty, even thirty years ago, although they have been doing exercises all of this time. The very language of their grumbling is still the same.

Then there are those who try to apply external means that can have certain effects in esotericism. For example, they become vegetarians. But there are people who go about it with utmost seriousness, really attempt to break a habit, yet achieve no results at all despite decades of exercises. Such people will think: If only I could experience a tiny fragment of the spiritual world! It is as if they have returned to the fleshpots of Egypt. For them, as for the Israelites in the desert longing for luxuries they had left behind in Egypt, the old sympathy for meat has not been suppressed. Others, thinking that they perhaps need meat, may say, "My brain needs meat...," for the old sympathy for meat was not suppressed. People will come up with all kinds of other reasons, thinking that they perhaps need meat. Let us not imagine that it is an easy thing to transform one's sympathies and antipathies. To quote a passage from *Faust*, "Easy it is, yet it is the easy that is hard." This is an apt expression of the situation of the evolving soul trying to rise to the higher worlds.

It is not a question of changing this or that particular sympathy or antipathy, but of changing *anything* whatsoever. If we do, then after certain exercises we can enter the domain of dream life in such a way that we bring nothing into it of our everyday sense experiences. Thereby, in a certain sense, new experiences have room to enter. When, through esoteric development, we have really gone through such experiences in practice, we become aware of a certain layer of consciousness in us lying behind the everyday consciousness with which we are all familiar. In ordinary life our dreams take place in this second layer of conscious-ness, "dream consciousness," but it only becomes such through our carrying into it what we experience from our waking consciousness. If, however, we hold back all of our everyday experiences from this region, then experiences from the higher worlds can enter. These higher expe-riences are present every day in our surrounding world. When they first arise, we begin to realize that our everyday consciousness itself seems like a dream compared to the *reality* of those experiences. We find that reality only begins on that higher level.

Returning to the example of suffering a blow of fate that subse-quently caused such bitter feelings, let us try to understand how one actually comes to realize the beginning of higher consciousness. Along with this bitterness we notice that *something* in us sought out this misfortune; we even feel its necessity for our development. Now for the first time, we realize in practice what karma is. We entered this incarnation with an imperfection in our soul. We felt it deeply, and thus were drawn by a magnetic power toward this blow of fate. By fully experiencing it, we have mastered and done away with the imperfection. That is something real and important. How superficial then is everyday judgment in creating a feeling of antipathy toward the misfortune. Here, rather, is the higher reality: Our soul goes forward from one life to another. How short is the time in which it can feel antipathy toward a blow of fate! When it looks out beyond the horizon of this incarnation, it feels one thing only to be necessary, to become ever more perfect. This feeling is stronger than any we have in our ordinary consciousness, which, when confronted by this blow of fate, would have slunk past it like a coward, would not have chosen the compensating necessity. But the deeper consciousness, of which we know nothing, does not do this. Instead, it seeks its destiny, and feels it as a process of growth toward perfection. It says, "I entered into this life. I was aware of an imperfection that has been in my soul since birth. If I would develop my soul, this imperfection must be remedied, but to do this I must go on to meet this misfortune. I must seek it out."

There we have the stronger element in the soul, compared to which the web of ordinary life, with all its sympathies and antipathies, is like a dream. In that realm of the beyond, we enter a life and feeling of which we can say, "It knows us better, it is stronger in us than our ordinary consciousness." Now we notice another thing. If we really have the experience just described, if we do not merely know it in theory but truly experience it, then of necessity we have another experience at the same time. While we feel we can already enter into those regions where everything is different from what it is in ordinary consciousness, a feeling arises in us: "I do not want to enter." This feeling is very deep. As a rule, the curiosity that impels people to enter the spiritual worlds is not nearly strong enough to overcome the feeling of revulsion that says, "I will not enter." The aversion we feel at this particular stage arises with tremendous force, and all sorts of misunderstandings about it are possible. Suppose that someone has even received personal instructions. He comes to his instructor and says, "I cannot get on at all, your instructions are of no use." Indeed he may honestly think so. If the instructor gave him the answer due him, however, he would not be able to understand it at all. This answer would have to be, "You can enter perfectly well, but you do not want to." Because his reluctance remains hidden in his subconsciousness, the pupil honestly believes he has the will to enter. Indeed, the moment one begins to realize this reluctance, one checks it. The idea that one does not want to enter is so horrifying that one immediately begins to damp down one's unwillingness. This reluctance is a subtle and insidious thing. We feel that we cannot enter with the ego, the self that we have acquired in this world. A person who wants to evolve to higher things feels very strongly that he or she must *leave this self behind*. That, however, is a difficult thing to do, because we would never have developed this self if we did not feel in our daily consciousness that we have this self in order to develop it here. Our ordinary ego has come into this world in order to evolve. Thus, when we want to enter the real world, we feel we must leave behind what we were able to evolve in the ordinary world. Then there is only one way. We must have developed this self more strongly than is required for ordinary consciousness. As a rule, we only develop it as far as needed for ordinary life.

Now, if you observe the second point in *How to Know Higher Worlds*, you will find that it amounts to this: that the self must be made stronger than is necessary for the purposes of daily life. Only then are we able to go out of our body at night and still retain something that we have not exhausted. It is only when we have fortified our ordinary self by our exercises, and have an excess of self-reliance in us, that we no longer want to shrink back from the higher worlds.

But then a new and considerable danger arises. We perhaps no longer bring the recollections of ordinary life into our dreams, but we bring something else—our expanded and strengthened self-consciousness. It would be as though we filled that realm with it. Anyone who carries through such exercises as given in my book, and thus comes to have inner soul experiences like Arjuna's, enters the realm of dream life with an expanded, strengthened self. The result is the same whether we have done a special training or were destined to expand the self at a definite period in our life. Arjuna is in this position. He stands at the boundary between the everyday world and that of dreams. He lives his way into that higher region because through his destiny he has a more powerful self in that realm than he needs for ordinary life.

I shall have to elaborate this point still further, showing that Arjuna has this more powerful consciousness, because now, as soon as he penetrates into that realm, Krishna at once receives him. Krishna lifts him out of the self he has acquired in ordinary life, and thus he becomes a different man from what he would have been if his expanded self had not met Krishna. In that case he would certainly have said to himself, "Blood relations are fighting against one another, events are taking place that must ruin the ancient holy caste distinctions and the service to our ancestors—events that must corrupt our womankind, and conditions that will prevent us from kindling the fires of sacrifice to our forefathers." All of this was part of Arjuna's everyday consciousness, from which his destiny tore him away. He would have had to stand on ground where he would have had to break with all these accustomed feelings connected with old traditions. He would have had to say to himself, "Away with all I hold sacred, with all the traditions that have been handed down to me. I will hurl myself into the battle."

But that is not what happens. Krishna appears, and what he says must appear to Arjuna as utmost unscrupulousness, as egoism driven beyond all bounds. The excess of force that Arjuna would otherwise have experienced, that he would have used to live through his own life, Krishna uses as a power whereby he makes himself visible to Arjuna. To make this thought still clearer, we may say that if Arjuna had simply met Krishna, even though the latter had actually come to him, he would have known nothing of him, just as we would know nothing of the sense world if we had not received something from the sense world itself that formed our senses for perceiving it. Similarly, Krishna must take from Arjuna his expanded and strengthened consciousness. He must, in a sense, remove Arjuna's self, so that with the help of what he has torn out he may show himself to Arjuna. Thus he makes from what he has torn out, so to speak, a mirror in which to show himself to Arjuna.

We have sought to explain what in Arjuna's consciousness enabled Krishna to meet him. This still leaves unexplained how Arjuna came to his higher consciousness in the first place. Nowhere do we see the statement that Arjuna had done esoteric exercises. In fact he had not done any. How then is he able to meet Krishna? What was it that gave Arjuna a higher and stronger self-consciousness? We shall start from this question in the next lecture.

4

Helsinki, May 31, 1913

W<small>E</small> have seen that if one would enter into the realm to which, among other things, the woven fabric of our dreams belongs, one must take from the ordinary world something we described as an intensified self-consciousness. There must be a stronger and fuller life in the ego than one needs for one's purposes on the physical plane. In our age this excess of self-consciousness is drawn forth from our soul by the experiences we gain through esoteric exercises such as I have given. Thus the first step consists in strengthening and intensifying one's inner self.

Human beings instinctively feel that they need this strengthening, and if they have not yet attained it, a kind of fear and shyness comes over them. They tend to shrink from the prospect of experiencing higher worlds. We must continually bear in mind that in the course of evolution, the human soul has passed through many different stages. Thus, in the period of the Bhagavad Gita, it was not yet possible for a human soul to intensify its self-consciousness by such esoteric exercises as may be practiced today. In that ancient time, however, something else was still present in the self, namely, primeval clairvoyance. This is also a faculty that humans do not really need for ordinary life on the physical plane, if we can be content with what our epoch offers us. But the people of that ancient time still had the remnants of primeval clairvoyance.

So we can look far back and put ourselves in the place of a person living at the time when the Bhagavad Gita originated. Such a person would express his or her experience this way: "When I look out into the world around me, I receive impressions through my senses. These impressions can be combined by the intellect, of which the brain is the organ. Apart from that, I still have another faculty, a clairvoyant power that enables me to acquire knowledge of other worlds. This power tells me that humanity belongs to other realms, that my human nature extends far beyond the ordinary physical world." This very power, by means of which there arises in the soul the instinctive knowledge that it belongs not only to the physical world, is actually a stronger kind of self-consciousness. It is as though these last remnants of ancient clairvoyance still had the power to surcharge the soul with selfhood. Nowadays, humans can again develop in themselves such surplus forces if they will undergo the right esoteric exercises.

Now, some objections may be made. You know that in anthroposophical lectures we must always forestall objections of which the true esotericist is well aware. Someone may ask: "Why should it occur to present day people to want to undertake esoteric exercises at all? Why shouldn't we be content with what our ordinary intellect offers us?" That, my friends, is a big question because it touches upon an actual fact for every thoughtful soul in the present cycle of evolution. If we did not reach out to anything more than what our senses and our brain-bound intellect can show us, we would certainly be content with our existence. We would observe the things and events around us, their relationships, and how they come into being and pass away again, but we would ask no questions about this ebb and flow of activity. We would be content with it as an animal may be content with its existence. In fact, if humans were really the beings that materialistic thinking considers us to be, we could quite well accept our life as such and ask no questions. This is the life of the animal, content with all that arises and passes before its senses. Why isn't this the case with us?

Remember that we are speaking of present day humanity, for even in ancient Greece the human soul was different in this respect from what it is today. When we today give ourselves with our whole soul to the study of natural science, or when we consider all the events of historical evolution and gain a knowledge of the external science of history—with all this, something else finds its way almost imperceptibly into our soul, something that has no purpose nor any sense for physical life. Many comparisons have been made to illustrate this fact. I would like to mention one of them, because people often make use of it without considering its deeper significance. A famous medical authority in the last third of the nineteenth century, wishing to enhance the honor of pure science, once drew attention to the Greek philosopher Pythagoras, who was asked: "What do you think of philosophers who spend their time speculating on the meaning and purpose of life? How does their occupation compare with the activities of ordinary men who pursue some useful calling and play a useful part in community life?" The philosopher replied, "Look at a fair or market; people come to buy and sell and everyone is busy, but there are a few among them who do not want to buy or sell but simply want to stroll about and watch what is going on." The philosopher implied that the market represented life, people busy in all sorts of ways, but the philosophers are not busy with such affairs. Instead, they look at what is happening and try to learn all about it.

Somehow a great respect for philosophers has penetrated deeply into the minds of an intellectual humanity precisely because philosophers do not obviously take part in any productive activity. The philosophers are honored just *because* their science is independent, detached, self-sufficient. Yet this comparison ought to give us food for thought, for it is by no means as banal as it might appear at first sight. After all, it is curious that philosophers should be compared to idlers in the marketplace of life, useless folk watching others labor. One might indeed think of it in this way, but we must realize that judgments are passed that originally are quite correct but become altogether wrong if they linger on for centuries, or as in this case for thousands of years. Therefore we ask again if these people who stroll about in life are really to be judged as idlers. That depends upon the standards by which we value human life. Certainly there are those who regard the philosophers as useless loiterers and think they would do better to perform some productive work. From their point of view they may be quite right, but when we today observe life through the senses and consider it by means of the brain-bound intellect, something steals into the soul that obviously has no connection with the outer world of the senses. That is the point.

This can be seen clearly in books that try to construct a satisfactory picture of the world and life on a purely materialistic basis. It usually turns out that the big questions do not arise until the end. The books claiming to solve the riddles of the universe actually only begin to set forth those riddles in their concluding pages. In effect, when one begins today to study the external world that is the subject treated in such books, the thought slips in that either humans exist for other worlds besides this world, or else the physical world deceives us and makes fools of us because it is continually raising questions for which we have no answer.

If life really ends with death, if humans have no part in and no connection with a higher world, an enormous part of our soul life is meaningless. Indeed, it is not the longing for something we do not have, but the lack of understanding what we do have that impels us to follow up these questions and ask what it is that comes into the soul that does not belong to this world of the senses. Thus we are driven to cultivate something which is evidently without foundation in the external world. We are impelled to take up esoteric exercises. We would not say humankind has an inward longing for immortality and therefore invents the idea of it, but rather that the external world has implanted in our soul something that would be meaningless, unreal, if the whole of our existence were limited to the time between birth and death. Human beings are impelled to ask the nature of something they have, not of something they do not have.

In fact, present day humans are no longer quite in the position of mere loiterers or onlookers, so they cannot appeal now to the Greek philosopher. In those times, the comparison held good, but today it does not. Today, we might say that buyers and sellers come and go. When at length they close the market and make up accounts, they find something that certainly could neither have been bought nor sold, nor can they discover whence it came. That never happens in an ordinary market, but so it is in the market of life. (Every comparison has its flaw, and this one is all the better for it.) As we go on living, we are continually finding things that life opens to view, yet no explanation for them is to be found in the world of sense. That is the deeper reason for why there are people in the world today who despair of life, yet at the same time have vague, unrecognized longings. Something is active in them that does not belong to the physical world, but keeps on putting forth questions about other worlds. For this reason, we now have to acquire a *spiritual* culture. Otherwise we shall be overcome by hopelessness and despair.

What we now must acquire, someone like Arjuna possessed simply because he lived in the ancient age of primeval clairvoyance. Yet it also was a period of transition, because he belonged to that time in evolution when only the last remnants and echoes of that clairvoyance remained. If we are to understand the Bhagavad Gita, it is important to realize that at the time of its appearance, humans were entering an age in which this old clairvoyance gradually became lost. In this lies the deep undercurrent of that sublime poem; or we may say, the source of the breath poured out through it. For this song resounds with tones of a great turning point in time, when, from the twilight of the old clairvoyance, a night was to begin in which a new force could be born to humankind. Only in that night could a force be born that the soul of today possesses, but which souls of that time did not yet possess. About Arjuna, then, we can say that ancient clairvoyance is still present in his soul, but it is flickering out. It is no longer a strong, spontaneous force. Rather, it requires a harrowing experience such as I have described to reawaken it. What then can Arjuna perceive through this awakening of the ancient power of vision, which at other times was dying away within him? He sees the spiritual being called Krishna.

Here it is necessary to point out that though humans may lift their souls today into that realm where dreams are woven, this is no longer enough to give a full understanding of Krishna's being. Even if we develop the forces enabling us to consciously pass into the region of dream consciousness, we still are unable today to fully discover what Krishna is. Referring again to what I said yesterday, let us call our everyday consciousness the lowest realm. Above it lies a realm of which we are unconscious in daily life, or rather a world that becomes conscious only in a kind of illusory image as maya or dream consciousness. But when we, so to speak, wipe out the dreams, erase the maya, then impressions from another world enter this region of human consciousness.

Into all the experiences we have of our physical environment, something now enters that is like a kind of overflow in the soul and really belongs to *other* worlds, to inner supersensible worlds. Now we have an experience that cannot be described as a reminiscence of ordinary life. The world now has a different aspect from anything known on the physical plane. We discover that we are *seeing* something we do not see in the ordinary world. Though we often imagine that we see light, in reality it is not so. On the physical plane, we never see light, only color and different shades of color, darker and lighter colors. We see the effects of light, but light itself speeds invisibly through space. We can easily convince ourselves of this fact. When a ray of light strikes through the window, we see a kind of streak of light rays in the room, caused by dust in the air. We see reflections of light from the glittering particles of dust, the light itself remaining invisible.

After lifting our experience to the higher realm we have spoken of, we really do begin to see the light itself. There we are surrounded by flowing light, just as in the physical world we live in flowing air. Only we do not enter this world with a physical body. We have no need to breathe there. One enters that world with the part of one's being that needs light, as in the physical world one's body needs air. In this region light is the element of life—light-air, we might call it—and it is a necessity for existence.

Further, that light is permeated and transfused with something not unlike the cloud forms shaping and reshaping in our atmosphere. The clouds are water, but up there what meets us like floating forms is nothing other than the weaving life of *sound*, the music of the spheres. Still further we shall perceive the flowing of *life* itself. Thus we may begin to describe the world into which our souls enter, but the terms of our description must remain meaningless for the physical world. Perhaps those who use words most lacking in meaning for the physical world will best describe that other world that has a far higher reality.

Of course, our materialistically minded friends will find it easy to object to these ideas. Their arguments against what the esotericist has to say are plausible enough. The esotericist knows how easily such objections are made, for the very reason that the higher worlds are best described by words not suitable for things of the physical plane. For example, the esotericist would speak of light-air, or air-light. On the physical plane, there is no such thing, but over there, there is. Indeed, when we penetrate into that realm, we also discover what it is to be deprived of this life element, to have insufficient light-air. We feel a pain of suffocation in our soul comparable to losing our breath for lack of air on the physical plane. There we also find the opposite condition, a fullness of pure, holy light-air in which we can live and perceive spiritual beings that live there, too, manifesting themselves in full clearness. Those are the beings that stand under Lucifer's guidance. The moment we enter that realm without sufficient preparation, without proper training, Lucifer gains the power to deprive us of the light-air we need. We can say that he suffocates our souls.

The effect is not quite the same as suffocation on the physical plane. But, like a polar bear transported south, we thirst and long for something that can reach us from the spiritual treasure, the spiritual light of the physical plane. That is just what Lucifer desires, for then we do not pay attention to all that comes from the upper hierarchies, but thirstily cleave to all that Lucifer has brought onto the physical plane. This is what happens if we have insufficiently trained ourselves in preparation. Then when we stand before Lucifer, he takes the light-air away from us. We crave breath, and long for the spiritual that comes from the physical plane.

Let us suppose that a person goes through a training that brings him far enough to enter the higher worlds, to reach this upper region. But suppose he has not done all that belongs to the training. Suppose he has forgotten that with all his exercises he must at the same time be ennobling his moral sense, his moral feelings. Suppose that he must let go of all earthly ambitions and all lust for power in his soul. Indeed, one can reach the higher worlds even if he is vain and ambitious, but he takes these qualities with him. When a person has not purified his moral feelings, Lucifer takes the light-air away from him, so that he perceives nothing of what is really there, and instead he longs for things on the physical plane. He breathes in, so to speak, what he has been able to perceive on the physical plane. So he may *imagine* that he perceives something only to be seen spiritually in the light-air. He imagines that he sees the different incarnations of various human beings. But it is not so. He does *not* see them, because he lacks the air-light. Instead, like a thirsty being, he sucks up into that realm things of the physical plane below, and describes all manner of things acquired there as though they were processes in the higher region. There is no more harmful way of raising one's soul into the higher worlds than by means of vain and earthly love of power! If one does this, one will forever remain unable to bring down true results of cognition. What one brings will be mere reflections, a phantom picture of the speculations and conjectures one may have made in the physical world.

We have been describing what might be called the general scenery of that realm. There are also beings we meet there, whom we may call elemental beings. In the physical world, we often speak of forces of nature. In that higher realm, these forces manifest themselves as real beings. There we make a definite discovery. Through the actual facts that meet us, we discover that whereas on the physical plane good and evil exist together, in that higher realm there are separate, specific forces of good and evil. Here in the physical world, good and evil are combined and interwoven in each human soul. One has more of a tendency to good, another less. In that realm, there are evil beings who exist to battle against the work of good beings. Consequently, on entering that realm, we already have occasion to make use of the strengthened self-consciousness we mentioned yesterday. We have need of the more acute power of judgment that must come with our enhanced self. Then we may really be in a position to say that here in the higher realm, there must be beings who have the mission of evil. Such beings have to exist alongside those who have the mission of good.

We often hear it asked, "Why didn't the all wise God of the universe simply create the good alone? Why isn't it everywhere, always?" Now we gain this conviction, however, that if only the good were present, the world would become one-sided; it would not bring forth all the fullness of life that it does yield. The good must have something to oppose it. This, in fact, can already be realized on the physical plane, but in that higher realm we perceive it with far greater force. There we see that only people who are content with a merely sentimental and dreamy outlook can imagine that good beings alone could bring about the purposes of the universe. In the realm of everyday life we might do with sentimentality, but we cannot tolerate it when we enter the stern realities of the supersensible world. There we know that the good beings alone could not have made the world. They would be too weak to mold this universe. In the totality of evolution, those forces must be included which come from the evil beings. There is great wisdom in this fact that evil is mingled in cosmic evolution. Thus, we have to get rid of sentimentality when we enter spiritual life. Bravely and unflinchingly, we must approach the dangerous truths that dawn upon us when we perceive the battle that is fought in just this realm— the battle between the good and evil beings that can there be revealed to us. All these are experiences we have when we have trained and adapted our souls to enter consciously into this realm.

So far we have only entered the realm of dreams. We human beings live in still another realm, one for which we are so little adapted in ordinary life that we generally have no perceptions whatsoever of it. It is the realm through which we live in dreamless sleep. Here an absolute paradox appears, for sleep, after all, is characterized by the complete cessation of consciousness. In normal human life today, people cease to be conscious when they fall asleep, and they do not regain consciousness until they wake up again. In the age of primeval clairvoyance, this realm too was something the soul could experience. If we go back into those ancient periods of evolution, however, there was actually a condition of life corresponding to our sleep in which people could perceive in a still higher, still more spiritual world than the world of dreams. This was true even in early post-Atlantean times. There we find conditions that, in regard to the usual human processes, are exactly like the condition of sleep, but are not, because they are permeated by consciousness. When we have reached this height we do not see the physical world, even though we still see the world of light air, of sound, of cosmic harmony, and of the battle between the good and evil beings. The world we see may be said to be still more fundamentally different [than what I have described so far] from all that exists in the physical world. So it is yet more difficult to describe than the world we find on entering the region of dream consciousness. I would like now to give you an idea of how one's consciousness in this realm works, and of its actual effects.

Anyone who describes that sublime world into which our dreams find their way, and about which I have given the merest hint, will be labeled a fantastic visionary by the prejudiced intellectualism of today. If anyone begins to speak of that still higher realm through which the human being ordinarily sleeps, then people, if they take any notice at all, will not stop at abusing that person as a visionary. They altogether lose their heads. We have already had an example of this. When my books were first published in Germany, the critics, who are supposed to represent the intellectual culture of today, attacked them with all sorts of insinuations. In one point, however, their criticism ran absolutely wild. In fact, they became foolish in their fury to the point where I had to call attention to something that could only originate in the spiritual realm we are now considering. This was the question of the two Jesus children mentioned in my book *The Spiritual Guidance of the Individual and Humanity.*[48]

For those of our friends who have not heard of this, I may say once more that it appeared as a result of esoteric research, namely, that at the beginning of our era not one but two Jesus children were born. One was descended from the so called Nathan line of the House of David, the other from the Solomon line. These two children grew up side by side. In the body of the Solomon child lived the soul of Zarathustra. In the twelfth year of the child's life this soul passed over into the other Jesus child and lived in that body until its thirtieth year. Here we have a matter of the deepest significance. Zarathustra's soul went on living in the body that, until its twelfth year, had been occupied by a mysterious soul. And then, only from the thirtieth year onward, there lived in this body the being whom we call the Christ, who remained on Earth altogether for three years.

---

48. Hudson, NY: Anthroposophic Press, 1992, pp. 63–67; see also Robert McDermott, "Rudolf Steiner's Ten Lectures on the Gospel of Luke: A Descriptive Outline," Rudolf Steiner, *According to Luke* (Great Barrington, MA: SteinerBooks, 2001), pp. 232–38.

We really cannot take amiss the critics' reaction to this statement. It is natural that they should want to have something to say about the matter from their scholarly viewpoint. But what they set out to criticize comes from a realm in which they are always fast asleep! So we cannot expect them to know anything about it. Yet a healthy human understanding is able to grasp this fact. When people do not give themselves a chance to understand, in their haste they change their power of understanding into bitterness and fury.

Such truths as these about the two Jesus children, which are to be found in this higher realm, never have anything to do with sympathy and antipathy. We *find* such truths; we never experience them in the way we gain experience in the usual manner of knowledge in the physical world, or even in the realm of dream life. In both these areas *we are there*, so to speak. We are present at the origin of our knowing or perception. This is true also of those esotericists who are conscious only as far as the realm of dreams. We can say that a person witnesses the birth of his or her knowledge, of his or her perceptions, in that realm, but truths like this concerning the two Jesus children can never be found in this way. When truths come to us in that higher realm and enter our consciousness, the moment in which we actually acquired them has long since passed. We experienced them long before we met them with our full consciousness, as we have to do in our time. We have them already in us, so that when we reach these truths—the most important, the most living and essential of all truths—we distinctly have the feeling that when we gained them we were in an earlier time than the present, that we are now drawing out of the depths of our soul what we acquired in an earlier time and are bringing it into our consciousness. Such truths we *discover in ourselves*, just as in the outer world we come across a flower or any other object. Even as in the outer world we can think about an object that is simply there before us, so can we think about these truths in this way when we have discovered them in ourselves, in our own self.

In the outer world we can only judge an object after we have perceived it. In the same way we find those sublime truths *objectively in ourselves*, and only then do we study them in ourselves. We inwardly investigate them as we would investigate the external facts of nature.

Just as it would have no meaning to ask of a flower whether it is true or false, there would be no sense in asking of these truths that we simply come upon in ourselves, whether they are true or false. Truth and falsehood only come into the picture when it is a question of our power to describe what we find or what arises in our consciousness. *Descriptions can be true or false.* Truth and falsehood do not concern the facts; they concern the manner in which any thinking being approaches or deals with those facts. When we do research and get results in this realm, we are really looking into a region of the soul we have lived in before but did not look there consciously.

In carrying on our esoteric exercises we are best able to enter this realm if we pay positive attention to those moments when from the depths of our soul arise not mere judgments, but facts—facts that we know we did not consciously take part in originating. The more we are able to wonder at the things there unveiled, as with the objective things of the outer world, the more astonishing it all is for us, and the better we are prepared to enter into this realm. So, as a general rule, we do not make a good entrance if we have all sorts of conjectures and constructions in our minds. For example, there is no better way of finding nothing at all about the previous incarnations of some person than to speculate as to who they might have been earlier. Let us say you wanted to investigate the earlier incarnations of Robespierre. The best way of finding out nothing at all about him would be to search about for historical personalities you think might possibly have been his previous incarnations. In that way you never can discover the truth. You must get out of the habit of making conjectures and theories, and forming opinions.

Those who would become true esotericists should set themselves to making as few judgments as possible about the world. In that way they will most quickly attain the condition in which the facts can meet them. The more you cultivate silence in your conjectures and opinions, the more your soul will be filled with the actual truths of the spiritual world. Someone, for example, who had grown up with a particular religious bias, with definite feelings and ideas or perhaps views about the Christ—such a person, in general, would not be the most adapted to discover a truth like the history of the two Jesus children. Only when one feels a little bit neutral about the Christ event is one well prepared for such a discovery, provided of course one has made all the other necessary preparations. People with a Buddhist bias will least be able to talk sense about Buddha, just as those with a Christian bias will least be able to talk sense about Christ. This is always true.

If we would enter the third realm just described, it is necessary that we go through all the bitterness—for in ordinary life we cannot help feeling this way—of becoming, so to say, a twofold person. We are, in fact, twofold beings in ordinary life, even if we make no conscious use of half of our existence, for we are both waking and sleeping beings. Different as these two conditions are, so is that third realm in the higher worlds different from this physical world. That realm has a peculiar existence of its own. There, also, we are surrounded by a world, but one so altogether new and different that we get to know it best if we extinguish not only the sense impressions of this world of ours but even our feelings and sentiments and all the things that have the power to arouse our passions and enthusiasms. In ordinary life, one is so little fitted for conscious experience of that higher world that one's consciousness is extinguished every night. One can only attain experience there if one can become a twofold person. Those who have the power at will to forget and to blot out all their interests in this physical world are then able to enter that higher realm. The world between—that is to say, where our dreams are woven—is made of the materials of both worlds. It is penetrated by reflections of the higher worlds of which we are generally not aware, and by reminiscences of ordinary consciousness. That is why no one can perceive the true causes of events in the physical world who is not able to penetrate with understanding into that third realm.

Now, if people today wish to discover through their own experience who Krishna is, they can only make that discovery in the third realm. Arjuna's impressions, which in the sublime Gita are described to us through the words of Krishna, have their origin in that world. For this reason, I have had to prepare the way today by speaking of humanity's ascent into the third realm. Only through this knowledge will you be able to understand the origin of the strange and wondrous truths that Krishna speaks to Arjuna—truths that sound so altogether different from anything that is spoken in ordinary life.

These lectures are to help us gain knowledge of Krishna, that is to say, of the very essence of the Bhagavad Gita. Also, the esoteric principles of this wonderful Song are to give you something that, if you really make use of it, can enable you to find your way into the higher worlds, because the way is open to every human being. We have only to realize that the grain of gold with which we must begin is ours, once we become aware of the many ways in which the highest spiritual beings live and work and are interwoven in our everyday life.

5

HELSINKI, JUNE 1, 1913

If we wish to penetrate into the mysteries of human life, we must fix our attention on a great law of existence: what is called the cyclic law. As a rule, it is better to characterize and describe than to define. In this case, also, I prefer not to use a definition of what is meant here by the cyclical course of life, for by comparison with actual reality, definitions must always appear insubstantial. A Greek philosophical school wishing to gain insight into the nature of definitions once set out to give a definition of the human being. As you know, definitions are intended to provide concepts corresponding to experienced phenomena, but those who have logical insight cannot help feeling the poverty and unfruitfulness of this process. The members of the Greek school eventually agreed to define the human being as a featherless biped.[49] While this particular definition sounds rather like a silly epigram, it does represent human nature in certain respects. The next day, one of the members of this school brought in a plucked hen and said to the company, "According to your definition this is

---

49. In an effort to formulate an adequate definition of the human being, Plato dialogically defined man as a featherless biped animal; subsequently, Diogenes the Cynic presented a plucked chicken with the remark, "here is Plato's human being."

a human being"—a silly way to show the unreality of attempts to define things. Being concerned with realities, we will proceed then to describe things in their essential characteristics.

To begin, we will consider a cycle familiar in everyday life, that of our waking and sleeping. What does it really signify? We can only understand the nature of sleep if we realize that in the present epoch the soul activity of human waking life brings about a continual destruction of delicate structures in the nervous system. With our every thought and every impulse of will arising in us under the stimulus of the outside world, we are destroying delicate forms in our brain. In the near future, it will more and more be realized how sleep must supplement our waking day-life. We are approaching the point where natural science will join with spiritual science in these matters. Natural science has already produced more than one theory to the effect that our waking life operates in a kind of destructive way in the nerves and brain. Owing to this fact, we have to allow the corresponding reverse process—the compensation—to take place during sleep.

While we are asleep, forces of which we remain unconscious are at work in us that do not otherwise manifest themselves. They are busy reconstructing the finer nerve structures of our brain. Now, it is this very destruction that enables us to have processes of thought, and to acquire knowledge. Ordinary knowledge would not be possible if processes of disintegration did not take place in us during our waking hours. Two opposite processes are at work in our nervous system— while we are awake a process of destruction, and during sleep a repairing process. Since it is to the destructive process that we owe our consciousness, it is that process we perceive. Our waking life consists in perceiving disintegrating processes. When we sleep, we are not conscious because no destructive process is at work in us. The force that at other times creates our consciousness is used up in constructive work when we sleep. There you have a cycle.

Let us now consider what happens during sleep. Because of this alternating cycle of buildup and breakdown processes we see why it is so dangerous to health to go without proper sleep. Certainly human life is so arranged that the danger is not immediately apparent, because what is present in us at any one time has been built up for a considerable time before. Abnormal processes cannot affect our nature as deeply as we might imagine. We could expect people who suffer from sleeplessness to go to pieces quickly, but they do not. The reason for this is the same as that which holds for people both blind and deaf, like the famous Helen Keller, whose intellect could nevertheless be developed. In the present age, this should theoretically be impossible, for what constitutes the greater part of our intelligence enters the brain through eyes and ears. The reason for Miss Keller's intellectual development is that, though the portals of her senses are closed, she has inherited a brain that has the potential for development. If humans were not hereditary beings, a case like hers would be impossible. Which is to say, if humans did not have a much healthier brain through heredity than we generally give them credit for, sleeplessness would in a very short time completely undermine health. But most people have so much inherited strength that insomnia can persist for a long time without seriously injuring them. Nevertheless, the cycle of construction takes place, with its resulting unconsciousness in sleep, and destruction accompanying consciousness in waking life.

In the totality of human life, we perceive not only these smaller cycles but larger ones as well. Here I will call your attention to a cycle I have often mentioned before. Anyone who follows the course of life in the Western world will observe a quite definite configuration of the spiritual life of humankind in the period from the fourteenth, fifteenth, and sixteenth centuries to the last third of the nineteenth. In ordinary life, these developments are observed vaguely and even inaccurately, but if we examine them in sufficient depth we shall see how, since the last third of the nineteenth century, there have been in all directions signs of an altogether different form of Western spiritual life. Of course, we are at the beginning of this new trend, so people do not notice it in its full significance. Just imagine someone trying to speak before an audience such as this, for instance in the 1840s or '50s, about the same things I am putting before you here. It is unthinkable, absurd. It would have been out of the question to speak of these things as we do now, at any time from the fourteenth century to the last third of the nineteenth. This was the period when the natural scientific mode of thought, the way of thinking that produced the great materialistic achievements, reached its height. The stragglers of scientific intellectualism will go on adhering to it for some time to come, but the actual epoch of materialism is past.

Just as the era of scientific thought began around the fifteenth century, so the era of spiritual thought is now beginning. These two sharply differentiated epochs meet in the very time in which we are living. It will become more and more evident that the new mode of thought must get in touch with the reality of things. Thought will become very different from the thought of the last four centuries, though the latter had to be so in its time. During this period, humanity's gaze had to be directed outward into the far spaces of the universe. I have often spoken of the great significance for Western spiritual evolution of the moment when Copernicus,[50] Galileo,[51] Kepler,[52] and Giordano Bruno[53] together burst open the blue vault of heaven. Until their time, it was believed that the blue cup of the heavens was suspended over our Earth. These great thinkers declared that this hollow cup did not really exist. They taught humankind to look out into the infinite distances of cosmic space.

Now, what was it that was so significant about Bruno's deed in explaining to humanity how the blue sphere they had set as the boundary of their power of sight was not really there, and that "You have only to realize that it is you yourselves who project it out into space"? It marked the beginning of an epoch that came to an end with the discovery that the spectroscope allowed one to investigate the material composition of the farthest heavenly bodies. A marvelous epoch, this epoch of materialism! Now we are at the starting point of another epoch, one that, though it has its origin in the same laws of growth as the preceding one, will be be the epoch of spirituality. Just as the epoch of natural science was prepared by Bruno's work in

---

50. 1473–1543.
51. 1564–1642.
52. 1571–1630.
53. 1548–1600.

breaking through the limits of space, so will the firmament of *time* be broken through in the age now beginning. Humankind, imagining life to be enclosed between birth and death, or conception and death, will learn that these are merely boundaries set by the human soul itself. Just as in earlier times, humans had set as the boundary of their senses a blue sphere above them, and then suddenly their vision expanded into the infinite spheres of space, so will the boundaries of time, of birth and death, be broken through. Set free of these, there will lie before our gaze in the infinite sea of time all the changes in the kernel of the human being as we follow it through its repeated incarnations. Thus a new age is beginning, the age of spiritual thought.

Now, if we can recognize the esoteric basis of these transitions from one age to another, where shall we see the cause of this change in human thought? It is not anything that philosophy or external physiology or anatomy can detect on its own. Yet forces have entered the active human soul and are being used today to gather spiritual knowledge—the same forces that have been working during the last four centuries as constructive energies in the human organism. These mysterious forces worked, just as constructive forces work in the nervous system during sleep, throughout the period from Copernicus to the last third of the nineteenth century. These forces were building up a definite structure in certain parts of the brain. The brains of Westerners are different from what they were five centuries ago. What is under our skulls today does not have the same appearance as it had then. Even though this cannot be proved externally, under the human forehead a delicate organ has developed, and the forces building it have now fulfilled their task. In the next cycle of history now approaching it will become evident in more and more people. Now that it is there, the forces that built it are liberated, and Western humanity can use them to gain spiritual knowledge. Here we have the esoteric physiological foundation of the matter. Already we are beginning to work with the forces that humans could not use during the last four hundred years, because they were spent in building up the organ needed to allow spiritual knowledge to take its place in the world.

Let us imagine a man of the seventeenth or eighteenth century. As he stands there before us, we know that certain esoteric forces are at work behind his forehead, transforming his brain. These forces were perpetually at work in all the people of the West. Now let us assume that this man had managed to suspend these forces for a moment, made them cease their work. The same thing would have happened to him—and it did happen in certain cases—as takes place when in the middle of sleep one suspends the forces that ordinarily work at building up the nerve structures of the brain, and lets them run loose. It is possible to experience moments when we seem to awaken in sleep, and yet do not awaken; for we remain motionless, we cannot move our limbs, we have no external perception. But we are awake. In the moments of free play of those regenerating forces we can use them for clairvoyant vision; we can see into the spiritual worlds. A similar thing happened if a man two hundred years ago suspended the constructive activity of his brain. He allowed these forces to remain inactive for a moment, and became briefly clairvoyant. What did he see? What did he perceive? He saw the forces working into the brain from the spiritual world, the forces that were preparing human beings from around the fifteenth century to the nineteenth century, so that from the twentieth century onward humans might rise to spiritual vision. There were always isolated individuals who had such experiences— experiences of truly momentous force, indescribably impressive. There were always people who for brief moments lived in the supersensible forces working to bring forth in the sense world what did not exist in former cycles of evolution: the finer organ in the frontal cavity. Such individuals saw the gods. They saw spiritual beings at work in the building process of the human organism.

In this, we see clairvoyance described from a fresh aspect. We can bring about such moments during sleep by practicing the exercises I have given in my book *How to Know Higher Worlds*, and thereby gain glimpses of spiritual life such as are described in my book *A Way of Self-Knowledge*. It is possible during a given cycle of evolution for the forces at work preparing the future to become free for a moment and become clairvoyantly visible.

We may also call it by another name, and designate as the forces of Gabriel these forces working at the subtle reconstruction of the human brain structure. We say "Gabriel," but the point is to gain a brief insight into the supersensible, where we perceive a spiritual being working from those worlds into the human organism. We perceive a sum of forces, in fact, directed by a being, Gabriel, of the hierarchy of the archangeloi. From the fifteenth century to the last third of the nineteenth century, the Gabrielic force was at work on the human physical organism, and because of this, the power to understand the spiritual world was dormant for a while. It was this dormancy of spiritual understanding that brought forth the great triumphs of natural science. Now this force has reawakened. The spirit has done its work; we stand at the beginning of a spiritual age; the Gabrielic forces have been liberated. We can now use them, for they have become forces for the soul.

Here we have a cycle of somewhat greater significance than that of waking and sleeping. There are, however, even mightier cycles in human evolution. We may note how self-consciousness, the pride of humankind in this era of our post-Atlantean age, was not always there but had to be developed gradually. Today the word *evolution* is often heard, but people seldom take it in real earnest.

Occasionally very curious experiences show how naive people can be in regard to the world surrounding them. For in their naiveté, people allow all kinds of things to emerge from the subconscious, but find it hard to resolve to really attribute a supersensible origin to what enters their known world from the unknown. In the last few days, I have again come across a curious instance of this logic that stops halfway. We can well understand why the anthroposophical outlook meets with so much resistance when we bear in mind that it takes a particular habit of thought to understand Anthroposophy, namely, the habit of never stopping halfway along any line of thinking. I have here a *Freethinker's Calendar*, published in Germany. The first edition came out last year. In it, a perfectly sincere person attacks the custom of teaching children religious ideas. He points out that this is contrary to the child's nature, since he himself has observed that when children are allowed to grow up on their own, they develop no religious ideas. It is therefore unnatural to inculcate these ideas into children. Now, we can be certain that this calendar will reach hundreds of people who will henceforth imagine that they understand how senseless it is to teach children religion. There are many such arguments today, and people never notice their complete lack of logic. In reply we need only ask, "If children for some reason have lived all their lives on an island alone and have not learned to speak, ought we therefore to refrain from teaching them to speak?" That would be the same kind of logic. Of course, people will not admit it is the same since they found it so profound in the first instance. It is curious to observe on the broad horizon of external life today things that represent some aftereffect of the passing materialist age.

I have yet another example: some remarkable essays recently published by Woodrow Wilson, President of the United States of America. There is one on the laws of human progress. He points out that people are influenced by the dominant thought of their age, so that, for example, in Newton's time, when everything was permeated with the idea of gravity, the effects of Newton's theories could be felt in social concepts, even in political terminology, though actually these theories are only applicable to the heavenly bodies. The idea of gravity was especially influential. All this is true. We need only read the literature of Newton's time to find everywhere words like "attraction" and "repulsion." Wilson develops this point very ingeniously. He says how unsatisfactory it is to apply purely mechanical concepts, as of celestial mechanism, to human life and conditions. He shows how these ideas were completely imbedded in human life at that time, and how widely they influenced political and social affairs. He rightly denounces this application of purely mechanical laws in an age when Newtonism drew all thought under its yoke. "We must think along different lines," says Wilson, and then he proceeds to construct his own concept of the state. Now, the way he does it is that after all he has said about Newtonism, he himself allows Darwinism to speak through every page of his writing. In fact, he is naïve enough to admit it. He says the Newtonian concepts were insufficient; we must apply the Darwinian laws of the organism. Here we have a living instance of the way people march through the world today with half-baked logic, because in reality the laws derived purely from the living organism are *also* insufficient. We need laws of the soul and spirit. Thus, we understand how objections are piled up against anthroposophical thought, for it requires an all-pervading thinking, a logic that penetrates to the core and does not stop halfway. This is just the virtue of the anthroposophical outlook. It forces its followers to think in an orderly manner.

So we must think of evolution in the spiritual sense, not in Wilson's Darwinian sense. We must bear in mind that the self-consciousness that is the essential characteristic of today's humanity, this firm rooting in the ego, has only gradually developed. It too needed to be prepared, just as our spiritual thinking was being prepared in the last four centuries. Spiritual forces had to work down from the supersensible worlds in order to develop what later found expression in the self-conscious life of humans. In this connection, we can speak of a break in evolution, with a preceding and a succeeding epoch. We will call the latter the age of self-consciousness.[54]

This period[55] is preceded in the cyclic interchange by one[56] in which the organ of self-consciousness was being built into the human being from the supersensible worlds. What now works as a soul force in self-consciousness was then working unrecognizably in the depths of human nature. The junction of these two great epochs is an important point in evolution. Before this time, most people had no self-consciousness at all. Even in the most advanced, it was comparatively weak. People then did not think as they do today, with the awareness, "I am thinking this thought." Their thoughts rose up like living dreams. Nor did their impulses of will and feeling enter their consciousness as they do today. They lived more of an instinctive life in their souls. From the spiritual worlds, however, beings were working into the human organism, preparing it for a later time when it would be capable of self-consciousness. Meanwhile, people had to live quite differently then, even as external experience is quite

---

54. In many of his books and lectures Steiner gives the dates of these ages, each approximately 2100 years, as follows: sentient soul age, third millennium to mid-eighth century B.C.E.; intellectual soul age, mid-eighth century to 1413; consciousness soul age, 1413 to the mid-fourth millennium.
55. The consciousness soul age.
56. The intellectual soul age.

different between the fifteenth and twentieth centuries C.E. from what it will become later on. So we must say that until the period when self-consciousness entered the human soul, everything that could prepare the way for it had been flowing into human life.

Now let us imagine that toward the end of that ancient epoch a mighty shock in one man's life suddenly cut off all that was binding him to the forces I just described, the forces of an earlier epoch, suspending their action for a moment. He would have experienced what we experience when in sleep we temporarily withdraw from the constructive forces and become clairvoyant—what an eighteenth-century person would have experienced in suspending the forces then at work on his or her brain structure. If in that ancient time, one withheld one's understanding and feeling for the sacrificial fires and reverence for the ancestors, one could for a moment use the forces normally used by understanding and gaze into the supersensible worlds. One could then see how human self-consciousness was being prepared from the spiritual world. This is what Arjuna did when at the moment of battle he experienced such a shock. The usually constructive forces stood still in him, and he could look upward to the divine being preparing the way for self-consciousness. This divinity was Krishna.

In the region where self-consciousness first made its appearance, people were strictly divided into castes. They respected this division. Those born in lower castes felt it as their highest endeavor to order their lives within their castes so that in later incarnations they might raise themselves to higher ones. It was a mighty driving force in the evolution of the human soul. People knew that by developing their soul forces they were making themselves fit to rise for their next life in a higher caste. So too they looked up to their ancestors, seeing in them something that is not bound to one particular body. People honored the ancestors because they had died, leaving behind the Manes, the spiritual quality working after death from the higher spheres. Seeing in the cult of the ancestors something that is already present in us, unbound to the physical body—the self-conscious soul that goes through the gates of death into the spiritual world—was good preparation for the great goal of human nature. For four hundred years, the best education in spirituality had been one that forced humans to think in natural-scientific terms. Similarly, in ancient times, instillation of the respect for caste was a wonderful preparation for the development of self-consciousness. Each person stood within a caste and developed a very special connection to the caste system. The pious reverence for ancestors and caste was an extraordinarily active force, working deep into human life. Spiritual beings were at work, preparing for a future when a person would be able to feel with every thought, "*I* think," with every feeling, "*I* feel," with every impulse of will, "*I* will."

Krishna, then, is that being who has worked through centuries—from the seventh and eighth centuries B.C.E. onward—on the human organism, to make humans capable of gradually entering the epoch of self-consciousness. What kind of impression does he make, this master builder of the human ego-nature? He must speak to Arjuna in words saturated through and through with self-consciousness.

Thus, from another side, we understand Krishna as the divine architect of what prepared and brought about self-consciousness in humanity. The Bhagavad Gita tells us how, in particular circumstances, a man could come into the presence of this divine builder of his nature. There we have one aspect of Krishna's nature. In the succeeding lectures we shall learn to know yet another aspect.

6

HELSINKI, JUNE 2, 1913

It really is exceedingly difficult in our Western civilization to speak intelligently and intelligibly about such a work as the Bhagavad Gita. This is because the currently dominant tendency is to interpret any spiritual work of this kind as a kind of doctrine, an abstract teaching or a philosophy, which makes it hard for people to come to a sound judgment in such matters. They like to approach such spiritual creations from the ideal or conceptual point of view. Here we touch upon something that makes it most difficult in our time to gain a true judgment about the great historical impulses in human evolution. How often, for instance, do people point out that this or that saying occurring in the gospels as the teaching of Christ can be found in some earlier work no less profoundly expressed? Then they say, "You see, it is the same teaching after all." Certainly, that is not incorrect, because in countless instances it can be shown that the teachings of the gospels occur in earlier spiritual works. Yet, while the statement is not incorrect, it may be nonsense from the standpoint of a truly fundamental knowledge of human evolution. People's thinking will have to get accustomed to this and realize that a statement can be perfectly correct and yet nonsense. Until we stop seeing this as a contradiction in terms, we will remain unable to judge certain matters in a truly unbiased way.

For instance, one could call the Bhagavad Gita one of the greatest creations of the human spirit, a creation that has not been surpassed in later times. If one were to add that what entered the world with the revelation inherent in the Christ impulse is something altogether different, something to which the Bhagavad Gita could not attain even if its beauty and greatness were increased a hundred times, these two statements do not contradict each other. They may seem to do so according to the habits of modern abstract thinking, yet in no sense is it truly a contradiction. Indeed, one might go further, and ask, "When was that mightiest word spoken that may be regarded as giving the impulse to the human ego, so that it may take its place in the evolution of humankind?" That significant word was uttered at the moment Krishna spoke to Arjuna, when he poured into Arjuna's ears the most powerful, incisive, burning words to quicken the consciousness of self in humanity. In the whole history of human life we cannot find anything that kindled the human self more mightily than the living force of Krishna's words to Arjuna. Of course, we must not take those words in the way words are so often taken in Western countries, where the noblest words are given merely abstract, philo-sophic interpretations. Any such interpretation would certainly miss the essence of the Bhagavad Gita. In this way Western scholars today have outrageously misused and tortured the Bhagavad Gita. They have even gone so far as to dispute whether it is more representative of the Sankhya philosophy or of some other school of thought. In fact, a distinguished scholar, in his edition of this poem, has actually printed certain lines in small type because in his view they ought to be expunged altogether, having crept in by mistake. He thinks nothing is really a part of the Gita except what accords with the Sankhya, or at the most with the Yoga philosophy. It may be said, though, that there is no trace in this great poem of what we understand by "philosophy" today. At most, one could say that in ancient India certain basic dispo-sitions of soul developed into certain philosophic tendencies. These really have nothing to do with the Bhagavad Gita, at least not in the sense of being an interpretation or exposition of it.

It is altogether unfair to the intellectual and spiritual life of the East to set it side by side with what the West knows as philosophy because there was no philosophy in the East in the same sense that there is philosophy in the West. In this respect the spirit of our age, just beginning, is as yet imperfectly understood. In the last lecture we spoke of what humanity still has to learn. Above all we must firmly realize how the human soul, under certain conditions, can meet the being whom we tried to describe from a certain aspect, calling him Krishna. Far more important than any dispute as to whether Sankhya or Vedic philosophy is contained in the Bhagavad Gita is the realization that, under certain conditions, Arjuna meets that Spirit who prepared the age of self consciousness.[57] To understand it as a real description of world history—of history and of the color and temper of a particular age in which living, individual beings are placed before us—is the important point. We have tried to describe their natures, speaking of Arjuna's thoughts and feelings as characteristic of that time, trying to throw light on the new age of self consciousness, and showing how a creative spiritual being preparing for a new age appeared before Arjuna. Now, if we seek a living picture of spiritual beings in their relation to each other, we need to know this Krishna being more exactly. The following may therefore help us complete our picture of him.

To penetrate into the region where we can perceive such a mighty being as Krishna, one must have progressed far enough to be able to have real perceptions and real experiences in the spiritual world. That may seem obvious. Yet when we consider what people generally expect of the higher worlds, the matter is by no means self-evident. I have often indicated that innumerable misunderstandings arise from the fact that people wish to lift their lives into the supersensible world while carrying a mass of prejudices with them. They desire to be led along the path into the supersensible toward something already familiar to them in the sense world. In that higher realm a person perceives forms, for instance, not of dense matter perhaps, but forms that appear as forms of light. One finds that people expect to hear sounds like the

---

57. Steiner seems here to be using the term "age of self-consciousness" for what he more usually refers to as the intellectual soul age (eighth century B.C.E. to fifteenth century C.E.).

sounds of the physical world. They do not realize that by *expecting* such things, by entering the higher world with such preconceived ideas, they want a spiritual world just like the sense world, though in a refined form. In the here and now, we are accustomed to color and brightness, so we imagine we will only reach the higher realities if the beings there appear to us in the same way. It ought not to be necessary to say all this, since the supersensible beings are far above all attributes of the senses and in their true form do not appear at all with sensory qualities, because this would presuppose eyes and ears, that is, sense organs. In the higher worlds, we do not perceive by means of sense organs, but by soul organs.

What can happen in this connection I can illustrate by a childish comparison. Suppose I am describing something to you verbally. Then I feel impelled to represent it with a few strokes on the blackboard, thereby materializing what I have expressed in words. No one would dream of taking the diagram for the reality. It is the same when we express what we have experienced supersensibly by giving it form and color and stamping it in words borrowed from the sense world. In doing so we do not use our ordinary intellect, but a higher faculty of feeling that translates the supersensible into sense terms. In such a way our souls live into invisible worlds, for instance, into that of the Krishna being. Then they feel the need of representing to themselves that being. What they represent, however, is not the being himself but a kind of sketch, a supersensible diagram. Such sketches, supersensible illustrations, so to speak, are imaginations. The misunderstanding that so often arises amounts to this, that we sensualize what the higher forces of the soul sketch out before us. By interpreting it sensually we lose its real essence. The essence is not contained in these pictures, but through them it must be dimly felt at first, until by slow degrees we actually begin to see it.

I have already mentioned in the second lecture the wonderful dramatic composition of the Bhagavad Gita. I tried to give an idea of the form of the first four discourses. This same dramatic impulse increases from one discourse to the next as we penetrate on and on into the realms of esoteric vision. A sound idea of the artistic composition of this poem may be suggested by looking to see if there is not a central point, a *climax* to this increase of force and feeling. There are eighteen discourses; therefore we might look for the climax in the ninth. In fact, in the ninth chapter, in the very middle, we read these striking words, "Because of your faith I will tell you the most profound of secrets" [IX.1]. Here indeed is a strange saying that seems to sound abstract, yet has deep significance. Then there follows this most profound mystery: "All creatures find their existence in me, but I am not limited by them" [IX.4].

How often people ask today, "What is the judgment of true mystic wisdom about this or that?" They want absolute truths, but actually there are no such truths. There are only truths that hold good in certain contexts; in definite circumstances and under definite conditions, they *are* true. The statement, "I am in all beings, yet they are not in me," cannot be taken as an abstractly, absolutely true statement. Yet this was spoken out of the deepest wisdom of Krishna at the time when he stood before Arjuna, and its truth is real and immediate, referring to Him who is the creator of our inmost being, of our consciousness of self.

Through this wonderful approach, we are carried on to the central point of the *Gita*, to the ninth discourse where these words are poured out to Arjuna. Then, in the eleventh discourse, another element enters. What may we expect here, realizing the artistic form of the poem and the deep esoteric truths contained in it? When we take up the ninth and tenth discourses, the very middle of the poem, we notice a remarkable thing—a peculiar difficulty in imagining and bringing to life in our souls the ideas presented to us in this part of the song.

As you begin the first discourse, your soul is borne along by the continually increasing currents of feeling and idea. First, immortality is the subject. Then you are uplifted and inspired by the concepts awakened through Yoga. All the while, your feeling is being borne along by something in which, one might say, it can feel at home. We go on and the poem proceeds in a wonderful way to the concept of the one who inspired the age of self consciousness. Our enthusiasm is kindled as we approach this being. All this time we are living in definite, familiar feelings. Then comes a still greater climax. We are told how the soul can become ever freer of the outer bodily life. We are led on to the idea, so familiar to Indian culture, that the soul can withdraw into itself, realizing inaction in the midst of actions experienced by the body. The soul can become a complete whole, independent of the outer world as it gradually attains Yoga and becomes one with Brahma. In the succeeding discourses we see how our certainty of feeling—the feeling that can still gain nourishment from daily life—gradually vanishes. Then, as we approach the ninth discourse, our soul seems to rise to inspired heights of unknown experience. If now, in the ninth and tenth discourses, we try to make the ideas borrowed from ordinary life suffice, we fail. As we reach this part of the song we feel as if we are standing on a summit of human attainment, born directly out of the esoteric depths of life. If we are to understand it, we must bring to it something that our developing soul must first attain by its own effort.

It is remarkable how fine and unerring the composition of the Bhagavad Gita is in this respect. We can get as far as the fifth, sixth, or seventh discourse by developing the concepts given us at the very beginning, in the first discourse. In the second, our soul is awakened to realize the presence of the eternal in the ever-changing flow of appearance. Then follows all that passes into the depths of Yoga, from the third song onward. After this, an altogether new mood begins to appear. Whereas the first discourses still have an intellectual quality, reminding us at times of the Western philosophic mode of thinking, something enters now that requires Yoga, the devotional mood, for its understanding. As we continue purifying more and more this mood of devotion, our soul rises higher in reverence. The Yoga of the first discourses no longer carries us. It ceases, and an altogether new mood of soul bears us up into the ninth and tenth discourses, because the words here spoken are no more than a dry, empty sound echoing in our ear if we approach them intellectually. But they radiate warmth to us if we approach them devotionally. One who would understand this sublime poem may start with intellectual understanding and so follow the opening discourses, but as the song proceeds toward the ninth, a deep devotional mood must be awakened. Then the words of the mighty Krishna will be like wonderful music echoing and re-echoing in the soul. Whoever reaches this ninth song may feel this devotional mood as if taking off one's shoes before treading on holy ground, where one feels one must walk with reverence. Then follows the eleventh discourse. What can come next, now that we have reached the climax of this devotional mood?

When one has risen to the summit where Krishna has led Arjuna—a height that cannot be attained except in esoteric vision or in reverent devotion—it can only be the holy and formless, the supersensible, that appears before one. Then the supersensible can be poured out into imagination. Following this, the uplifted and strengthened soul force that belongs not to the realm of the intellect but to imaginative perception, can cast into living pictures what in its essential being is without form or likeness. This is what happens at the beginning of the second half of the sublime song—that is to say, around the eleventh discourse. Here, after due preparation, the Krishna being to whom Arjuna has been led step by step is conjured up before his soul in imagination. This is where the majestic description in the Indian poem appears in its fullness, where Krishna finally appears in a picture, an imagination.

We may truly say that experiences such as this, which only the innermost power of the human soul can undergo, have almost nowhere else been described in such a wonderful way, so filled with meaning. For those who are able to realize it, the imagination of Krishna as Arjuna now describes it will always be of most profound significance. Up to the tenth discourse, we are led by Krishna as by an inspiring being. Now the radiant bliss of Arjuna's opened vision comes before us. Arjuna becomes the narrator, and describes his imagination in words so wonderful that one fears to reproduce them.

O Lord, I see within your body all the gods and every kind of living creature. I see Brahma, the Creator, seated on a lotus; I see the ancient sages and the celestial serpents.

I see infinite mouths and arms, stomachs and eyes, and you are embodied in every form. I see you everywhere, without beginning, middle, or end. You are the Lord of all creation, and the cosmos is your body.

You wear a crown and carry a mace and discus; your radiance is blinding and immeasurable. I see you, who are so difficult to behold, shining like a fiery sun blazing in every direction.

You are the supreme, changeless Reality, the one thing to be known. You are the refuge of all creation, the immortal spirit, the eternal guardian of eternal dharma.

You are without beginning, middle or end; you touch everything with your infinite power. The sun and moon are your eyes, and your mouth is fire; your radiance warms the cosmos.

O Lord, your presence fills the heavens and the earth and reaches in every direction. I see the three worlds trembling before this vision of your wonderful and terrible form.

The gods enter your being, some calling out and greeting you in fear. Great saints sing your glory, praying, "May all be well."

The multitudes of gods, demigods, and demons are all overwhelmed by the sight of you. O mighty Lord, at the sight of your myriad eyes and mouths, arms and legs, stomachs and fearful teeth, I and the entire universe shake in terror.

O Vishnu, I can see your eyes shining; with open mouth, you glitter in an array of colors, and your body touches the sky. I look at you and my heart trembles; I have lost all courage and all peace of mind.

When I see your mouths with their fearful teeth, mouths burning like the fires at the end of time, I forget where I am and have no place to go. O Lord, you are the support of the universe, have mercy on me! [XI.15–25]

Such is the imagination that Arjuna beholds when his soul has been raised to that height where an imagination of Krishna is possible. Then we hear what Krishna is echoing across to Arjuna once more as a mighty inspiration. In reality it is as if it were not merely sounding for the spiritual ear of Arjuna, but echoing down through all the ages that followed. At this point we begin dimly to perceive what it means when a new impulse is given for a new epoch in the world's history, and when the author of this impulse appears to the clairvoyant gaze of Arjuna. We feel with Arjuna. We remind ourselves that he is in the midst of the turmoil of battle where brother-blood is pitted against its kin. We know that what Krishna has to give depends above all upon the end of the old clairvoyant epoch, together with all that was holy in it, and the beginning of a new epoch. When we reflect on the impulse of this new epoch that was to begin with fratricide, when we rightly understand the impulse that forced its way in through all the swaying concepts and institutions of the preceding epoch, then we get a correct concept of what Krishna lets Arjuna hear.

> I am time, the destroyer of all; I have come to consume the world. Even without your participation, all the warriors gathered here will die.
>
> Therefore arise, Arjuna; conquer your enemies and enjoy the glory of sovereignty. I have already slain all these warriors; you will only be my instrument.
>
> Bhisma, Drona, Jayadratha, Karna, and many others are already slain. Kill those whom I have killed. Do not hesitate. Fight in this battle and you will conquer your enemies. [XI.32–34]

It was not in order to bring to human ears the voice that spoke of slaying that these words were uttered, but to make them hear the voice that tells of the center in the human being that has to develop in the age to come. Into this center there were focused the highest impulses realizable by humanity at that time, and that there is nothing in human evolution with which the human ego is not connected. Here we find in the Bhagavad Gita something that lifts us up and sets us on the horizon of the whole of human evolution.

When we think of the evolution of humanity over all the Earth, and trace it as we are able to do by means of what is given, for example, in our esoteric science; when in this sense we see the Earth as the place where humanity has first been brought to the ego through many different stages following one another and developing from age to age; when we thus follow the course of evolution through the epochs of time, then we may say to ourselves that, having been planted here on Earth, the highest these souls can attain is to become *free souls*. Free—that is what we will become if we bring to full development all the forces latent within us as individual souls. In order to make this possible Krishna was active, indirectly and almost imperceptibly at first, then ever more definitely, and at last quite directly in the period we have been describing. In all of earthly evolution there is no being who could give *the individual human soul* so much as Krishna. If we let the changing moods of this great poem work upon us, we shall gain much more than those who try to read into it pedantic doctrines of Sankhya or Yoga philosophies. If we can only dimly feel the dazzling heights that can be reached through Yoga, we shall begin to lay hold of the meaning and spirit of such a mighty imagination as that of Arjuna's presented to us here. Even as an image, it is so sublime and forceful that we are able to form some conception of the creative spirit, which in Krishna is grafted onto the world. The highest impulse that can speak to the individual speaks through Krishna to Arjuna. The highest to which one can lift oneself by raising to their full pitch all the powers that reside within one's being—that is Krishna. The highest to which one can soar by training oneself and working on oneself with wisdom—that is Krishna.

I say expressly the individual soul because—and I say this deliberately—on Earth there exists not only the individual human soul but also *humankind*. Consider this in connection with all I have tried to give about Krishna, because on Earth there are all those concerns that do not belong to the individual alone. Imagine a person feeling the inner impulse to perfect him- or herself as far as a human soul can. Then imagine each person separately going on to develop indefinitely. And then there is humankind. For this earthly planet there are matters that bring humankind into connection with the whole universe. With the Krishna impulse coming into each individual soul, let us assume that every soul would have developed in itself a higher impulse, not immediately, nor even up to the present time, but sometime in the future. So that from the age of self-consciousness onward, the stream of humankind's collective evolution would have split apart. Individual souls would have progressed and unfolded to the highest point, but separately, dispersed, broken apart from each other. Their paths would have diverged further and further as the Krishna impulse worked in each one. Human existence would have been uplifted in the sense that souls individualized themselves and so lifted themselves out of the common current, developing their self-life to the utmost. In this way the ancient time would have shone into the future like many, many rays from a single star. Every one of these rays would have proclaimed the glory of Krishna far into future cosmic eras. This is the path on which humankind was traveling in the sixth or eighth centuries before the foundation of Christianity.

Then from the opposite side something else came in. The Krishna impulse comes into the human soul when from the depths of its own inner being the soul works, creates, and draws forth its powers more and more until it may rise to those realms where it may reach Krishna. But something came toward humanity *from outside*, which humans could never have reached through the forces that lived within themselves, something bending down to each individual. The souls that were separating and isolating themselves encountered the same being who came down out of the cosmic universe into the age of self-consciousness from outside. It came in such a way that it belonged to the whole of humanity, to all the Earth. This other impulse came from the opposite side. It was the Christ.

Though put rather abstractly for the present, we see how a continually increasing individualization was prepared and brought about in humankind, and how then those souls that had the impulse to individualize themselves more and more were met by the Christ impulse, leading them once more together into a common humanity. What I have tried to indicate has been a rather preliminary description of the two impulses from the Christ and Krishna. I have tried to show how closely the two impulses come together in the age of the midpoint of evolution, even though they come from diametrically opposite directions. We can make very great mistakes by confusing these two revelations. What I have developed today in a rather general way, we will make more concrete in the succeeding lectures. But I would close today with a few words that may simply and clearly summarize what these two impulses are—truly the most important in human evolution.

If we look back to all that happened between the tenth century before Christ and the tenth century afterward, we may say that into the universe the Krishna impulse flowed for every individual human soul, and into the Earth the Christ impulse came for all humankind.

Observe that for those who can think specifically, "all of humankind" by no means signifies the same as the mere sum total of all individual human souls.

7

Helsinki, June 3, 1913

It is a fact of nature, though usually ignored by science, that the makeup of human beings makes it impossible for us to know one particular part of our being. As we look upon the world, it roughly shows itself as an ascending scale from the mineral kingdom through the plant and animal kingdoms up to man. It goes without saying that we must assume some *creative force* behind all the forms we perceive around us in the kingdoms of nature. The point is, however, that as human beings we can gain knowledge of the world we live in just because the mineral, plant, and animal kingdoms are outside of us and we can observe them. As to all that is within ourselves, we can only know insofar as the same forces are at work in us as are active in the three kingdoms of nature outside us. The forces active within us that *transcend* those three kingdoms, we cannot know using habitual methods for knowing nature—not in the least. Yet it is just what humans have over and above the kingdoms of nature that enables them to systematically build up knowledge of those kingdoms. Just as little as the eye, whose purpose it is to see outwardly, can see itself, just so little can humans know what there is in themselves by which they may acquire knowledge. This is a very simple idea, but sound.

It is impossible for the eye to see itself because its function is to look out, and it is impossible for those forces in us that help us acquire outer knowledge, to acquire self-knowledge. Further, these very forces represent what it is in the human being that makes it something more than an animal. Materialistic Darwinism easily disposes of this fact by simply leaving out the fact that this special human power to know itself cannot be known by our usual cognitive instruments. Recognizing that this power is unknowable, science denies its existence and accordingly considers humans only insofar as they are still animal. You can see on what peculiar fallacy the illusion of materialistic Darwinism rests. Humans cannot know in themselves those forces that are the actual means of knowledge. But the eye *can* see another eye, and for this reason, other things being equal, it can believe in itself. With cognition this is not the case. It would be *logically* possible for a human being to face another human being and perceive the cognitive faculty that raises human beings above animals. But even that is *actually* impossible, for the very reasons implied in what we have said previously about the effects of thinking.

What does ordinary cognition involve in the outer world? We saw already that it involves a perpetual destruction, a wearing down of the nerve structures in the brain. In other words, if we were to look in life, on the physical plane, for the facts of cognition, one would find a destructive process in the nervous system; one would not find any creative, constructive process. But the creative forces without which human beings don't even begin to rise above animals cannot unfold in the waking state, in ordinary life, which is normally associated with cognition. So these forces must come into effect in such a way as not to interfere with the destruction of the nervous structure. This means that they rest, they are dormant, during our waking time.

Consider the important implications of this recognition: the forces one would need in order to recognize the nonsense of materialistic Darwinism are actually asleep from the time we awake to the time we go to sleep, and instead, during that time we have a destructive process, whereas the creative forces raising humans above animals are resting. The creative forces that form the animal organism are much less perfect than those working on the human organism. During the waking hours, these constructive processes are not active at all, but instead another process continuously destroys precisely that which raises humans above the animal. These creative forces are paralyzed in waking life. They are just not there. So during the waking hours, the forces that raise humans above animality are asleep; they come into action when we sleep. Everything that was destroyed is restored, and completed. Thus it is only in a sleeping person that we can find these creative forces raising humans above animality. We are forced to say: that which restores during human sleep the forces that were eroded in the waking hours, these forces must be the ones that raise humans above animality. True, natural science doesn't know these forces; there is only beginning to be an intuition about them. But science is on its way to revealing these forces with entirely external means. They could only be truly observed if one were to observe the reorganization process that takes place during sleep. Once science learns to distinguish those forces in the human being that go beyond the realm of animality, then it will physically observe, precisely in the sleeping body, the transcendence of animality by human beings, because one will recognize that the same forces that work creatively during sleep work destructively during waking life. Once science learns to distinguish the human forces of regeneration from what is present in animal bodies, it will recognize that the creative forces active in human life are only awake when the human being sleeps. This means that in true self-knowledge human creative forces, the truly human forces, can only be perceived when human beings become clairvoyant during sleep, i.e., in a person that awakens clairvoyantly in a state resembling sleep. We already mentioned this in the fifth lecture.

I said today that, to some extent, from the processes observable in a person during sleep, science will in time find indications of the forces whereby the human being transcends the animal, but they will only be indications. When these forces appear to clairvoyant consciousness today, they are seen to be of such a nature that they cannot be revealed to the senses in their true form. It will be possible to deduce their existence from certain scientific facts. Apart from their not being perceptible in their essence, there is quite another reason why it will become possible to discover them, although not to perceive them. These human creative forces have a very special relation to all the other forces of nature. We are here approaching a very difficult subject, but I may possibly clarify it in the following way.

Let us imagine we have here the receptacle of an air pump, say a bell jar, and suppose we succeed in making a perfect vacuum inside it. Everyone whose intellect is bound to the world of senses will now say, "There is no air inside, only an empty space; we cannot go any farther, there cannot be less than no air inside." Actually, that is not true. We can pump until no air at all is left, then go on pumping until we get a space still emptier of air than a vacuum. People dependent on the material world will find it difficult to imagine this "less than nothing."

It is a bit easier to imagine this in regard to our sensations. Just imagine we are in a forest where many, many birds are singing. We stand in the midst of the birdsong. Let us assume we walk farther and farther away, we go out of the woods, we hear the birdsong less and less, until the point where we cannot hear it any more—but let us go farther, and the sense of being surrounded in our hearing will fade also. We come to silence, and when we go farther, we come to something that is less than the birdsong, less than the silence, less than the complete peace. As you can see, this second thought, this second image, is much easier to follow than the first. We find it easy to imagine a boundary past which we no longer hear anything. And we can also imagine that we can go farther, and hear less than nothing.

It is sometimes remarkable how things can be accepted as self-evidences, axioms. Thus we can read in many Western philosophical treatises: There is no such thing as less than nothing. It just can't be. Actually, some people even claim that Nothing itself cannot truly exist.—Let me turn, however, to a really trivial example. In real life, people have no trouble knowing that in some areas there is indeed such a thing as "nothing," and even "less than nothing." Suppose you have ten dollars in your pocket. You can gradually spend them until you have nothing left. In this domain of life there is a real "less than nothing." It is often one of the strongest realities—you can go into *debt* for a few dollars. Everybody is presumably much happier having two, three, four, five dollars in their pocket, than if they owe two, three, four, five dollars. In practical life, less than nothing is often more intensely real than the reality of possession.

Yet "less than nothing" exists in the universe as well as in the above illustration. All philosophical dicta about "nothing," however pretentious their form, are really rubbish. They are themselves a kind of ill-defined nothingness. It is true that the physical something that surrounds us can be reduced to nothing, and then still further to *less than nothing*. We must imagine the world that surrounds us, which we know in the forces of nature throughout the mineral, plant, and animal kingdoms, reduced to nothing, then below nothing. It is then that those forces arise that are creatively active in the sleeping human being. Natural science knows only the external side of these forces. In fact, it holds fast to a mere abstraction about them and therefore cannot penetrate or appreciate them because ordinary science is to the reality in the forces of nature as the abstract number ten, for example, is to ten beans or ten apples. If we eliminate quality and say that all of these are "ten" and nothing else, we are doing what natural science does, making no distinctions, touching only the surface of things.

If we form the idea that regenerative forces must build up the organism again in sleep, then science will treat these forces in the same way as a man who, when someone meets him saying, "I have fifteen dollars in my pocket," replies, "Never mind the dollar part; you have *fifteen*." The speaker leaves out of account the very thing that matters.

I mention all this to show how difficult it is, and must be, for external science to know the truth. It will draw certain conclusions and thus come *near* the truth. For some persons this will not be necessary, because science will gradually be supplemented by clairvoyant perception that experiences the difference between these forces and those active in the three kingdoms of nature. At present I cannot deal fully with the superficial objection that animals also sleep. Such objections have little logical value, but people do not notice this, for they judge according to abstract concepts instead of the real nature of things. Introducing animal sleep into the argument would be the same error as if someone were to say, "I sharpen my pencil with a knife, and I also shave with a knife," and another person replied, "That is impossible, knives are there to cut meat." People are always making that kind of judgment. They think that a given thing must have the same function in different realms of nature. Sleep is an altogether different function in humans from what it is in animals.

I wanted to call your attention to forces at work in human nature that we find at first in the regeneration of the sleeping organism. Now, these forces are closely related to other forces that also develop in humans with a certain unconsciousness: the forces having to do with reproduction. We know that up to a certain age human consciousness is filled with a pure and straightforward unconsciousness of these forces, the innocence of childhood. Then at a certain age this consciousness awakens. From that time onward the human organism is permeated by an awareness of the forces henceforth known as sexual love.

What lives as a sleeping force in earlier life and only awakens at puberty, seen in its original and essential form, is the very same as the forces that in sleep regenerate the outworn forces in the human being. It, however, is hidden by the other parts of human nature in which it is mingled. These invisible forces at work in the human being become capable of either good or evil only when they awaken, but they sleep, or at most dream, until the time of puberty. Since the forces that manifest themselves later must first be prepared, they are intermingled, though not yet awake, with the remaining forces in the organism from birth onward. During this time, human nature is permeated by these sleeping forces. This is what meets us in the child as such a wonderful mystery. It is the sleeping generative forces that only awaken later on. Those who are sensitive to these things feel something like a gentle divine breath when they find, behind the naughtiness, obstinacy, and other more or less unpleasant characteristics a child may have, the same forces that awaken later, at puberty, but are held back in childhood. The child's innocent qualities are those of the grown-up person, but in childlike form. One who recognizes them as generative forces feels the breath of divine powers. While in later life they appear in a person's lower nature, they are so wonderful because they really breathe the pure breath of God so long as they work in unconscious innocence. We must feel these things and be sensitive to them, and then we shall perceive how wonderfully human nature is composed. The generative forces, sleeping during the tender age of childhood, awaken around the time of puberty, and from then on are still innocently active when at night we sink back into sleep.

Thus human nature falls into two parts. In every human being, two persons confront us—the one that we are from the time we awaken until we go to sleep, the other, from going to sleep to waking again. In our waking state we are continually at pains to wear and worry our nature down to the animal level with all that is not pure knowledge, pure spiritual activity. What raises us above humanity holds sway like a pure, sublime force within the generative powers as they were during innocent childhood, and then in sleep it is awakened in the regeneration of what was worn away in the daytime. So we have in ourselves one person who is related to the creative forces in humanity, and another who destroys them.

The deeply significant thing in the double nature of the human being is that behind all that the senses perceive we have to surmise another person in whom creative forces dwell. This second person is really never there in a pure, unmixed form during waking life, or even in sleep, because in sleep the physical and etheric bodies still remain permeated by the aftereffects of waking life, by the disturbing and destructive forces. When at last the latter have been removed altogether, we wake up again.

So it has been since what we call the Lemurian age, the beginning, strictly speaking, of present day humankind's evolution. At that time, as I describe in greater detail in my *Outline of Esoteric Science*, the luciferic influence in human nature set in. From this influence there came, among other things, what today compels humans continually to wear and tear themselves down to the animal nature. The other element in human nature, which humans as now constituted do not yet know about—the creative forces in them—came into play in the early Lemurian time before the luciferic impulses entered. We rise in thought from human "completion" to human "becoming"; from human created to human being re-created. In so doing, we have to look back to that distant Lemurian time when the human being was as yet wholly permeated by the creating forces. At that time humans came into being as they are today, and entered a kind of lower nature. If we follow the human race from that epoch onward, we have this double nature continually before us in all that has happened since. Humanity then entered a kind of lower nature.

At the same time, as we can see clairvoyantly by looking back into the akashic record, there appeared beside ordinary people, who themselves were permeated by the human creative forces, something like a brother or sister soul, a definite soul. It was as though this sister soul was held back, not thrown into the current of human evolution. It remained permeated through and through by human creative forces *only*, and by nothing else. Thus a certain brother or sister soul (in that ancient time there was no difference)—Adam's brother soul—remained behind. It could not enter the physical process of human evolution. It lived on, invisible to the physical world. It was not born the way human beings are born, in the flowing stream of this life, because if it had gone through birth and death it would have been part of the physical human process. It could only be perceived by those who rose to the heights of clairvoyance, who developed those forces that awaken in the state we otherwise know as sleep. In that state, human beings are near the pure forces that live and work in the sister soul.

The human being entered evolution, but holding sway above this life there lived, in sacrifice, a soul that throughout all the processes of human life never came down in bodily form. It did not strive like ordinary human souls for birth and death in successive incarnations, and it could only show itself to them when in their sleep they attained clairvoyant vision. Yet it worked on humankind wherever they could meet it with special clairvoyant gifts. There were humans who either by nature or special training in schools of initiation had this power and were able to recognize the creative forces. Wherever such schools are mentioned in history we can always find evidence that they were aware of a soul accompanying humankind. In most instances, it was only recognizable in those special conditions of clairvoyance that expand human spiritual vision into sleep consciousness.

When Arjuna stood on the battlefield with the Kurus and Pandavas arrayed against each other, when he felt all that was going on around him and deeply realized the unique situation in which he was placed, it came about that this sister soul spoke to him through the soul of his charioteer. The manifestation of this special soul, speaking through a human soul, is none other than Krishna.[58] For what soul was it that

---

58. See fns. 22 and 33, and pp. 112 and 116.

could instill into humanity the impulse to consciousness of self? It was the soul that had remained behind in the old Lemurian age when humans entered actual earthly evolution.

This soul had often been visible in manifestations before, but in a far more spiritual form. At the moment of which the Bhagavad Gita tells us, we have to imagine a kind of embodiment of this soul of Krishna, though much concealed in maya. Later on in history a definite incarnation takes place. This soul actually incarnated in the body of a child. Those of our friends to whom I have spoken of this before know that at the time when Christianity was founded two children were born in different families, both from the house of David. The one child is mentioned in Matthew's Gospel, the other in Luke's. This is the true reason for the external discrepancies between the two gospels. Now this Jesus child of Luke's Gospel is an incarnation of the soul that had never before lived in a human body but is nevertheless a human soul, having been one in the ancient Lemurian age. This is the soul that revealed itself as Krishna.

We touch here upon a wonderful mystery. We see how the human soul, as it was before humans descended into the course of earthly incarnations, enters the body of the Luke Jesus child. We understand that this soul could hold sway in the human body only until the twelfth year of its life. After that, another soul must take possession, the Zarathustra soul that had gone through all the transformations of humankind. This wonderful mystery is enacted that the innermost essence and self of humanity, which we have seen hailed as Krishna, permeates the Jesus child of the Luke Gospel. In this child are the innermost forces of humanity, the Krishna forces, for indeed we know their origin. This Krishna root takes us back into the Lemurian time, the very primeval age of humankind. At that time it was one with humanity, before the physical evolution of humankind began. In later time this root, these Krishna forces, flowing together and uniting in the unknown and unseen, worked to bring about the unfolding of each human's inner being from within. Concretely embodied, this root is present within a single being, the Luke Jesus child, and as the child grows up, it remains active beneath the surface of life in this special body after the Zarathustra soul has entered it. Thus, all that the Krishna impulse signifies is incarnated in the body of Luke's Jesus child. What was embodied is related to the forces that are asleep in every child in their sublime purity and innocence, until they awaken as the sexual forces. In this child they can manifest themselves and be active until the age of puberty, when one ordinarily becomes sexually mature. But the *body* of this child that had been taken from common humanity would no longer have been adapted to the forces related to the innocent sexual forces in the child. Thus the soul in the other Jesus child, which was the soul of Zarathustra, that had passed through many incarnations and reached its eminence by hard work and special striving, passed over into the body of the Luke Jesus child, and from then on dwelt in that body.

In the thirtieth year, at the time the Bible describes as the Baptism in the Jordan, there comes toward this special human body what now belongs to all humankind. This is the moment indicated in the words "This is my well beloved Son, this day have I begotten Him."[59] Christ now comes toward the physical body from the other side. In the body that stands before us here, we have in concrete form what yesterday we thought of abstractly. What belongs to all of humankind comes to the body that contains what, through another impulse, has brought the inner human being to the highest ideal of individual strength and will carry it to yet greater heights.

When you consider all that has been said today, leading up as it does to a certain understanding of that great moment pictorially represented as the baptism by John, you will have to admit that our anthroposophical outlook takes nothing away from the sublime majesty of the Christ idea. On the contrary, by shedding the light of understanding upon it, much is added to all that can be given to humankind exoterically. Today I have endeavored to present the matter in such a way as to give it sense and meaning for those who can consider it with an open mind, in the light of external human history. That is not the way, however, by which this secret was found. Someone might ask, in view of the lectures about Luke's Gospel I delivered years ago

---

59. Luke 3.22; Matthew 3.17. Virtually all translations of this text read as follows: "Thou art my beloved son, with thee I am well pleased."

in Basel,[59] when for the first time I drew attention to the different genealogies of the two Jesus children, "Why did you not explain then all you have added to it now?" That depends on the whole way these things were discovered. Actually, this truth has not yet been found in one single and complete whole by the human understanding. It was not discovered in the form in which I have tried to convey it today. The truth itself was there first, as I indicated in a lecture a few days ago, and the rest followed of its own accord, adding itself to the main body of this piece of knowledge about the two Jesus children. From this you may gather that in the Anthroposophical Movement for which I am permitted to stand before you, there is nothing of the nature of intellectual or logical construction. I do not mean to lay this down as a general rule for everybody, but I do regard it as my own personal task to say nothing that is given by the intellect as such, but to take things in the way they are directly and immediately given to esoteric vision. Only afterward are they permeated with the power of understanding. The truth about the two Jesus children was not discovered by external historical research, but from the beginning it was an esoteric fact. Afterward, the connection with the Krishna mystery was revealed.

You see in this how the science of the human being will have to work into the esoteric realm in the age we are entering; how the fundamental impulses of earthly evolution will gradually be understood and realized by individual persons, and how this will throw more and more light on all that has happened in the past. True science will not only speak to the intellect, but will fill the whole soul. It is when we make ourselves acquainted with esoteric facts that we have a feeling for the real majesty, the greatness and wonder of these facts. Truly, the more deeply we penetrate the world of reality, the more we have this feeling of wonder. Not only our intellect and reason but our whole soul is illumined when we let truth come to us in this way. Especially at such a point as this, the wondrous event when the

---

59. Basel, September 15–25, 1909. See *According to Luke: The Gospel of Compassion and Love Revealed*. Introduction and Notes by Robert McDermott (Great Barrington, MA: SteinerBooks, 2001).

whole inwardness of humanity lived in a human body, when a soul that had developed upward to this point through the whole course of earthly life took possession of this body, into which there came during three years of its life something that was vouchsafed to all humankind from the great universe beyond. Truly, this can stir our souls to their depths. The spiritual age that is dawning will in time make it possible to deepen our understanding still more.

One thing is essential to the coming spiritual age. We must learn to take a different attitude toward the great riddles and secrets of the cosmos, to approach them not as in the past with reason and intellect alone, but with all the faculties of our soul. Then we shall ourselves become partakers in the whole of human evolution. It will be for us like a fountain of sublime, all-human consciousness. We shall have fullness of soul. We shall feel that we may belong to that humanity that over all the Earth is to develop such impulses as have been the subject of our thoughts today.

8

HELSINKI, JUNE 4, 1913

I F we want to approach such a creation as the sublime Bhagavad Gita with full understanding, it is necessary for us to attune our souls to it, so to speak, to shift into the manner of thought and feeling that really lies at the basis of such a work. This is especially true for people who, by situation and circumstances, are as far removed from this great poem as Westerners are. It is natural for us to make a contemporary work our own without much difficulty. It is also natural that those who belong to a certain nation should always have an immediate feeling for a work that has sprung directly out of the substance of that nation, even though it might belong to a previous age. The population of the West, however, is altogether remote in sentiment and feeling from the Bhagavad Gita.

If we would approach it then with understanding, we must prepare ourselves for the very different mood of soul, the different spirit that pervades it. Appalling misunderstandings can arise when people imagine they can approach this poem without first working on their own souls. A creation coming over to us from India, from the ninth or tenth century[60]

---

60. Steiner usually refers to the Gita as originating in the sixth century B.C.E.; there is no historical evidence for its origin in the ninth or tenth centuries B.C.E., but the historic and mythic sources of the *Mahabharata*, in which the Bhagavad Gita originated, probably do date to these centuries.

before the foundation of Christianity, cannot be understood as directly by Westerners as, say, the Finnish *Kalevala* or the Greeks Homeric poems. If we would go into the matter further, we must once more bring together different materials that can show us the way to enter the spirit of this wonderful poem.

Here I would like first and foremost to draw attention to something: The summits of spiritual life have always been concealed from the wide plain of human intelligence, in a certain sense right up to the present age. It is true that one of the characteristics of our age, which is only now dawning and which we have somewhat described, will be that certain things hitherto kept secret and really known to only a few will be spread abroad into large circles. That is the reason why you are present here, because our movement is the beginning of this spreading abroad of facts that until now have remained secret from the masses. Perhaps one subconscious reason that brought you to the anthroposophical view of the world and into this spiritual movement came precisely from the feeling that certain secrets must today be poured out into all people. Until our time, however, these facts remained secret not because they were deliberately kept so, but because it lay in the natural course of human development that they had to remain secret. It is said that the secrets of the old Mysteries were protected from the profane by certain definite, strictly observed rules. Far more than by rule, these secrets were protected by a fundamental characteristic of humankind in olden times, namely, that people simply could not have understood these secrets. This fact was a much more powerful protection than any external rule could be.

For certain facts, this has been especially the case during the materialistic age. What I am about to say is extreme heresy from the point of view of our time. For example, there is nothing better protected in the regions of central Europe than Fichte's philosophy.[61] Not that it is kept secret, for his teachings are printed and are read. But they are not

---

61. Johann Gotlieb Fichte (1762–1814), whom Steiner discussed in his doctoral dissertation, 1892, published as *Truth and Knowledge: An Introduction to "Philosophy of Spiritual Activity"* (Great Barrington, MA: SteinerBooks, 2007).

understood. They remain secret. In this way much of what pertains to the general development of humanity will remain esoteric knowledge, even though it is published and revealed in broad daylight.

Not only in this sense, but in a rather different one, too, there is an important peculiarity of human evolution concerning the ideas we must have in order to understand the Bhagavad Gita. Everything we may call the mood, the mode of feeling, the mental habit of ancient India from which the Gita sprang, was also accessible in its full spirituality to the understanding of only a few. What one age has produced through the activity of a few, remains secret, in regard to its real depth, even afterward when it passes over and becomes the property of a whole people. Again, this is a peculiar trait in human evolution that is full of wisdom, though it may seem paradoxical at first. Even for the contemporaries of the Bhagavad Gita and for their followers, for the whole race to which this high point of spiritual achievement belongs, and for its posterity, its teaching remained a secret. The people who came later did not know the real depth of this spiritual current. It is true that in the following centuries there grew up a certain religious belief in its teachings, combined with great fervor of feeling, but with this there was no deepening of perception. Neither the contemporaries nor those who followed developed a truly penetrating understanding of this poem. In the intervening time, only a few have really understood it.

Thus it comes about that in the judgment of posterity, what was once present as a strong and special spiritual movement is greatly distorted and falsified. As a rule, we cannot find the way to approach an understanding of a given reality by studying the judgments of the descendants of the race that produced it. So we will find no real understanding for the spiritual tendency that in the deepest sense permeates the Bhagavad Gita in the sentiments and feelings of the people of India today.[62] We will find enthusiasm, strong feeling, and fervent belief in abundance, but not a deep perception of the poem's meaning. This is especially true of the age just passed, from the fourteenth and fifteenth to the nineteenth century. As a matter of fact, it

---

62. Sri Aurobindo began to write his *Essays on the Gita* one year after this lecture.

is especially true for the people who profess that religion. There is one anecdote that, like many others, reveals a deep truth—how a great European thinker said on his deathbed, "Only one person understood me, and he misunderstood me."

It can also be said of this age that has just run its course that it contained some spiritual substance that represents a great height of achievement, but has widely remained unknown as to its real nature, even to its contemporaries. Here is something to which I would like to draw your attention. Some exceptionally clever people can undoubtedly be found among the present people of the East, and of India. By the whole configuration of their mind and soul, however, they are already far from understanding the feelings poured out in the Bhagavad Gita. Consider how these people receive from Western civilization a way of thought that does not reach to the depths, but is merely superficial understanding. This has a double result. For one, it is easy for the people of India to develop something that may easily make them feel how far behind a superficial Western culture is in relation to what has already been given by their great poem. In effect, they still have *more* ways to approach the meaning of that poem than to approach the deeper contents of Western spiritual and intellectual life. Then there are others in India who would gladly be ready to receive such spiritual substance as is contained, let us say, in the works of Soloviev,[63] Hegel, and Fichte, to mention a few of many spiritualized thinkers. Many Indian thinkers would like to make these ideas their own.[64]

I once experienced something of this kind. At the beginning of our founding of the German Section in our movement,[65] an Indian thinker sent me a dissertation. He sent it to many other Europeans besides. In this, he tried to combine what Indian philosophy offers with important European concepts, such as might be gained in real

---

63. Vladimir Soloviev (1853–1900), Russian mystical philosopher and sophiologist.
64. Sri Aurobindo absorbed Hegelian philosophy at King's College, Cambridge, 1890–92.
65. That is, the Theosophical Society, of which Steiner was the general secretary of the German branch.

truth—so he implied—if one entered deeply into Hegel and Fichte. In spite of the man's honest effort, the whole essay was of no use whatsoever. I do not mean to sound hostile; rather, I would praise his effort, but the fact is, what this man produced could only appear as utter dilettantism to anyone who had access to the real concepts of Fichte and Hegel. There was nothing to be done with the whole thing.

Here we have a person who honestly endeavors to penetrate a later spiritual stream altogether different from his own point of view, but he cannot get through the hindrances that time and evolution put in his way. When he attempts nevertheless to penetrate them, the result is untrue and impossible thoughts. I later heard a lecture by another person, one who does not know what European spiritual evolution really is, and what its depths contain. He lectured in support of the same Indian thinker. He was a European who had learned the arguments of the Indian thinker and was bringing them forward as spiritual wisdom before his followers. They too, of course, were ignorant of the fact that they were listening to something that rested on the wrong intellectual basis. For one who could look keenly into what the European produced, it was simply terrible. If you will forgive the expression, it was enough to give one the creeps. It was misunderstanding grafted onto misunderstanding. So difficult is it to comprehend all that the human soul can produce. We must make it our ideal to truly understand all the masterpieces of the human spirit. If we feel this ideal through and through and keep in mind what I just said, we shall gain a ray of light to show us how truly difficult it is to access the Bhagavad Gita. Also, we shall realize how untold misunderstandings are possible, and how harmful they can be.

We in the West can well understand how the people of India look up to the old creative spirits of earlier times whose activity flows through the Vedantic philosophy and permeates the Sankhya philosophy with its deep meaning. We can understand how Indian people look up with reverence to that climax of spiritual achievement that appears in Shankaracharya[64] seven or eight centuries after the foundation of Christianity. But we must think of it in another way as well if we want to attain a truly deep understanding. To do so we must set up a kind of hypothesis, for it has not yet been realized in evolution.

Let us imagine that those who were the creators of the sublime spirituality that permeates the Vedas, the Vedantic literature, and the philosophy of Shankaracharya were to appear again in our time with the same spiritual faculty, the same keenness of perception they had when they were in the world in that ancient epoch. They would have come in touch with spiritual creations like those of Soloviev, Hegel, and Fichte. What would they have said? We are assuming that what the adherents of those ancient philosophies say does not concern us, but only what those spirits themselves would say. I am aware that I am going to say something paradoxical, but we must think of what Schopenhauer[66] once said: "There is no getting away from it; it is the sad fate of truth that it must always become paradoxical in the world. Truth is unable to sit on the throne of error; therefore it sits on the throne of time, and appeals to the guardian angel of time. So great, however, is the spread of that angel's mighty wings that the individual dies within a single beat." So we must not shrink from the fact that truth must appear paradoxical. The following does also, and is true.

If the poets of the Vedas, the founders of Sankhya philosophy, even Shankaracharya himself, had returned in the nineteenth century and seen the works of Soloviev, Hegel, and Fichte, all those great men would have said, "These three men have achieved by the very quality and tenor of their minds what we were striving for back in that era, what we hoped our gift of spiritual vision would reveal to us. We thought we must rise to heights of clairvoyant vision, then in these heights there would appear before us what permeates the souls of these nineteenth-century men *quite naturally*, almost as a matter of course!"

This sounds paradoxical to those Western people who with childlike lack of consciousness look to the people of the East, comparing themselves with them, all the while misunderstanding what the *West* actually contains. A peculiarly strange picture! We imagine those founders of Indian philosophy looking up fervently to Fichte and other Western

---

66. Arthur Schopenhauer (1788–1860), German philosopher of pessimism and the will, and one of the earliest European interpreters of Hindu and Buddhist scriptures.

thinkers, and along with them we see a number of people today who do not value the spiritual substance of Europe, but grovel in the dust before Shankaracharya and those before him while they themselves are unconcerned with the achievements of such thinkers as Hegel, Fichte, and Soloviev. We do so because only by such a hypothesis can we understand all the facts history presents to us.

We shall understand this if we imagine those times from which the spiritual substance of the Bhagavad Gita flowed. Let us imagine human beings of that period somewhat as follows. What appears to a person today in varied ways in dream consciousness—the pictorial imagination of dream life—was in that ancient time the normal content of the soul, everyday consciousness. It was a dreamlike, pictorial consciousness, by no means the same as in the Old Moon⁶⁷ epoch, but much more evolved. This was the condition out of which human souls were passing on in the descending line of evolution. Still earlier was what we call sleep consciousness, a state wholly closed to us today, from which a kind of dreamlike inspiration came to human beings. It was the state closed to us today during our sleep. As dream consciousness is for us, so was this sleep consciousness for that ancient humanity. It found its way into normal picture consciousness much as dream consciousness does for us, but more rarely. In yet another respect, it was somewhat different in those times. Our current dream consciousness generally brings up recollections of ordinary life. Then, when sleep consciousness could still penetrate the higher worlds, it allowed people to recollect those spiritual worlds. Then, gradually, this consciousness descended lower and lower.

Anyone who at that time was striving as we do today in our esoteric education, aimed for something quite different. When we today go through our esoteric development we are aware that we have gone downhill to our everyday consciousness and are now striving upward. Those seekers were also striving upward, from their everyday dream

---

67. For Steiner's account of the three phases of the evolution of consciousness prior to Earth evolution, which he refers to as Old Saturn, Old Sun, Old Moon, see his *Outline of Esoteric Science* (Hudson, NY: Anthroposophic Press, 1997), pp. 165–97.

consciousness. What was it then that they attained? With all their pains, it was something altogether different from what we are trying to attain. If someone had offered those people my book *How to Know Higher Worlds*, they would have had no use for it at all. Its contents would have been foolishness for that ancient time; it only makes sense for humankind today. Then, everything they did with their Yoga and Sankhya was a striving toward a height that we have reached in the most profound works of our time, in those of the three European thinkers I have mentioned. They were striving to grasp the world in ideas and concepts. Therefore, one who really penetrates the matter finds no difference—apart from differences of time, mood, form, and quality of feeling—between our three thinkers and the Vedantic philosophy. At that time the Vedantic philosophy was that to which men were striving upward; today it has come down and is accessible to everyday consciousness.

If we wish to describe the condition of our souls in this connection we may start out by saying that sleep consciousness is closed for us, but for the ancient people of India it was still permeated by the light of spiritual vision. What we are now striving for lay hidden in the depths of the future for them. I mean what we call imaginative knowledge, fully conscious picture consciousness, permeated by the sense of the ego. I mean fully conscious imagination as it is described in *How to Know Higher Worlds*. So much for the technical point that should be inserted here. In these abstract technicalities lies something far more important: that if a person today were to make vigorous use of the forces present in the soul, what the people of the Bhagavad Gita era strove for with all their might lies right at hand. It really does, even if only for a Soloviev, a Fichte, or a Hegel. One more thing: What today can be found right at hand was in ancient times attained by applying all the keen vision of Sankhya, and the deep penetration of Yoga. It was attained with effort and pain, a sublime effort to lift the mind.

Now imagine how different life is for a person who lives at the top of a mountain and is continually enjoying the magnificent view, compared with a person who has never once seen the view but has to toil upward with trouble and pain from the valley. If you have the view every day, you get accustomed to it. It is not in the concepts, in their content, that the achievements of Shankaracharya, of the Vedic poets, and of their successors are different from those of Hegel and Fichte. The difference lies in the fact that Shankaracharya's predecessors were striving upward from the valley to the summit. It was their keenness of mind in Sankhya philosophy, their deepening of soul in Yoga, that led them there. It was in this work, this overcoming of the soul, that the experience lay. It is the experience, not the content of thought, that is important here.

This is the immensely significant thing, something from which we may in a certain sense derive comfort, because Europeans do not value what they can find right at hand. Europeans prefer the form in which it meets them in Vedantic and Sankhya philosophies, because there, without knowing it, they value the great efforts that achieved it. That is the personal side of the matter. It makes a difference whether you find a certain content of thought here or there, or whether you attain it by the severe effort of the soul. It is the soul's work that gives a thing its life. We must take this into account. What was once attained alone by Shankaracharya and by the deep training of Yoga can be found today right at hand, even if only by people like those we have named.

This is not a matter for abstract commentaries. We only need the power to transplant ourselves into the living feelings of that time. We then begin to understand that the external expressions themselves, the outer forms of the ideas, were experienced quite differently from the way we can experience them. We must study those forms of expression that belong to the feeling, the mood, the mental habit of a human soul in the time of the Gita who might have lived through what that great poem contains. We must study the Gita not in an external philological sense, not in order to provide academic commentaries, but to show how different its whole configuration of feeling and idea is from what we have now. Regarding the conceptual explanations of the world, which today, to use a graphic term, lie below but used to lie above: though the content of thought is the same, the form of expression is different. Whoever would stop with the abstract contents of these thoughts may find them easy to understand, but working one's way through to the real, living experience will not be easy. It will cost great pains to go this way again and feel with the ancient Indians, because it was in this fashion that concepts first arose such as flowed into the words *sattva, rajas, tamas.*[68] I do not attach any importance to the ideal concepts these words imply in the Bhagavad Gita, but indeed we are inclined today to take them much too easily, thinking we understand them.

We may add something further. We shall never reach an understanding beyond the limits of abstract concepts if we consider only the concepts of science regarding the activity of living beings. Sleep, for example, is not the same for humans and animals. Simply to define sleep would be like defining a knife as the same thing whether used for shaving or cutting meat. If we would keep an open mind and approach the concepts of *tamas, rajas,* and *sattva* once more from a different aspect, we can add something else taken from our present-day life. Let us consider the way humans experience nature when they enter intellectually the three kingdoms that surround them. The mode and quality of knowledge is different in each case. I am not trying to make you understand *sattva, rajas,* and *tamas* exhaustively. I only want to help you come a little nearer to an idea of their meaning. When humans today approach the mineral kingdom, they feel they can penetrate it and its laws with their thinking, that they can in a certain sense live together with it. This kind of understanding at the time of the Gita would have been called a *sattva* understanding of the mineral kingdom. In the plant kingdom we always encounter an obstacle, namely, that with our present intelligence we cannot penetrate life. The ideal now is to investigate and analyze nature from a physical-chemical standpoint, and to comprehend it in this manner. In fact, some scientists spin their threads of thought so far as to imagine they have come nearer to the idea of life by producing external forms that imitate as closely as possible the appearance of the generative process. This is idle fantasy. In our pursuit of knowledge, we do not penetrate the plant kingdom as far as we do the mineral. All we can do is *observe* plant life. What we can only observe, but not penetrate with intellectual understanding, is

---

68. The three *gunas,* respectively truth or light; energy; and darkness or lethargy.

rajas understanding. When we come to the animal kingdom, its form of consciousness escapes our everyday intelligence far more than the life of plants. We do not perceive what the animal actually lives and experiences. What we can understand about the animal kingdom with today's science is a *tamas* understanding.

What is it that actually lies in these words? Without a living sympathy for what was felt in them, we cannot follow a single line of the poem with the right quality of feeling, particularly in its later sections. At a higher stage, our inability to feel our way into these concepts is something like trying to read a book in a language we don't understand. For such a person there would be no question of seeking out the meaning of concepts in commentaries. One would just set to work to learn the language. So here it is not a matter of interpreting and commenting on the words *sattva, rajas, tamas* in an academic way. In them lies the feeling of the whole period of the Gita, something of immense significance because it led humans to an understanding of the world and its phenomena. If we would describe the way they were led, we must first free ourselves from many ideas that cannot be found in the writings of Soloviev, Hegel, and Fichte, yet lie in the widespread, fossilized thinking of the West. By *sattva, rajas, tamas* is meant a certain kind of finding one's way into the different conditions of universal life, in its varied kingdoms. It would be abstract and wrong to interpret these words simply on the basis of the ancient Indian quality of thought and feeling. It is easier to take them in the true sense of the life of that time, but to interpret them as much as possible through our own life. It is better to choose the external contour and coloring of these conceptions freely out of our own experience.

Human beings today feed themselves with various substances: animal, plant, and mineral. These foods of course have different effects on their constitution. When they eat plants, they permeate themselves with *sattva* conditions. When they try to understand them, they are for them a *rajas* condition. Nourishment from the assimilation of mineral substance—salts and the like—represents a *rajas* condition; that brought about by eating meat represents *tamas*. Notice that we cannot keep the same order of sequence as if we were starting from an abstract definition. We have to keep our concepts fluid. I have not told you this to inspire horror in those who feel bound to eating meat. In a moment I shall mention another matter where the connection is again different.

Let us imagine that a man is trying to assimilate the outer world, not through ordinary science but by that kind of clairvoyance that is legitimate for our age. Suppose that he now brings the facts and phenomena of the surrounding world into his clairvoyant consciousness. All this will call forth a certain condition in him, just as for ordinary understanding the three kingdoms of nature call forth *sattva, rajas,* and *tamas* conditions. In effect, what can enter the purest form of clairvoyant perception corresponding to purified clairvoyance calls forth *tamas*. (I use the word "purified," although not in the moral sense.) A man who would truly see spiritual facts objectively, with the kind of clairvoyance we can attain today, must by this activity bring about in himself the *tamas* condition. Then when he returns into the ordinary world where he immediately forgets his clairvoyant knowledge, he feels that with his ordinary approach he enters a new condition, a new relation to knowledge, namely the *sattva* condition. Thus in our present age everyday knowledge is the *sattva* condition. In the intermediate stage of belief building on authority, we are in the *rajas* condition.

Knowledge in the higher worlds brings about *tamas* in the human soul. Knowledge in our everyday environment is the condition of *sattva*; while faith, religious belief resting on authority, brings about the condition of *rajas*. So you see, those whose constitution compels them to eat meat need not be horrified at the fact that meat puts them in a *tamas* condition, for the same condition is brought about by purified clairvoyance. It is that condition of an external thing when by some natural process it is most detached from the spiritual. If we call the spirit "light," then the *tamas* condition is devoid of light. It is "darkness." So long as our organism is permeated by the spirit in the normal way, we are in the *sattva* condition, that of our ordinary perception of the external world. When we are asleep we are in *tamas*. We have to bring about this condition in sleep in order that our spirit may leave our body and enter the higher spirituality around us. If we would reach the higher worlds—and the Evangelist[69] already tells us what humanity's darkness is—our human nature must be in the condition of *tamas*. Since humanity is in the condition of *sattva*, not of *tamas*, which is darkness, the words of the Evangelist, "The light shineth in darkness and the darkness comprehendeth it not,"[70] can be rendered somewhat as follows, "The higher light penetrated as far as humanity, but they were filled by a natural *sattva* that they would not give up." Thus, the higher light couldn't find entrance because it can only shine in darkness.

If we seek knowledge of such living concepts as *sattva, rajas,* and *tamas*, we must get accustomed to *not* taking them in an absolute sense. They are always, one might say, turning this way and that. For a right concept of the world, there is no absolute higher or lower, only a relative sense. A European professor took objection to this. He translated *sattva* as "goodness" and objected to another man who translated it as "light," though he translated *tamas* as "darkness." Such things truly express the source of all misunderstanding. When humanity is in the condition of *tamas*—whether by sleep or clairvoyant perception, to take only these two cases—then, in effect, it is in darkness as far as the external human is concerned. So ancient Indian thought was right, yet it could not use a word like "light" in place of the word *sattva*. *Tamas* may always be translated "darkness," but for the external world the *sattva* condition could not *always* be interpreted simply as "light."

Suppose we are describing light. It is entirely correct to call the light colors. Red, orange, and yellow, according to Sankhya philosophy, are the *sattva* colors. In this sense, too, green must be called a *rajas* color, and blue, indigo, and violet, *tamas* colors. One may say that effects of light and of clairvoyance in general fall under the concept of *sattva*. Under the same concept we must also place, for example, goodness, kindness, and loving human behavior. It is true that light falls under the concept of *sattva*, but this concept is broader; light is

---

69. John, the author of the fourth Gospel and three letters, was an important object of Steiner's esoteric research.
70. Prologue to the Gospel of John.

not really identical with it. Therefore it is wrong to translate *sattva* as "light," though it is quite possible to translate *tamas* as "darkness." Nor is it correct, however, to say that "light" does not convey the idea of *sattva*.

The criticism that the professor made of a man who may have been well aware of this is also not quite justified, for the simple reason that if someone said, "Here is a lion," nobody would attempt to correct him by saying, "No, here is a beast of prey." Both are correct. This comparison hits the nail right on the head. As regards external appearance, it is correct to associate *sattva* with what is full of light, but it is wrong to say *sattva* is only of light. It is a more general concept than light, just as "beast of prey" is more general than "lion."

The same cannot be said of darkness for the reason that, in *tamas*, things that are different and specific in *rajas* and *sattva* merge into something more general. After all, a lamb and a lion are two very different creatures. If I wanted to describe them as to their *sattva* characters—the form that the natural element of life and force and spirit takes in lambs and lions—I would describe them very differently. But if I wished to describe them in the *tamas* condition, the differences do not come into consideration, because in the *tamas* condition the lamb or lion is simply lying lazily on the ground. In the *sattva* condition, lambs and lions are very different, but on a cosmic level the indolence of both is, after all, one and the same.

Our power of truly looking into such concepts must therefore adapt to great differentiation. As a matter of fact, the three concepts with the qualities of feeling in them are among the most illuminating components in the whole of Sankhya. In all that Krishna puts before Arjuna, when he presents himself as the founder of the age of self-consciousness, he has to speak in words altogether permeated by those shades of feeling derived from the concepts *sattva, rajas, tamas*. About these three concepts, and what at length leads to a climax in the Bhagavad Gita, we shall speak more fully in the last lecture of this course.

9

Helsinki, June 5, 1913

The latter part of the Bhagavad Gita is permeated by feelings and shades of meaning saturated with ideas of *sattva, rajas* and *tamas*. In these last chapters our whole mode of thinking and feeling must be attuned so as to understand what is meant by those three conditions. In the last lecture I sought to give an idea of those important concepts by making use of present-day experiences. Certainly anyone who enters the poem in depth must perceive that since the time when it arose those concepts have shifted to some extent. Nevertheless, it would not be incorrect to refer to them simply by verbal quotations from the poem. Our mode of feeling is different from what is contained there and we are unable to make those very different feelings our own. If we tried to do so, we would only be describing the unknown by the unknown.

So in the Bhagavad Gita you will find, with regard to food, that the concepts we developed last time have shifted a little. What is true for us today about plant food was true for the ancient Indian of the food Krishna calls "mild" or "gentle" food. Whereas *rajas* food, which we described correctly for us today as mineral food (salt, for instance), would have been designated at that time as "sour" or "sharp." For our constitution, meat is essentially a *tamas* food; but the Indian meant by this something that could hardly be considered food at present, which gives us an idea of how different people were then. They meant food that had become rotten, had stood too long and had a foul smell. In our present incarnation we could not properly call that *tamas* food, because the human organism has changed, even as far as our physical body.

In order to understand these feelings of *sattva, rajas,* and *tamas,* so fundamental in the Gita, it is well for us to apply them to our own conditions. Now, if we wish to consider what *sattva* really is, it is best to begin by taking the most striking conception of it. In our time the person who can give him- or herself up to knowledge as penetrating as our present knowledge of the mineral kingdom is a *sattva* person. For the Indian, such a person was not one who had such knowledge, but one who went through the world with intelligent understanding— we would say, with heart and head in the right place—a person who takes on without prejudice or bias the phenomena the world offers; a person who always perceives the world with sympathy and conceives it with intelligence; one who receives the light of ideas, of feelings and sentiments streaming out from all the beauty and loveliness of the world; one who avoids all that is ugly, developing him- or herself rightly. One who does all this in the physical world is a *sattva* person. In the inorganic world, a *sattva* impression is that of a surface not too brilliant—bright, yet illuminated in such a way that its details of color can be seen in their right lustre.

A *rajas* person is in a certain way prevented by his or her own emotions, impulses and reactions, or by the thing itself, from fully penetrating his or her surroundings, so that one does not give oneself up to the world, but meets it with what one is oneself. For example, one becomes acquainted with the plant kingdom. One can admire it, but one brings one's own emotions to bear on it and therefore cannot penetrate it to its depths.

A *tamas* person is altogether given up to the bodily life, so that he or she is blunt and apathetic toward the environment, as we might be toward a consciousness different from our own. While we dwell on the physical plane, we know nothing of the consciousness of a dog or a horse, not even of another human being. In this respect the human being, as a rule, is blunt and dull, withdrawing into his or her own bodily life. Humans live in impressions of *tamas*. But humans must gradually become apathetic to the physical world in order to have access to the spiritual worlds in clairvoyance. In this way we can best read the ideas of *sattva, rajas,* and *tamas.* In external nature a *rajas* impression would be that of a moderately bright surface, say of green, a uniform green shade. A dark-colored surface would represent a *tamas* impression. Where we look out into the darkness of universal space, when the beautiful spectacle of the free heavens appears to us, the blue color we see is almost a *tamas* color.

If we saturate ourselves with the feeling these ideas give, we can apply them to everything that surrounds us. These ideas are really comprehensive. For the ancient Indians, to comprehend this three-fold nature of their surroundings meant not only a certain understanding of the outer world, it also meant bringing to life their own inner being. They felt it somewhat as follows. Imagine an ancient countryman who sees the glory of nature around him—the early morning sky, the Sun and stars, everything he can see. He does not think about it, however. He does not build up concepts and ideas about the world but just lives in utmost harmony with it. If he begins to feel himself as an individual person, distinguishing his soul from his environment, he has to do so by learning to understand his surroundings through ideas about them.

To set one's environment objectively before one is always a certain way of grasping the reality of one's own being. The Indian of the time of the Bhagavad Gita said, "So long as one does not penetrate and perceive the *sattva, rajas,* and *tamas* conditions in one's environment, one continues merely to live in it. One is not yet there, independently in one's own being, but is bound up with one's own surroundings. However, when the world around one becomes so objective that one can pursue it everywhere with the awareness that this is a *sattva* condition, this a *rajas,* that a *tamas,* then one becomes ever freer of the world, more independent in oneself. This, therefore, is one way of bringing about consciousness of self. At bottom, this is Krishna's concern—to free Arjuna's soul from all those things that surround him and are characteristic of the time in which he lives. So Krishna explains, 'Behold all the life there on the bloody field of battle, where brothers confront brothers, with all that thou feelest thyself bound to, dissolved in, a part of. Learn to know that all that is there outside you runs its course in conditions of *sattva, rajas,* and *tamas.* Then wilt thou contrast thyself with it. Know that in thine own highest self thou dost not belong to it, and wilt experience thy separate being within thyself, the spirit in thee.'"[71]

Here we have another of the beautiful elements in the dramatic composition of the Bhagavad Gita. At first we are gradually made acquainted with its ideas as abstract concepts, but then afterward, these become more and more vivid. The concepts of *sattva, rajas,* and *tamas* take on living shape and form in the most varied spheres of life. Then, at length, the separation of Arjuna's soul from it all is accomplished, so to speak, before our spiritual gaze. Krishna explains to him how we must free ourselves from all that is bound up with these three conditions.

There are *sattva* people who are so bound up with existence as to be attached to all the happiness and joy they can draw from their environment. They speed through the world, drinking in their blissfulness from all that can give it to them. *Rajas* people are diligent, people of action, but they act because they are attached to the consequences of their action. They depend on the joy of action, on the impression action makes upon them. *Tamas* people are attached to laziness; they want to be comfortable. They really do not want to act at all. All of those whose souls and spirits are bound into external conditions belong to one or other of these three groups.

"But thine eyes shall see the daybreak of the age of self-consciousness. Thou shalt learn to hold thy soul apart. Thou shalt be neither *sattva, rajas,* nor *tamas*" [see XVII.53–66]. Thus is Krishna the great educator of the human ego. He shows its separation from its environment. He explains soul activities according to how they partake of *sattva, rajas* or *tamas.* If one raises one's belief to the divine creators of the world, one is a *sattva* person. In the time of the Gita, however,

---

71. Rather than a quotation, this passage seems to be Steiner's summary of Krishna's teaching concerning the *gunas,* for which, see especially chapters 14 and 18.

there were those who knew nothing of the divine beings guiding the universe. They were completely attached to the so-called nature spirits, those behind the immediate beings of nature. Such people are *rajas* people. The *tamas* people are those who in viewing the world get only so far as what we may call the ghostlike, which in its spiritual nature is nearest to the material. So these three groups may also be distinguished in regard to religious feeling.

If we wished to apply these concepts to religious feeling in our time we should say that those who strive after Anthroposophy are *sattva* people, those attached to external faith are *rajas* people, and those who, in a material or spiritual sense, will only believe in what has bodily shape and form—the materialists and spiritualists—are the *tamas* people. Spiritualists do not ask for spiritual beings in whom they may believe. They are quite prepared to believe in them, but they do not want to lift themselves up to the spiritual beings. They want the beings to come down. Spiritual beings must rap, because rapping can be heard with physical ears. They must appear in clouds of light because clouds can be seen with physical eyes. Hence spiritualists and materialists are *tamas* people, quite in the sense of the *tamas* people of Krishna's time.

There are also unconscious *tamas* people, the materialistic thinkers of our time, who deny all that is spiritual. When materialists meet in conference today, they persuade themselves that they adhere to materialism on logical grounds, but this is an illusion. Materialists are people who remain so not on the basis of logic, but for fear of the spiritual. They deny the spirit because they are afraid of it. They are in effect compelled to deny it by the logic of their own unconscious soul, which penetrates to the door of the spiritual but cannot pass through it. One who can see reality can see in a materialistic congress how each person in the depths of his or her soul is afraid of the spirit. Materialism is not logic; it is cowardice before the spiritual. All its arguments are nothing but an opiate to damp down this fear. Actually, Ahriman—the giver of fear—has every materialist by the neck. This is a grotesque but an austere and fundamental truth that one may recognize if one goes to any materialistic meeting. Why is such a meeting called? The illusion is that people there discuss views of the universe, but in reality it is a meeting to conjure up the devil Ahriman, to beckon him into their chambers.

Krishna, then, indicates to Arjuna how the different religious beliefs may be classified, and speaks to him of the different ways human beings may approach the gods in actual prayer. In all cases the temper of the human soul can be described in terms of these three conditions. *Sattva, rajas,* and *tamas* people are different in the way they relate to their gods. *Tamas* people may be priests whose priesthood depends on a kind of habit. They have their office, but no living connection with the spiritual world. So they repeat *Aum, Aum, Aum,* which proceeds from the dullness, the *tamas* condition of their spirit. They pour forth their subjective nature in the *Aum.*

Rajas people look out on the surrounding world and begin to feel that it has something in it akin to themselves, that it is related to them and therefore that it is worthy of worship. They are the people of *"Tat"* who worship the "That," the Cosmos, as being akin to themselves. *Sattva* people perceive that what lives within us is one with all that surrounds us in the universe outside. In their prayer they have a sense for *"Sat,"* the All Being, the unity without and within, unity of the objective and the subjective. Krishna says that one who would truly become free in the soul, one who does not wish to be merely a *sattva,* a *rajas,* or a *tamas* person in any single respect or another, must attain to a transformation of these conditions within the self so that one wears them like a garment, while in one's real self one grows out beyond them.

This is the impulse that Krishna as the creator of self-consciousness must give. He stands before Arjuna and teaches him to "Look upon all the conditions of the world, with all that is to humankind highest and deepest, but free thyself from the highest and deepest of the three conditions and in thine own self become as one who lays hold of the self. Learn and know that thou canst live without feeling thyself bound up with *rajas,* or *tamas,* or *sattva*" [see XVIII.11–12]. One had to *learn* this at that time, because it was the beginning of the dawn of self-liberation. But here again, what then required the greatest effort can today be found right at hand. This is the tragedy of present life. There are too many today who stand in the world and burrow down into their own soul, finding no connection with the outer world. In their feelings and all their inner experiences they are lonely souls. They neither feel themselves bound up with the conditions of *sattva, rajas* or *tamas,* nor are they free from them, but are cast out into the world like an endlessly, aimlessly revolving wheel. Such people who live only in themselves and cannot understand the world, who are unhappy because in their soul life they are separated from all external existence—these represent the shadow side of the fruit that it was Krishna's task to develop in Arjuna and in all of his contemporaries and successors. What had to be Arjuna's highest endeavor has become the greatest suffering for many people today.

Thus do successive ages change. Today we must say that we are at the end of the age that began with the time of the Bhagavad Gita. This may penetrate our feelings with deep significance. It may also tell us that just as in that ancient time those seeking self-consciousness had to hear what Krishna told Arjuna, those seeking their soul's salvation today—in whom self-consciousness is developed to a morbid degree—these too should listen, to hear what can lead them once more to an understanding of the three external conditions. What might this teaching be?

Let us put forward some more preliminary ideas before we set out to answer this question. Let us ask again, what is it that Krishna really wants for Arjuna, whose relation to external conditions was right for his time? What is it that he says with divine simplicity and naïveté? He reveals what he wishes to be even to our present time. We have described how a kind of picture consciousness, a living imagery, lit up the human soul, how there was hovering above it, so to speak, what today is self-consciousness, which people at that time had to strive for with all their might, but which today is right at hand. Try to live into the soul condition of that time before Krishna introduced the new age. The world did not call forth clear concepts and ideas, but pictures, like those of our dreams today. The lowest region of soul life was a picture-like consciousness, and this was illumined from the higher region—of sleep consciousness—through inspiration. In this way souls could rise to still higher conditions. This ascent was called "entering into Brahma." To ask a soul today, living in the West, to enter into Brahma would be a senseless anachronism. It would be like requiring a person who is halfway up a mountain to reach the top by the same way as one still down in the valley. To ask a soul today to do Hindu (or Yogic) exercises and "enter into Brahma" presupposes that a person is at the stage of picture consciousness, which as a matter of fact certain Asians still are. What those people of the Gita age found in rising into Brahma, Westerners already have in their concepts and ideas. Truly, Shankaracharya would today introduce the ideas of Soloviev, Hegel, and Fichte to his reverent disciples as the first stage of rising into Brahma. It is not the content, however, but the pains of the way that are important.

Krishna indicates a main characteristic of this rising into Brahma, through which we have a beautiful characterization by Krishna himself. At that time the constitution of the soul was entirely passive. The world of pictures came to you, and you gave yourself up to these flowing pictures. Compare this with the altogether different nature of *our* everyday world. Devotion, giving ourselves up to things, does not help us to understand them, even though there are many who do not wish to advance to what must necessarily take place in our time. Nevertheless, for our age we have to exert ourselves, we have to be alive and active, in order to achieve ideas and concepts of our surrounding world. Herein lies all the trouble in our education. We have to educate children so that their minds are awake when their concepts of the surrounding world are being formed. Today the soul must be more active than it was in the age before the origin of the Bhagavad Gita. We can put it so:

Bhagavad Gita age—rising to Brahma with passive souls.
Consciousness soul age (our present age)—actively working our way up into the higher worlds.

What then must Krishna say when he wishes to introduce that new age in which the active way of gaining an understanding of the universe is gradually to begin? He must say, "I have to come; I have to give thee the 'I'-human, a gift that shall impel thee to activity." If it had all remained passive as before—the human being interwoven with the world, devoted to the world—the new age would never have begun. Everything connected with the entry of the soul into the spiritual world before the time of the Gita, Krishna calls "devotion." "All is devotion to Brahma" [see XVIII.65–70]. This he compares to the feminine in humankind; while what is the self in humans, the active working element that pushes up from within as the generator of the self-consciousness that is to come, Krishna calls the masculine in humankind. What human beings can attain in Brahma must be fertilized by Krishna. So his teaching to Arjuna is, "All human beings until now were Brahma people. Brahma is all that is spread out as the mother-womb of the whole world. But I am the father, who came into the world to fertilize the maternal womb."[72]

Thus the consciousness of self is created, which is to work on all human beings. This is indicated as clearly as possible. Krishna and Brahma are related to each other as father and mother in the world. Together they produce the self-consciousness that human beings must have in the further course of their evolution—the self-consciousness that makes it possible for them to become ever more perfect as individual beings. The Krishna faith has altogether to do with the single person, the individual person. To follow his teaching exclusively means to strive for the perfection of oneself as an individual. This can be achieved only by liberating the self, loosening it from all that adheres to external conditions. Fix your attention on this backbone of Krishna's teaching, on the way it directs human beings to put aside all externals, to become free from the life that takes its course in continually changing conditions of every kind; to comprehend oneself in the self alone, that it may be borne ever onward to higher perfection. See how this perfection depends on human beings leaving behind the external configuration of things, casting off the whole of outer life like a shell, becoming free and ever more inwardly alive. Tearing the self away from the environment, no longer asking what goes on in external processes of

72. See XIV.3: "My womb is *prakriti*; in that I place the seed. Thus all created things are born. Everything born, Arjuna, comes from the womb of *prakriti*, and I am the seed-giving father."

perfection, but asking how shall one perfect *oneself.* This is the teaching of Krishna.

Lucifer directed human attention to the outer world. By his instigation, humans had to learn to know the external, and therefore had to go through the long course of evolution down to the time of Christ. Then he who was once withdrawn from Lucifer came, in Krishna and later in the Luke Jesus child. In two stages he gave that teaching that from another side was to be the antithesis of the teaching of Lucifer in Paradise. "He wanted to open your eyes to the conditions of *sattva, rajas,* and *tamas.* Shut your eyes to these conditions and you will find yourselves as human beings, as self-conscious human beings." Thus does the imagination appear before us. On the one side the imagination of Paradise, where Lucifer opens our eyes to the three conditions in the external world, when for a while the opponent of Lucifer withdraws. Then humans go through their evolution and reach the point where in two stages another teaching is given them, of self consciousness, which bids them close their eyes to the three external conditions. Both teachings are one-sided. If the Krishna-Jesus influence alone had continued, one one-sidedness would have been added to another. Humankind would have taken leave of all that surrounds it, and would have lost all interest in external evolution. Each person would only have sought his or her own perfection. Striving for perfection is right, but such striving bought at the price of a lack of interest in the whole of humanity is one sided, even as the luciferic influence was one sided. Hence the all embracing Christ impulse entered, the higher synthesis of the two one-sided tendencies. Krishna—that is, the spirit who worked through Krishna—appeared again in the Jesus child of the Nathan line of the House of David, described in Luke's Gospel. Thus, fundamentally, this child embodied the impulse, all the forces that tend to make human beings independent and loosen them from external reality. What was the intention of this soul that did not enter human evolution but worked in Krishna and again in this Jesus child? At a far-distant time, this soul had had to go through the experience of remaining outside human evolution because the antagonist Lucifer had come, he who said, "Your eyes will be opened and you will distinguish good and evil, and be as God." In the ancient Indian sense Lucifer said to humanity, "You will be as the gods, and will have power to find the *sattva, rajas,* and *tamas* conditions in the world."

In the personality of the Luke Jesus child himself, the Christ impulse lived for three years, the Christ who came to humankind to bring together these two extremes. Through each of them humankind would have fallen into weakness and sin. Through Lucifer, humanity would have been condemned to live one-sidedly in the external conditions of *sattva, rajas,* and *tamas.* Through Krishna, they were to be educated for the other extreme, to close their eyes and seek only their own perfection. Christ took sin upon himself. He gave to humanity what reconciles the two one-sided tendencies. He took upon himself the sin of self-consciousness, which would close its eyes to the world outside. He took upon himself the sin of Krishna, and of all who would commit his sin. He took upon himself the sin of Lucifer and of all who would commit the sin of fixing their attention on externalities. By taking both extremes upon himself, he makes it possible for humanity by degrees to find a harmony between the inner and the outer world, because in that harmony alone the salvation of humanity is to be found.

An evolution that has once begun, however, cannot end suddenly. The urge to self-consciousness that began with Krishna went on and on, increasing and intensifying self-consciousness more and more, bringing about estrangement from the outer world. In our time too this course is tending to continue. At the time when the Krishna impulse was received by the Luke Jesus child, humankind was in the midst of this development—an increase of self-consciousness and estrangement from the outer world. It was this that was brought home to those who received the baptism of John in the Jordan, so that they understood the Baptist when he said to them, "Change your disposition; walk no longer in the path of Krishna"—though he did not use this word. The path on which humankind had then entered we may call the Jesus path, if we would speak in an esoteric sense. In effect, the pursuit of this Jesus path alone went on and on through the following centuries. In many respects, human civilization in the centuries following the foundation of Christianity was only related to Jesus, not to the Christ who lived in Jesus for the three years from the baptism by John until the Mystery of Golgotha.

Every line of evolution, however, works its way onward up to a certain tension. In the course of time this longing for individual perfection was driven to such a pitch that humanity was in a certain sense brought more and more into the tragedy of estrangement from the divine in nature, from the outer world. Today we are experiencing this in many ways. So many people today have little understanding left of our environment. Therefore, it is just in our time that an understanding of the Christ impulse must break in upon us. The Christ path must be added to the Jesus path. The path of one sided striving for perfection has become too strong. In many respects we are so remote from our surroundings that certain movements, when they arise, overreach themselves immediately, and the longing for the opposite is awakened. Many human souls now feel how little they can escape from this enhanced self-consciousness, and this creates an impulse to know the divinity of the outer world. It is such souls as these who in our time will seek the understanding of the Christ impulse that is opened up by true Anthroposophy, the force that does not merely strive for the one sided perfection of the individual soul but belongs to the whole progress of humanity. To understand the Christ means not merely to strive toward perfection, but to receive in oneself something expressed by St. Paul, "Not I, but Christ in me." "I" is the Krishna word. "Not I, but Christ in me," is the Christian word.

So we see how every spiritual movement in history has its justification in a certain sphere. No one should ever imagine that the Krishna impulse could have been dispensed with. No one should ever think either that one human spiritual movement is fully justified in its one-sidedness. The two extremes—the Luciferic and the Krishna impulses—had to find their higher unity in the mission of the Christ.

One who would understand in the true anthroposophic sense the impulse necessary for the further evolution of humankind must realize how Anthroposophy has to become a means of shedding light on all religions. He or she must learn to see how the different streams in evolution all flow into the one main current of development. It would be a dilettante beginning if one tried to find again in the Krishna stream what can be found in the stream of Christianity. Only when we regard the matter in this way do we understand what it means to seek a unity in all religions. There is, however, another way of doing so. One may repeat over and over, "In all religions the same fundamental essence is contained." In effect, the same essence is contained in the root of a plant, in the stem, leaves, flowers, the pollen and the fruit. That is true, but it is an abstract truth. It is no more profound than if one were to say, "Why make any distinctions? Salt, pepper, vinegar, and milk all have their place on the table; all are one, for all are substance." Here you can tell how futile such a way of thought can be, but you do not notice it so easily when it comes to comparing religions. It will not do to compare the Chinese, Hindu, Buddhist, Zoroastrian, Muslim, and Christian faiths in this abstract way, saying, "Look, everywhere we find the same principles. In each case there is a Savior."

Abstractions can indeed be found in countless places and in countless ways, but this is a dilettante method, because it leads to nothing. One may form societies to pursue the study of all religions, and do so in the same sense as saying pepper, salt, etc. are one because they are all substance. That has no importance. What is important is to regard things as they really are. To persist in declaiming the equality of all religions is an example of esoteric dilettantism. It is as though it were one and the same whether what lived in the Christ were the pivot of the whole of evolution or whether it could be found in the first person you meet in the street. For one who wishes to guide his or her life by truth, it is an atrocity to associate the impulse in the world's history that is bound up with the Mystery of Golgotha, and for which the name Christ has been preserved, with any other impulse in history, because in truth it is the central point of the whole of earthly evolution.

In these lectures I have tried by means of a particular instance to indicate how present day esotericism must try to throw light on the different spiritual movements that have appeared in the course of human history. Though each has its right and proper point of contact, one must distinguish between them as between the stem of a plant and the green leaf, and between the green leaf and the colored petal, though all together form a unity. If one tries with this truly modern esotericism to penetrate with one's soul into what has flowed into humanity in diverse currents, one recognizes how the different religious faiths lose nothing of their greatness and majesty. How sublime was the greatness that appeared to us in the figure of Krishna, even when we simply tried to get a definite view of his place in evolution! All such lines of thought as we can give only in outline are indeed imperfect, and you may be assured that no one is more aware of their imperfection than the present speaker. But the endeavor has been to show in what spirit a true consideration of the spiritual movement toward individuality in humankind must be carried out. I purposely tried to derive our thoughts from a spiritual creation remote from us, the Bhagavad Gita, to show how Western minds can perceive and feel what they owe to Krishna—what he, through the continued working of his impulse, still signifies for their own upward striving.

However, the spiritual movement we represent here necessarily demands that we enter concretely, and with real love, into the special nature of every current in humanity's spiritual history. This is a bit inconvenient, because it brings us all too near to the humble thought of how little, after all, we really penetrate into their depths. Another idea follows upon this, namely, that we must continue striving further and ever further. Both of these ideas are inconvenient. It is the sad fate of that movement we call Anthroposophy that it produces inconvenient results for many souls. It requires that we actively lay hold of the definite, separate facts of the world's development. At the same time it requires all of us to say earnestly to ourselves, "I can indeed reach something higher, and I will. Whatever I have attained, it is always only a certain stage and standpoint. I must forever go on striving—on and on, without end."

Thus all along it has been not quite comfortable to belong to the spiritual movement that by our efforts is endeavoring to take its place in what is called the Theosophical Movement.[73] It has not been easy, because we demand that people shall learn to strive ever more deeply

---

73. This is a reference to Steiner's break with the Theosophical Society in 1912 and the formation of the Anthroposophical Society. See Guenther Wachsmuth, *The Life and Work of Rudolf Steiner: From the Turn of the Century to His Death* (NY: Whittier Books, 1955), and Christopher Bamford's introduction to *Spiritualism, Madame Blavatsky, and Theosophy—An Eyewitness View of Occult History* (Great Barrington, MA: Anthroposophic Press, 2001).

to penetrate the sacred mysteries. We could not supply you with anything so easy as introducing some person's son or daughter, saying, "You need only wait, the Savior of humankind will appear physically embodied in this boy or girl."[74] We could not do this because we must be true. Yet one who perceives what is happening cannot but regard these latest proceedings as the final grotesque outcome of the dilettante comparison of religions that can also be put forward so easily, and that continually repeats what should be taken as a matter of course, the tritest of all sayings, "All religions contain the same essence."[75]

The last weeks and months have shown—and my speaking here on this significant subject has shown it again—that a circle of people can be found at the present time who are ready to seek spiritual truths. We have no other concern than to put these truths forward, though many, or even everyone, may leave us. If so, it will make no difference in the way the spiritual truths are here proclaimed. The sacred obligation to truth will guide the movement that underlies this cycle of lectures. Whoever would go with us must do so under the conditions that have now become necessary. It is certainly more convenient to proceed otherwise, not entering into another side of the matter as we do by pointing out the reality in all things. But that also is part of our obligation to truth. It is simpler to inform people of the equality and unity of religions, or tell them they are to wait for the incarnation of a savior who is predestined, whom they are to recognize not by themselves but on someone's authority.

Human souls today will themselves have to decide how far a spiritual movement can be carried on and upheld by pure devotion to the ideal of truthfulness. In our time, it had to come to that sharp cleavage whose climax was reached when those who had no other desire than to set forth what is true and genuine in evolution, were described as

---

74. This would seem to be a reference to the claim in 1911 by Annie Besant and C. W. Leadbeater that J. Krishnamurti (1895–1986), who was then sixteen years old, was the reincarnation of Jesus. This claim, and the creation of the Order of the Star of the East, beginning in 1909, contributed to the break, perhaps inevitable, between Rudolf Steiner and Annie Besant, then president of the Theosophical Society.
75. H. P. Blavatsky taught the unity of all religions.

Jesuits.[76] This was a convenient way of separating, but the external evidence was the work of objective falsehood. This cycle of lectures may once more have shown you that we have been working out of no one-sided tendency, since it comprises the present, the past, and the primal past, in order to reveal the unique, fundamental impulse of human evolution. So I too may say that it fills me with the deepest satisfaction to have been able to give these lectures here before you. This shows me there is hope because there are souls here who have the impulse, the urge toward what works also in the supersensible with nothing but simple, honest truthfulness.

I was forced to add this final word to these lectures, for it is necessary in view of all that has happened to us in the course of time down to the point of being excluded from the Theosophical Society. Considering all we have suffered, and all that is now being falsely asserted in numerous pamphlets, it was necessary to say something, although a discussion of these matters is always painful to me.

Those who desire to work with us must know that we have taken for our banner the humble, yet unconditional, honest striving for truth, striving ever upward into the higher worlds.

---

76. During the years of tension between the teaching of Rudolf Steiner and the leaders of the Theosophical Society, Annie Besant repeated the accusation, which was without foundation, that Rudolf Steiner was a student of the Jesuits.

APPENDIX: From *The Gospel of St. Mark*

Lecture 5

BASEL, SEPTEMBER 19, 1912

Y ESTERDAY[77] we endeavored to place before our minds from a certain point of view the world-historical position that existed at the moment in time when the Mystery of Golgotha occurred. We tried to do this by presenting the picture of two significant leaders of humankind, the Buddha and Socrates, both of whom lived several centuries before the Mystery of Golgotha. In doing this we remarked that the Buddha represented something like the significant conclusion of one stream of evolution. In the fifth or sixth century before the Mystery of Golgotha, he proclaimed what has since then been recognized as a deeply significant teaching. The revelation of Benares, which in a certain way encompasses and renews all that had been able to flow into human souls during thousands of years, was proclaimed in the only way it could be proclaimed half a millennium before the Mystery of Golgotha. We can see even more clearly how far the Buddha represented the great conclusion of one cosmic stream when we place before our minds his great predecessor who recedes far back into the twilight

---

77. Basel, September 19, 1912. See *The Gospel of St. Mark* (Hudson, NY: Anthroposophic Press, 1986).

of human evolution: Krishna, who in quite a different sense appears to us as the final moment of a revelation thousands of years old. Krishna can be placed several centuries before the Buddha,[78] but that is not the issue here. The main point is that the more we allow the being of Krishna and the being of the Buddha to affect us, the more clearly we recognize that in Krishna what was later to be proclaimed by the Buddha appears in an even brighter light, whereas with Buddha, as we wish to demonstrate in a moment, in a certain way that impulse comes to an end.

The name Krishna embraces something that for many thousands of years has shone into the spiritual development of humankind. If we immerse ourselves in all that is meant by the proclamation of Krishna, we look up into the sublime heights of human spiritual evolution, instilling the feeling within us that nothing can possibly surpass or enhance what resounds from Krishna's revelation. What resounds from this revelation of Krishna is a kind of climax. In saying this we are attributing to the person of Krishna what also was revealed by others before him. For everything that had been given out gradually for thousands of years before his time by those who were given the task of becoming the bearers of knowledge was renewed, summed up, and brought to a conclusion in the revelations of Krishna to his people. If we take into consideration how Krishna speaks about the divine spiritual worlds and the relation of these worlds to humankind, and about the course of cosmic events, and if we also consider the spirituality to which we ourselves must rise if we wish to penetrate the deeper meaning of the teaching of Krishna, then we may say that only one event in the whole subsequent development of humanity can in even a slight degree be compared with it.

---

78. Contemporary scholarship typically places the birth of Gotama Buddha at approximately 624 B.C.E., and his death eighty years later, in 544 B.C.E. For a scholarly account of Buddha's life, see Hajime Nakamura, *Gotama Buddha: A Biography Based on the Most Reliable Texts*, trans. Gaynor Sekimori, Vol. 1 (Tokyo: Kosei Publishing Co., 2000). Steiner presumably refers here to the appearance of Krishna in the Bhagavad Gita, the text of which is typically placed at approximately the third century B.C.E., but was presumably evolving from the *Mahabharata* for several centuries prior.

We may say of the revelation of Krishna that it is in a certain sense an esoteric teaching. Why esoteric? It is esoteric for the simple reason that few people can achieve the inner capacity to ascend to those spiritual heights where understanding can be gained. There is no need to keep secret what Krishna revealed in an external way, to lock it up in a safe, so that it stays "esoteric." It remains esoteric for no other reason than that too few people rise to the heights to which they must rise if they are to understand it. However widely such revelations as those of Krishna are disseminated among the people and put into their hands, they still remain esoteric. For they can be brought out of the realm of the esoteric not by disseminating them among the people, but only when there are souls who can rise high enough to be able to unite with them. It is true that such revelations hover above us at a certain spiritual height, yet they speak to us as if from a high point of spirituality. Those who simply pick up the words that are contained in such revelations should by no means believe they understand them, not even if they are learned, twentieth-century people. It is widely asserted today that there is no esoteric teaching. This is understand-able because those who say such things do indeed possess the words, and with them think they have everything. But it is in the very nature of esoteric teaching that they do not understand what they possess.

Consider, as another example of this phenomenon, everything that in recent years has been linked to the names of Fichte, Schelling, and Hegel, whose teachings have a slight resemblance to other "esoteric teachings" of humankind. For though we can undoubtedly acquire the writings of Fichte, Schelling, and Hegel, it cannot be denied that in the widest sense of the word they have remained esoteric teaching. Truly, they have remained esoteric to this day. There are very few people who wish to achieve any kind of relation to what these three men have written. From a certain kind of what I may call philosophical courtesy, there is today in certain circles some talk about Hegel again. If some-thing is said like what I have just said myself, then the reply is made that after all there really are some people who busy themselves with Hegel. However, if one listens to what these people say and what they contribute to the understanding of Hegel, then we are all the more compelled to the view that for these people Hegel has remained an esoteric teaching. What shines out toward us from India from Krishna appears again in Fichte, Schelling, and Hegel in an abstract conceptual way, and it is not easy to notice the similarity. Indeed, it requires a special constitution of soul to be able to do so. I should like to speak candidly about this and state clearly what is required.

When people today who believe they have enjoyed not an average but a superior education take up a philosophical work by Fichte or Hegel, they believe they are reading something concerned only with the development of advanced concepts. Most people will agree that it is difficult to warm up to it, if, for example, they turn to Hegel's *Encyclopaedia of the Philosophical Sciences* and read for the first time about being, nonbeing, becoming, existence, and the like. We have probably heard it said that in this work a man has cooked up a collection of highly abstract concepts, beautiful enough, no doubt, but providing nothing capable of kindling warmth in heart or soul. I have known many people who after three or four pages of this particular work have promptly closed the book. But they are not at all prepared to admit that perhaps the guilt lies in themselves that they do not warm up, and that they have avoided the struggles that have to be endured in going from hell to heaven. This they do not willingly admit. Yet it is possible by means of these so called "abstract concepts" to experience a veritable life struggle, and to feel not only a living warmth but the whole range of feeling from the most extreme cold to the highest soul warmth. Then one can come to feel that these things are written not in simple abstract concepts but in the heart's blood.

We may compare what radiates over us from Krishna with what is regarded as the newest evolutionary phase of the human ascent toward the spiritual heights. Yet there is a significant difference. What we meet with in Fichte, Schelling, and Hegel, these most mature thinkers of Christianity, we meet with in a pre-Christian era, in the form it had to take then, in Krishna. For what is Krishna's revelation? It is something that can never again be repeated, the greatness and quality of which can never be surpassed. If we have an understanding for such things, we may develop a conception, an idea, of the strength of that spiritual light that radiates out to us; that is, if we let such things affect us as are connected with the culture from which Krishna emerged.

To take a few examples from the Bhagavad Gita, in the tenth canto
Krishna speaks as follows:

> I am the spirit of creation, its beginning, its center, and its end.
> Among all beings I am always the noblest of all that has come into
> being; among spiritual beings I am Vishnu, I am the sun among
> the stars; among the lights I am the moon; among the elements
> I am fire; among the mountains I am the lofty Meru; among
> the water I am the great cosmic sea; among the rivers I am the
> Ganges; among the multitude of trees I am the Ashvattha tree; in
> the true sense of the word I am the ruler of humankind and of
> all the beings that live; among the serpents I am the one that is
> eternal, the very ground of existence itself! [See X.20–27]

Let us take another example from the same culture, which we
find in the Vedas. The Devas were gathered around the throne of
the Almighty, and in deep reverence they asked who He was. Then
the Almighty, that is to say the cosmic God in the old Indian sense,
answered:

> If there were another than I, I would describe myself through him.
> I have been from all eternity and through all eternity I shall be. I
> am the primal cause of everything, of all that is in West, in East,
> in North and South; I am the cause of all that is in the heights
> above and in the depths below. I am all; I am more ancient than
> anything that is. I am the ruler of rulers; I am the truth itself. I
> am revelation itself, and the cause of revelation. I am knowledge,
> I am piety, I am the law. I am almighty!

And when, as the ancient document records, it was asked what was
the cause of all things, the answer was given:

> The cause of the world, it is fire; it is the Sun and it is also the
> Moon. It is also this pure Brahman and this water and this high-
> est of all creatures. All moments and all weeks and all months
> and all centuries and all millennia and all millions of years have

proceeded from him, have emerged from his radiant personality which no one can comprehend, neither above nor below nor in the circumference, nor in the center, here where we stand!

Such words sound over to us from very ancient times, and we surrender ourselves to them. They speak of Krishna, of the cosmic God, and of cosmic origins. If we approach these words without preconceptions, how do we feel? From the tone of these thoughts, as they sound forth through these words, things are said that could never have been expressed in a greater or more significant way. And we know that they never could have been spoken in a greater or more significant manner. That is to say, something was placed into human evolution that must stand just as it is and be accepted as it is, since it has come to a conclusion. And wherever people in later times have thought about such things, and may perhaps have believed in accordance with methods employed in these later times that one thing or another could have been expressed in clearer concepts or could have been modified in one way or another, they have nevertheless been unable to say it with more clarity. They have never done so. Indeed, if anyone wished to say something more clearly about precisely these things, it would be sheer presumption.

Let us first consider the passage of the Bhagavad Gita where Krishna characterizes his own nature. What is he really characterizing? His way of speaking is truly remarkable. He says of his nature that he is the spirit of all that has come into being, that among the heavenly spirits he is Vishnu, among the stars he is the Sun, among the lights the Moon, among the elements the fire, and so on. If we wish to paraphrase this and compress it into a formula, we can say that Krishna points to himself as the essence, the entity of all things. He is this entity in such a way that it represents always the purest, the most divine kind of nature. Hence, according to this passage, if we penetrate beyond the actual things and seek to find behind them the nature of their true being, we arrive at the being of Krishna. If we take a number of plants of the same species and look for the entity of this species, which is not in itself visible but comes to expression in the single plant forms, and ask what lies behind them as their essence, the answer is: Krishna! But we must not think of this being as identical with any single plant, but must think of him as the highest and purest element in the form.

So what is Krishna actually speaking of? Of nothing else but what one can recognize as one's own essence when one sinks into oneself, not one's being as it appears to one in ordinary life, but something that lies *behind* the human being and the human soul as they manifest themselves in life. He speaks of the human essence that is within us because the true human essence is at one with the universe. This is by no means a knowledge that works egotistically within Krishna. It is something in Krishna that wishes to point to the highest in humanity, something that may perceive itself as identical and at-one with what lives as being in all things.

Just as we speak today for our own age, so Krishna spoke to his own age of what he had in mind for his culture. If today we look into our own being, we first of all glimpse the ego as you will find it pictured in the book *How to Know Higher Worlds*. We distinguish the ordinary ego from the higher, supersensible ego, which does not appear in the world of sense. This supersensible ego is not only in us but is at the same time poured out over the being of all things. It is not what we mean when we say in our customary manner "I am," although in our language it has the same sound. In Krishna's mouth it would not have had the same sound. He is speaking of the nature of the human soul as it would have been interpreted in that day, in the same way as we today speak of the ego.

How did it come about that what Krishna expresses is so similar to what we express when we speak of the highest of which we have knowledge today? This was possible because the culture out of which Krishna emerged was preceded for thousands of years by a clairvoyant culture, because human beings were accustomed to rising to clairvoyant vision when they looked into the being of things. And we can understand a language such as resounds to us from the Bhagavad Gita when we look upon it as the close of the old clairvoyant view of the world, when we recognize that when people in those ancient times passed into the intermediate state between sleeping and waking, which was at that time common to all human beings, they did not experience ordinary sense perception. They felt themselves poured out over all things, felt themselves in all beings and at one with them. They felt themselves to be at one with the best of things, and their best was in all things. And if you do not start out from an abstract feeling and an abstract perception, as is customary today, but rather start out from the old way of feeling and perception as we have just characterized them, then you will understand such words as resound to us from Krishna in the Bhagavad Gita. If then you ask how people with the old clairvoyance perceived themselves, you will understand them and realize that in the same way that a person, when the etheric body is freed through spiritual-scientific training, feels him- or herself spread and poured out into everything, so did the people of former times experience this as a natural condition, although not in the same way as would now be the case as a result of spiritual-scientific training. Ancient people felt themselves to be inside things, and this condition came about by itself without their volition. And when these revelations were shaped into forms and what had been seen was expressed in beautiful, wonderful words, then something appeared like, for example, these revelations of Krishna. For this reason it could also be said that Krishna spoke to his fellow beings in this way, "I wish to proclaim in words what the best of us have perceived when they were in the supersensible worlds and how the best of us have perceived their relationship to the world. In future times such people as these will no longer be found, and you yourselves cannot be as your ancestors were. I wish to put into words what these ancestors perceived, so that it will endure, because humanity can no longer possess this as a natural condition."

Something that had belonged to humankind for thousands of years was brought in words such as were possible at that time in the form of the revelations of Krishna, so that people in subsequent ages might possess this revelation of what they were no longer able to perceive for themselves.

Other sayings can be interpreted in a similar manner. Let us suppose that at a period when Krishna was giving his revelations a pupil had stood before his initiate teacher and asked him, "What lies behind the things which my eyes see? Can you, my initiated teacher tell me?" The initiated teacher might well have answered, "Behind what your external, material eyes can see lies the spiritual, the supersensible. But in former times people could still see the supersensible while they were in their normal condition. They were able to look into the nearest supersensible world, the etheric world that borders on our material world. Here in this world is to be found the cause of everything that is material, and these ancient people were able to see this cause. In our time I can do no more than express in words what could in earlier times be seen: 'It is fire, it is the Sun!' But not the Sun as it now appears, for what can now be seen by the eye was precisely what for ancient clairvoyants could least of all be seen. The white fiery globe of the Sun was darkness for them, while the effects of the Sun were spread over all space. The radiations of the Sun's aura in many colored light pictures flowed in and out of each other, coming forth from each other in such a way that when they merged into things they became immediately creative light. It is the Sun and also the Moon (though this too was seen in a different manner), for pure Brahman is altogether in it."

What is pure Brahman? When we breathe in the air and breathe it out again, materialistic people believe they are only inhaling oxygen. But that is a delusion; with every breath we inhale and exhale spirit. The spirit that lives in the air we breathe penetrates into us and goes out from us again. And when the old clairvoyants saw that, they did not, like the materialists, believe that they were breathing in oxygen. That is a materialistic prejudice. The clairvoyants of ancient times were aware that the etheric element of the spirit, Brahman, from whom all life comes, was being inhaled. In the same way that today we believe that life comes from the oxygen in the air, so did ancient people know that life comes from Brahman; by taking in Brahman, we live. The purest Brahman is the source of our life.

And of what nature are the conceptual heights to which this very ancient, this ether-like, light-like wisdom aspires? Today people believe they are able to think with great subtlety. But when we see how people jumble up and confuse everything as soon as they try to explain something, then we lose all respect for the thinking of today, especially for *logical* thinking. At this point I really must engage in a short discussion that may seem abstract. I shall make it as short as possible.

Let us suppose that we encounter an animal that has a mane and is yellow; then we call this animal a lion. Now we begin to ask, "What is a lion?" The answer, "A beast of prey." Next we ask, "What is a beast of prey?" Answer, "A mammal." We ask further, "What is a mammal?" Answer, "A living creature." And so we continue describing one thing through another. Most people believe they are being very lucid when they go on asking ever more questions in the same way as they asked about the lion, the mammal, and so on. And people often ask similar questions about spiritual matters, even about the highest spiritual things, in just the same way as they ask what a lion is, what a beast of prey is, and the rest. And at the end of lectures, when slips of paper are handed in with questions, questions such as these are asked countless numbers of times, for example, "What is God?" "How did the world begin?" "How will the world end?" There are many people who have no wish to know anything at all beyond these questions. They ask them in just the same way as they ask, "What is a lion?" and so on.

People think that what is valid for everyday life must also be equally valid for the highest things. They do not take into consideration that the highest things are of such a nature that we cannot ask such questions about them. If we proceed from one thing to another, from the lion to the beast of prey and so on, we must eventually come to something that cannot be described in this way, when there is no longer any sense in asking, "What is this?" For in this kind of questioning, a predicate is sought for the subject. But when we reach the highest being, this being can be comprehended only through itself. From a logical point of view it is absolutely meaningless to ask the question, "What is God?" Everything can be led upward to the highest, but to the highest no predicate can be added, for the answer would have to be: God is..., and God would then have to be described in terms of something higher. So the question itself would involve the strangest contradiction possible.

The fact that this question is still invariably asked today shows how highly exalted Krishna was when he appeared in a very early epoch and spoke as follows, "The Devas gather around the throne of the Almighty, and in deep devotion ask who He is. Then He answers, 'If there were anyone else other than I myself, I should describe myself through him' " [see X.20–41]. But this He does not do; He does not describe himself through another. So we also, as we could say, like the Devas, are led in devotion and humility to this ancient and holy culture, and admire its logical elevation, which it did not achieve through thinking but through the old clairvoyance. In those times people knew at once that when they reached the causes then questioning must cease. The causes must be *perceived*. At this point we stand in admiration in front of the teachings that have come down to us from those very ancient times, as though the spirits who transmitted them to us wished to say to us, "The times are past when people could see directly into the spiritual worlds, nor will they be able to do so in the future. But we wish to record what we can aspire to, something that at one time was granted to human clairvoyance."

So we find recorded in the Bhagavad Gita and in the Vedas all those things that were brought together by Krishna as a kind of conclusion. Such things cannot be surpassed, though they will be perceived again when clairvoyance is renewed. But they will never be perceived through those faculties that people have attained in subsequent times. For this reason it is always correct to say that if we remain within the realm of contemporary culture, an external culture whose content is determined by sense perception, we shall never again attain to the ancient sacred revelation that found its conclusion in Krishna, unless we do so through a trained clairvoyance. But in its own evolution through spiritual science, the soul can again raise itself and attain it again. What was at one time given to humanity in a normal way, one might say, is not now given to humankind in ordinary life, and we cannot attain it under natural conditions. It is for this reason that these truths came down to us. When there are thinkers like Fichte, Schelling, and Hegel, who reached the highest possible purity in their thinking, then we can meet with these things again, in the form of ideas—not indeed as life-filled as they were, nor with the direct personal impact of Krishna, and never in the way in which they were understood in the time of the old clairvoyance. Yet, as I have often stated, it was a spiritual necessity that the old clairvoyance should slowly and gradually die out in the post-Atlantean era.

If we look back to the ancient Indian civilization,[79] the first post-Atlantean cultural period, we may say that no records are extant from this epoch, for at that time people could still see into the spiritual world. Only through the akashic chronicle can we rediscover what was then revealed to humankind. It was a sublime revelation. But then humankind sank lower and lower. In the old Persian epoch,[80] the second post-Atlantean cultural period, though the revelations still continued, they had lost their original purity. They were still less pure in the third cultural period, that of ancient Egypt. If we wish to visualize what were the real conditions of the time, we must bear in mind that as far as the first cultural epochs are concerned no records exist (and this is true for all the peoples of that age, whether or not a cultural epoch has been named after them). If we speak of the ancient Indian culture we are referring to a culture from which nothing has come down to us in writing. It is just the same with the primeval Persian culture. Written records exist only from the Egyptian-Babylonian-Chaldean culture, which belongs to the third cultural period. But during the period of the unfolding of the primeval Persian culture within Indian culture there was a second Indian period, running parallel to the old Persian. And yet a third period began in India contemporary with the Egyptian-Babylonian-Chaldean culture, and it was during this period that the first written records were kept. These first records date from the latter part of this third culture. Such records are, for example, those contained in the Vedas, which then penetrated into external life. It is these records which also speak of Krishna.

So no one should believe that written records go back to the first Indian cultural epoch. Everything contained in the documents are records first written down in the third period of ancient India, for the reason that precisely in the third period the old clairvoyance was dying out more and more. These are the records assembled around

---

79. This reference is not to the period of the Vedas and Upanishads, approximately 1000 B.C.E. to 500 B.C.E., but to a period Steiner places in the eighth to the sixth millennia B.C.E.
80. The sixth to the fourth millennia B.C.E.

the person of Krishna. Thus ancient India tells us something that can be externally investigated. If we examine things fundamentally, everything agrees with what can be discovered in the external documents. As the third world age came to an end and humanity lost what it had originally possessed, Krishna appeared on the scene to preserve what otherwise would have been lost.

When tradition[81] says that Krishna appeared in the third world age, what age is meant by this? This age is what we call the Egypto-Chaldean cultural epoch. The Indian teaching of Krishna accords perfectly with what we have been characterizing. When the old clairvoyance and all its treasures were on the point of being lost, then Krishna appeared and revealed them so that they could be preserved into later times. Krishna, then, is the conclusion of something great and powerful. And everything that has been said here over the years agrees entirely with what is given also in the ancient Indian documents if we read them rightly. It is pure nonsense to talk in this context of "Eastern" and "Western," because this is only a matter of language, of vocabulary. What is important is that we speak with a full understanding of that which we proclaim. And the more you go into what has been given out over the years, the more you will see that it is in complete agreement with all the documents of ancient India.

So Krishna stands there as a conclusion. Then, a few centuries later, comes the Buddha. In what sense is the Buddha, if we may so express it, the other pole of this conclusion? In what relation does the Buddha stand to Krishna?

Let us place before our souls what we have just spoken of as characteristic of Krishna: great powerful clairvoyant revelations of primordial ages, couched in such words that people in future times will be able to understand and feel and sense in them the ancient clairvoyance of humanity. Krishna's revelation, as he stands before us, is something

81. It is not immediately clear to which tradition Steiner is referring. As his audience were Theosophists in the process of joining the newly formed Anthroposophical Society, he might have been referring to the esoteric writings of early Theosophists, particularly H. P. Blavatsky.

that people can accept as containing the wisdom of the spiritual world that lies behind the sense world, the world of causes and spiritual facts. This wisdom is expressed in great, powerful words in Krishna's revelations. If we immerse ourselves in the Vedas, in all that we can summarize in conclusion as the revelation of Krishna, then we may say that this is the world in which humanity is at home, the world that lies behind what our eyes can see, our ears hear, our hands grasp, and so on. Yes, the human soul belongs to the world revealed by Krishna.

How could the human soul itself feel in the course of subsequent centuries? It could perceive how these marvelous revelations of an older time spoke about the true, spiritual, celestial home of humankind. It could then look into all that surrounded it. It saw with eyes, heard with ears, grasped things with the sense of touch. It could think with the intellect about things, the intellect that never penetrates into the spiritual element proclaimed in the revelation of Krishna. And the soul could say to itself, "There is an ancient holy teaching from times past that tells of a world, our spiritual home which lies all around us, around that world which is all that we now recognize. We no longer live in that spiritual home; we have been expelled from that world of which Krishna spoke so magnificently."

Then comes the Buddha. What does he say of the marvels of the world spoken of by Krishna to human souls that could perceive only what eyes can see and ears hear? He says, "Certainly you live in the world of the senses. The yearning that drives you from incarnation to incarnation has led you into this world. But I am telling you of that path which can lead you out of this world and into that world of which Krishna spoke. I am telling you about the path through which you will be redeemed from the world that is not the world of Krishna." Buddha's teaching in these later centuries resounds like a kind of nostalgia for the world of Krishna. In this respect the Buddha seems to us like the last successor of Krishna, as Krishna's successor who had to come. And if the Buddha himself had spoken of Krishna, how would he have been able to speak about him? He would have said something like this: "I have come to proclaim to you again the greater one who was my predecessor. Turn your mind backward to the Krishna who was greater than I, and you will see what you can attain if you leave this world which is not your true spiritual home. I will show you the path by which you can redeem yourselves from the world of sense. I lead you back to Krishna."

The Buddha could have spoken in this way, but he did not use these exact words. Nevertheless, he did say them in a somewhat different form when he said, "In the world in which you live there is suffering, there is suffering, there is suffering. Birth is suffering. Age is suffering. Illness is suffering. Death is suffering. To be apart from that which one loves is suffering. To be bound to that which one does not love is suffering. The longing for that which one loves but may not attain is suffering."[82] And so he gave his Eightfold Path. It was a teaching that did not go beyond that of Krishna because in fact it was the same teaching as the one given by Krishna. "I have come after him who is greater than I, and I will show you the way back to him who is greater than I." These are the world-historical tones that ring forth to us from the land of the Ganges.[83]

Now let us go a little further toward the West, and place once more before our souls the figure of the Baptist, and remember the words that the Buddha could have spoken: "I have come after Krishna who is greater than I; and I will show you the way back to him, away from the world bereft of the divine of which Krishna spoke. Turn your minds backward!"

Now consider the figure of the Baptist. How did he speak, how did he express his views? How did he express the facts he had received from the spiritual world? He too pointed to another, but he did not say, as the Buddha could have said, "I have come after him." On the contrary, he said, "*After* me there will come one greater than I" (Mark 1: 7). This

---

82. This summary of Buddha's teaching, immediately following his enlightenment experience, includes a reference to the three sorrows that Gotama experienced prior to his leaving home, namely illness, old age, and death. It also refers to the first noble truth, *dukkha*, meaning that life is characterized by an unsatisfactory quality. After teaching the first three noble truths—suffering, the cause (desiring), and the fact that suffering is curable—Buddha taught the fourth noble truth, which is the eightfold path.
83. There are almost certainly no extant documents that indicate that Buddha made such a statement concerning his relation to Krishna.

is what the Baptist said. Nor did he say, "Here in the world is suffering, and I wish to lead you to something that is not of this world." No, he said, "Change your way of thinking. Do not continue to look backward, but look forward. When He comes who is greater than I, the time will be fulfilled. Then the divine world will enter into the world of suffering. And what was lost of the revelations of past times will enter in a new way into human souls" (Matt. 5: 2).

So the successor of Krishna is the Buddha, and John the Baptist is the forerunner of Christ Jesus. Thus everything is reversed. We are faced with the six hundred years that elapsed between these two events, and we have before us the two comets, with their nuclei: the one comet pointing backward with Krishna as nucleus, together with the one who leads men backward, the Buddha. Then we have the other comet pointing forward, with Christ as its nucleus, together with him who stands before us as the forerunner. If, in the best sense, you recognize the Buddha as the successor of Krishna, and John the Baptist as the forerunner of Christ Jesus, then this formula expresses in the simplest way what took place in human evolution around the time of the Mystery of Golgotha. It is in this way that we should look at things, and then we can understand them.

All this has no bearing on any religious confession, nor should it be linked with any particular religion. These are facts of world history. No one who understands them in their innermost depths can present them or will ever present them in a different way. Do such statements impair in any way any revelation ever given to humankind? It is curious that it is sometimes said that we assign in some way a higher place to Christianity than to other religions. Do such words as "higher" or "deeper" have any meaning in this context? Are not such words as "higher" or "lower," "larger" or "smaller," the most abstract words we can use? Are we praising Krishna any less than do those who put him higher than Christ? We refrain from using such words as "higher" or "less high," and wish only to characterize these matters in accordance with the truth. It is not a matter of whether we place Christianity higher or lower, but whether we characterize in the right way what belongs to Krishna. Look up all that has been said about Krishna, and ask yourselves whether anyone else has ever said anything about

Krishna "higher" than what has been presented here. Everything else is idle talk. But truth comes to light when there begins to be active that feeling for truth that goes to the essence of things.

Here when we are characterizing the simplest and grandest of the gospels, we have the opportunity of studying the whole position of the Christ as a cosmic and earthly being. It was therefore necessary to go into the greatness of what came to its conclusion centuries before the Mystery of Golgotha in which the new morning glow of the future of humanity dawned.

PART III

The Bhagavad Gita

Translated by Eknath Easwaran

CONTENTS

1. The War Within

DHRITARASHTRA

[1] O Sanjaya, tell me what happened at
Kurukshetra, the field of dharma, where my
family and the Pandavas gathered to fight.

SANJAYA

[2] Having surveyed the forces of the Pandavas arrayed
for battle, prince Duryodhana approached his teacher,
Drona, and spoke. [3] "O my teacher, look at this mighty
army of the Pandavas, assembled by your own gifted
disciple, Yudhishthira. [4] There are heroic warriors
and great archers who are the equals of Bhima and
Arjuna: Yuyudhana, Virata, the mighty Drupada,
[5] Dhrishtaketu, Chekitana, the valiant king of Kashi,
Purujit, Kuntibhoja, the great leader Shaibya, [6] the
powerful Yudhamanyu, the valiant Uttamaujas,
and the son of Subhadra, in addition to the sons of
Draupadi. All these command mighty chariots.
[7] "O best of brahmins, listen to the names of those
who are distinguished among our own forces: [8]
Bhishma, Karna, and the victorious Kripa;
Ashvatthama, Vikarna, and the son of Somadatta.

[9] "There are many others, too, heroes giving up their
lives for my sake, all proficient in war and armed
with a variety of weapons. [10] Our army is unlimited
and commanded by Bhishma; theirs is small and
commanded by Bhima. [11] Let everyone take his
proper place and stand firm supporting Bhishma!"

[12] Then the powerful Bhishma, the grandsire, oldest of all the Kurus, in order to cheer Duryodhana, roared like a lion and blew his conch horn. [13] And after Bhishma, a tremendous noise arose of conchs and cow horns and pounding on drums.

[14] Then Sri Krishna and Arjuna, who were standing in a mighty chariot yoked with white horses, blew their divine conchs. [15] Sri Krishna blew the conch named Panchajanya, and Arjuna blew that called Devadatta. The mighty Bhima blew the huge conch Paundra. [16] Yudhishthira, the king, the son of Kunti, blew the conch Anantavijaya; Nakula and Sahadeva blew their conchs as well. [17] Then the king of Kashi, the leading bowman, the great warrior Shikhandi, Dhrishtadyumna, Virata, the invincible Satyaki, [18] Drupada, all the sons of Draupadi, and the strong-armed son of Subhadra joined in, [19] and the noise tore through the heart of Duryodhana's army. Indeed, the sound was tumultuous, echoing throughout heaven and earth.

[20] Then, O Dhritarashtra, lord of the earth, having seen your son's forces set in their places and the fighting about to begin, Arjuna spoke these words to Sri Krishna:

ARJUNA

[21] O Krishna, drive my chariot between the two armies. [22] I want to see those who desire to fight with me. With whom will this battle be fought? [23] I want to see those assembled to fight for Duryodhana, those who seek to please the evil-minded son of Dhritarashtra by engaging in war.

SANJAYA

[24] Thus Arjuna spoke, and Sri Krishna, driving his splendid chariot between the two armies, [25] facing Bhishma and Drona and all the kings of the earth, said: "Arjuna, behold all the Kurus gathered together." [26] And Arjuna, standing between the two armies, saw fathers and grandfathers, teachers, uncles, and brothers, sons and grandsons, [27]in-laws and friends. Seeing his kinsmen established in opposition, [28]Arjuna was overcome by sorrow. Despairing, he spoke these words:

ARJUNA

[21] O Krishna, I see my own relations here anxious to fight, [29] and my limbs grow weak; my mouth is dry, my body shakes, and my hair is standing on end. [30] My skin burns, and the bow Gandiva has slipped from my hand. I am unable to stand; my mind seems to be whirling. [31] These signs bode evil for us. I do not see that any good can come from killing our relations in battle. [32] O Krishna, I have no desire for victory, or for a kingdom or pleasures. Of what use is a kingdom or pleasure or even life, [33] if those for whose sake we desire these things — [34] teachers, fathers, sons, grandfathers, uncles, in-laws, grandsons, and others with family ties — are engaging in this battle, renouncing their wealth and their lives? [35] Even if they were to kill me, I would not want to kill them, not even to become ruler of the three worlds. How much less for the earth alone? [36] O Krishna, what satisfaction could we find in killing Dhritarashtra's sons? We would become sinners by slaying these men, even though they are

evil. [37] The sons of Dhritarashtra are related to us; therefore, we should not kill them. How can we gain happiness by killing members of our own family?

[38] Though they are overpowered by greed and see no evil in destroying families or injuring friends, we see these evils. [39] Why shouldn't we turn away from this sin? [40] When a family declines, ancient traditions are destroyed. With them are lost the spiritual foundations for life, and the family loses its sense of unity. [41] Where there is no sense of unity, the women of the family become corrupt; and with the corruption of its women, society is plunged into chaos. [42] Social chaos is hell for the family and for those who have destroyed the family as well. It disrupts the process of spiritual evolution begun by our ancestors. [43] The timeless spiritual foundations of family and society would be destroyed by these terrible deeds, which violate the unity of life.

[44] It is said that those whose family dharma has been destroyed dwell in hell. [45] This is a great sin! We are prepared to kill our own relations out of greed for the pleasures of a kingdom. [46] Better for me if the sons of Dhritarashtra, weapons in hand, were to attack me in battle and kill me unarmed and unresisting.

SANJAYA

[47] Overwhelmed by sorrow, Arjuna spoke these words. And casting away his bow and his arrows, he sat down in his chariot in the middle of the battlefield.

2. Self-Realization

SANJAYA

[1] These are the words that Sri Krishna spoke
to the despairing Arjuna, whose eyes were
burning with tears of pity and confusion.

KRISHNA

[2] This despair and weakness in a time of crisis are
mean and unworthy of you, Arjuna. How have you
fallen into a state so far from the path to liberation?
[3] It does not become you to yield to this weakness.
Arise with a brave heart and destroy the enemy.

ARJUNA

[4] How can I ever bring myself to fight against Bhishma
and Drona, who are worthy of reverence? How can
I, Krishna? [5] Surely it would be better to spend my
life begging than to kill these great and worthy souls!
If I killed them, every pleasure I found would be
tainted. [6] I don't even know which would be better,
for us to conquer them or for them to conquer us.
The sons of Dhritarashtra have confronted us; but
why would we care to live if we killed them?

[7] My will is paralyzed, and I am utterly confused.
Tell me which is the better path for me. Let me be
your disciple. I have fallen at your feet; give me
instruction. [8] What can overcome a sorrow that
saps all my vitality? Even power over men and
gods or the wealth of an empire seem empty.

SANJAYA

⁹ This is how Arjuna, the great warrior, spoke
to Sri Krishna. With the words, "O Krishna,
I will not fight," he fell silent. ¹⁰ As they stood
between the two armies, Sri Krishna smiled and
replied to Arjuna, who had sunk into despair.

KRISHNA

¹¹ You speak sincerely, but your sorrow has no
cause. The wise grieve neither for the living nor
for the dead. ¹² There has never been a time when
you and I and the kings gathered here have not
existed, nor will there be a time when we will
cease to exist. ¹³ As the same person inhabits the
body through childhood, youth, and old age, so
too at the time of death he attains another body.
The wise are not deluded by these changes.

¹⁴ When the senses contact sense objects, a person
experiences cold or heat, pleasure or pain. These
experiences are fleeting; they come and go.
Bear them patiently, Arjuna. ¹⁵ Those who are
unaffected by these changes, who are the same
in pleasure and pain, are truly wise and fit for
immortality. Assert your strength and realize this!

¹⁶ The impermanent has no reality; reality lies in the
eternal. Those who have seen the boundary between
these two have attained the end of all knowledge.
¹⁷ Realize that which pervades the universe and is
indestructible; no power can affect this unchanging,
imperishable reality. ¹⁸ The body is mortal, but
that which dwells in the body is immortal and
immeasurable. Therefore, Arjuna, fight in this battle.

[19] One believes he is the slayer, another believes he is the slain. Both are ignorant; there is neither slayer nor slain. [20] You were never born; you will never die. You have never changed; you can never change. Unborn, eternal, immutable, immemorial, you do not die when the body dies. [21] Realizing that which is indestructible, eternal, unborn, and unchanging, how can you slay or cause another to slay?

[22] As one abandons worn-out clothes and acquires new ones, so when the body is worn out a new one is acquired by the Self, who lives within.

[23] The Self cannot be pierced by weapons or burned by fire; water cannot wet it, nor can the wind dry it. [24] The Self cannot be pierced or burned, made wet or dry. It is everlasting and infinite, standing on the motionless foundations of eternity. [25] The Self is unmanifested, beyond all thought, beyond all change. Knowing this, you should not grieve.

[26] O mighty Arjuna, even if you believe the Self to be subject to birth and death, you should not grieve. [27] Death is inevitable for the living; birth is inevitable for the dead. Since these are unavoidable, you should not sorrow. [28] Every creature is unmanifested at first and then attains manifestation. When its end has come, it once again becomes unmanifested. What is there to lament in this?

[29] The glory of the Self is beheld by a few, and a few describe it; a few listen, but many without understanding. [30] The Self of all beings, living within the body, is eternal and cannot be harmed. Therefore, do not grieve.

^{31} Considering your dharma, you should not
vacillate. For a warrior, nothing is higher than a
war against evil. ^{32} The warrior confronted with
such a war should be pleased, Arjuna, for it comes
as an open gate to heaven. ^{33} But if you do not
participate in this battle against evil, you will incur
sin, violating your dharma and your honor.

^{34} The story of your dishonor will be repeated
endlessly: and for a man of honor, dishonor is
worse than death. ^{35} These brave warriors will
think you have withdrawn from battle out of fear,
and those who formerly esteemed you will treat
you with disrespect. ^{36} Your enemies will ridicule
your strength and say things that should not be
said. What could be more painful than this?

^{37} Death means the attainment of heaven; victory
means the enjoyment of the earth. Therefore
rise up, Arjuna, resolved to fight! ^{38} Having
made yourself alike in pain and pleasure, profit
and loss, victory and defeat, engage in this
great battle and you will be freed from sin.

^{39} You have heard the intellectual explanation of
Sankhya, Arjuna; now listen to the principles
of yoga. By practicing these you can break
through the bonds of karma. ^{40} On this path
effort never goes to waste, and there is no failure.
Even a little effort toward spiritual awareness
will protect you from the greatest fear.

^{41} Those who follow this path, resolving deep within
themselves to seek me alone, attain singleness

of purpose. For those who lack resolution, the
decisions of life are many-branched and endless.

[42] There are ignorant people who speak flowery
words and take delight in the letter of the law,
saying that there is nothing else. [43] Their hearts
are full of selfish desires, Arjuna. Their idea of
heaven is their own enjoyment, and the aim of
all their activities is pleasure and power. The
fruit of their actions is continual rebirth. [44] Those
whose minds are swept away by the pursuit of
pleasure and power are incapable of following
the supreme goal and will not attain samadhi.

[45] The scriptures describe the three gunas. But
you should be free from the action of the gunas,
established in eternal truth, self-controlled, without
any sense of duality or the desire to acquire and hoard.

[46] Just as a reservoir is of little use when the
whole countryside is flooded, scriptures
are of little use to the illumined man or
woman, who sees the Lord everywhere.

[47] You have the right to work, but never to the
fruit of work. You should never engage in action
for the sake of reward, nor should you long for
inaction. [48] Perform work in this world, Arjuna,
as a man established within himself — without
selfish attachments, and alike in success and
defeat. For yoga is perfect evenness of mind.

[49] Seek refuge in the attitude of detachment and
you will amass the wealth of spiritual awareness.

Those who are motivated only by desire for the fruits of action are miserable, for they are constantly anxious about the results of what they do. [50] When consciousness is unified, however, all vain anxiety is left behind. There is no cause for worry, whether things go well or ill. Therefore, devote yourself to the disciplines of yoga, for yoga is skill in action.

[51] The wise unify their consciousness and abandon attachment to the fruits of action, which binds a person to continual rebirth. Thus they attain a state beyond all evil.

[52] When your mind has overcome the confusion of duality, you will attain the state of holy indifference to things you hear and things you have heard. [53] When you are unmoved by the confusion of ideas and your mind is completely united in deep samadhi, you will attain the state of perfect yoga.

ARJUNA

[54] Tell me of those who live established in wisdom, ever aware of the Self, O Krishna. How do they talk? How sit? How move about?

KRISHNA

[55] They live in wisdom who see themselves in all and all in them, who have renounced every selfish desire and sense craving tormenting the heart. [56] Neither agitated by grief nor hankering after pleasure, they live free from lust and fear and anger. Established in meditation, they are truly wise. [57] Fettered no more by selfish attachments, they are neither elated by good fortune nor

depressed by bad. Such are the seers.

58 Even as a tortoise draws in its limbs, the wise can
draw in their senses at will. 59 Aspirants abstain
from sense pleasures, but they still crave for
them. These cravings all disappear when they see
the highest goal. 60 Even of those who tread the
path, the stormy senses can sweep off the mind.
61 They live in wisdom who subdue their senses
and keep their minds ever absorbed in me.

62 When you keep thinking about sense objects,
attachment comes. Attachment breeds desire, the
lust of possession that burns to anger. 63 Anger
clouds the judgment; you can no longer learn
from past mistakes. Lost is the power to choose
between what is wise and what is unwise, and your
life is utter waste. 64 But when you move amidst the
world of sense, free from attachment and aversion
alike, 65 there comes the peace in which all sorrows
end, and you live in the wisdom of the Self.
66 The disunited mind is far from wise; how can
it meditate? How be at peace? When you know
no peace, how can you know joy? 67 When you
let your mind follow the call of the senses, they
carry away your better judgment as storms
drive a boat off its charted course on the sea.

68 Use all your power to free the senses from
attachment and aversion alike, and live in the full
wisdom of the Self. 69 Such a sage awakes to light
in the night of all creatures. That which the world
calls day is the night of ignorance to the wise.

70 As rivers flow into the ocean but cannot make
the vast ocean overflow, so flow the streams of the

sense-world into the sea of peace that is the sage.
But this is not so with the desirer of desires.
[71] They are forever free who renounce all
selfish desires and break away from the ego-
cage of "I," "me," and "mine" to be united with
the Lord. [72] This is the supreme state. Attain to
this, and pass from death to immortality.

3. Selfless Service

ARJUNA

[1] O Krishna, you have said that knowledge is greater than action; why then do you ask me to wage this terrible war? [2] Your advice seems inconsistent. Give me one path to follow to the supreme good.

KRISHNA

[3] At the beginning of time I declared two paths for the pure heart: *jnana yoga*, the contemplative path of spiritual wisdom, and *karma yoga*, the active path of selfless service.

[4] One who shirks action does not attain freedom; no one can gain perfection by abstaining from work. [5] Indeed, there is no one who rests for even an instant; all creatures are driven to action by their own nature.

[6] Those who abstain from action while allowing the mind to dwell on sensual pleasure cannot be called sincere spiritual aspirants. [7] But they excel who control their senses through the mind, using them for selfless service.

[8] Fulfill all your duties; action is better than inaction. Even to maintain your body, Arjuna, you are obliged to act. [9] Selfish action imprisons the world. Act selflessly, without any thought of personal profit.

[10] At the beginning, mankind and the obligation of selfless service were created together.

"Through selfless service, you will always
be fruitful and find the fulfillment of your
desires": this is the promise of the Creator.

[11] Honor and cherish the devas as they honor and
cherish you; through this honor and love you will
attain the supreme good. [12] All human desires are
fulfilled by the devas, who are pleased by selfless
service. But anyone who enjoys the things given by the
devas without offering selfless acts in return is a thief.

[13] The spiritually minded, who eat in the spirit of
service, are freed from all their sins; but the selfish,
who prepare food for their own satisfaction, eat sin.
[14] Living creatures are nourished by food, and food
is nourished by rain; rain itself is the water of life,
which comes from selfless worship and service.

[15] Every selfless act, Arjuna, is born from Brahman,
the eternal, infinite Godhead. Brahman is present
in every act of service. [16] All life turns on this law,
O Arjuna. Those who violate it, indulging the
senses for their own pleasure and ignoring the
needs of others, have wasted their life. [17] But those
who realize the Self are always satisfied. Having
found the source of joy and fulfillment, they no
longer seek happiness from the external world.
[18] They have nothing to gain or lose by any action;
neither people nor things can affect their security.

[19] Strive constantly to serve the welfare of the
world; by devotion to selfless work one attains
the supreme goal of life. [20] Do your work with
the welfare of others always in mind. It was
by such work that Janaka attained perfection;
others too have followed this path.

21 What the outstanding person does, others will
try to do. The standards such people create will be
followed by the whole world. 22 There is nothing in
the three worlds for me to gain, Arjuna, nor is there
anything I do not have; I continue to act, but I am not
driven by any need of my own. 23 If I ever refrained
from continuous work, everyone would immediately
follow my example. 24 If I stopped working I would
be the cause of cosmic chaos, and finally of the
destruction of this world and these people.

25 The ignorant work for their own profit, Arjuna;
the wise work for the welfare of the world,
without thought for themselves. 26 By abstaining
from work you will confuse the ignorant,
who are engrossed in their actions. Perform
all work carefully, guided by compassion.

27 All actions are performed by the gunas of prakriti.
Deluded by identifi cation with the ego, a person
thinks, "*I* am the doer." 28 But the illumined man or
woman understands the domain of the gunas and is
not attached. Such people know that the gunas interact
with each other; they do not claim to be the doer.

29 Those who are deluded by the operation of
the gunas become attached to the results of
their action. Those who understand these truths
should not unsettle the ignorant. 30 Performing
all actions for my sake, completely absorbed
in the Self, and without expectations, fight!
— but stay free from the fever of the ego.

31 Those who live in accordance with these divine
laws without complaining, firmly established in
faith, are released from karma. 32 Those who violate

these laws, criticizing and complaining, are utterly
deluded, and are the cause of their own suffering.

³³ Even the wise act within the limitations of their
own nature. Every creature is subject to prakriti;
what is the use of repression? ³⁴ The senses have
been conditioned by attraction to the pleasant
and aversion to the unpleasant. Do not be ruled
by them; they are obstacles in your path.

³⁵ It is better to strive in one's own dharma than to
succeed in the dharma of another. Nothing is ever
lost in following one's own dharma, but competition
in another's dharma breeds fear and insecurity.

ARJUNA

³⁶ What is the force that binds us to selfish
deeds, O Krishna? What power moves us,
even against our will, as if forcing us?

KRISHNA

³⁷ It is selfish desire and anger, arising from
the guna of rajas; these are the appetites and
evils which threaten a person in this life.

³⁸ Just as a fire is covered by smoke and a mirror is
obscured by dust, just as the embryo rests deep within
the womb, knowledge is hidden by selfish desire
— ³⁹ hidden, Arjuna, by this unquenchable fire for
self-satisfaction, the inveterate enemy of the wise.

⁴⁰ Selfish desire is found in the senses, mind,
and intellect, misleading them and burying
the understanding in delusion. ⁴¹ Fight

with all your strength, Arjuna! Controlling
your senses, conquer your enemy, the
destroyer of knowledge and realization.

42 The senses are higher than the body, the mind
higher than the senses; above the mind is the
intellect, and above the intellect is the Atman.
43 Thus, knowing that which is supreme, let the
Atman rule the ego. Use your mighty arms to
slay the fierce enemy that is selfish desire.

4. Wisdom in Action

KRISHNA

[1] I told this eternal secret to Vivasvat. Vivasvat
taught Manu, and Manu taught Ikshvaku. [2] Thus,
Arjuna, eminent sages received knowledge of
yoga in a continuous tradition. But through time
the practice of yoga was lost in the world.

[3] The secret of these teachings is profound.
I have explained them to you today because
you are my friend and devotee.

ARJUNA

[4] You were born much after Vivasvat; he
lived very long ago. Why do you say that
you taught this yoga in the beginning?

KRISHNA

[5] You and I have passed through many births, Arjuna.
You have forgotten, but I remember them all.
[6] My true being is unborn and changeless. I am the
Lord who dwells in every creature. Through the power
of my own maya, I manifest myself in a finite form.

[7] Whenever dharma declines and the purpose
of life is forgotten, I manifest myself on earth.
[8] I am born in every age to protect the good,
to destroy evil, and to reestablish dharma.

⁹ Those who know me as their own divine Self
break through the belief that they are the body
and are not reborn as separate creatures. Such a
one, Arjuna, is united with me. ¹⁰ Delivered from
selfish attachment, fear, and anger, filled with me,
surrendering themselves to me, purified in the fire of
my being, many have reached the state of unity in me.

¹¹ As they approach me, so I receive them.
All paths, Arjuna, lead to me.

¹² Those desiring success in their actions worship
the gods; through action in the world of mortals,
their desires are quickly fulfilled. ¹³ The distinctions
of caste, guna, and karma have come from me. I am
their cause, but I myself am changeless and beyond
all action. ¹⁴ Actions do not cling to me because I am
not attached to their results. Those who understand
this and practice it live in freedom. ¹⁵ Knowing this
truth, aspirants desiring liberation in ancient times
engaged in action. You too can do the same, pursuing
an active life in the manner of those ancient sages.

¹⁶ What is action and what is inaction? This question
has confused the greatest sages. I will give you the
secret of action, with which you can free yourself from
bondage. ¹⁷ The true nature of action is difficult to
grasp. You must understand what is action and what is
inaction, and what kind of action should be avoided.

¹⁸ The wise see that there is action in the
midst of inaction and inaction in the midst
of action. Their consciousness is unified, and
every act is done with complete awareness.

254 * THE BHAGAVAD GITA AND THE WEST

The awakened sages call a person wise when all
his undertakings are free from anxiety about results;
all his selfish desires have been consumed in the
fire of knowledge. 20 The wise, ever satisfied, have
abandoned all external supports. Their security is
unaffected by the results of their action; even while
acting, they really do nothing at all. 21 Free from
expectations and from all sense of possession, with
mind and body firmly controlled by the Self, they do
not incur sin by the performance of physical action.

22 They live in freedom who have gone beyond
the dualities of life. Competing with no one,
they are alike in success and failure and content
with whatever comes to them. 23 They are free,
without selfish attachments; their minds are
fixed in knowledge. They perform all work in the
spirit of service, and their karma is dissolved.

24 The process of off ering is Brahman; that which
is offered is Brahman. Brahman offers the sacrifice
in the fire of Brahman. Brahman is attained by
those who see Brahman in every action.

25 Some aspirants offer material sacrifices to the gods.
Others offer selfless service as sacrifice in the fire
of Brahman. 26 Some renounce all enjoyment of the
senses, sacrificing them in the fire of sense restraint.
Others partake of sense objects but offer them in
service through the fire of the senses. 27 Some offer the
workings of the senses and the vital forces through the
fire of self-control, kindled in the path of knowledge.

28 Some offer wealth; others offer sense restraint
and suffering. Some take vows and offer knowledge
and study of the scriptures; and some make the

offering of meditation. ²⁹ Some offer the forces of
vitality, regulating their inhalation and exhalation,
and thus gain control over these forces. ³⁰ Others
offer the forces of vitality through restraint of
their senses. All these understand the meaning of
service and will be cleansed of their impurities.

³¹ True sustenance is in service, and through it
a man or woman reaches the eternal Brahman.
But those who do not seek to serve are without
a home in this world. Arjuna, how can they
be at home in any world to come?

³² These offerings are born of work, and each guides
mankind along a path to Brahman. Understanding
this, you will attain liberation. ³³ The offering of
wisdom is better than any material offering, Arjuna;
for the goal of all work is spiritual wisdom.

³⁴ Approach those who have realized the purpose of
life and question them with reverence and devotion;
they will instruct you in this wisdom. ³⁵ Once you
attain it, you will never again be deluded. You
will see all creatures in the Self, and all in me.

³⁶ Even if you were the most sinful of sinners, Arjuna,
you could cross beyond all sin by the raft of spiritual
wisdom. ³⁷ As the heat of a fire reduces wood to
ashes, the fire of knowledge burns to ashes all karma.
³⁸ Nothing in this world purifies like spiritual wisdom.
It is the perfection achieved in time through the path
of yoga, the path which leads to the Self within.

³⁹ Those who take wisdom as their highest
goal, whose faith is deep and whose senses are
trained, attain wisdom quickly and enter into

perfect peace. [40] But the ignorant, indecisive and lacking in faith, waste their lives. They can never be happy in this world or any other.

[41] Those established in the Self have renounced selfish attachments to their actions and cut through doubts with spiritual wisdom. They act in freedom. [42] Arjuna, cut through this doubt in your own heart with the sword of spiritual wisdom. Arise; take up the path of yoga!

5. Renounce & Rejoice

ARJUNA

[1] O Krishna, you have recommended both the path of selfless action and *sannyasa*, the path of renunciation of action. Tell me definitely which is better.

KRISHNA

[2] Both renunciation of action and the selfless performance of action lead to the supreme goal. But the path of action is better than renunciation.

[3] Those who have attained perfect renunciation are free from any sense of duality; they are unaffected by likes and dislikes, Arjuna, and are free from the bondage of self-will. [4] The immature think that knowledge and action are different, but the wise see them as the same. The person who is established in one path will attain the rewards of both. [5] The goal of knowledge and the goal of service are the same; those who fail to see this are blind. [6] Perfect renunciation is difficult to attain without performing action. But the wise, following the path of selfless service, quickly reach Brahman.

[7] Those who follow the path of service, who have completely purified themselves and conquered their senses and self-will, see the Self in all creatures and are untouched by any action they perform.

[8] Those who know this truth, whose consciousness is unified, think always, "I am not the doer." While

seeing or hearing, touching or smelling; eating,
moving about, or sleeping; breathing [9] or speaking,
letting go or holding on, even opening or closing
the eyes, they understand that these are only the
movements of the senses among sense objects.

[10] Those who surrender to Brahman all selfish
attachments are like the leaf of a lotus floating
clean and dry in water. Sin cannot touch them.
[11] Renouncing their selfish attachments, those who
follow the path of service work with body, senses,
and mind for the sake of self-purification.

[12] Those whose consciousness is unified abandon
all attachment to the results of action and attain
supreme peace. But those whose desires are
fragmented, who are selfishly attached to the results
of their work, are bound in everything they do.

[13] Those who renounce attachment in all their
deeds live content in the "city of nine gates,"
the body, as its master. They are not driven to
act, nor do they involve others in action.

[14] Neither the sense of acting, nor actions, nor the
connection of cause and effect comes from the
Lord of this world. These three arise from nature.

[15] The Lord does not partake in the good and evil
deeds of any person; judgment is clouded when
wisdom is obscured by ignorance. [16] But ignorance
is destroyed by knowledge of the Self within.
The light of this knowledge shines like the sun,
revealing the supreme Brahman. [17] Those who cast
off sin through this knowledge, absorbed in the

Lord and established in him as their one goal and
refuge, are not reborn as separate creatures.

18 Those who possess this wisdom have equal
regard for all. They see the same Self in a spiritual
aspirant and an outcaste, in an elephant, a cow, and
a dog. 19 Such people have mastered life. With even
mind they rest in Brahman, who is perfect and is
everywhere the same. 20 They are not elated by good
fortune nor depressed by bad. With mind established
in Brahman, they are free from delusion. 21 Not
dependent on any external support, they realize
the joy of spiritual awareness. With consciousness
unifi ed through meditation, they live in abiding joy.

22 Pleasures conceived in the world of the senses have
a beginning and an end and give birth to misery,
Arjuna. The wise do not look for happiness in them.
23 But those who overcome the impulses of lust
and anger which arise in the body are made whole
and live in joy. 24 They find their joy, their rest, and
their light completely within themselves. United
with the Lord, they attain nirvana in Brahman.

25 Healed of their sins and conflicts, working for the
good of all beings, the holy sages attain nirvana in
Brahman. 26 Free from anger and selfish desire, unified
in mind, those who follow the path of yoga and realize
the Self are established forever in that supreme state.

27 Closing their eyes, steadying their breathing, and
focusing their attention on the center of spiritual
consciousness, 28 the wise master their senses,
mind, and intellect through meditation. Self-
realization is their only goal. Freed from selfish

desire, fear, and anger, they live in freedom always.
[29] Knowing me as the friend of all creatures, the
Lord of the universe, the end of all offerings and
all spiritual disciplines, they attain eternal peace.

6. The Practice of Meditation

KRISHNA

[1] It is not those who lack energy or refrain from
action, but those who work without expectation
of reward who attain the goal of meditation.
Theirs is true renunciation. [2] Therefore, Arjuna,
you should understand that renunciation and
the performance of selfless service are the same.
Those who cannot renounce attachment to the
results of their work are far from the path.

[3] For aspirants who want to climb the mountain
of spiritual awareness, the path is selfless work;
for those who have ascended to yoga the path
is stillness and peace. [4] When you have freed
yourself from attachment to the results of work,
and from desires for the enjoyment of sense
objects, you will ascend to the unitive state.
[5] Reshape yourself through the power of your
will; never let yourself be degraded by self-
will. The will is the only friend of the Self,
and the will is the only enemy of the Self.

[6] To those who have conquered themselves,
the will is a friend. But it is the enemy of those
who have not found the Self within them.

[7] The supreme Reality stands revealed in the
consciousness of those who have conquered
themselves. They live in peace, alike in cold and
heat, pleasure and pain, praise and blame.

⁸ They are completely fulfilled by spiritual wisdom and
Self-realization. Having conquered their senses, they
have climbed to the summit of human consciousness.
To such people a clod of dirt, a stone, and gold are
the same. ⁹ They are equally disposed to family,
enemies, and friends, to those who support them and
those who are hostile, to the good and the evil alike.
Because they are impartial, they rise to great heights.

¹⁰ Those who aspire to the state of yoga should seek
the Self in inner solitude through meditation. With
body and mind controlled they should constantly
practice one-pointedness, free from expectations
and attachment to material possessions.

¹¹ Select a clean spot, neither too high nor too low,
and seat yourself firmly on a cloth, a deerskin, and
kusha grass. ¹² Then, once seated, strive to still your
thoughts. Make your mind one-pointed in meditation,
and your heart will be purified. ¹³ Hold your body,
head, and neck firmly in a straight line, and keep
your eyes from wandering. ¹⁴ With all fears dissolved
in the peace of the Self and all actions dedicated to
Brahman, controlling the mind and fixing it on me, sit
in meditation with me as your only goal. ¹⁵ With senses
and mind constantly controlled through meditation,
united with the Self within, an aspirant attains
nirvana, the state of abiding joy and peace in me.

¹⁶ Arjuna, those who eat too much or eat too little,
who sleep too much or sleep too little, will not
succeed in meditation. ¹⁷ But those who are temperate
in eating and sleeping, work and recreation, will
come to the end of sorrow through meditation.
¹⁸ Through constant effort they learn to withdraw

the mind from selfish cravings and absorb it in
the Self. Thus they attain the state of union.

[19] When meditation is mastered, the mind is
unwavering like the flame of a lamp in a windless
place. [20] In the still mind, in the depths of meditation,
the Self reveals itself. Beholding the Self by means
of the Self, an aspirant knows the joy and peace
of complete fulfillment. [21] Having attained that
abiding joy beyond the senses, revealed in the
stilled mind, they never swerve from the eternal
truth. [22] They desire nothing else and cannot be
shaken by the heaviest burden of sorrow.

[23] The practice of meditation frees one from
all affliction. This is the path of yoga. Follow it
with determination and sustained enthusiasm.
[24] Renouncing wholeheartedly all selfish desires and
expectations, use your will to control the senses.
[25] Little by little, through patience and repeated
eff ort, the mind will become stilled in the Self.

[26] Wherever the mind wanders, restless and diffuse
in its search for satisfaction without, lead it within;
train it to rest in the Self [27] Abiding joy comes to
those who still the mind. Freeing themselves from
the taint of self-will, with their consciousness
unified, they become one with Brahman.

[28] The infinite joy of touching Brahman is easily
attained by those who are free from the burden
of evil and established within themselves. [29] They
see the Self in every creature and all creation in
the Self. With consciousness unified through
meditation, they see everything with an equal eye.

[30] I am ever present to those who have realized me in every creature. Seeing all life as my manifestation, they are never separated from me. [31] They worship me in the hearts of all, and all their actions proceed from me. Wherever they may live, they abide in me.

[32] When a person responds to the joys and sorrows of others as if they were his own, he has attained the highest state of spiritual union.

ARJUNA

[33] O Krishna, the stillness of divine union which you describe is beyond my comprehension. How can the mind, which is so restless, attain lasting peace? [34] Krishna, the mind is restless, turbulent, powerful, violent; trying to control it is like trying to tame the wind.

KRISHNA

[35] It is true that the mind is restless and difficult to control. But it can be conquered, Arjuna, through regular practice and detachment. [36] Those who lack self-control will find it difficult to progress in meditation; but those who are self-controlled, striving earnestly through the right means, will attain the goal.

ARJUNA

[37] Krishna, what happens to one who has faith but who lacks self-control and wanders from the path, not attaining success in yoga? [38] If he becomes deluded on the spiritual path, will he

lose the support of both worlds, like a cloud
scattered in the sky? [39] Krishna, you can dispel all
doubts; remove this doubt which binds me.

KRISHNA

[40] Arjuna, my son, such a person will not be destroyed.
No one who does good work will ever come to a
bad end, either here or in the world to come.

[41] When such people die, they go to other realms
where the righteous live. They dwell there for
countless years and then are reborn [42] into a home
which is pure and prosperous. Or they may be born
into a family where meditation is practiced; to be
born into such a family is extremely rare. [43] The
wisdom they have acquired in previous lives will be
reawakened, Arjuna, and they will strive even harder
for Self-realization. [44] Indeed, they will be driven
on by the strength of their past disciplines. Even
one who inquires after the practice of meditation
rises above those who simply perform rituals.

[45] Through constant effort over many lifetimes,
a person becomes purified of all selfish desires
and attains the supreme goal of life.

[46] Meditation is superior to severe asceticism and the
path of knowledge. It is also superior to selfless service.
May you attain the goal of meditation, Arjuna! [47] Even
among those who meditate, that man or woman who
worships me with perfect faith, completely absorbed
in me, is the most firmly established in yoga.

7. Wisdom from Realization

KRISHNA

[1] With your mind intent on me, Arjuna,
discipline yourself with the practice of yoga.
Depend on me completely. Listen, and I
will dispel all your doubts; you will come to
know me fully and be united with me.

[2] I will give you both jnana and vijnana.
When both these are realized, there is
nothing more you need to know.

[3] One person in many thousands may seek perfection,
yet of these only a few reach the goal and come to
realize me. [4] Earth, water, fire, air, *akasha*, mind,
intellect, and ego — these are the eight divisions
of my prakriti. [5] But beyond this I have another,
higher nature, Arjuna; it supports the whole
universe and is the source of life in all beings.
[6] In these two aspects of my nature is the womb of
all creation. The birth and dissolution of the cosmos
itself take place in me. [7] There is nothing that exists
separate from me, Arjuna. The entire universe is
suspended from me as my necklace of jewels.

[8] Arjuna, I am the taste of pure water and the
radiance of the sun and moon. I am the sacred
word and the sound heard in air, and the courage
of human beings. [9] I am the sweet fragrance in the
earth and the radiance of fire; I am the life in every
creature and the striving of the spiritual aspirant.

¹⁰ My eternal seed, Arjuna, is to be found in every creature. I am the power of discrimination in those who are intelligent, and the glory of the noble. ¹¹ In those who are strong, I am strength, free from passion and selfish attachment. I am desire itself, if that desire is in harmony with the purpose of life.

¹² The states of sattva, rajas, and tamas come from me, but I am not in them. ¹³ These three gunas deceive the world: people fail to look beyond them to me, supreme and imperishable. ¹⁴ The three gunas make up my divine maya, difficult to overcome. But they cross over this maya who take refuge in me. ¹⁵ Others are deluded by maya; performing evil deeds, they have no devotion to me. Having lost all discrimination, they follow the way of their lower nature.

¹⁶ Good people come to worship me for different reasons. Some come to the spiritual life because of suffering, some in order to understand life; some come through a desire to achieve life's purpose, and some come who are men and women of wisdom. ¹⁷ Unwavering in devotion, always united with me, the man or woman of wisdom surpasses all the others. To them I am the dearest beloved, and they are very dear to me. ¹⁸ All those who follow the spiritual path are blessed. But the wise who are always established in union, for whom there is no higher goal than me, may be regarded as my very Self.

¹⁹ After many births the wise seek refuge in me, seeing me everywhere and in everything. Such great souls are very rare. ²⁰ There are others whose discrimination is misled by many desires. Following their own nature, they worship lower gods, practicing various rites. ²¹ When a person is devoted to something with

complete faith, I unify his faith in that. [22] Then, when faith is completely unified, one gains the object of devotion. In this way, every desire is fulfilled by me. [23] Those whose understanding is small attain only transient satisfaction: those who worship the gods go to the gods. But my devotees come to me.

[24] Through lack of understanding, people believe that I, the Unmanifest, have entered into some form. They fail to realize my true nature, which transcends birth and death. [25] Few see through the veil of maya. The world, deluded, does not know that I am without birth and changeless. [26] I know everything about the past, the present, and the future, Arjuna; but there is no one who knows me completely.

[27] Delusion arises from the duality of attraction and aversion, Arjuna; every creature is deluded by these from birth. [28] But those who have freed themselves from all wrongdoing are firmly established in worship of me. Their actions are pure, and they are free from the delusion caused by the pairs of opposites.

[29] Those who take refuge in me, striving for liberation from old age and death, come to know Brahman, the Self, and the nature of all action. [30] Those who see me ruling the cosmos, who see me in the *adhibhuta*, the *adhidaiva*, and the *adhiyajna*, are conscious of me even at the time of death.

8. The Eternal Godhead

ARJUNA

[1] O Krishna, what is Brahman, and what is the nature
of action? What is the *adhyatma*, the *adhibhuta*,
the *adhidaiva*? 2 What is the *adhiyajna*, the supreme
sacrifice, and how is it to be offered? How are the
self-controlled united with you at the time of death?

KRISHNA

[3] My highest nature, the imperishable Brahman,
gives every creature its existence and lives in
every creature as the adhyatma. My action is
creation and the bringing forth of creatures. 4 The
adhibhuta is the perishable body; the adhidaiva is
Purusha, eternal spirit. The adhiyajna, the supreme
sacrifice, is made to me as the Lord within you.

[5] Those who remember me at the time of death
will come to me. Do not doubt this. 6 Whatever
occupies the mind at the time of death determines
the destination of the dying; always they will
tend toward that state of being. 7 Therefore,
remember me at all times and fight on. With your
heart and mind intent on me, you will surely
come to me. 8 When you make your mind one-
pointed through regular practice of meditation,
you will find the supreme glory of the Lord.

[9] The Lord is the supreme poet, the first cause, the
sovereign ruler, subtler than the tiniest particle,
the support of all, inconceivable, bright as the

sun, beyond darkness. [10] Remembering him in
this way at the time of death, through devotion
and the power of meditation, with your mind
completely stilled and your concentration fixed
in the center of spiritual awareness between the
eyebrows, you will realize the supreme Lord.

[11] I will tell you briefly of the eternal state all
scriptures affirm, which can be entered only
by those who are self-controlled and free from
selfish passions. Those whose lives are dedicated
to Brahman attain this supreme goal.

[12] Remembering me at the time of death, close
down the doors of the senses and place the mind
in the heart. Then, while absorbed in meditation,
focus all energy upwards to the head. [13] Repeating
in this state the divine name, the syllable *Om* that
represents the changeless Brahman, you will go
forth from the body and attain the supreme goal.

[14] I am easily attained by the person who always
remembers me and is attached to nothing else. Such
a person is a true yogi, Arjuna. [15] Great souls make
their lives perfect and discover me; they are freed from
mortality and the suffering of this separate existence.
[16] Every creature in the universe is subject to rebirth,
Arjuna, except the one who is united with me.

[17] Those who understand the cosmic laws know that
the Day of Brahma ends after a thousand yugas and
the Night of Brahma ends after a thousand yugas.
[18] When the day of Brahma dawns, forms are brought
forth from the Unmanifest; when the night of Brahma
comes, these forms merge in the Formless again.
[19] This multitude of beings is created and destroyed

again and again in the succeeding days and nights
of Brahma. [20] But beyond this formless state there
is another, unmanifested reality, which is eternal
and is not dissolved when the cosmos is destroyed.
[21] Those who realize life's supreme goal know that
I am unmanifested and unchanging. Having come
home to me, they never return to separate existence.

[22] This supreme Lord who pervades all existence, the
true Self of all creatures, may be realized through
undivided love. [23] There are two paths, Arjuna,
which the soul may follow at the time of death.
One leads to rebirth and the other to liberation.

[24] The six months of the northern path of the sun, the
path of light, of fire, of day, of the bright fortnight,
leads knowers of Brahman to the supreme goal.
[25] The six months of the southern path of the sun, the
path of smoke, of night, of the dark fortnight, leads
other souls to the light of the moon and to rebirth.

[26] These two paths, the light and the dark, are said
to be eternal, leading some to liberation and others
to rebirth. [27] Once you have known these two
paths, Arjuna, you can never be deluded again.
Attain this knowledge through perseverance in
yoga. [28] There is merit in studying the scriptures,
in selfless service, austerity, and giving, but the
practice of meditation carries you beyond all
these to the supreme abode of the highest Lord.

9. The Royal Path

KRISHNA

¹ Because of your faith, I shall tell you the most
profound of secrets: obtaining both jnana
and vijnana, you will be free from all evil.

² This royal knowledge, this royal secret, is the
greatest purifier. Righteous and imperishable, it is
a joy to practice and can be directly experienced.
³ But those who have no faith in the supreme
law of life do not find me, Arjuna. They return
to the world, passing from death to death.

⁴ I pervade the entire universe in my unmanifested
form. All creatures find their existence in me,
but I am not limited by them. ⁵ Behold my divine
mystery! These creatures do not really dwell in me,
and though I bring them forth and support them,
I am not confined within them. ⁶ They move in me
as the winds move in every direction in space.
⁷ At the end of the eon these creatures return to
unmanifested matter; at the beginning of the next
cycle I send them forth again. ⁸ Controlling my
prakriti, again and again I bring forth these myriad
forms and subject them to the laws of prakriti. ⁹ None
of these actions binds me, Arjuna. I am unattached
to them, so they do not disturb my nature.

¹⁰ Under my watchful eye the laws of nature take
their course. Thus is the world set in motion; thus
the animate and the inanimate are created.

¹¹ The immature do not look beyond physical
appearances to see my true nature as the Lord of all
creation. ¹² The knowledge of such deluded people
is empty; their lives are fraught with disaster and
evil, and their work and hopes are all in vain.

¹³ But truly great souls seek my divine nature.
They worship me with a one-pointed mind,
having realized that I am the eternal source of
all. ¹⁴ Constantly striving, they make firm their
resolve and worship me without wavering. Full
of devotion, they sing of my divine glory.
¹⁵ Others follow the path of jnana, spiritual
wisdom. They see that where there is One,
that One is me; where there are many, all
are me; they see my face everywhere.

¹⁶ I am the ritual and the sacrifice; I am true medicine
and the mantram. I am the offering and the fire which
consumes it, and the one to whom it is offered.

¹⁷ I am the father and mother of this universe, and its
grandfather too; I am its entire support. I am the sum
of all knowledge, the purifier, the syllable *Om*; I am
the sacred scriptures, the Rig, Yajur, and Sama Vedas.

¹⁸ I am the goal of life, the Lord and support
of all, the inner witness, the abode of all. I am
the only refuge, the one true friend; I am the
beginning, the staying, and the end of creation;
I am the womb and the eternal seed.

¹⁹ I am heat; I give and withhold the
rain. I am immortality and I am death;
I am what is and what is not.

[20] Those who follow the rituals given in the
Vedas, who offer sacrifices and take soma, free
themselves from evil and attain the vast heaven
of the gods, where they enjoy celestial pleasures.
[21] When they have enjoyed these fully, their merit
is exhausted and they return to this land of death.
Thus observing Vedic rituals but caught in an
endless chain of desires, they come and go.

[22] Those who worship me and meditate on
me constantly, without any other thought
— I will provide for all their needs.

[23] Those who worship other gods with faith and
devotion also worship me, Arjuna, even if they do
not observe the usual forms. [24] I am the object of all
worship, its enjoyer and Lord. But those who fail to
realize my true nature must be reborn. [25] Those who
worship the devas will go to the realm of the devas;
those who worship their ancestors will be united with
them after death. Those who worship phantoms will
become phantoms; but my devotees will come to me.

[26] Whatever I am offered in devotion with a pure heart
— a leaf, a flower, fruit, or water — I partake of that love
offering. [27] Whatever you do, make it an offering to me
— the food you eat, the sacrifices you make, the help
you give, even your suffering. [28] In this way you will be
freed from the bondage of karma, and from its results
both pleasant and painful. Then, firm in renunciation
and yoga, with your heart free, you will come to me.

[29] I look upon all creatures equally; none are less dear
to me and none more dear. But those who worship
me with love live in me, and I come to life in them.

30 Even sinners become holy when they worship
me alone with firm resolve. 31 Quickly their souls
conform to dharma and they attain to boundless
peace. Never forget this, Arjuna: no one who
is devoted to me will ever come to harm.

32 All those who take refuge in me, whatever their
birth, race, sex, or caste, will attain the supreme
goal; this realization can be attained even by those
whom society scorns. 33 Kings and sages too seek
this goal with devotion. Therefore, having been
born in this transient and forlorn world, give all
your love to me. 34 Fill your mind with me; love
me; serve me; worship me always. Seeking me in
your heart, you will at last be united with me.

10. Divine Splendor

KRISHNA

[1] Listen further, Arjuna, to my supreme teaching,
which gives you such joy. Desiring your welfare,
O strong-armed warrior, I will tell you more.

[2] Neither gods nor sages know my origin, for I
am the source from which the gods and sages
come. [3] Whoever knows me as the Lord of all
creation, without birth or beginning, knows
the truth and frees himself from all evil.

[4] Discrimination, wisdom, understanding,
forgiveness, truth, self-control, and peace of
mind; pleasure and pain, birth and death, fear
and courage, honor and dishonor; [5] nonviolence,
charity, equanimity, contentment, and perseverance
in spiritual disciplines — all the different qualities
found in living creatures have their source in me.

[6] The seven great sages and the four ancient
ancestors were born from my mind and received
my power. From them came all the creatures of
this world. [7] Whoever understands my power
and the mystery of my manifestations comes
without doubt to be united with me.

[8] I am the source from which all creatures evolve.
The wise remember this and worship me with loving
devotion. [9] Their thoughts are all absorbed in me, and
all their vitality flows to me. Teaching one another,
talking about me always, they are happy and fulfilled.

¹⁰ To those steadfast in love and devotion I give
spiritual wisdom, so that they may come to me.
¹¹ Out of compassion I destroy the darkness of their
ignorance. From within them I light the lamp of
wisdom and dispel all darkness from their lives.

ARJUNA

¹² You are Brahman supreme, the highest abode,
the supreme purifier, the self-luminous, eternal
spirit, first among the gods, unborn and infinite.
¹³ The great sages and seers — Narada, Asita,
Devala, and Vyasa too — have acclaimed you
thus; now you have declared it to me yourself.

¹⁴ Now, O Krishna, I believe that everything you
have told me is divine truth. O Lord, neither gods
nor demons know your real nature. ¹⁵ Indeed,
you alone know yourself, O supreme spirit. You
are the source of being and the master of every
creature, God of gods, the Lord of the universe.

¹⁶ Tell me all your divine attributes, leaving
nothing unsaid. Tell me of the glories with which
you fill the cosmos. ¹⁷ Krishna, you are a supreme
master of yoga. Tell me how I should meditate
to gain constant awareness of you. In what things
and in what ways should I meditate on you?
¹⁸ O Krishna, you who stir up people's hearts,
tell me in detail your attributes and your powers;
I can never tire of hearing your immortal words.

KRISHNA

¹⁹ All right, Arjuna, I will tell you of my
divine powers. I will mention only the most

glorious; for there is no end to them.

20 I am the true Self in the heart of every
creature, Arjuna, and the beginning,
middle, and end of their existence.

21 Among the shining gods I am Vishnu; of
luminaries I am the sun; among the storm gods I
am Marichi, and in the night sky I am the moon.

22 Among scriptures I am the Sama Veda, and among
the lesser gods I am Indra. Among the senses I am
the mind, and in living beings I am consciousness.

23 Among the Rudras I am Shankara. Among
the spirits of the natural world I am Kubera,
god of wealth, and Pavaka, the purifying
fire. Among mountains I am Meru.

24 Among priests I am Brihaspati, and among
military leaders I am Skanda. Among
bodies of water I am the ocean.

25 Among the great seers I am Bhrigu, and among
words, the syllable *Om*; I am the repetition of the holy
name, and among mountains I am the Himalayas.

26 Among trees I am the *ashvattha*, the sacred fig;
among the *gandharvas*, the heavenly musicians,
I am Chitraratha. Among divine seers I am
Narada, and among sages I am Kapila.
27 I was born from the nectar of immortality
as the primordial horse and as Indra's noble
elephant. Among human beings, I am the king.

28 Among weapons I am the thunderbolt.

I am Kamadhuk, the cow that fulfills all
desires; I am Kandarpa, the power of sex,
and Vasuki, the king of snakes.

29 I am Ananta, the cosmic serpent, and Varuna,
the god of water; I am Aryaman among the
noble ancestors. Among the forces which
restrain I am Yama, the god of death.

30 Among animals I am the lion; among birds, the
eagle Garuda. I am Prahlada, born among the
demons, and of all that measures, I am time.

31 Among purifying forces I am the wind; among
warriors, Rama. Of water creatures I am the
crocodile, and of rivers I am the Ganges.

32 I am the beginning, middle, and end of creation.
Of all the sciences I am the science of Self-
knowledge, and I am logic in those who debate.
33 Among letters I am A; among grammatical
compounds I am the *dvandva.* I am infinite time,
and the sustainer whose face is seen everywhere.

34 I am death, which overcomes all, and the
source of all beings still to be born. I am the
feminine qualities: fame, beauty, perfect speech,
memory, intelligence, loyalty, and forgiveness.

35 Among the hymns of the Sama Veda I am the
Brihat; among poetic meters, the Gayatri. Among
months I am Margashirsha, first of the year; among
seasons I am spring, that brings forth flowers.

36 I am the gambling of the gambler and the
radiance in all that shines. I am effort, I am

victory, and I am the goodness of the virtuous.

37 Among the Vrishnis I am Krishna, and among
the Pandavas I am Arjuna. Among sages I
am Vyasa, and among poets, Ushanas.

38 I am the scepter which metes out punishment, and
the art of statesmanship in those who lead. I am the
silence of the unknown and the wisdom of the wise.

39 I am the seed that can be found in every
creature, Arjuna; for without me nothing can
exist, neither animate nor inanimate.

40 But there is no end to my divine attributes,
Arjuna; these I have mentioned are only a
few. 41 Wherever you find strength, or beauty,
or spiritual power, you may be sure that these
have sprung from a spark of my essence.

42 But of what use is it to you to know all this, Arjuna?
Just remember that I am, and that I support the
entire cosmos with only a fragment of my being.

11. The Cosmic Vision

ARJUNA

[1] Out of compassion you have taught me the
supreme mystery of the Self. Through your words
my delusion is gone. [2] You have explained the origin
and end of every creature, O lotus-eyed one, and
told me of your own supreme, limitless existence.

[3] Just as you have described your infinite glory,
O Lord, now I long to see it. I want to see you
as the supreme ruler of creation. [4] O Lord,
master of yoga, if you think me strong enough
to behold it, show me your immortal Self.

KRISHNA

[5] Behold, Arjuna, a million divine forms, with an
infinite variety of color and shape. [6] Behold the gods
of the natural world, and many more wonders never
revealed before. [7] Behold the entire cosmos turning
within my body, and the other things you desire to see.
[8] But these things cannot be seen with your
physical eyes; therefore I give you spiritual
vision to perceive my majestic power.

SANJAYA

[9] Having spoken these words, Krishna, the master of
yoga, revealed to Arjuna his most exalted, lordly form.

[10] He appeared with an infinite number of faces,
ornamented by heavenly jewels, displaying unending

miracles and the countless weapons of his power.
[11] Clothed in celestial garments and covered with
garlands, sweet-smelling with heavenly fragrances,
he showed himself as the infinite Lord, the source
of all wonders, whose face is everywhere.

[12] If a thousand suns were to rise in the heavens
at the same time, the blaze of their light would
resemble the splendor of that supreme spirit.

[13] There, within the body of the God of gods,
Arjuna saw all the manifold forms of the universe
united as one. [14] Filled with amazement, his hair
standing on end in ecstasy, he bowed before the
Lord with joined palms and spoke these words.

ARJUNA

[15] O Lord, I see within your body all the
gods and every kind of living creature. I see
Brahma, the Creator, seated on a lotus; I see
the ancient sages and the celestial serpents.

[16] I see infinite mouths and arms, stomachs
and eyes, and you are embodied in every form.
I see you everywhere, without beginning,
middle, or end. You are the Lord of all
creation, and the cosmos is your body.

[17] You wear a crown and carry a mace and discus;
your radiance is blinding and immeasurable. I
see you, who are so difficult to behold, shining
like a fiery sun blazing in every direction.

[18] You are the supreme, changeless Reality,
the one thing to be known. You are the

refuge of all creation, the immortal spirit,
the eternal guardian of eternal dharma.

19 You are without beginning, middle, or end;
you touch everything with your infinite power.
The sun and moon are your eyes, and your mouth
is fire; your radiance warms the cosmos.

20 O Lord, your presence fills the heavens and
the earth and reaches in every direction. I see
the three worlds trembling before this vision
of your wonderful and terrible form.

21 The gods enter your being, some calling
out and greeting you in fear. Great saints sing
your glory, praying, "May all be well!"

22 The multitudes of gods, demigods, and demons
are all overwhelmed by the sight of you. 23 O
mighty Lord, at the sight of your myriad eyes
and mouths, arms and legs, stomachs and fearful
teeth, I and the entire universe shake in terror.

24 O Vishnu, I can see your eyes shining; with open
mouth, you glitter in an array of colors, and your
body touches the sky. I look at you and my heart
trembles; I have lost all courage and all peace of mind.

25 When I see your mouths with their fearful teeth,
mouths burning like the fires at the end of time,
I forget where I am and I have no place to go. O Lord,
you are the support of the universe; have mercy on me!

26 I see all the sons of Dhritarashtra; I see Bhishma,
Drona, and Karna; I see our warriors and all the kings
who are here to fight. 27 All are rushing into your awful

jaws; I see some of them crushed by your teeth. ²⁸ As
rivers flow into the ocean, all the warriors of this
world are passing into your fiery jaws; ²⁹ all creatures
rush to their destruction like moths into a flame.

³⁰ You lap the worlds into your burning mouths and
swallow them. Filled with your terrible radiance,
O Vishnu, the whole of creation bursts into flames.

³¹ Tell me who you are, O Lord of terrible form.
I bow before you; have mercy! I want to know
who you are, you who existed before all creation.
Your nature and workings confound me.

KRISHNA

³² I am time, the destroyer of all; I have come to
consume the world. Even without your participation,
all the warriors gathered here will die.

³³ Therefore arise, Arjuna; conquer your enemies and
enjoy the glory of sovereignty. I have already slain
all these warriors; you will only be my instrument.

³⁴ Bhishma, Drona, Jayadratha, Karna, and
many others are already slain. Kill those whom
I have killed. Do not hesitate. Fight in this
battle and you will conquer your enemies.

SANJAYA

³⁵ Having heard these words, Arjuna trembled
in fear. With joined palms he bowed before
Krishna and addressed him stammering.

ARJUNA

³⁶ O Krishna, it is right that the world delights
and rejoices in your praise, that all the saints
and sages bow down to you and all evil flees
before you to the far corners of the universe.

³⁷ How could they not worship you, O Lord? You
are the eternal spirit, who existed before Brahma
the Creator and who will never cease to be. Lord
of the gods, you are the abode of the universe.
Changeless, you are what is and what is not, and
beyond the duality of existence and nonexistence.

³⁸ You are the first among the gods, the timeless spirit,
the resting place of all beings. You are the knower and
the thing which is known. You are the final home;
with your infinite form you pervade the cosmos.

³⁹ You are Vayu, god of wind; Yama, god of
death; Agni, god of fire; Varuna, god of water.
You are the moon and the creator Prajapati,
and the great-grandfather of all creatures. I bow
before you and salute you again and again.

⁴⁰ You are behind me and in front of me; I bow to
you on every side. Your power is immeasurable.
You pervade everything; you are everything.

⁴¹ Sometimes, because we were friends, I rashly said,
"Oh, Krishna! Say, friend!" — casual, careless remarks.
Whatever I may have said lightly, whether we were
playing or resting, alone or in company, sitting
together or eating, ⁴² if it was disrespectful, forgive

me for it, O Krishna. I did not know the greatness
of your nature, unchanging and imperishable.

[43] You are the father of the universe, of the
animate and the inanimate; you are the object of
all worship, the greatest guru. There is none to
equal you in the three worlds. Who can match
your power? [44] O gracious Lord, I prostrate
myself before you and ask for your blessing. As
a father forgives his son, or a friend a friend, or
a lover his beloved, so should you forgive me.

[45] I rejoice in seeing you as you have never been
seen before, yet I am filled with fear by this vision
of you as the abode of the universe. Please let me
see you again as the shining God of gods. [46] Though
you are the embodiment of all creation, let me see
you again not with a thousand arms but with four,
carrying the mace and discus and wearing a crown.

KRISHNA

[47] Arjuna, through my grace you have been
united with me and received this vision of my
radiant, universal form, without beginning
or end, which no one else has ever seen.

[48] Not by knowledge of the Vedas, nor
sacrifice, nor charity, nor rituals, nor even by
severe asceticism has any other mortal seen
what you have seen, O heroic Arjuna.

[49] Do not be troubled; do not fear my terrible
form. Let your heart be satisfied and your fears
dispelled in looking at me as I was before.

SANJAYA

⁵⁰ Having spoken these words, the Lord once
again assumed the gentle form of Krishna and
consoled his devotee, who had been so afraid.

ARJUNA

⁵¹ O Krishna, now that I have seen your
gentle human form my mind is again
composed and returned to normal.

KRISHNA

⁵² It is extremely difficult to obtain the vision you
have had; even the gods long always to see me in
this aspect. ⁵³ Neither knowledge of the Vedas, nor
austerity, nor charity, nor sacrifice can bring the vision
you have seen. ⁵⁴ But through unfailing devotion,
Arjuna, you can know me, see me, and attain union
with me. ⁵⁵ Those who make me the supreme goal
of all their work and act without selfish attachment,
who devote themselves to me completely and are
free from ill will for any creature, enter into me.

12. *The Way of Love*

ARJUNA

[1] Of those steadfast devotees who love you and
those who seek you as the eternal formless
Reality, who are the more established in yoga?

KRISHNA

[2] Those who set their hearts on me and
worship me with unfailing devotion and
faith are more established in yoga.

[3] As for those who seek the transcendental Reality,
without name, without form, contemplating
the Unmanifested, beyond the reach of thought
and of feeling, [4] with their senses subdued and
mind serene and striving for the good of all
beings, they too will verily come unto me.

[5] Yet hazardous and slow is the path to the Unrevealed,
difficult for physical creatures to tread. [6] But they
for whom I am the supreme goal, who do all work
renouncing self for me and meditate on me with
single-hearted devotion, [7] these I will swiftly rescue
from the fragment's cycle of birth and death,
for their consciousness has entered into me.

[8] Still your mind in me, still your intellect in me, and
without doubt you will be united with me forever.
[9] If you cannot still your mind in me, learn to do so
through the regular practice of meditation. [10] If you
lack the will for such self-discipline, engage yourself

in my work, for selfless service can lead you at last to complete fulfillment. ¹¹ If you are unable to do even this, surrender yourself to me, disciplining yourself and renouncing the results of all your actions.

¹² Better indeed is knowledge than mechanical practice. Better than knowledge is meditation. But better still is surrender of attachment to results, because there follows immediate peace.

¹³ That one I love who is incapable of ill will, who is friendly and compassionate. Living beyond the reach of *I* and *mine* and of pleasure and pain, ¹⁴ patient, contented, self-controlled, firm in faith, with all their heart and all their mind given to me — with such as these I am in love.

¹⁵ Not agitating the world or by it agitated, they stand above the sway of elation, competition, and fear: that one is my beloved.

¹⁶ They are detached, pure, efficient, impartial, never anxious, selfless in all their undertakings; they are my devotees, very dear to me.

¹⁷ That one is dear to me who runs not after the pleasant or away from the painful, grieves not, lusts not, but lets things come and go as they happen.

¹⁸ That devotee who looks upon friend and foe with equal regard, who is not buoyed up by praise nor cast down by blame, alike in heat and cold, pleasure and pain, free from selfish attachments, ¹⁹ the same in honor and dishonor, quiet, ever full, in harmony everywhere, firm in faith — such a one is dear to me.

[20] Those who meditate upon this immortal dharma as I have declared it, full of faith and seeking me as life's supreme goal, are truly my devotees, and my love for them is very great.

13. *The Field & the Knower*

KRISHNA

[1] The body is called a field, Arjuna; the one who knows it is called the Knower of the field. This is the knowledge of those who know. [2] I am the Knower of the field in everyone, Arjuna. Knowledge of the field and its Knower is true knowledge.

[3] Listen and I will explain the nature of the field and how change takes place within it. I will also describe the Knower of the field and his power. [4] These truths have been sung by great sages in a variety of ways, and expounded in precise arguments concerning Brahman.

[5] The field, Arjuna, is made up of the following: the five areas of sense perception; the five elements; the five sense organs and the five organs of action; the three components of the mind: *manas, buddhi,* and *ahamkara*; and the undifferentiated energy from which all these evolved. [6] In this field arise desire and aversion, pleasure and pain, the body, intelligence, and will.

[7] Those who know truly are free from pride and deceit. They are gentle, forgiving, upright, and pure, devoted to their spiritual teacher, filled with inner strength, and self-controlled. [8] Detached from sense objects and self-will, they have learned the painful lesson of separate birth and suffering, old age, disease, and death.

[9] Free from selfish attachment, they do not get
compulsively entangled even in home and family.
They are even-minded through good fortune and bad.
[10] Their devotion to me is undivided. Enjoying solitude
and not following the crowd, they seek only me. [11] This
is true knowledge, to seek the Self as the true end of
wisdom always. To seek anything else is ignorance.

[12] I will tell you of the wisdom that leads to
immortality: the beginningless Brahman, which
can be called neither being nor non-being.

[13] It dwells in all, in every hand and foot and head,
in every mouth and eye and ear in the universe.
[14] Without senses itself, it shines through the
functioning of the senses. Completely independent, it
supports all things. Beyond the gunas, it enjoys their
play.

[15] It is both near and far, both within and without
every creature; it moves and is unmoving. [16] In its
subtlety it is beyond comprehension. It is indivisible,
yet appears divided in separate creatures. Know it
to be the creator, the preserver, and the destroyer.

[17] Dwelling in every heart, it is beyond darkness.
It is called the light of light, the object and
goal of knowledge, and knowledge itself.

[18] I have revealed to you the nature of the
field and the meaning and object of true
knowledge. Those who are devoted to me,
knowing these things, are united with me.

[19] Know that prakriti and Purusha are both without
beginning, and that from prakriti come the

gunas and all that changes. [20] Prakriti is the agent,
cause, and effect of every action, but it is Purusha
that seems to experience pleasure and pain.

[21] Purusha, resting in prakriti, witnesses the play of
the gunas born of prakriti. But attachment to the
gunas leads a person to be born for good or evil.

[22] Within the body the supreme Purusha
is called the witness, approver, supporter,
enjoyer, the supreme Lord, the highest Self.

[23] Whoever realizes the true nature of Purusha,
prakriti, and the gunas, whatever path he or
she may follow, is not born separate again.

[24] Some realize the Self within them through the
practice of meditation, some by the path of wisdom,
and others by selfless service. [25] Others may not know
these paths; but hearing and following the instructions
of an illumined teacher, they too go beyond death.

[26] Whatever exists, Arjuna, animate or inanimate, is
born through the union of the field and its Knower.

[27] They alone see truly who see the Lord the
same in every creature, who see the deathless
in the hearts of all that die. [28] Seeing the same
Lord everywhere, they do not harm themselves
or others. Thus they attain the supreme goal.

[29] They alone see truly who see that all actions
are performed by prakriti, while the Self remains
unmoved. [30] When they see the variety of
creation rooted in that unity and growing out
of it, they attain fulfillment in Brahman.

[31] This supreme Self is without a beginning,
undiff erentiated, deathless. Though it dwells in
the body, Arjuna, it neither acts nor is touched
by action. [32] As akasha pervades the cosmos
but remains unstained, the Self can never be
tainted though it dwells in every creature.

[33] As the sun lights up the world, the Self dwelling in
the field is the source of all light in the field. [34] Those
who, with the eye of wisdom, distinguish the field
from its Knower and the way to freedom from the
bondage of prakriti, attain the supreme goal.

14. The Forces of Evolution

KRISHNA

[1] Let me tell you more about the wisdom that
transcends all knowledge, through which the
saints and sages attained perfection. [2] Those who
rely on this wisdom will be united with me. For
them there is neither rebirth nor fear of death.

[3] My womb is prakriti; in that I place the seed.
Thus all created things are born. [4] Everything
born, Arjuna, comes from the womb of
prakriti, and I am the seed-giving father.

[5] It is the three gunas born of prakriti — sattva, rajas,
and tamas — that bind the immortal Self to the body.
[6] Sattva — pure, luminous, and free from sorrow
— binds us with attachment to happiness and wisdom.
[7] Rajas is passion, arising from selfish desire and
attachment. These bind the Self with compulsive
action. [8] Tamas, born of ignorance, deludes all
creatures through heedlessness, indolence, and sleep.

[9] Sattva binds us to happiness; rajas
binds us to action. Tamas, distorting our
understanding, binds us to delusion.

[10] Sattva predominates when rajas and tamas
are transformed. Rajas prevails when sattva
is weak and tamas overcome. Tamas prevails
when rajas and sattva are dormant.

¹¹ When sattva predominates, the light of wisdom shines through every gate of the body. ¹² When rajas predominates, a person runs about pursuing selfish and greedy ends, driven by restlessness and desire. ¹³ When tamas is dominant a person lives in darkness — slothful, confused, and easily infatuated.

¹⁴ Those dying in the state of sattva attain the pure worlds of the wise. ¹⁵ Those dying in rajas are reborn among people driven by work. But those who die in tamas are conceived in the wombs of the ignorant.

¹⁶ The fruit of good deeds is pure and sattvic. The fruit of rajas is suffering. The fruit of tamas is ignorance and insensitivity.

¹⁷ From sattva comes understanding; from rajas, greed. But the outcome of tamas is confusion, infatuation, and ignorance.

¹⁸ Those who live in sattva go upwards; those in rajas remain where they are. But those immersed in tamas sink downwards.

¹⁹ The wise see clearly that all action is the work of the gunas. Knowing that which is above the gunas, they enter into union with me.

²⁰ Going beyond the three gunas which form the body, they leave behind the cycle of birth and death, decrepitude and sorrow, and attain to immortality.

ARJUNA

²¹ What are the characteristics of those who have gone beyond the gunas, O Lord? How do they act?

How have they passed beyond the gunas' hold?

KRISHNA

22 They are unmoved by the harmony of sattva, the
activity of rajas, or the delusion of tamas. They feel
no aversion when these forces are active, nor do
they crave for them when these forces subside.

23 They remain impartial, undisturbed by the actions
of the gunas. Knowing that it is the gunas which act,
they abide within themselves and do not vacillate.

24 Established within themselves, they are equal in
pleasure and pain, praise and blame, kindness and
unkindness. Clay, a rock, and gold are the same to
them. 25 Alike in honor and dishonor, alike to friend
and foe, they have given up every selfish pursuit.
Such are those who have gone beyond the gunas.

26 By serving me with steadfast love, a man or
woman goes beyond the gunas. Such a one is fit
for union with Brahman. 27 For I am the support of
Brahman, the eternal, the unchanging, the deathless,
the everlasting dharma, the source of all joy.

15. The Supreme Self

KRISHNA

[1] Sages speak of the immutable ashvattha
tree, with its taproot above and its branches
below. On this tree grow the scriptures; seeing
their source, one knows their essence.

[2] Nourished by the gunas, the limbs of this
tree spread above and below. Sense objects
grow on the limbs as buds; the roots hanging
down bind us to action in this world.

[3] The true form of this tree — its essence, beginning,
and end — is not perceived on this earth. Cut
down this strong-rooted tree with the sharp ax
of detachment; [4] then find the path which does
not come back again. Seek That, the First Cause,
from which the universe came long ago.

[5] Not deluded by pride, free from selfish attachment
and selfish desire, beyond the duality of pleasure
and pain, ever aware of the Self, the wise go
forward to that eternal goal. [6] Neither the sun
nor the moon nor fire can add to that light.
This is my supreme abode, and those who enter
there do not return to separate existence.

[7] An eternal part of me enters into the world,
assuming the powers of action and perception
and a mind made of prakriti. [8] When the divine
Self enters and leaves a body, it takes these along
as the wind carries a scent from place to place.

⁹ Using the mind, ears, eyes, nose, and the senses
of taste and touch, the Self enjoys sense objects.

¹⁰ The deluded do not see the Self when it leaves the
body or when it dwells within it. They do not see
the Self enjoying sense objects or acting through the
gunas. But they who have the eye of wisdom see.

¹¹ Those who strive resolutely on the path of
yoga see the Self within. The thoughtless,
who strive imperfectly, do not.

¹² The brightness of the sun, which lights up the world,
the brightness of the moon and of fire — these are my
glory. ¹³ With a drop of my energy I enter the earth and
support all creatures. Th rough the moon, the vessel of
life-giving fluid, I nourish all plants. ¹⁴ I enter breathing
creatures and dwell within as the life-giving breath.
I am the fire in the stomach which digests all food.

¹⁵ Entering into every heart, I give the power
to remember and understand; it is I again who
take that power away. All the scriptures lead
to me; I am their author and their wisdom.

¹⁶ In this world there are two orders of being: the
perishable, separate creature and the changeless
spirit. ¹⁷ But beyond these there is another, the
supreme Self, the eternal Lord, who enters into
the entire cosmos and supports it from within.

¹⁸ I am that supreme Self, praised by the scriptures
as beyond the changing and the changeless. ¹⁹ Those
who see in me that supreme Self see truly. They
have found the source of all wisdom, Arjuna,
and they worship me with all their heart.

[20] I have shared this profound truth with you, Arjuna. Those who understand it will attain wisdom; they will have done that which has to be done.

16. *Two Paths*

KRISHNA

[1] Be fearless and pure; never waver in your
determination or your dedication to the spiritual
life. Give freely. Be self-controlled, sincere, truthful,
loving, and full of the desire to serve. Realize the
truth of the scriptures; learn to be detached and
to take joy in renunciation. [2] Do not get angry or
harm any living creature, but be compassionate
and gentle; show good will to all. [3] Cultivate vigor,
patience, will, purity; avoid malice and pride. Then,
Arjuna, you will achieve your divine destiny.

[4] Other qualities, Arjuna, make a person more
and more inhuman: hypocrisy, arrogance,
conceit, anger, cruelty, ignorance.

[5] The divine qualities lead to freedom; the
demonic, to bondage. But do not grieve, Arjuna;
you were born with divine attributes.
[6] Some people have divine tendencies, others
demonic. I have described the divine at length,
Arjuna; now listen while I describe the demonic.

[7] The demonic do things they should avoid and
avoid the things they should do. They have
no sense of uprightness, purity, or truth.

[8] "There is no God," they say, "no truth, no spiritual
law, no moral order. The basis of life is sex; what else
can it be?" [9] Holding such distorted views, possessing

scant discrimination, they become enemies of
the world, causing suffering and destruction.

[10] Hypocritical, proud, and arrogant, living in
delusion and clinging to deluded ideas, insatiable
in their desires, they pursue their unclean ends.
[11] Although burdened with fears that end only with
death, they still maintain with complete assurance,
"Gratification of lust is the highest that life can offer."

[12] Bound on all sides by scheming and anxiety, driven
by anger and greed, they amass by any means they can
a hoard of money for the satisfaction of their cravings.

[13] "I got this today," they say; "tomorrow I shall get that.
This wealth is mine, and that will be mine too. [14] I have
destroyed my enemies. I shall destroy others too! Am
I not like God? I enjoy what I want. I am successful.
I am powerful. I am happy. [15] I am rich and well-born.
Who is equal to me? I will perform sacrifices and give
gifts, and rejoice in my own generosity." This is how
they go on, deluded by ignorance. [16] Bound by their
greed and entangled in a web of delusion, whirled
about by a fragmented mind, they fall into a dark hell.

[17] Self-important, obstinate, swept away by the
pride of wealth, they ostentatiously perform
sacrifices without any regard for their purpose.
[18] Egotistical, violent, arrogant, lustful, angry,
envious of everyone, they abuse my presence within
their own bodies and in the bodies of others.

[19] Life after life I cast those who are malicious, hateful,
cruel, and degraded into the wombs of those with
similar demonic natures. [20] Birth after birth they find
themselves with demonic tendencies. Degraded in this

way, Arjuna, they fail to reach me and fall lower still.
²¹ There are three gates to this self-destructive
hell: lust, anger, and greed. Renounce these three.

²² Those who escape from these three gates of
darkness, Arjuna, seek what is best and attain life's
supreme goal. ²³ Others disregard the teachings of
the scriptures. Driven by selfish desire, they miss
the goal of life, miss even happiness and success.

²⁴ Therefore let the scriptures be your guide in
what to do and what not to do. Understand their
teachings; then act in accordance with them.

17. The Power of Faith

ARJUNA

¹ O Krishna, what is the state of those who
disregard the scriptures but still worship with
faith? Do they act from sattva, rajas, or tamas?

KRISHNA

² Every creature is born with faith of some
kind, either sattvic, rajasic, or tamasic.
Listen, and I will describe each to you.

³ Our faith conforms to our nature,
Arjuna. Human nature is made of faith.
A person is what his shraddha is.

⁴ Those who are sattvic worship the forms of God;
those who are rajasic worship power and wealth.
Those who are tamasic worship spirits and ghosts.
⁵ Some invent harsh penances. Motivated by hypocrisy
and egotism, ⁶ they torture their innocent bodies and
me who dwells within. Blinded by their strength
and passion, they act and think like demons.

⁷ The three kinds of faith express themselves
in the habits of those who hold them: in the
food they like, the work they do, the disciplines
they practice, the gift s they give. Listen, and
I will describe their different ways.

⁸ Sattvic people enjoy food that is mild, tasty,
substantial, agreeable, and nourishing, food that

promotes health, strength, cheerfulness, and longevity. ⁹ Rajasic people like food that is salty or bitter, hot, sour, or spicy — food that promotes pain, discomfort, and disease. ¹⁰ Tamasic people like overcooked, stale, left over, and impure food, food that has lost its taste and nutritional value.

¹¹ The sattvic perform sacrifices with their entire mind fixed on the purpose of the sacrifice. Without thought of reward, they follow the teachings of the scriptures. ¹² The rajasic perform sacrifices for the sake of show and the good it will bring them. ¹³ The tamasic perform sacrifices ignoring both the letter and the spirit. They omit the proper prayers, the proper offerings, the proper food, and the proper faith.

¹⁴ To offer service to the gods, to the good, to the wise, and to your spiritual teacher; purity, honesty, continence, and nonviolence: these are the disciplines of the body. ¹⁵ To offer soothing words, to speak truly, kindly, and helpfully, and to study the scriptures; these are the disciplines of speech. ¹⁶ Calmness, gentleness, silence, self-restraint, and purity: these are the disciplines of the mind.

¹⁷ When these three levels of self-discipline are practiced without attachment to the results, but in a spirit of great faith, the sages call this practice sattvic. ¹⁸ Disciplines practiced in order to gain respect, honor, or admiration are rajasic; they are undependable and transitory in their effects. ¹⁹ Disciplines practiced to gain power over others, or in the confused belief that to torture oneself is spiritual, are tamasic.

²⁰ Giving simply because it is right to give, without thought of return, at a proper time, in proper

circumstances, and to a worthy person, is sattvic giving. [21] Giving with regrets or in the expectation of receiving some favor or of getting something in return is rajasic. [22] Giving at an inappropriate time, in inappropriate circumstances, and to an unworthy person, without affection or respect, is tamasic.

[23] *Om Tat Sat*: these three words represent Brahman, from which come priests and scriptures and sacrifice. [24] Those who follow the Vedas, therefore, always repeat the word *Om* when offering sacrifices, performing spiritual disciplines, or giving gifts. [25] Those seeking liberation and not any personal benefit add the word *Tat* when performing these acts of worship, discipline, and charity. [26] *Sat* means "that which is"; it also indicates goodness. Therefore it is used to describe a worthy deed.

[27] To be steadfast in self-sacrifice, self-discipline, and giving is *sat*. To act in accordance with these three is *sat* as well. [28] But to engage in sacrifice, self-discipline, and giving without good faith is *asat*, without worth or goodness, either in this life or in the next.

18. *Freedom & Renunciation*

ARJUNA

[1] O Krishna, destroyer of evil, please explain
to me *sannyasa* and *tyaga* and how one kind
of renunciation differs from another.

KRISHNA

[2] To refrain from selfish acts is one kind of
renunciation, called sannyasa; to renounce
the fruit of action is another, called tyaga.

[3] Among the wise, some say that all action should
be renounced as evil. Others say that certain
kinds of action — self-sacrifice, giving, and
self-discipline — should be continued. [4] Listen,
Arjuna, and I will explain three kinds of tyaga
and my conclusions concerning them.

[5] Self-sacrifice, giving, and self-discipline should
not be renounced, for they purify the thoughtful.
[6] Yet even these, Arjuna, should be performed
without desire for selfi sh rewards. This is essential.

[7] To renounce one's responsibilities is not fitting.
The wise call such deluded renunciation tamasic.
[8] To avoid action from fear of difficulty or physical
discomfort is rajasic. There is no reward in such
renunciation. [9] But to fulfill your responsibilities
knowing that they are obligatory, while at the same
time desiring nothing for yourself — this is sattvic
renunciation. [10] Those endowed with sattva clearly

understand the meaning of renunciation and do
not waver. They are not intimidated by unpleasant
work, nor do they seek a job because it is pleasant.

[11] As long as one has a body, one cannot renounce
action altogether. True renunciation is giving up all
desire for personal reward. [12] Those who are attached
to personal reward will reap the consequences of
their actions: some pleasant, some unpleasant, some
mixed. But those who renounce every desire for
personal reward go beyond the reach of karma.

[13] Listen, Arjuna, and I will explain the five elements
necessary for the accomplishment of every action,
as taught by the wisdom of Sankhya. [14] The body,
the means, the ego, the performance of the act,
and the divine will: [15] these are the five factors in all
actions, right or wrong, in thought, word, or deed.

[16] Those who do not understand this think of
themselves as separate agents. With their crude
intellects they fail to see the truth. [17] The person
who is free from ego, who has attained purity
of heart, though he slays these people, he does
not slay and is not bound by his action.

[18] Knowledge, the thing to be known, and the
knower: these three promote action. The means,
the act itself, and the doer: these three are the
totality of action. [19] Knowledge, action, and the doer
can be described according to the gunas. Listen,
and I will explain their distinctions to you.

[20] Sattvic knowledge sees the one indestructible Being
in all beings, the unity underlying the multiplicity

of creation. [21] Rajasic knowledge sees all things
and creatures as separate and distinct. [22] Tamasic
knowledge, lacking any sense of perspective, sees
one small part and mistakes it for the whole.

[23] Work performed to fulfill one's obligations,
without thought of personal reward or of whether
the job is pleasant or unpleasant, is sattvic. [24] Work
prompted by selfish desire or self-will, full of stress,
is rajasic. [25] Work that is undertaken blindly, without
any consideration of consequences, waste, injury
to others, or one's own capacities, is tamasic.

[26] Sattvic workers are free from egotism and selfish
attachments, full of enthusiasm and fortitude in
success and failure alike. [27] Rajasic workers have
strong personal desires and crave rewards for
their actions. Covetous, impure, and destructive,
they are easily swept away by fortune, good or
bad. [28] Tamasic workers are undisciplined, vulgar,
stubborn, deceitful, dishonest, and lazy. They are
easily depressed and prone to procrastination.

[29] Listen, Arjuna, as I describe the three
types of understanding and will.

[30] To know when to act and when to refrain
from action, what is right action and what is
wrong, what brings security and what insecurity,
what brings freedom and what bondage:
these are the signs of a sattvic intellect.
[31] The rajasic intellect confuses right and wrong
actions, and cannot distinguish what is to be
done from what should not be done. [32] The
tamasic intellect is shrouded in darkness, utterly
reversing right and wrong wherever it turns.

33 The sattvic will, developed through meditation, keeps prana, mind, and senses in vital harmony. 34 The rajasic will, conditioned by selfish desire, pursues wealth, pleasure, and respectability. 35 The tamasic will shows itself in obstinate ignorance, sloth, fear, grief, depression, and conceit.

36 Now listen, Arjuna: there are also three kinds of happiness. By sustained effort, one comes to the end of sorrow. 37 That which seems like poison at first, but tastes like nectar in the end — this is the joy of sattva, born of a mind at peace with itself. 38 Pleasure from the senses seems like nectar at first, but it is bitter as poison in the end. This is the kind of happiness that comes to the rajasic. 39 Those who are tamasic draw their pleasures from sleep, indolence, and intoxication. Both in the beginning and in the end, this happiness is a delusion.

40 No creature, whether born on earth or among the gods in heaven, is free from the conditioning of the three gunas. 41 The different responsibilities found in the social order — distinguishing brahmin, kshatriya, vaishya, and shudra — have their roots in this conditioning.

42 The responsibilities to which brahmins are born, based on their nature, are self-control, tranquility, purity of heart, patience, humility, learning, austerity, wisdom, and faith.

43 The qualities of kshatriyas, based on their nature, are courage, strength, fortitude, dexterity, generosity, leadership, and the firm resolve never to retreat from battle. 44 The occupations suitable for a vaishya are agriculture, dairying, and trade.

The proper work of a shudra is service.
[45] By devotion to one's own particular duty,
everyone can attain perfection. Let me tell you how.
[46] By performing one's own work, one worships
the Creator who dwells in every creature. Such
worship brings that person to fulfillment.
[47] It is better to perform one's own duties
imperfectly than to master the duties of another.
By fulfilling the obligations he is born with, a
person never comes to grief. [48] No one should
abandon duties because he sees defects in them.
Every action, every activity, is surrounded by
defects as a fire is surrounded by smoke.

[49] One who is free from selfish attachments, who
has mastered himself and his passions, attains
the supreme perfection of freedom from action.
[50] Listen and I shall explain now, Arjuna, how one
who has attained perfection also attains Brahman,
the supreme consummation of wisdom.

[51] Unerring in discrimination, sovereign of
the senses and passions, free from the clamor
of likes and dislikes, [52] such a one leads a
simple, self-reliant life based on meditation,
controlling speech, body, and mind.

[53] Free from self-will, aggressiveness, arrogance, anger,
and the lust to possess people or things, they are at
peace with themselves and others and enter into the
unitive state. [54] United with Brahman, ever joyful,
beyond the reach of desire and sorrow, they have equal
regard for every living creature and attain supreme
devotion to me. [55] By loving me they come to know
me truly; then they know my glory and enter into my
boundless being. [56] All their acts are performed in my

service, and through my grace they win eternal life.
⁵⁷ Make every act an offering to me; regard me as your
only protector. Relying on interior discipline, meditate
on me always. ⁵⁸ Remembering me, you shall overcome
all difficulties through my grace. But if you will not
heed me in your self-will, nothing will avail you.

⁵⁹ If you egotistically say, "I will not fight this battle,"
your resolve will be useless; your own nature will
drive you into it. ⁶⁰ Your own karma, born of your
own nature, will drive you to do even that which
you do not wish to do, because of your delusion.

⁶¹ The Lord dwells in the hearts of all creatures
and whirls them round upon the wheel of maya.
⁶² Run to him for refuge with all your strength, and
peace profound will be yours through his grace.

⁶³ I give you these precious words of wisdom; reflect
on them and then do as you choose. ⁶⁴ These are the
last words I shall speak to you, dear one, for your
spiritual fulfillment. You are very dear to me.

⁶⁵ Be aware of me always, adore me, make every
act an offering to me, and you shall come to me;
this I promise; for you are dear to me. ⁶⁶ Abandon
all supports and look to me for protection. I shall
purify you from the sins of the past; do not grieve.

⁶⁷ Do not share this wisdom with anyone who lacks
in devotion or self-control, lacks the desire to learn,
or scoff s at me. ⁶⁸ Those who teach this supreme
mystery of the Gita to all who love me perform the
greatest act of love; they will come to me without
doubt. ⁶⁹ No one can render me more devoted
service; no one on earth can be more dear to me.

⁷⁰ Those who meditate on these holy words worship
me with wisdom and devotion. ⁷¹ Even those who
listen to them with faith, free from doubts, will
find a happier world where good people dwell.

⁷² Have you listened with attention? Are you
now free from your doubts and confusion?

ARJUNA

⁷³ You have dispelled my doubts and delusions,
and I understand through your grace. My
faith is firm now, and I will do your will.

SANJAYA

⁷⁴ This is the dialogue I heard between Krishna,
the son of Vasudeva, and Arjuna, the great-
hearted son of Pritha. The wonder of it makes
my hair stand on end! ⁷⁵ Through Vyasa's grace,
I have heard the supreme secret of spiritual union
directly from the Lord of yoga, Krishna himself.

⁷⁶ Whenever I remember these wonderful, holy words
between Krishna and Arjuna, I am filled with joy.
⁷⁷ And when I remember the breathtaking form of
Krishna, I am filled with wonder and my joy overflows.

⁷⁸ Wherever the divine Krishna and the mighty
Arjuna are, there will be prosperity, victory,
happiness, and sound judgment. Of this I am sure!

Notes

CHAPTER ONE

1 The phrase "on the field of dharma" (*dharma-kshetre*) gives a hint that the battle is to be an allegorical one, a fight of dharma, justice, against adharma, evil. The battle takes place not only at Kurukshetra, the "field of the Kurus," but also on the elusive "field of dharma," the spiritual realm where all moral struggles are waged.

40-44 These verses are particularly difficult to translate, because they revolve around the complex word *dharma*: law, justice, or simply something's inner nature. To try to capture the word in English we might say "God's law" or "eternal truth." Dharma is divinely given; it is the force that holds things together in a unity, the center that must hold if all is to go well. The opposite of dharma is *adharma*: evil, injustice, chaos. In these verses Arjuna gives expression to his fears of a coming chaos, an evil world where good people will be confused and violated. "Sense of unity" here translates *dharma*; the phrase "loses its sense of unity" would be more literally translated as "is overcome by *adharma*."

The translation speaks in a general way of the chaos that overcomes society when dharma is weak—when ancient spiritual truths are ignored. Thus *varna-samkara*, literally "confusion of caste," is more meaningful as "society [is] plunged into chaos." The subject here is not the observance of caste restrictions, but the essential cohesion of the social fabric.

42 The Sanskrit refers to the ancient pinda rites that offer homage to dead ancestors. These rites maintained the traditions of the family by respecting and worshipping those who had gone before. Again, the rather liberal rendering "the spiritual evolution begun by our ancestors" seems preferable to a narrower translation.

CHAPTER TWO

17 *Tat*, "that," is an ancient name for Brahman, the supreme reality. Brahman is neither masculine nor feminine; in fact, it has no attributes at all. It is impossible to describe Brahman in words, so it is simply pointed to: *tat*.

72 The state of immortality is *brahma-nirvana*, "the nirvana that is Brahman." This is the state of release or liberation, union with the divine ground of existence. The word *nirvana* comes from the Sanskrit root *va* "to blow" with the prefix *nir* "out"; it means "to extinguish," as a fire is said to be "blown out." Thus it indicates the extinction of the old, limited personality. By adding the word *brahman*, complete union with the universal Godhead is indicated. *Brahma-nirvana* then means the mystic state of extinction of self in the union with God. *Nirvana* is a Buddhist term as well. Some misconceptions are unfortunately current about this rather esoteric concept. Nirvana is wrongly presented as a kind of empty nothingness, even a spiritual death. We get exactly the opposite impression if we approach the Hindus and Buddhists themselves. It is true there is much talk of extinguishing the petty ego and going beyond self-will—the mask that hides the creative, wise, loving Self underneath. This "death" of the old person to make way for the new is one purpose of spiritual disciplines. It can be painful, but the death of the old does not lead to annihilation but to a spiritual rebirth.

CHAPTER THREE

9 Here and later *yajna* is translated as "selfless work" or "selfless service." The literal meaning is sacrifice: essentially, self-sacrifice, giving up something one greatly values for the sake of a higher purpose. Some translators give a very narrow translation of *yajna* as a ritualistic sacrifice, but this is inaccurate.

39 *Kama* can be translated as selfish desire or pleasure, and often carries a connotation of sensual desire or sexual passion. It means

essentially a personal desire for ease or pleasure, not "desire" of a more altruistic kind.

CHAPTER FOUR

37 This is a well-known verse. The meanings of *karma* are complex, but the verse is widely taken to mean that true knowledge destroys the effects of past errors, which generate further karma. When consciousness is unified and illumined, one is released from the bondage of karma.

CHAPTER FIVE

6 *Yoga* has many meanings in the Gita. Here *yoga* is translated as "action" and "selfless service" because a contrast is being made between Sankhya and yoga: that is, between philosophical explanation and the actual practice of the spiritual life.

9 The word for "senses" in Sanskrit is *indriya*, literally "faculty" or "power." The indriyas are not only the five faculties of perception (seeing, hearing, touching, smelling, and tasting) but also those of action, whose organs are the hands, the feet, the tongue, and the organs of excretion and reproduction.

13 "The city of nine gates" is the body. The gates are the two eyes, the two nostrils, the two ears, the mouth, and the organs of excretion and reproduction. In some lists these gates are expanded to eleven by adding the navel and the *brahmarandhra* or sagittal suture, the opening at the top of the skull.

27-28 The area "of spiritual consciousness" between the eyebrows is one of the seven centers of awareness or *chakras* described in yoga literature. These seven chakras, though not physical, are said to lie along a channel for awakened spiritual energy (*kundalini*) that corresponds with the spine; the chakras are located at the level of the anus, sex organs, stomach, heart, throat, eyebrows, and the top of the head. Kundalini circulates among these centers, but it is usually confined to the lowest three chakras, corresponding to the main preoccupations of life on the physical level. In yogic concentration the vital energy (kundalini) rises; samadhi is said to take place when it reaches the chakras at the brow or head.

CHAPTER SIX

11 This describes the traditional seat used for meditation. The Gita is not concerned with the outer forms of the spiritual life, but here we do get a mention of the grass and deerskin used by the ancient sages. Perhaps the point is that they used what was available in their forest retreats, and that the seat should be what Patanjali calls *sukhasana*: comfortable enough to forget about your body.

14 "All actions dedicated to Brahman" is a literal translation of the those of action, whose organs are the hands, the feet, the tongue, and the organs of excretion and reproduction.

CHAPTER SEVEN

16 *Artharthi* has given translators some difficulties. "Those who desire to achieve their purpose" captures the basic meaning of the word. *Artha* is goal or purpose; the second word of the compound, *arthi*, means "one who has a goal." So *artharthi* probably refers to those who take to the spiritual life with a particular purpose in view. *Artha* also means wealth or worldly goods, but to translate this phrase as "those who desire wealth" would go against the entire tenor of the Gita.

23 "The gods" here are the *devas*, the lower, celestial deities such as Indra.

30 These obscure terms (*adhibhuta*, *adhidaiva*, and *adhiyajna*) are taken up in the next chapter.

CHAPTER EIGHT

6 Whatever is the content of the mind at the moment of death determines the direction of the soul's rebirth. The implication is that whatever has been the bedrock of consciousness during life will be remembered at the time of death and lead the soul on to fulfill that desire in the next life.

9-10 The eyebrow center is discussed in the note to 5:27–28.

CHAPTER NINE

5 *Yoga* here means "mysterious power." This is yet another meaning attached to the word *yoga*, for those who practiced *yoga* were sometimes thought of as concealing within themselves extraordinary powers developed through their disciplines. The folklore of India relates many stories about mysterious yogis who have strange, divine powers.

Krishna speaks here of his *yoga aishvaram*, his mysterious and majestic power. *Ishvara* means "lord" and *aishvaram* "lordly": Krishna's yoga is something he uses as Ishvara, the Lord of the world. Now he begins to show Arjuna something of the nature of the mystery.

17 Rig, Yajur, and Sama are the principal Vedas, the ancient scriptures that are Hinduism's orthodox authority.

20-21 These verses repeat the idea that heaven itself is an impermanent state. After exhausting the store of their good karma, the blessed souls in heaven must be reborn on earth. Only the liberated soul, the one who has found union with Krishna or *brahmanirvana*, escapes the round of rebirth and death as a separate, mortal creature.

CHAPTER TEN

18 *Amrita*, "immortal," comes from *a* "not" and *mrita* "mortal." The Greek word *ambrosia* is cognate and has the same meanings:

amrita is the *ambrosia* of the gods, the drink that makes them live forever, and in a general sense it means sweet or nectar-like. So the translation could also be "your words, which are like ambrosia."

22 The mind (*manas*) is here taken to be one of the senses or indriyas of perception; for example, it is really with the mind rather than with the eye that we see of India relates many stories about mysterious yogis who have strange, divine powers.

33 The Sanskrit alphabet, too, begins with the letter *a*; perhaps this is why Krishna declares that among letters he is *a*, the first. Another possible reason is that *a* is the most frequent sound in Sanskrit.

CHAPTER ELEVEN

14 Here Arjuna presses the palms of his hands together in the gesture called *anjali*, like the Western gesture of prayer. This is the usual form of respectful greeting in India, as well as being used in worship and prayer.

15 Brahma, the Creator (not to be confused with Brahman, the attributeless Godhead, which is beyond the Trinity of creation, preservation, and destruction) sits within a lotus that grows from the navel of Lord Vishnu.

17 Here Arjuna sees not his friend Krishna, but the Lord incarnate in Krishna: Vishnu, armed with his traditional weapons, a club (or mace) and a discus. Not mentioned in this verse are the two benign symbols he carries in his other hands, a conch and a lotus.

CHAPTER TWELVE

1 Arjuna is asking which path is superior, that of knowledge (jnana yoga) or love (bhakti yoga).

CHAPTER THIRTEEN

5 This is a list of all the twenty-four categories given in Sankhya philosophy to describe phenomena in the field of prakriti.

CHAPTER FIFTEEN

1 The *ashvattha* is the sacred pipal tree, a kind of fig often grown in temple compounds in India. The idea of a "world tree" appears in many ancient cultures. Here the Gita uses the image of the tree as "upside down," drawing on the fact that the pipal sends out aerial roots, making "branches above and below." The image illustrates the phenomenal world, rooted in Brahman, complete unity, and branching out into the apparent diversity of life.

13 *Rasatmaka soma* is here translated as "life-giving fluid," the nourishment of plants. In Hindu mythology it is the moon, sometimes called Soma, that nourishes plants, as the source of the life-giving nectar called Soma. In the Vedas, soma is an intoxicating, invigorating drink distilled from a plant grown high in the mountains and drunk by participants in a sacred ritual. Scholars have tried to discover what the soma plant might have been, but so far no conclusive identification has been made. Soma also appears as an important god in the Vedas.

CHAPTER SEVENTEEN

27-28 *Sat* means that which is real or true and that which is good; it derives from the Sanskrit verb *as*, to be, and is directly related to our English word *is*. It is noteworthy that this word *sat* links reality and goodness, reflecting the idea that good is eternal; it is merely covered from time to time by *asat*, evil, which is temporary and in that sense unreal. *Asat* is formed from *sat* by the addition of the prefix *a* "without," very much the way English forms words like amoral.

CHAPTER EIGHTEEN

1 *Sannyasa* and *tyaga* both mean renunciation, *sannyasa* from the root *as* "to cast aside" and *tyaga* from *tyaj* "to give up."

14 "The divine will" is a translation of *daivam*, which comes from notes the word *deva*, "god." *Daivam* is sometimes translated as "fate," but this is inappropriate in the Gita, which is not at all fatalistic. The Gita does, however, allow a place for God's will or Providence in the affairs of humankind—though of course the dominant force is usually karma, not daivam.

34 This verse uses the phrase *dharma-kama-artha*, "duty, pleasure, and wealth," traditionally considered the three goals of ordinary human life. The fourth and highest goal is *moksha*, salvation. The rajasic personality, as this verse points out, pursues the first three worldly goals; moksha is ignored.

41 The Vedas establish the fourfold division of society into the classes of brahmin, kshatriya, vaishya, and shudra — roughly priests and intellectuals; warriors and rulers; businessmen, farmers, and craftpeople; and workers and servants.

66 Dharma is not used here in the usual sense of law or inner nature, but in a rarer meaning: a thing's attribute, condition, or conditioning. Usually *dharma* is used in this sense only in the plural, as here: thus dharma is divine law; dharmas are the innumerable beings, things, emotions and mental states that make up everyday existence as we experience it. Here, following the root meaning (*dhri*, to support or hold up), *sarva-dharman* is translated as "all your supports," in the sense of external props, conditioned dependencies. Another translation would be: "Cast off your dependency on everything external, Arjuna, and rely on the Self alone."

GUIDE TO FURTHER READING

Translations of the Bhagavad Gita from Sanskrit to English continue to be published every year, as do commentaries by Indian and Western interpreters. The following guide does not claim to be comprehensive, but it does intend to give ample guidance to anyone interested in Steiner or in the Gita. In 1975, I published "Indian Spirituality in the West: A Bibliographical Mapping" in the scholarly journal *Philosophy East and West: A Quarterly of Asian and Comparative Thought* (Vol. 25, No. 2), pp. 213–39. The next month I happened to knock on the door of the Anthroposophical Library, then at 211 Madison Avenue in New York City, where I was introduced by Fred Paddock to two books of lectures on the Bhagavad Gita by Rudolf Steiner, who was at that time entirely unknown to me. These two books of lectures are published in the present volume.

A. Standard Editions

It is a pleasure to recommend for beginners and scholars alike several inexpensive, available, and very readable translations: *The Bhagavad Gita: Krishna's Counsel in Time of War*, introduction and afterword by Barbara Stoler Miller (NY: Bantam, 1986), and *The Bhagavad Gita*, translated with a general introduction by Eknath Easwaran (Tomales, CA: Nilgiri Press, 1985). Barbara Stoler Miller was a professor of Sanskrit and a deep student of the Indian spiritual tradition; Eknath Easwaran was a spiritual teacher with a scholar's knowledge of Sanskrit texts; for more on Eknath Easwaran, see B.3 below. *Bhagavad Gita Annotated and Explained*, translated by Shri Purohit Swami and annotation by Kendra Crossen Burroughs, foreword by the series editor Andrew Harvey (Woodstock, VT: Skylight Paths Publishing, 2001), is also very readable because it has a commentary facing each page of text. Another justly popular edition is *The Bhagavad Gita*, translation and introduction by Juan Mascaro (NY: Penguin, 1962). All of these can be recommended to virtually anyone interested in reading, rereading, or delving deeply into the Gita.

The next four books provide substantial scholarly commentary:

The Bhagavad Gita, translated and interpreted by Franklin Edgerton (NY: Harper Torchbooks, 1964)

The Bhagavad Gita, commentary by R. C. Zaehner (NY: Oxford University Press, 1966)

The Bhagavad Gita, translation, introduction, notes, by S. Radhakrishnan (London: George Allen and Unwin, 1948)

The Bhagavad Gita: translation and critical commentary by A. L. Herman (Springfield, IL: Charles C. Thomas, 1973).

J. A. B. van Buitenen, a distinguished Sanskritist and translator of the Mahabharata, argues that the Bhagavad Gita can only be properly understood within the context of the *Mahabharata*. See his *The Bhagavadgita in the Mahabharata: A Bilingual Edition* (Chicago, IL: University of Chicago Press, 1981).

Finally, as for most topics in the academic study of religion, an excellent essay on the Gita can be found in Mircea Eliade, ed., *The Encyclopedia of Religion* (NY: Macmillan, 1987; rev. ed., 2005).

B. COMMENTARIES FROM AN INTERPRETIVE FRAMEWORK

1. Classic American Tradition: Emerson to James

As there are no translations or commentaries by American thinkers from Emerson to James, it must be admitted that this is an odd section. The category is here simply because it would seem important for readers of this volume to be informed that the Gita has an influential history in the West. In America, serious interest in the Bhagavad Gita dates to the mid-nineteenth century. The influence of Indian thought, including prominently the Bhagavad Gita, on American thought, has been chronicled in three studies: Dale Riepe, *The Philosophy of India and Its Impact on American Thought* (Springfield, IL: Charles C. Thomas, 1970); Carl T. Jackson, *The Oriental Religions and American Thought: Nineteenth-Century Explorations* (Westport, CT: Greenwood Press, 1981); and Arthur Versluis, *American Transcendentalism and Asian Religions* (NY: Oxford University Press, 1993). Versluis is also the author of *The Esoteric Origins of the American Renaissance* (NY: Oxford University Press, 2001), a very important book, not particularly for the study of the Bhagavad Gita but for information on the little-known but very important influence of esotericism on the entire range of nineteenth-century American thought and literature. J. J. Clarke, *Oriental Enlightenment: The Encounter between Asian and Western Thought* (NY: Routledge, 1997), is a work of vast scholarly information and countless insights, all of which would be relevant to any effort to understand the history and contemporary impact on the West of south and east Asian thought.

2. Theosophical Interpretations

In his essay "A Lesson in Allegory: Theosophical Interpretations of the Bhagavadgita," in Robert Minor, ed., *Modern Indian Interpreters of the Bhagavad Gita* (NY: State University of New York Press, 1986), 11–33, Ronald Neufeldt suggests that allegory is the common element in commentaries on the Gita by prominent theosophists Annie Besant, William Q. Judge, and T. Subba Rowe (who exercised an important influenced on H.P.B.). In *The Secret Doctrine* (Pasadena, CA: The Theosophical University Press, 1999), H.P.B. refers to Rowe's *Notes on the Bhagavad Gita* II, 318n.

An essay by H.P.B. on "The Esoteric Character of the Gospels" is available in her *Studies in Occultism* (Pasadena, CA: Theosophical University Press, n.d.).

Though Irish born, Annie Besant, the third president of the Theosophical Society (1907–1932 or 1933), was an Indian nationalist—i.e., she worked very devotedly on behalf of the India's effort to free itself from British rule. Given the Gita's prominence in Indian cultural life, it is understandable that Besant would look to that text for support of the Nationalist movement. She saw the Gita as an allegory such that Krishna taught Arjuna the rightness of armed struggle. In 1905 Annie Besant published both *Esoteric Christianity* (Wheaton, IL: Theosophical Publishing House/Quest, 1977), which is both positive and esoteric, and, with Bhagavan Das, *The Bhagavad Gita* (Adyar Madras, India: The Theosophical Publishing House, 1962), a very detailed and well-informed translation and commentary.

Sylvia Cranston's *H. P. B.: The Extraordinary Life and Influence of Helena Blavatsky: Founder of the Modern Theosophical Movement* (New York: Jeremy P. Tarcher/Putnam, 1993), is a monumental, entirely sympathetic and inspiring biography. The most useful brief introduction to Theosophy is by Robert Ellwood, *Theosophy: A Modern Expression of the Wisdom of the Ages* (Wheaton, IL: Theosophical Publishing House, 1986).

3. Gandhian Interpretations

While in prison in 1929, Gandhi, having translated the Gita from English into his native Gujarati, finished his introduction to that translation. Entitled "Anasaktiyoga," this introduction was then translated into English by Gandhi and published in *The Gospel of Selfless Action or The Gita according to Gandhi* (Ahmedabad: Navajivan Publishing House, 1946). It includes a 125-page introductory essay by a scholar of Indian texts and follower of Gandhi, Mahadev Desai. Gandhi's essay and brief comments on the Gita have been republished in a slim paperback edition as M. K. Gandhi, *Anasaktiyoga: The Gospel of Selfless Action—The Gita according to Gandhi* (San Francisco, CA: Dry Bones Press, 1993). In addition to the essay on the allegorical interpretation of the Gita by prominent theosophists (above), Robert Minor, ed., *Modern Indian Interpreters of the Bhagavad Gita*, includes as well an excellent essay by J. T. F. Jordens, "Gandhi and the *Bhagavad Gita*," 88-109.

The text of the Bhagavad Gita included in this volume is a translation by Eknath Easwaran, a former professor of English in India, a Fulbright Professor in the United States, and founder of the Blue Mountain Center of Meditation in Berkeley, California. An accomplished Sanskritist and master of English prose, Easwaran has also translated the Upanishads and the Dhammapada. His *Gandhi the Man* (Nilgiri, 1978) is perhaps the best introduction to Gandhi's development as an inspiring moral and religious leader. Easwaran is also Gandhian in his interpretation of the Gita: his interpretation is the result of deep study of the text and an obvious ability to explain it in Gandhian terms—i.e., the civil war and Krishna's instruction to Arjuna to fight are not historical but rather reveal the struggle between selfish and selfless forces vying for the human heart. In addition to his translation and introduction to the Bhagavad Gita, Easwaran has written a three-volume, 1,300-page guide to the Gita "presented as a manual for daily use." Based on a deep knowledge of the text as well as of other Hindu foundational texts such as the *Upanishads* and the Indian Buddhist *Dhammapada*, Easwaran's three volumes offer a comprehensive, practical understanding of the Gita: the first volume, *The End of Sorrow*, which covers the first six chapters of the Gita, focuses on selfless action; the second volume, *Like a Thousand Suns*, which covers the middle six chapters of the Gita, focuses on Arjuna's transformative vision of Krishna; and the third volume, *To Know Is to Love Me*, focuses on the capacity for love in action made possible by the faithful practice of the Yogas of the Gita. These volumes by a highly respected spiritual teacher in the Gandhian tradition are spiritually profound and a pleasure to read.

4. Sri Aurobindo's Interpretations

Sri Aurobindo's *Essays on the Gita* is a masterpiece of elegance, insight, and inspiration. At 575 pages with sentences the length of paragraphs, it is as demanding to read as it is rewarding. Fortunately, there are three very similar volumes edited by disciples of Sri Aurobindo that combine his translation with selections of his commentary, mostly from *Essays on the Gita*, placed near the corresponding Gita verses. In addition to volumes edited by Shyam Sunder Jhunjhunwala (1974) and by Maheshwara (1978), a third volume, which has all of the positive features of the first two, first published in 1938, has been reissued and is easily available: Anilbaran Roy, ed., *Bhagavad Gita and Its Message: With Text, Translation, and Sri Aurobindo's Commentary* (Twin Lakes, WI: Lotus Press, 1995).

Synthesis of Yoga comprises volumes 20 and 21 of the 30-volume Sri Aurobindo Centenary Library. Volume 20 contains "The Yoga of the Divine Works" and "The Yoga of Integral Knowledge." Volume 21 contains "The Yoga of Divine Love" and "The Yoga of Self-Perfection." *Letters on Yoga*, which comprises volumes 22, 23, and 24 of the Centenary Library, includes Sri Aurobindo's notes to disciples on a wide range of theoretical and practical questions. For a clear and authoritative one-volume restatement of Sri Aurobindo's yoga teaching, see Haridas Chaudhuri, *Integral Yoga: The Concept of Harmonious and Creative Living* (London: George Allen & Unwin, 1990).

Thomas J. Hopkins, author of a scholarly introduction to Hinduism, *The Hindu Religious Tradition* (1971), also wrote a scholarly interpretation of Sri Aurobindo's *Essays on the Gita*: "The Vision of the Purushottama in *Essays on the Gita*," in Robert McDermott, ed., *Six Pillars: Introductions to the Major Works of Sri Aurobindo* (Chambersburg, PA: Wilson Books, 1974), pp. 63–96.

5. Commentaries from Other Spiritual Perspectives

Paramahansa Yogananda (author of the classic work, *Autobiography of a Yogi* and founder in 1920 of Self-Realization Fellowship in Los Angeles) is the author of a monumental commentary, *God Talks with Arjuna: The Bhagavad Gita—Royal Science of God-Realization* (Los Angeles, CA: Self-Realization Fellowship, 2001), 2 vols., boxed. Yogananda finds in the Gita all systems of Indian thought and essentially all extant spiritual wisdom. *Paths to God: Living the Bhagavad Gita* (NY: Harmony Books, 2004) is essentially the lecture course that Ram Dass gave at the founding of Naropa Institute in Boulder, 1974.

Bede Griffiths, a Benedictine monk who led an ashram in south India for several decades, has written on the Gita in the context of his inspiring effort to fuse the most spiritual elements of Hinduism and Roman Catholicism. See Bruno Barnhart, edited with commentary, *The One Light: Bede Griffiths' Principal Writings* (Springfield, IL: Templegate Publishers, 2001), especially 275-330.

C. WORKS BY RUDOLF STEINER AND OTHER ANTHROPOSOPHICAL WRITINGS RELEVANT TO HIS INTERPRETATION OF THE BHAGAVAD GITA

Rudolf Steiner's foundational books, all retranslated since 1990 and published by Anthroposophic Press/SteinerBooks, include *Theosophy* (1904), *How to Know Higher Worlds* (1904), and *An Outline of Esoteric Science* (1909). Preliminary to these works, written in 1894, approximately five years prior to the beginning of Rudolf Steiner's career as an esoteric teacher, is his carefully argued epistemology, *Intuitive Thinking as a Spiritual Path* (1995), previously translated as *Philosophy of Freedom* and *Philosophy of Spiritual Activity*.

In 1909 Steiner delivered ten lectures on the gospel of St. Luke in which he presented his esoteric understanding of what Luke, colleague of Paul and the author of one of the four canonical gospels and The Acts of the Apostles, experienced clairvoyantly as the basis for his gospel. Steiner finds that whereas Luke's gospel uses explanations, metaphors, images, and symbols known to his audience, the actual events included participation by Adam, Hermes, Moses, Krishna, Buddha, Zoroaster, and other great beings in service to the evolution of humanity. More particularly, this series of lectures focuses on one of the two Jesus children, the one described in the Gospel of Luke and constituted by Adam, Krishna, and Buddha (as distinct from the child described in Matthew who was constituted primarily by Zarathustra). These ten lectures have been republished as *According to Luke: The Gospel of Compassion and Love Revealed*, introduction and outline of the lectures by Robert McDermott (2001).

Valentin Tomberg, author of the highly regarded esoteric text *Meditations on the Tarot*, is also the author of three essays on aspects of Indian spirituality relevant for Anthroposophy and its relationship to the Gita: "Indian Yoga in Relation to the Christian-Rosicrucian Path, in *Inner Development* (Great Barrington, MA: Anthroposophic Press, 1992), 47-60; "Western Occultism, Vedanta, and Anthroposophy" (1930), and "Indian Yoga and Christian Occultism" (1939), both in Valentin Tomberg, *Early Articles: Spiritual Science and the World Situation* (Spring Valley, NY: Candeur Manuscripts, 1984).

Tyrone Anderson, a scholar of Indian as well as Western religious thought from an anthroposophical perspective, has contributed a fine essay titled "Krishna, Founder of the Age of Self-Consciousness: Rudolf Steiner's Occult Interpretation of the *Bhagavad Gita*" (*Journal for Anthroposophy*, Vol. 55, fall

1992), pp. 39–50. The conclusion of Anderson's essay serves as a link between Steiner's esoteric research concerning the Bhagavad Gita and the comparative study of religion. He writes:

> It was the innocent Adamic soul—the *Krishna* soul—which had prepared the Luke Jesus child's body for the Christ. Thus the Christ event itself depends directly upon the reality of Krishna! Apart from whatever we might think of this theology from a traditional dogmatic point of view, one fact is clear: this is a truly global Christology which assigns to the Christ deep roots in India and Persia long before any recorded revelations to the Hebrews. Perhaps this can be an indication for us of directions for creative comparative thinking in the future. (p. 47)

It appears that after 1913, Rudolf Steiner did not write about or lecture on Krishna or the Bhagavad Gita—or on Buddha (concerning whom another volume similar to this one on Krishna is forthcoming). One might assume that after his break from the Theosophical Society he did not need to continue speaking on one of the key topics that divided his esoteric teaching from that of Annie Besant and her colleagues. This idea may be true, but it needn't be. After all, Steiner similarly did not return to philosophy after 1914. Instead, he turned to the arts, including the building of the Goetheanum, to social and political topics (especially during the First World War), to education, sciences, medicine, and history. Whatever the practical reasons for his first taking up in 1909 and ending in 1913 his research on Krishna and the Bhagavad Gita, he surely made a significant contribution to the esoteric understanding of both Krishna and the Gita, and to their significance for a comprehensive understanding of the evolution of consciousness, of the Hindu tradition in relation to the West, of important differences between Theosophy and Anthroposophy, and for the comparative study of religion.

RUDOLF STEINER'S COLLECTED WORKS

The German Edition of Rudolf Steiner's Collected Works (the Gesamtausgabe [GA] published by Rudolf Steiner Verlag, Dornach, Switzerland) presently runs to over 354 titles, organized either by type of work (written or spoken), chronology, audience (public or other), or subject (education, art, etc.). For ease of comparison, the Collected Works in English [CW] follows the German organization exactly. A complete listing of the CWs follows with literal translations of the German titles. Other than in the case of the books published in his lifetime, titles were rarely given by Rudolf Steiner himself, and were often provided by the editors of the German editions. The titles in English are not necessarily the same as the German; and, indeed, over the past seventy-five years have frequently been different, with the same book sometimes appearing under different titles.

For ease of identification and to avoid confusion, we suggest that readers looking for a title should do so by CW number. Because the work of creating the Collected Works of Rudolf Steiner is an ongoing process, with new titles being published every year, we have not indicated in this listing which books are presently available. To find out what titles in the Collected Works are currently in print, please check our web site at www.steinerbooks.org, or write to SteinerBooks 610 Main Street, Great Barrington, MA 01230:

Written Work

CW 1	Goethe: Natural-Scientific Writings, Introduction, with Footnotes and Explanations in the text by Rudolf Steiner
CW 2	Outlines of an Epistemology of the Goethean World View, with Special Consideration of Schiller
CW 3	Truth and Science
CW 4	The Philosophy of Freedom
CW 4a	Documents to "The Philosophy of Freedom"
CW 5	Friedrich Nietzsche, A Fighter against His Own Time
CW 6	Goethe's Worldview
CW 6a	Now in CW 30
CW 7	Mysticism at the Dawn of Modern Spiritual Life and Its Relationship with Modern Worldviews
CW 8	Christianity as Mystical Fact and the Mysteries of Antiquity
CW 9	Theosophy: An Introduction into Supersensible World Knowledge and Human Purpose
CW 10	How Does One Attain Knowledge of Higher Worlds?
CW 11	From the Akasha-Chronicle
CW 12	Levels of Higher Knowledge

CW 13   Occult Science in Outline
CW 14   Four Mystery Dramas
CW 15   The Spiritual Guidance of the Individual and Humanity
CW 16   A Way to Human Self-Knowledge: Eight Meditations
CW 17   The Threshold of the Spiritual World. Aphoristic Comments
CW 18   The Riddles of Philosophy in Their History, Presented as an
         Outline
CW 19   Contained in CW 24
CW 20   The Riddles of the Human Being: Articulated and Unarticulated
         in the Thinking, Views and Opinions of a Series of German and
         Austrian Personalities
CW 21   The Riddles of the Soul
CW 22   Goethe's Spiritual Nature And Its Revelation In "Faust" and
         through the "Fairy Tale of the Snake and the Lily"
CW 23   The Central Points of the Social Question in the Necessities of
         Life in the Present and the Future
CW 24   Essays Concerning the Threefold Division of the Social
         Organism and the Period 1915-1921
CW 25   Cosmology, Religion and Philosophy
CW 26   Anthroposophical Leading Thoughts
CW 27   Fundamentals for Expansion of the Art of Healing according to
         Spiritual-Scientific Insights
CW 28   The Course of My Life
CW 29   Collected Essays on Dramaturgy, 1889-1900
CW 30   Methodical Foundations of Anthroposophy: Collected Essays on
         Philosophy, Natural Science, Aesthetics and Psychology, 1884-
         1901
CW 31   Collected Essays on Culture and Current Events, 1887-1901
CW 32   Collected Essays on Literature, 1884-1902
CW 33   Biographies and Biographical Sketches, 1894-1905
CW 34   Lucifer-Gnosis: Foundational Essays on Anthroposophy and
         Reports from the Periodicals "Lucifer" and "Lucifer-Gnosis,"
         1903-1908
CW 35   Philosophy and Anthroposophy: Collected Essays, 1904-1923
CW 36   The Goetheanum-Idea in the Middle of the Cultural Crisis of the
         Present: Collected Essays from the Periodical "Das Goetheanum,"
         1921-1925
CW 37   Now in CWs 260a and 251
CW 38   Letters, Vol. 1: 1881-1890
CW 39   Letters, Vol. 2: 1890-1925
CW 40   Truth-Wrought Words
CW 40a   Sayings, Poems and Mantras; Supplementary Volume
CW 42   Now in CWs 264-266

Lectures to the Members of the Anthroposophical Society

CW 267   Soul-Exercises: Vol. 1: Exercises with Word and Image Meditations for the Methodological Development of Higher Powers of Knowledge, 1904-1924

CW 268   Soul-Exercises: Vol. 2: Mantric Verses, 1903-1925

CW 269   Ritual Texts for the Celebration of the Free Christian Religious Instruction. The Collected Verses for Teachers and Students of the Waldorf School

CW 270   Esoteric Instructions for the First Class of the School for Spiritual Science at the Goetheanum 1924, 4 Volumes

CW 271   Art and Knowledge of Art. Foundations of a New Aesthetic

CW 272   Spiritual-Scientific Commentary on Goethe's "Faust" in Two Volumes. Vol. 1: Faust, the Striving Human Being

CW 273   Spiritual-Scientific Commentary on Goethe's "Faust" in Two Volumes. Vol. 2: The Faust-Problem

CW 274   Addresses for the Christmas Plays from the Old Folk Traditions

CW 275   Art in the Light of Mystery-Wisdom

CW 276   The Artistic in Its Mission in the World. The Genius of Language. The World of the Self-Revealing Radiant Appearances – Anthroposophy and Art. Anthroposophy and Poetry

CW 277   Eurythmy. The Revelation of the Speaking Soul

CW 277a   The Origin and Development of Eurythmy

CW 278   Eurythmy as Visible Song

CW 279   Eurythmy as Visible Speech

CW 280   The Method and Nature of Speech Formation

CW 281   The Art of Recitation and Declamation

CW 282   Speech Formation and Dramatic Art

CW 283   The Nature of Things Musical and the Experience of Tone in the Human Being

CW 284/285 Images of Occult Seals and Pillars. The Munich Congress of Whitsun 1907 and Its Consequences

CW 286   Paths to a New Style of Architecture. "And the Building Becomes Human"

CW 287   The Building at Dornach as a Symbol of Historical Becoming and an Artistic Transformation Impulse

CW 288   Style-Forms in the Living Organic

CW 289   The Building-Idea of the Goetheanum: Lectures with Slides from the Years 1920-1921

CW 290   The Building-Idea of the Goetheanum: Lectures with Slides from the Years 1920-1921

CW 291   The Nature of Colors

CW 291a   Knowledge of Colors. Supplementary Volume to "The Nature of Colors"

CW 292   Art History as Image of Inner Spiritual Impulses

SIGNIFICANT EVENTS
IN THE LIFE OF RUDOLF STEINER

1829: June 23: birth of Johann Steiner (1829-1910)—Rudolf Steiner's father—in Geras, Lower Austria.

1834: May 8: birth of Franciska Blie (1834-1918)—Rudolf Steiner's mother—in Horn, Lower Austria. "My father and mother were both children of the glorious Lower Austrian forest district north of the Danube."

1860: May 16: marriage of Johann Steiner and Franciska Blie.

1861: February 25: birth of *Rudolf Joseph Lorenz Steiner* in Kraljevec, Croatia, near the border with Hungary, where Johann Steiner works as a telegrapher for the South Austria Railroad. Rudolf Steiner is baptized two days later, February 27, the date usually given as his birthday.

1862: Summer: the family moves to Mödling, Lower Austria.

1863: The family moves to Pottschach, Lower Austria, near the Styrian border, where Johann Steiner becomes stationmaster. "The view stretched to the mountains...majestic peaks in the distance and the sweet charm of nature in the immediate surroundings."

1864: November 15: birth of Rudolf Steiner's sister, Leopoldine (d. November 1, 1927). She will become a seamstress and live with her parents for the rest of her life.

1866: July 28: birth of Rudolf Steiner's deaf-mute brother, Gustav (d. May 1, 1941).

1867: Rudolf Steiner enters the village school. Following a disagreement between his father and the schoolmaster, whose wife falsely accused the boy of causing a commotion, Rudolf Steiner is taken out of school and taught at home.

1868: A critical experience. Unknown to the family, an aunt dies in a distant town. Sitting in the station waiting room, Rudolf Steiner sees her "form," which speaks to him, asking for help. "Beginning with this experience, a new soul life began in the boy, one in which not only the outer trees and mountains spoke to him, but also the worlds that lay behind them. From this moment on, the boy began to live with the spirits of nature...."

1869: The family moves to the peaceful, rural village of Neudorfl, near Wiener-Neustadt in present-day Hungary. Rudolf Steiner attends the village school. Because of the "unorthodoxy" of his writing and spelling, he has to do "extra lessons."

1870: Through a book lent to him by his tutor, he discovers geometry: "To grasp something purely in the spirit brought me inner happiness. I know that I first learned happiness through geometry." The same tutor allows him to draw, while other students still struggle with their reading and writing. "An artistic element" thus enters his education.

1871: Though his parents are not religious, Rudolf Steiner becomes a "church child," a favorite of the priest, who was "an exceptional character." "Up to the age of ten or eleven, among those I came to know, he was far and away the most significant." Among other things, he introduces Steiner to Copernican, heliocentric cosmology. As an altar boy, Rudolf Steiner serves at Masses, funerals, and Corpus Christi processions. At year's end, after an incident in which he escapes a thrashing, his father forbids him to go to church.

1872: Rudolf Steiner transfers to grammar school in Wiener-Neustadt, a five-mile walk from home, which must be done in all weathers.

1873-75: Through his teachers and on his own, Rudolf Steiner has many wonderful experiences with science and mathematics. Outside school, he teaches himself analytic geometry, trigonometry, differential equations, and calculus.

1876: Rudolf Steiner begins tutoring other students. He learns bookbinding from his father. He also teaches himself stenography.

1877: Rudolf Steiner discovers Kant's *Critique of Pure Reason*, which he reads and rereads. He also discovers and reads von Rotteck's *World History*.

1878: He studies extensively in contemporary psychology and philosophy.

1879: Rudolf Steiner graduates from high school with honors. His father is transferred to Inzersdorf, near Vienna. He uses his first visit to Vienna "to purchase a great number of philosophy books"— Kant, Fichte, Schelling, and Hegel, as well as numerous histories of philosophy. His aim: to find a path from the "I" to nature.

October 1879-1883: Rudolf Steiner attends the Technical College in Vienna—to study mathematics, chemistry, physics, mineralogy, botany, zoology, biology, geology, and mechanics—with a scholarship. He also attends lectures in history and literature, while avidly reading philosophy on his own. His two favorite professors are Karl Julius Schröer (German language and literature) and Edmund Reitlinger (physics). He also audits lectures by Robert Zimmerman on aesthetics and Franz Brentano on philosophy. During this year he begins his friendship with Moritz Zitter (1861-1921), who will help support him financially when he is in Berlin.

1880: Rudolf Steiner attends lectures on Schiller and Goethe by Karl Julius Schröer, who becomes his mentor. Also "through a remarkable combination of circumstances," he meets Felix Koguzki, an "herb gatherer" and healer, who could "see deeply into the secrets of nature." Rudolf Steiner will meet and study with this "emissary of the Master" throughout his time in Vienna.

1881: January: "... I didn't sleep a wink. I was busy with philosophical problems until about 12:30 a.m. Then, finally, I threw myself down on my couch. All my striving during the previous year had been to research whether the following statement by Schelling was true or not: *Within everyone dwells a secret, marvelous capacity to draw back from the stream of time—out of the self clothed in all that comes to us from outside—into our innermost being and there, in the immutable form of the Eternal, to look into ourselves.* I believe, and I am still quite certain of it, that I discovered this capacity in myself; I had long had an inkling of it. Now the whole of idealist philosophy stood before me in modified form. What's a sleepless night compared to that!"

Rudolf Steiner begins communicating with leading thinkers of the day, who send him books in return, which he reads eagerly.

July: "I am not one of those who dives into the day like an animal in human form. I pursue a quite specific goal, an idealistic aim—knowledge of the truth! This cannot be done offhandedly. It requires the greatest striving in the world, free of all egotism, and equally of all resignation."

August: Steiner puts down on paper for the first time thoughts for a "Philosophy of Freedom." "The striving for the absolute: this human yearning is freedom." He also seeks to outline a "peasant philosophy," describing what the worldview of a "peasant"—one who lives close to the earth and the old ways—really is.

1881-1882: Felix Koguzki, the herb gatherer, reveals himself to be the envoy of another, higher initiatory personality, who instructs Rudolf Steiner to penetrate Fichte's philosophy and to master modern scientific thinking as a preparation for right entry into the spirit. This "Master" also teaches him the double (evolutionary and involutionary) nature of time.

1882: Through the offices of Karl Julius Schröer, Rudolf Steiner is asked by Joseph Kurschner to edit Goethe's scientific works for the *Deutschen National-Literatur* edition. He writes "A Possible Critique of Atomistic Concepts" and sends it to Friedrich Theodore Vischer.

1883: Rudolf Steiner completes his college studies and begins work on the Goethe project.

1884: First volume of Goethe's *Scientific Writings* (CW 1) appears (March). He lectures on Goethe and Lessing, and Goethe's approach to science. In July, he enters the household of Ladislaus and Pauline Specht as tutor to the four Specht boys. He will live there until 1890. At this time, he meets Josef Breuer (1842-1925), the coauthor with Sigmund Freud of *Studies in Hysteria*, who is the Specht family doctor.

1885: While continuing to edit Goethe's writings, Rudolf Steiner reads deeply in contemporary philosophy (Edouard von Hartmann, Johannes Volkelt, and Richard Wahle, among others).

1886: May: Rudolf Steiner sends Kurschner the manuscript of *Outlines of Goethe's Theory of Knowledge* (CW 2), which appears in October, and which he sends out widely. He also meets the poet Marie Eugenie Delle Grazie and writes "Nature and Our Ideals" for her. He attends her salon, where he meets many priests, theologians, and philosophers, who will become his friends. Meanwhile, the director of the Goethe Archive in Weimar requests his collaboration with the *Sophien* edition of Goethe's works, particularly the writings on color.

1887:   At the beginning of the year, Rudolf Steiner is very sick. As the year
        progresses and his health improves, he becomes increasingly "a man of
        letters," lecturing, writing essays, and taking part in Austrian cultural
        life. In August-September, the second volume of Goethe's *Scientific
        Writings* appears.
1888:   January-July: Rudolf Steiner assumes editorship of the "German
        Weekly" (*Deutsche Wochenschrift*). He begins lecturing more inten-
        sively, giving, for example, a lecture titled "Goethe as Father of a New
        Aesthetics." He meets and becomes soul friends with Friedrich Eckstein
        (1861-1939), a vegetarian, philosopher of symbolism, alchemist, and
        musician, who will introduce him to various spiritual currents (includ-
        ing Theosophy) and with whom he will meditate and interpret esoteric
        and alchemical texts.
1889:   Rudolf Steiner first reads Nietzsche (*Beyond Good and Evil*). He
        encounters Theosophy again and learns of Madame Blavatsky in the
        Theosophical circle around Marie Lang (1858-1934). Here he also
        meets well-known figures of Austrian life, as well as esoteric figures
        like the occultist Franz Hartman and Karl Leinigen-Billigen (translator
        of C.G. Harrison's *The Transcendental Universe.*) During this period,
        Steiner first reads A.P. Sinnett's *Esoteric Buddhism* and Mabel Collins's
        Light on the Path. He also begins traveling, visiting Budapest, Weimar,
        and Berlin (where he meets philosopher Edouard von Hartman).
1890:   Rudolf Steiner finishes volume 3 of Goethe's scientific writings. He
        begins his doctoral dissertation, which will become *Truth and Science*
        (CW 3). He also meets the poet and feminist Rosa Mayreder (1858-
        1938), with whom he can exchange his most intimate thoughts. In
        September, Rudolf Steiner moves to Weimar to work in the Goethe-
        Schiller Archive.
1891:   Volume 3 of the Kurschner edition of Goethe appears. Meanwhile,
        Rudolf Steiner edits Goethe's studies in mineralogy and scientific
        writings for the *Sophien* edition. He meets Ludwig Laistner of the
        Cotta Publishing Company, who asks for a book on the basic ques-
        tion of metaphysics. From this will result, ultimately, *The Philosophy
        of Freedom* (CW 4), which will be published not by Cotta but by Emil
        Felber. In October, Rudolf Steiner takes the oral exam for a doctorate
        in philosophy, mathematics, and mechanics at Rostock University,
        receiving his doctorate on the twenty-sixth. In November, he gives his
        first lecture on Goethe's "Fairy Tale" in Vienna.
1892:   Rudolf Steiner continues work at the Goethe-Schiller Archive and on
        his *Philosophy of Freedom. Truth and Science*, his doctoral dissertation,
        is published. Steiner undertakes to write introductions to books on
        Schopenhauer and Jean Paul for Cotta. At year's end, he finds lodging
        with Anna Eunike, née Schulz (1853-1911), a widow with four daugh-
        ters and a son. He also develops a friendship with Otto Erich Hartleben
        (1864-1905) with whom he shares literary interests.

1893: Rudolf Steiner begins his habit of producing many reviews and articles. In March, he gives a lecture titled "Hypnotism, with Reference to Spiritism." In September, volume 4 of the Kurschner edition is completed. In November, *The Philosophy of Freedom* appears. This year, too, he meets John Henry Mackay (1864-1933), the anarchist, and Max Stirner, a scholar and biographer.

1894: Rudolf Steiner meets Elisabeth Förster Nietzsche, the philosopher's sister, and begins to read Nietzsche in earnest, beginning with the as yet unpublished *Antichrist*. He also meets Ernst Haeckel (1834-1919). In the fall, he begins to write *Nietzsche, A Fighter against His Time* (CW 5).

1895: May, *Nietzsche, A Fighter against His Time* appears.

1896: January 22: Rudolf Steiner sees Friedrich Nietzsche for the first and only time. Moves between the Nietzsche and the Goethe-Schiller Archives, where he completes his work before year's end. He falls out with Elisabeth Förster Nietzsche, thus ending his association with the Nietzsche Archive.

1897: Rudolf Steiner finishes the manuscript of *Goethe's Worldview* (CW 6). He moves to Berlin with Anna Eunike and begins editorship of the *Magazin fur Literatur*. From now on, Steiner will write countless reviews, literary and philosophical articles, and so on. He begins lecturing at the "Free Literary Society." In September, he attends the Zionist Congress in Basel. He sides with Dreyfus in the Dreyfus affair.

1898: Rudolf Steiner is very active as an editor in the political, artistic, and theatrical life of Berlin. He becomes friendly with John Henry Mackay and poet Ludwig Jacobowski (1868-1900). He joins Jacobowski's circle of writers, artists, and scientists—"The Coming Ones" (*Die Kommenden*)—and contributes lectures to the group until 1903. He also lectures at the "League for College Pedagogy." He writes an article for Goethe's sesquicentennial, "Goethe's Secret Revelation," on the "Fairy Tale of the Green Snake and the Beautiful Lily."

1888-89: "This was a trying time for my soul as I looked at Christianity. . . . I was able to progress only by contemplating, by means of spiritual perception, the evolution of Christianity . . . . Conscious knowledge of real Christianity began to dawn in me around the turn of the century. This seed continued to develop. My soul trial occurred shortly before the beginning of the twentieth century. It was decisive for my soul's development that I stood spiritually before the Mystery of Golgotha in a deep and solemn celebration of knowledge."

1899: Rudolf Steiner begins teaching and giving lectures and lecture cycles at the Workers' College, founded by Wilhelm Liebknecht (1826-1900). He will continue to do so until 1904. Writes: *Literature and Spiritual Life in the Nineteenth Century; Individualism in Philosophy; Haeckel and His Opponents; Poetry in the Present;* and begins what will become (fifteen years later). *The Riddles of Philosophy* (CW 18). He also meets many artists and writers, including Käthe Kollwitz, Stefan

Zweig, and Rainer Maria Rilke. On October 31, he marries Anna Eunike.

1900: "I thought that the turn of the century must bring humanity a new light. It seemed to me that the separation of human thinking and willing from the spirit had peaked. A turn or reversal of direction in human evolution seemed to me a necessity." Rudolf Steiner finishes *World and Life Views in the Nineteenth Century* (the second part of what will become *The Riddles of Philosophy*) and dedicates it to Ernst Haeckel. It is published in March. He continues lecturing at *Die Kommenden*, whose leadership he assumes after the death of Jacobowski. Also, he gives the Gutenberg Jubilee lecture before 7,000 typesetters and printers. In September, Rudolf Steiner is invited by Count and Countess Brockdorff to lecture in the Theosophical Library. His first lecture is on Nietzsche. His second lecture is titled "Goethe's Secret Revelation." October 6, he begins a lecture cycle on the mystics that will become *Mystics after Modernism* (CW 7). November-December: "Marie von Sivers appears in the audience...." Also in November, Steiner gives his first lecture at the Giordano Bruno Bund (where he will continue to lecture until May, 1905). He speaks on Bruno and modern Rome, focusing on the importance of the philosophy of Thomas Aquinas as monism.

1901: In continual financial straits, Rudolf Steiner's early friends Moritz Zitter and Rosa Mayreder help support him. In October, he begins the lecture cycle *Christianity as Mystical Fact* (CW 8) at the Theosophical Library. In November, he gives his first "Theosophical lecture" on Goethe's "Fairy Tale" in Hamburg at the invitation of Wilhelm Hubbe-Schleiden. He also attends a tea to celebrate the founding of the Theosophical Society at Count and Countess Brockdorff's. He gives a lecture cycle, "From Buddha to Christ," for the circle of the *Kommenden*. November 17, Marie von Sivers asks Rudolf Steiner if Theosophy does not need a Western-Christian spiritual movement (to complement Theosophy's Eastern emphasis). "The question was posed. Now, following spiritual laws, I could begin to give an answer...." In December, Rudolf Steiner writes his first article for a Theosophical publication. At year's end, the Brockdorffs and possibly Wilhelm Hubbe-Schleiden ask Rudolf Steiner to join the Theosophical Society and undertake the leadership of the German section. Rudolf Steiner agrees, on the condition that Marie von Sivers (then in Italy) work with him.

1902: Beginning in January, Rudolf Steiner attends the opening of the Workers' School in Spandau with Rosa Luxemburg (1870-1919). January 17, Rudolf Steiner joins the Theosophical Society. In April, he is asked to become general secretary of the German Section of the Theosophical Society, and works on preparations for its founding. In July, he visits London for a Theosophical congress. He meets Bertram

Keightly, G.R.S. Mead, A.P. Sinnett, and Annie Besant, among others. In September, *Christianity as Mystical Fact* appears. In October, Rudolf Steiner gives his first public lecture on Theosophy ("Monism and Theosophy") to about three hundred people at the Giordano Bruno Bund. On October 19-21, the German Section of the Theosophical Society has its first meeting; Rudolf Steiner is the general secretary, and Annie Besant attends. Steiner lectures on practical karma studies. On October 23, Annie Besant inducts Rudolf Steiner into the Esoteric School of the Theosophical Society. On October 25, Steiner begins a weekly series of lectures: "The Field of Theosophy." During this year, Rudolf Steiner also first meets Ita Wegman (1876-1943), who will become his close collaborator in his final years.

1903: Rudolf Steiner holds about 300 lectures and seminars. In May, the first issue of the periodical *Luzifer* appears. In June, Rudolf Steiner visits London for the first meeting of the Federation of the European Sections of the Theosophical Society, where he meets Colonel Olcott. He begins to write *Theosophy* (CW 9).

1904: Rudolf Steiner continues lecturing at the Workers' College and elsewhere (about 90 lectures), while lecturing intensively all over Germany among Theosophists (about a 140 lectures). In February, he meets Carl Unger (1878-1929), who will become a member of the board of the Anthroposophical Society (1913). In March, he meets Michael Bauer (1871-1929), a Christian mystic, who will also be on the board. In May, *Theosophy* appears, with the dedication: "To the spirit of Giordano Bruno." Rudolf Steiner and Marie von Sivers visit London for meetings with Annie Besant. June: Rudolf Steiner and Marie von Sivers attend the meeting of the Federation of European Sections of the Theosophical Society in Amsterdam. In July, Steiner begins the articles in *Luzifer-Gnosis* that will become *How to Know Higher Worlds* (CW 10) and *Cosmic Memory* (CW 11). In September, Annie Besant visits Germany. In December, Steiner lectures on Freemasonry. He mentions the High Grade Masonry derived from John Yarker and represented by Theodore Reuss and Karl Kellner as a blank slate "into which a good image could be placed."

1905: This year, Steiner ends his non-Theosophical lecturing activity. Supported by Marie von Sivers, his Theosophical lecturing—both in public and in the Theosophical Society—increases significantly: "The German Theosophical Movement is of exceptional importance." Steiner recommends reading, among others, Fichte, Jacob Boehme, and Angelus Silesius. He begins to introduce Christian themes into Theosophy. He also begins to work with doctors (Felix Peipers and Ludwig Noll). In July, he is in London for the Federation of European Sections, where he attends a lecture by Annie Besant: "I have seldom seen Mrs. Besant speak in so inward and heartfelt a manner...." "Through Mrs. Besant I have found the way to H.P. Blavatsky."

September to October, he gives a course of thirty-one lectures for a small group of esoteric students. In October, the annual meeting of the German Section of the Theosophical Society, which still remains very small, takes place. Rudolf Steiner reports membership has risen from 121 to 377 members. In November, seeking to establish esoteric "continuity," Rudolf Steiner and Marie von Sivers participate in a "Memphis-Misraim" Masonic ceremony. They pay forty-five marks for membership. "Yesterday, you saw how little remains of former esoteric institutions." "We are dealing only with a 'framework'... for the present, nothing lies behind it. The occult powers have completely withdrawn."

1906: Expansion of Theosophical work. Rudolf Steiner gives about 245 lectures, only 44 of which take place in Berlin. Cycles are given in Paris, Leipzig, Stuttgart, and Munich. Esoteric work also intensifies. Rudolf Steiner begins writing *An Outline of Esoteric Science* (CW 13). In January, Rudolf Steiner receives permission (a patent) from the Great Orient of the Scottish A & A Thirty-Three Degree Rite of the Order of the Ancient Freemasons of the Memphis-Misraim Rite to direct a chapter under the name "Mystica Aeterna." This will become the "Cognitive Cultic Section" (also called "Misraim Service") of the Esoteric School. (See: *From the History and Contents of the Cognitive Cultic Section* (CW 264). During this time, Steiner also meets Albert Schweitzer. In May, he is in Paris, where he visits Edouard Schuré. Many Russians attend his lectures (including Konstantin Balmont, Dimitri Mereszkovski, Zinaida Hippius, and Maximilian Woloshin). He attends the General Meeting of the European Federation of the Theosophical Society, at which Col. Olcott is present for the last time. He spends the year's end in Venice and Rome, where he writes and works on his translation of H.P. Blavatsky's *Key to Theosophy*.

1907: Further expansion of the German Theosophical Movement according to the Rosicrucian directive to "introduce spirit into the world"—in education, in social questions, in art, and in science. In February, Col. Olcott dies in Adyar. Before he dies, Olcott indicates that "the Masters" wish Annie Besant to succeed him: much politicking ensues. Rudolf Steiner supports Besant's candidacy. April-May: preparations for the Congress of the Federation of European Sections of the Theosophical Society—the great, watershed Whitsun "Munich Congress," attended by Annie Besant and others. Steiner decides to separate Eastern and Western (Christian-Rosicrucian) esoteric schools. He takes his esoteric school out of the Theosophical Society (Besant and Rudolf Steiner are "in harmony" on this). Steiner makes his first lecture tours to Austria and Hungary. That summer, he is in Italy. In September, he visits Edouard Schuré, who will write the introduction to the French edition of *Christianity as Mystical Fact* in Barr, Alsace. Rudolf Steiner writes the autobiographical statement known as the "Barr Document." In *Luzifer–Gnosis*, "The Education of the Child" appears.

1908:   The movement grows (membership: 1150). Lecturing expands. Steiner makes his first extended lecture tour to Holland and Scandinavia, as well as visits to Naples and Sicily. Themes: St. John's Gospel, the Apocalypse, Egypt, science, philosophy, and logic. *Luzifer-Gnosis* ceases publication. In Berlin, Marie von Sivers (with Johanna Mücke (1864-1949) forms the *Philosophisch-Theosophisch* (after 1915 *Philosophisch-Anthroposophisch*) *Verlag* to publish Steiner's work. Steiner gives lecture cycles titled *The Gospel of St. John* (CW 103) and *The Apocalypse* (104).

1909:   *An Outline of Esoteric Science* appears. Lecturing and travel continues. Rudolf Steiner's spiritual research expands to include the polarity of Lucifer and Ahriman; the work of great individualities in history; the Maitreya Buddha and the Bodhisattvas; spiritual economy (CW 109); the work of the spiritual hierarchies in heaven and on Earth (CW 110). He also deepens and intensifies his research into the Gospels, giving lectures on the Gospel of St. Luke (CW 114) with the first mention of two Jesus children. Meets and becomes friends with Christian Morgenstern (1871-1914). In April, he lays the foundation stone for the Malsch model—the building that will lead to the first Goetheanum. In May, the International Congress of the Federation of European Sections of the Theosophical Society takes place in Budapest. Rudolf Steiner receives the Subba Row medal for *How to Know Higher Worlds*. During this time, Charles W. Leadbeater discovers Jiddu Krishnamurti (1895-1986) and proclaims him the future "world teacher," the bearer of the Maitreya Buddha and the "reappearing Christ." In October, Steiner delivers seminal lectures on "anthroposophy," which he will try, unsuccessfully, to rework over the next years into the unfinished work, *Anthroposophy (A Fragment)* (CW 45).

1910:   New themes: *The Reappearance of Christ in the Etheric* (CW 118); *The Fifth Gospel; The Mission of Folk Souls* (CW 121); *Occult History* (CW 126); the evolving development of etheric cognitive capacities. Rudolf Steiner continues his Gospel research with *The Gospel of St. Matthew* (CW 123). In January, his father dies. In April, he takes a month-long trip to Italy, including Rome, Monte Cassino, and Sicily. He also visits Scandinavia again. July-August, he writes the first mystery drama, *The Portal of Initiation* (CW 14). In November, he gives "psychosophy" lectures. In December, he submits "On the Psychological Foundations and Epistemological Framework of Theosophy" to the International Philosophical Congress in Bologna.

1911:   The crisis in the Theosophical Society deepens. In January, "The Order of the Rising Sun," which will soon become "The Order of the Star in the East," is founded for the coming world teacher, Krishnamurti. At the same time, Marie von Sivers, Rudolf Steiner's coworker, falls ill. Fewer lectures are given, but important new ground is broken. In Prague, in March, Steiner meets Franz Kafka (1883-1924) and Hugo Bergmann (1883-1975). In April, he delivers his paper to the

Philosophical Congress. He writes the second mystery drama, *The Soul's Probation* (CW 14). Also, while Marie von Sivers is convalescing, Rudolf Steiner begins work on *Calendar 1912/1913*, which will contain the "Calendar of the Soul" meditations. On March 19, Anna (Eunike) Steiner dies. In September, Rudolf Steiner visits Einsiedeln, birthplace of Paracelsus. In December, Friedrich Rittelmeyer, future founder of the Christian Community, meets Rudolf Steiner. The *Johannes-Bauverein*, the "building committee," which would lead to the first Goetheanum (first planned for Munich), is also founded, and a preliminary committee for the founding of an independent association is created that, in the following year, will become the Anthroposophical Society. Important lecture cycles include *Occult Physiology* (CW 128); *Wonders of the World* (CW 129); *From Jesus to Christ* (CW 131). Other themes: esoteric Christianity; Christian Rosenkreutz; the spiritual guidance of humanity; the sense world and the world of the spirit.

1912:   Despite the ongoing, now increasing crisis in the Theosophical Society, much is accomplished: *Calendar 1912/1913* is published; eurythmy is created; both the third mystery drama, *The Guardian of the Threshold* (CW 14) and *A Way of Self-Knowledge* (CW 16) are written. New (or renewed) themes included life between death and rebirth and karma and reincarnation. Other lecture cycles: *Spiritual Beings in the Heavenly Bodies and the Kingdoms of Nature* (CW 136); *The Human Being in the Light of Occultism, Theosophy, and Philosophy* (CW 137); *The Gospel of St. Mark* (CW 139); and *The Bhagavad Gita and the Epistles of Paul* (CW 142). On May 8, Rudolf Steiner celebrates White Lotus Day, H.P. Blavatsky's death day, which he had faithfully observed for the past decade, for the last time. In August, Rudolf Steiner suggests the "independent association" be called the "Anthroposophical Society." In September, the first eurythmy course takes place. In October, Rudolf Steiner declines recognition of a Theosophical Society lodge dedicated to the Star of the East and decides to expel all Theosophical Society members belonging to the order. Also, with Marie von Sivers, he first visits Dornach, near Basel, Switzerland, and they stand on the hill where the Goetheanum will be. In November, a Theosophical Society lodge is opened by direct mandate from Adyar (Annie Besant). In December, a meeting of the German section occurs at which it is decided that belonging to the Order of the Star of the East is incompatible with membership in the Theosophical Society. December 28: informal founding of the Anthroposophical Society in Berlin.

1913:   Expulsion of the German section from the Theosophical Society. February 2-3: Foundation meeting of the Anthroposophical Society. Board members include: Marie von Sivers, Michael Bauer, and Carl Unger. September 20: Laying of the foundation stone for the *Johannes Bau* (Goetheanum) in Dornach. Building begins immediately. The third mystery drama, *The Soul's Awakening* (CW 14), is completed.

Also: *The Threshold of the Spiritual World* (CW 147). Lecture cycles include: *The Bhagavad Gita and the Epistles of Paul* and *The Esoteric Meaning of the Bhagavad Gita* (CW 146), which the Russian philosopher Nikolai Berdyaev attends; *The Mysteries of the East and of Christianity* (CW 144); *The Effects of Esoteric Development* (CW 145); and *The Fifth Gospel* (CW 148). In May, Rudolf Steiner is in London and Paris, where anthroposophical work continues.

1914: Building continues on the *Johannes Bau* (Goetheanum) in Dornach, with artists and coworkers from seventeen nations. The general assembly of the Anthroposophical Society takes place. In May, Rudolf Steiner visits Paris, as well as Chartres Cathedral. June 28: assassination in Sarajevo ("Now the catastrophe has happened!"). August 1: War is declared. Rudolf Steiner returns to Germany from Dornach—he will travel back and forth. He writes the last chapter of *The Riddles of Philosophy*. Lecture cycles include: *Human and Cosmic Thought* (CW 151); *Inner Being of Humanity between Death and a New Birth* (CW 153); *Occult Reading and Occult Hearing* (CW 156). December 24: marriage of Rudolf Steiner and Marie von Sivers.

1915: Building continues. Life after death becomes a major theme, also art. Writes: *Thoughts during a Time of War* (CW 24). Lectures include: *The Secret of Death* (CW 159); *The Uniting of Humanity through the Christ Impulse* (CW 165).

1916: Rudolf Steiner begins work with Edith Maryon (1872-1924) on the sculpture "The Representative of Humanity" ("The Group"—Christ, Lucifer, and Ahriman). He also works with the alchemist Alexander von Bernus on the quarterly *Das Reich*. He writes *The Riddle of Humanity* (CW 20). Lectures include: *Necessity and Freedom in World History and Human Action* (CW 166); *Past and Present in the Human Spirit* (CW 167); *The Karma of Vocation* (CW 172); *The Karma of Untruthfulness* (CW 173).

1917: Russian Revolution. The U.S. enters the war. Building continues. Rudolf Steiner delineates the idea of the "threefold nature of the human being" (in a public lecture March 15) and the "threefold nature of the social organism" (hammered out in May-June with the help of Otto von Lerchenfeld and Ludwig Polzer-Hoditz in the form of two documents titled *Memoranda*, which were distributed in high places). August-September: Rudolf Steiner writes *The Riddles of the Soul* (CW 20). Also: commentary on "The Chemical Wedding of Christian Rosenkreutz" for Alexander Bernus (*Das Reich*). Lectures include: *The Karma of Materialism* (CW 176); *The Spiritual Background of the Outer World: The Fall of the Spirits of Darkness* (CW 177).

1918: March 18: peace treaty of Brest-Litovsk—"Now everything will truly enter chaos! What is needed is cultural renewal." June: Rudolf Steiner visits Karlstein (Grail) Castle outside Prague. Lecture cycle: *From Symptom to Reality in Modern History* (CW 185). In mid-November,

Emil Molt, of the Waldorf-Astoria Cigarette Company, has the idea of founding a school for his workers' children.

1919: Focus on the threefold social organism: tireless travel, countless lectures, meetings, and publications. At the same time, a new public stage of Anthroposophy emerges as cultural renewal begins. The coming years will see initiatives in pedagogy, medicine, pharmacology, and agriculture. January 27: threefold meeting: " We must first of all, with the money we have, found free schools that can bring people what they need." February: first public eurythmy performance in Zurich. Also: "Appeal to the German People" (CW 24), circulated March 6 as a newspaper insert. In April, *Toward Social Renewal* (CW 23)—"perhaps the most widely read of all books on politics appearing since the war"—appears. Rudolf Steiner is asked to undertake the "direction and leadership" of the school founded by the Waldorf-Astoria Company. Rudolf Steiner begins to talk about the "renewal" of education. May 30: a building is selected and purchased for the future Waldorf School. August-September, Rudolf Steiner gives a lecture course for Waldorf teachers, *The Foundations of Human Experience (Study of Man)* (CW 293). September 7: Opening of the first Waldorf School. December (into January): first science course, the *Light Course* (CW 320).

1920: The Waldorf School flourishes. New threefold initiatives. Founding of limited companies *Der Kommenden Tag* and *Futurum A.G.* to infuse spiritual values into the economic realm. Rudolf Steiner also focuses on the sciences. Lectures: *Introducing Anthroposophical Medicine* (CW 312); *The Warmth Course* (CW 321); *The Boundaries of Natural Science* (CW 322); *The Redemption of Thinking* (CW 74). February: Johannes Werner Klein—later a cofounder of the Christian Community—asks Rudolf Steiner about the possibility of a "religious renewal," a "Johannine church." In March, Rudolf Steiner gives the first course for doctors and medical students. In April, a divinity student asks Rudolf Steiner a second time about the possibility of religious renewal. September 27-October 16: anthroposophical "university course." December: lectures titled *The Search for the New Isis* (CW 202).

1921: Rudolf Steiner continues his intensive work on cultural renewal, including the uphill battle for the threefold social order. "University" arts, scientific, theological, and medical courses include: *The Astronomy Course* (CW 323); *Observation, Mathematics, and Scientific Experiment* (CW 324); the *Second Medical Course* (CW 313); *Color*. In June and September-October, Rudolf Steiner also gives the first two "priests' courses" (CW 342 and 343). The "youth movement" gains momentum. Magazines are founded: *Die Drei* (January), and—under the editorship of Albert Steffen (1884-1963)—the weekly, *Das Goetheanum* (August). In February-March, Rudolf Steiner takes his first trip outside Germany since the war (Holland). On April 7, Steiner receives a letter regarding "religious renewal," and May 22-23, he agrees to address the question in a practical way. In June, the Klinical-Therapeutic Institute opens in Arlesheim under the direction of Dr. Ita Wegman. In August, the Chemical-Pharmaceutical Laboratory opens in Arlesheim (Oskar Schmiedel and Ita Wegman, directors). The Clinical Therapeutic Institute is inaugurated in Stuttgart (Dr. Ludwig Noll, director); also the Research Laboratory in Dornach (Ehrenfried Pfeiffer and Gunther Wachsmuth, directors). In November-December, Rudolf Steiner visits Norway.

1922: The first half of the year involves very active public lecturing (thousands attend); in the second half, Rudolf Steiner begins to withdraw and turn toward the Society—"The Society is asleep." It is "too weak" to do what is asked of it. The businesses—*Die Kommenden Tag* and *Futura A.G.*—fail. In January, with the help of an agent, Steiner undertakes a twelve-city German tour, accompanied by eurythmy performances. In two weeks he speaks to more than 2,000 people. In April, he gives a "university course" in The Hague. He also visits England. In June, he is in Vienna for the East-West Congress. In August-September, he is back in England for the Oxford Conference on Education. Returning to Dornach, he gives the lectures *Philosophy, Cosmology, and Religion* (CW 215), and gives the third priest's course (CW 344). On September 16, The Christian Community is founded. In October-November, Steiner is in Holland and England. He also speaks to the youth: *The Youth Course* (CW 217). In December, Steiner gives lectures titled *The Origins of Natural Science* (CW 326), and *Humanity and the World of Stars: The Spiritual Communion of Humanity* (CW 219). December 31: Fire at the Goetheanum, which is destroyed.

1923: Despite the fire, Rudolf Steiner continues his work unabated. A very hard year. Internal dispersion, dissension, and apathy abound. There is conflict—between old and new visions—within the society. A wake-up call is needed, and Rudolf Steiner responds with renewed lecturing vitality. His focus: the spiritual context of human life; initiation science; the course of the year; and community building. As a foundation for an artistic school, he creates a series of pastel sketches. Lecture cycles: *The Anthroposophical Movement; Initiation Science* (CW 227) (in England at the Penmaenmawr Summer School); *The Four Seasons and the Archangels* (CW 229); *Harmony of the Creative Word* (CW 230); *The Supersensible Human* (CW 231), given in Holland for the founding of the Dutch society. On November 10, in response to the failed Hitler-Ludendorf putsch in Munich, Steiner closes his Berlin residence and moves the *Philosophisch-Anthroposophisch Verlag* (Press) to Dornach. On December 9, Steiner begins the serialization of his *Autobiography: The Course of My Life* (CW 28) in *Das Goetheanum*. It will continue to appear weekly, without a break, until his death. Late December-early January: Rudolf Steiner refounds the Anthroposophical Society (about 12,000 members internationally) and takes over its leadership. The new board members are: Marie Steiner, Ita Wegman, Albert Steffen, Elizabeth Vreede, and Guenther Wachsmuth. (See *The Christmas Meeting for the Founding of the General Anthroposophical Society* (CW 260). Accompanying lectures: *Mystery Knowledge and Mystery Centers* (CW 232); *World History in the Light of Anthroposophy* (CW 233). December 25: the Foundation Stone is laid (in the hearts of members) in the form of the "Foundation Stone Meditation."

1924: January 1: having founded the Anthroposophical Society and taken over its leadership, Rudolf Steiner has the task of "reforming" it. The process begins with a weekly newssheet ("What's Happening in the Anthroposophical Society") in which Rudolf Steiner's "Letters to Members" and "Anthroposophical Leading Thoughts" appear (CW 26). The next step is the creation of a new esoteric class, the "first class" of the "University of Spiritual Science" (which was to have been followed, had Rudolf Steiner lived longer, by two more advanced classes). Then comes a new language for Anthroposophy—practical, phenomenological, and direct; and Rudolf Steiner creates the model for the second Goetheanum. He begins the series of extensive "karma" lectures (CW 235-40); and finally, responding to needs, he creates two new initiatives: biodynamic agriculture and curative education. After the middle of the year, rumors begin to circulate regarding Steiner's health. Lectures: January-February, *Anthroposophy* (CW 234); February: *Tone Eurythmy* (CW 278); June: *The Agriculture Course* (CW 327); June-July: Speech [?] Eurythmy (CW 279); *Curative Education* (CW 317); August: (England, "Second International Summer School"), *Initiation Consciousness: True and False Paths in Spiritual Investigation* (CW 243); September: *Pastoral Medicine* (CW 318). On September 26, for the first time, Rudolf Steiner cancels a lecture. On September 28, he gives his last lecture. On September 29, he withdraws to his studio in the carpenter's shop; now he is definitively ill. Cared for by Ita Wegman, he continues working, however, and writing the weekly installments of his *Autobiography* and *Letters to the Members/Leading Thoughts* (CW 26).

1925: Rudolf Steiner, while continuing to work, continues to weaken. He finishes *Extending Practical Medicine* (CW 27) with Ita Wegman. On March 30, around ten in the morning, Rudolf Steiner dies.

INDEX

VISTA SERIES

Robert McDermott, Series Editor

The following volumes have been generously supported by a grant from Laurance S. Rockefeller (1910-2004), who was a visionary with a deep commitment to spiritual ideals:

A Life for the Spirit: Rudolf Steiner in the
Crosscurrents of Our Time
HENRY BARNES

A Western Approach to Reincarnation and Karma
Edited and Introduced by
RENÉ QUERIDO

Art as Spiritual Activity
Rudolf Steiner's Contribution to the Visual Arts
Edited and Introduced by
MICHAEL HOWARD

Rhythms of Learning
What Waldorf Education Offers Children, Parents & Teachers
Edited and Introduced by
ROBERTO TROSTLI

The Bhagavad Gita and the West
*The Esoteric Significance of the Bhagavad Gita and
Its Relation to the Epistles of Paul*
Edited and Introduced by
ROBERT MCDERMOTT